Too Busy to Cook?
Volume Two

Too Busy to Cook?

Volume Two

THE KNAPP PRESS
Publishers
Los Angeles

Copyright © 1988 by Knapp Communications Corporation

Published by The Knapp Press
5900 Wilshire Boulevard, Los Angeles, California 90036

BON APPETIT and TOO BUSY TO COOK? are registered trademarks of Bon Appétit
Publishing Corp. Used with permission.

Library of Congress Cataloging-in-Publication Data
(Revised for vol. 2)

Too busy to cook?

   Includes index.
   1. Quick and easy cookery. I. Bon appétit.
TX652.T657 1981   641.5'55   81-5959
ISBN 0-89535-049-1 (v. 1)
ISBN 0-89535-214-1 (v. 2)

On the Cover: Spaghettini Primavera. Photographed by Brian Leatart

Printed and bound in the United States of America
10 9 8 7 6 5 4 3 2 1

❖ Contents

Foreword

In 1981 we compiled the first collection of recipes from the *Too Busy to Cook?* column in *Bon Appétit* magazine. You, our readers, responded with overwhelming enthusiasm; to date, over 500,000 copies are in print, and we continue to get requests for more of *Too Busy to Cook?*

Here it is—an exciting new collection of time-saving recipes and entertaining ideas designed for busy people who enjoy serving terrific meals that don't take hours to prepare. In this volume, we present over 600 recipes from talented cooks with limited time and an abundance of creativity—our readers. We've gathered the most outstanding recipes that have appeared in the "Too Busy to Cook?" column since 1981. From Zucchini Appetizer Squares to Chocolate Chip-Peanut Butter Pie, you'll find recipes for both casual family dining and elegant entertaining, along with every occasion in between.

Organized for quick reference, each chapter offers dozens of recipes for easy dishes that pare down preparation time without sacrificing taste or pizzazz. And to make menu-planning and entertaining even easier, do-ahead tips are indicated within the recipes wherever possible. Although some recipes use the time-saving advantages of the microwave or food processor, you don't need any special equipment to use this book—just good-quality ingredients and a desire to make fresh, delicious and fast meals for friends and family.

Suggested menus for all occasions are listed at the back of the book, following the recipes, to provide imaginative ideas when planning special meals. You'll find everything from a Casual Sunday Supper for Eight to a Holiday Cocktail Party for Sixteen.

So, if a lack of time has kept you from cooking as much as you'd like, don't worry—we can't give you a 25-hour day, but we can provide you with fabulous recipes, ideas and inspiration for those days when you find yourself too busy to cook.

1 ❖ Appetizers and Beverages

Nothing sets the tone of a special meal like a terrific appetizer—the perfect prelude heightens the anticipation of the meal to follow. The appetizers in this chapter include creamy spreads and mousses, crisp vegetable fritters and light puffs, zesty stuffed shrimp and oysters, tangy meatballs and won tons, and crunchy cheese crisps. There's something here to suit any meal or occasion and—equally as important to the busy cook—to suit any schedule. We've also included a selection of refreshing beverages, some of which would provide ideal accompaniments to the appetizers in the chapter.

As you'll see, there's no need to skip the appetizer because you're short on time—those included here are incomparably easy to prepare, and many can be made in advance. For instance, the Lemon-Anchovy Dipping Sauce can be prepared several days ahead, to be served with snow peas for a pretty, piquant beginning. Sausage-Nut Pâté should be prepared one day ahead to allow the flavors to mellow, and Steamed Pork-filled Won Tons can be made a day ahead and re-steamed for just five minutes before serving. Florentine Appetizer Puffs are another ideal do-ahead—they can be made one week in advance, frozen, then baked just before serving. Or, if your schedule lends itself more to quick, last-minute preparations than to advance planning, try the crowd-pleasing Chicken Nacho Platter or the olive-studded Cheddar Wedges, which use English muffins for a quick, easy tidbit.

All of the appetizers here are delicious as hors d'oeuvres, but some are also substantial enough to provide a welcome first course that's perfect for turning a middle-of-the-week dinner into something special, or for kicking off a weekend dinner party. Golden-brown Quick Crab Cakes served on a bed of fresh greens is a delicious, down-home starter. Mussels Vinaigrette topped with chopped avocado, tomato and green onions makes a sparkling stage-setter for an elegant meal.

To toast the occasion with something a little out of the ordinary, try Sparkling Apple Sangria or Fresh Strawberry-Champagne Spritzers. We end the chapter as you might cap off a special dinner, with traditional Irish Coffee and Cognac-laced Café Brûlot. Either one finishes the meal just as it started—with style and perfect ease.

Appetizers

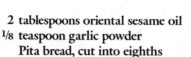

GUACAMOLE PICANTE

Sour cream can be added to this spicy dip to make it smoother.

Makes about 4 cups

- 4 medium avocados, peeled, pitted and sliced
- 1 medium tomato, coarsely chopped
- 1 small onion, chopped
- 2 tablespoons hot salsa
- 2 tablespoons Worcestershire sauce
- 2 tablespoons fresh lime juice
- 1 small jalapeño chili, seeded and finely chopped
- 1 teaspoon chili powder
- 1 teaspoon salt
  Crudités
  Tortilla chips

Combine first 9 ingredients in large bowl and mash with fork until slightly chunky. Serve with fresh vegetables and crisp tortilla chips.

EASY ARTICHOKE DIP

Makes about 2 1/2 cups

- 2 8 1/2-ounce cans artichoke hearts, drained
- 6 tablespoons plain yogurt
  Salt and freshly ground white pepper
  Crudités or assorted crackers

Combine artichoke hearts and yogurt in blender and puree until smooth. Taste and season with salt and pepper. Serve with crudités or crackers.

HUMMUS DIP

Makes about 2 1/2 cups

- 2 15 1/2-ounce cans chick-peas (garbanzo beans), drained
- 1/4 cup fresh lemon juice

- 2 tablespoons oriental sesame oil
- 1/8 teaspoon garlic powder
  Pita bread, cut into eighths

Puree all ingredients except bread in blender or processor. (*Can be prepared 1 day ahead. Cover and chill.*) Transfer to bowl. Serve with pita bread.

SNOW PEAS WITH LEMON-ANCHOVY DIPPING SAUCE

This tangy sauce can be prepared several days ahead and refrigerated.

Makes about 1 1/4 cups

Dipping Sauce
- 2 egg yolks
- 3 to 4 tablespoons Dijon mustard
- 1 2-ounce can anchovies, undrained
  Juice of 1 lemon or to taste
- 1 shallot, chopped
- 1 cup vegetable oil
- 1/4 cup sour cream (optional)
  Salt and freshly ground pepper
- 1 tablespoon capers, rinsed and drained
  Additional capers (optional garnish)

- 1 1/4 pounds fresh snow peas or 2 pounds small, young sugar snap peas

For sauce: Combine egg yolks, mustard, anchovies, lemon juice and shallot in processor and mix until foamy and pale. With machine running, slowly drizzle in oil, stopping occasionally to make sure oil is being absorbed. If sauce is very stiff, mix in sour cream. Season to taste with salt and pepper. Turn into storage container. Stir in capers. Chill until shortly before serving. Top with capers if desired.

String snow peas or sugar snaps and crisp in ice water. Drain well and

arrange in sunburst pattern on flat basket or serving platter. Place bowl of dipping sauce in center.

SNOW PEAS WITH GARLIC DIP

Makes about 1 cup

- 3/4 cup sour cream
- 1/4 cup mayonnaise
- 2 tablespoons minced green onion
- 2 small garlic cloves, minced
- 1 tablespoon Dijon mustard
- 1 teaspoon fresh lemon juice
- 1/4 teaspoon salt
- 1/8 teaspoon freshly ground pepper
- 1/2 pound snow peas, trimmed

Combine first 8 ingredients in bowl and mix well. Refrigerate 1 hour. Serve with trimmed snow peas.

FIESTA DIP SAN LUCAS

More than just a delicious chip and vegetable dip—stir some into scrambled eggs or spread it on a tortilla to microwave for a quick quesadilla.

Makes 3 cups

- 2 cups grated cheddar cheese, room temperature
- 1 8-ounce package cream cheese, room temperature
- 4 teaspoons fresh lemon juice
- 1 teaspoon instant chicken bouillon powder
  Hot pepper sauce
- 1 medium tomato, seeded and finely chopped
- 1 4-ounce can diced green chilies, drained and rinsed
- 3 tablespoons finely chopped onions
  Crudités
  Tortilla chips

Blend first 5 ingredients in blender or processor 30 seconds. Stop and scrape sides of work bowl. Blend 15 more seconds. Transfer to medium bowl. Stir in tomato, chilies and onions. Cover and refrigerate at least 1 hour. (*Can be prepared 3 days ahead.*) Serve dip with crudités and tortilla chips.

CHUNKY CHILI CON QUESO

You will need a fondue pot and forks to present this appealing appetizer.

4 to 6 servings

 2 tablespoons (¼ stick) butter
 1 large onion, chopped
 2 cups grated longhorn cheddar cheese
 1 1-pound can peeled tomatoes, drained, diced
 1 4-ounce can diced green chilies, drained
 1 4-ounce can mushroom pieces and stems, drained and chopped
 ½ teaspoon dried marjoram, crumbled
 ½ teaspoon salt
  Day-old French bread, cubed and toasted

Melt butter in large skillet over low heat. Add onion and stir until translucent, about 5 minutes. Mix in cheese, tomatoes, chilies, mushrooms, marjoram and salt. Continue stirring until cheese melts, about 3 minutes. Transfer mixture to fondue pot and place over low heat. Serve, passing bread separately to dip into cheese mixture.

CURRIED CHEESE SPREAD

Serve with crackers or toast.

Makes about 1½ cups

 2 3-ounce packages cream cheese, room temperature
 1 cup grated sharp cheddar cheese
 ¼ cup minced onion
 1 tablespoon dry Sherry
 1 teaspoon curry powder
 ¼ teaspoon salt
 2 tablespoons mango chutney, chopped

Blend cream cheese with cheddar in medium bowl. Mix in onion, Sherry, curry powder and salt. Stir in chutney. Serve cheese spread at room temperature. (*Can be prepared 2 days ahead. Cover tightly and refrigerate.*)

VIENNESE LIPTAUER

Makes 1½ cups

 1 cup cream cheese, room temperature
 ½ cup (1 stick) butter, room temperature
 3 tablespoons sour cream
 2 anchovy fillets
 1 teaspoon capers, drained
 1 tablespoon finely chopped onion
 1 tablespoon Dijon mustard
 1½ teaspoons paprika
 1 teaspoon caraway seeds
 ½ teaspoon salt

Blend cheese, butter and sour cream in medium bowl. Mash anchovies and capers in small bowl. Mix into cheese. Stir in remaining ingredients. Transfer to serving bowl or mound on plate. Cover and refrigerate at least 1 hour or overnight. Serve at room temperature.

WARM MUSHROOM SPREAD

Makes about 2½ cups

 4 slices bacon
 8 ounces mushrooms, chopped (about 3 cups)
 1 medium onion, finely chopped
 1 garlic clove, minced
 2 tablespoons all purpose flour
 ⅛ teaspoon freshly ground pepper
 1 8-ounce package cream cheese, cubed
 2 teaspoons Worcestershire sauce
 1 teaspoon soy sauce
 ½ cup sour cream
 1 teaspoon fresh lemon juice
  Cocktail rye or assorted crackers

Cook bacon in large skillet over medium heat until crisp. Transfer to small bowl, crumble and set aside. Pour off all but 2 tablespoons drippings from skillet. Add mushrooms, onion and

garlic to skillet and sauté over medium-high heat until liquid evaporates. Stir in flour and pepper and mix well. Add cream cheese, Worcestershire sauce and soy sauce and continue cooking until cheese is melted. Blend in sour cream, lemon juice and bacon and cook until heated through; *do not boil.* Serve with cocktail rye or crackers.

HOT CRAB DIP

8 servings

 1 8-ounce package cream cheese, room temperature
 1 6-ounce can crabmeat, drained
 2 tablespoons minced green onions
 1 tablespoon milk
 1 teaspoon prepared horseradish
 ⅛ teaspoon freshly ground pepper
  Crudités

Preheat oven to 350°F. Oil 1-quart soufflé dish. Mix all ingredients except crudités in medium bowl. Turn into prepared dish. Bake until bubbly, about 30 minutes. Serve with crudités.

CHOPPED EGGPLANT-ONION SPREAD

Makes about 2¾ cups

 1 medium eggplant (about 1¼ pounds)
 1 medium-size green or red bell pepper
 1 medium garlic clove
 2 tablespoons chopped onion
 ¼ cup vegetable oil
 3 tablespoons cider vinegar
 ¾ teaspoon salt
 ½ teaspoon sugar
  Freshly ground pepper
  Sliced pumpernickel bread

Preheat oven to 400°F. Prick eggplant and bell pepper with fork in several places. Arrange on baking sheet. Bake bell pepper until tender, about 30 minutes. Let cool. Continue baking eggplant until tender, about 30 minutes. Remove from oven and let cool.

  Mince garlic in processor by dropping through feed tube with machine running. Add onion and mince using on/off turns. Peel eggplant and add to processor. Peel bell pepper, cut into fourths, core and remove seeds. Add bell pepper, oil, vinegar, salt, sugar and pepper to processor and mix well; do not over process, some texture should remain. Transfer to bowl. Serve with pumpernickel bread.

SMOKED OYSTER SPREAD

Makes about 1 cup

- 1 3.66-ounce can smoked oysters, drained and minced
- 1/2 cup whipped cream cheese
- 1 medium-size green onion, minced
- 1 tablespoon chili sauce
  Cucumber slices
  Crackers

Mix oysters, cream cheese, green onion and chili sauce in small bowl. Cover and refrigerate overnight. Serve with cucumber slices and crackers.

GORGONZOLA-PISTACHIO LOAF

16 servings

- 2 8-ounce packages cream cheese, room temperature
- 1/2 pound Gorgonzola cheese, room temperature
- 1 cup (2 sticks) unsalted butter, room temperature
- 1 cup chopped fresh parsley
- 1 cup shelled pistachios

  Fresh parsley sprigs
  Shelled pistachios
  Thinly sliced baguettes or crackers

Moisten well two 18-inch cheesecloth squares. Line 8x4-inch loaf pan, draping excess cloth over sides. Combine cream cheese, Gorgonzola and butter in large bowl and blend with rubber spatula. Spread 1/3 of cheese mixture into prepared pan. Sprinkle with chopped parsley. Cover with half of remaining cheese mixture. Sprinkle with 1 cup pistachios. Cover with remaining cheese mixture. Fold ends of cloth over

and press down lightly. Refrigerate until firm, about 1 hour.

Invert onto serving plate. Carefully remove cheesecloth. Garnish with parsley sprigs and pistachios. Serve cheese loaf at room temperature with sliced baguettes or crackers.

CAVIAR AND CHOPPED EGG APPETIZER

Makes about 3 cups

- 6 hard-cooked eggs, finely chopped
- 1/2 cup (1 stick) butter, room temperature
- 1/2 cup mayonnaise
- 1/4 cup minced green onions
- 2 teaspoons fresh lemon juice
- 1 cup sour cream
- 6 ounces caviar

Line small bowl with plastic wrap and set aside. Combine first 5 ingredients in medium bowl and mix thoroughly. Transfer to prepared bowl, packing tightly. Cover and refrigerate several hours or overnight. Unmold onto platter. Spread sour cream over egg mixture. Cover with caviar and serve.

SAUSAGE-NUT PATE

Makes about 2 cups

- 1/2 pound bulk pork sausage
- 1 pound mushrooms, sliced
- 3/4 cup chopped onions
- 1 garlic clove, minced
- 1/4 cup slivered almonds, toasted
- 1/3 cup coarsely chopped walnuts, toasted
- 1 tablespoon safflower oil
- 1/2 teaspoon dried sage, crumbled
- 1/4 teaspoon dried thyme, crumbled
- 1/8 teaspoon salt
- 1/8 teaspoon cayenne pepper
  Crackers

Cook sausage in heavy medium saucepan over medium heat until well browned, stirring frequently, about 8 minutes. Transfer to processor using slotted spoon. Pour off all but 2 teaspoons drippings from skillet. Add mushrooms, onions and garlic to same

skillet and cook over medium heat until all liquid evaporates, stirring occasionally, about 10 minutes. Transfer to processor with sausage. Add nuts and mix using 6 on/off turns. Add oil, sage, thyme, salt and cayenne. Process continually until smooth, about 3 minutes. Transfer to 2-cup crock. Cover and chill overnight. Serve at room temperature with crackers.

BRANDIED LIVER TERRINE

6 servings

- 2 tablespoons vegetable oil
- 2 medium onions, chopped
- 1 pound beef or calf's liver, cut into 1-inch strips
- 2 hard-cooked eggs, chopped
- 1 tablespoon brandy
- 1 tablespoon mayonnaise
- 1 tablespoon chopped fresh parsley
  Salt and freshly ground pepper
  Parsley sprigs
  Thinly sliced French bread and cornichons

Heat oil in medium skillet over medium heat. Add onions and sauté until translucent, about 5 minutes. Add liver and sauté until browned, 6 to 8 minutes. Transfer to processor and chop finely. Add eggs, brandy, mayonnaise and chopped parsley and mix until smooth. Season with salt and pepper. Spoon into terrine or other serving bowl, spreading evenly. Garnish with parsley sprigs. Chill. Serve with French bread and cornichons.

STUFFED SNOW PEAS

A pretty, low-calorie appetizer.

Makes 50

- 2 cups plain nonfat yogurt
- 2 teaspoons coarse-grained mustard
  Salt and freshly ground pepper
- 50 snow peas, stemmed and strings removed
- 1 cup chopped pecans

Line colander or sieve with cheesecloth. Place 2 cups plain yogurt in colander over bowl; cover and let drain in refrigerator overnight.

Combine yogurt and mustard in small bowl. Season with salt and pepper. (*Can be prepared 1 day ahead. Cover and refrigerate.*) Using sharp paring knife, slice open each pea pod along straight side. Spoon yogurt mixture into pastry bag. Pipe into pea pods. Place nuts in shallow dish. Dip stuffing edge of peas into nuts. Place on serving platter. Cover and refrigerate until ready to serve. (*Can be prepared 8 hours ahead.*)

SNOW PEAS STUFFED WITH HERB CHEESE

Makes 40 hors d'oeuvres

- **40 snow peas, stemmed and blanched**
- **1 8-ounce package cream cheese, room temperature**
- **1 medium garlic clove, minced**
- **2 teaspoons chopped fresh chives**
- **1 teaspoon dried basil, crumbled**
- **1/2 teaspoon caraway seeds**
- **1/2 teaspoon dried dillweed**
- **1/2 teaspoon lemon pepper**

Split snow peas open lengthwise with small paring knife. Blend remaining ingredients in processor. Pipe cheese mixture into each snow pea using pastry bag fitted with small tip, or spread in snow peas using small knife. Refrigerate until chilled and serve.

PARMESAN-COATED FRIED BRIE

Offer an assortment of crackers or slices of French bread alongside.

8 to 10 servings

- **1 egg, beaten to blend**
- **1 tablespoon water**
- **1 cup seasoned dry breadcrumbs**
- **1/4 cup freshly grated Parmesan cheese**
- **1 1-pound wheel Brie cheese**
- **1/4 cup vegetable oil**

Combine egg and water in bowl. Combine breadcrumbs and Parmesan in another bowl. Dip Brie in egg mixture, coating well. Coat with breadcrumb mixture. Chill until firm, at least 1 hour. (*Can be prepared up to this point 8 hours ahead.*)

Heat oil in heavy medium skillet over medium heat. Add Brie and cook until browned and softened, about 2 minutes per side.

BRIE AND HERB CHEESES IN PASTRY

Use the pastry scraps to cut out hearts, leaves or other shapes to decorate the top of this impressive appetizer.

8 to 10 servings

- **1 10x9-inch sheet frozen puff pastry, thawed**
- **1 14-ounce wheel Brie cheese**
- **2 4-ounce packages garlic and herb semisoft cheese**
- **1 egg, beaten to blend**
- **1 tablespoon water**

Lightly flour baking sheet. Place puff pastry on prepared sheet and roll out gently to remove fold lines. Place Brie in center of pastry. Spread 1 package semisoft cheese on Brie. Turn Brie over. Spread remaining semisoft cheese on second side of Brie. Bring pastry up around sides and over cheese, wrapping completely and trimming excess pastry. Turn over and place seam side down. Gather pastry scraps; reroll and cut out decorations to place on top of pastry if desired. (*Can be prepared 1 day ahead. Cover and refrigerate. Bring to room temperature before baking.*) Combine beaten egg and 1 tablespoon water. Brush over top.

Preheat oven to 375°F. Bake pastry until golden brown, 30 to 35 minutes. Let stand 10 minutes. Serve warm.

FRENCH-FRIED CHEDDAR STICKS

Makes 25 to 30

- **3/4 pound sharp cheddar cheese, cut into 1 1/2x1-inch sticks**
- **1 cup warm milk**
- **1/2 cup all purpose flour Cayenne pepper**
- **2 eggs, beaten to blend**
- **1/2 cup Italian seasoned breadcrumbs**

  Safflower oil (for deep frying)

Soak cheese sticks in warm milk 10 minutes. Mix flour with cayenne. Drain cheese and roll in flour mixture, covering completely. Dip in eggs, then coat with breadcrumbs.

Heat oil in large saucepan to 365°F. Add cheese in batches and fry until golden brown, 10 to 20 seconds. Drain on paper towels. Serve warm.

STUFFED CUCUMBER CANAPES

Makes 2 dozen

- **1 8-ounce package cream cheese, room temperature**
- **2 medium-size green onions, minced**
- **1/4 teaspoon Worcestershire sauce**
- **1/8 teaspoon garlic powder**
- **1/8 teaspoon freshly ground white pepper**
- **1 medium cucumber, scored, cored and drained**
- **24 cocktail bread rounds Chopped fresh dill or capers**

Beat cream cheese, green onions, Worcestershire sauce, garlic powder and pepper in small bowl until smooth and creamy. Cut cucumber into thirds. Fill hollowed core of each piece with some of cream cheese mixture. Wrap cucumber pieces in foil. Refrigerate at least 1 hour or overnight.

Slice cucumber 1/4 inch thick. Arrange on bread rounds. Garnish with chopped dill or capers.

CHEESE-STUFFED MUSHROOMS

Makes 18 hors d'oeuvres

- **18 large mushrooms**
- **3 ounces mozzarella cheese, grated**
- **6 tablespoons mayonnaise**
- **2 tablespoons chopped fresh parsley**
- **1 teaspoon Worcestershire sauce**
- **1/8 teaspoon garlic powder**
- **1/8 teaspoon dried oregano, crumbled**
  Salt and freshly ground pepper

Preheat oven to 350°F. Lightly grease 9x13-inch baking dish. Separate mushroom stems from caps and arrange caps in prepared baking dish. Chop stems finely and transfer to large bowl. Add remaining ingredients and mix well. Spoon mixture into caps, mounding slightly. Bake until tender, about 20 minutes. Serve immediately.

MUSHROOM-SAUSAGE CROUSTADES

Makes 18 appetizers

Croustades
    Butter
18 **slices white bread, cut into 3-inch rounds**

Filling
1/4 **cup (1/2 stick) butter**
  3 **tablespoons finely chopped shallot**
1/2 **pound mushrooms, finely chopped**
  2 **tablespoons all purpose flour**
1 1/2 **tablespoons finely chopped fresh chives**
  1 **tablespoon finely chopped fresh parsley**
1/2 **teaspoon salt**
    Cayenne pepper
1/4 **pound sweet Italian sausage, cut into pieces**
  1 **cup whipping cream**
1/2 **teaspoon fresh lemon juice**

  2 **tablespoons freshly grated Parmesan cheese**

For croustades: Preheat oven to 400°F. Butter small muffin tin. Roll each bread round out on work surface to flatten. Carefully fit bread into muffin tin, pressing gently to form cup. Bake until lightly brown, about 8 minutes. Remove from tin and let cool on wire rack. (*Can be prepared ahead, sealed tightly in plastic bags and frozen.*)

For filling: Melt butter in large heavy skillet over medium-high heat. Add shallot and sauté until browned. Blend in mushrooms, stirring constantly until liquid is evaporated, about 10 to 15 minutes. Sprinkle with flour, chives, parsley, salt and cayenne pepper. Add sausage, stirring constantly until browned and crumbly. Pour in cream and bring to low boil.

Reduce heat and simmer until mixture thickens, about 10 minutes. Remove from heat and stir in lemon juice. Let mixture cool slightly.

To assemble: Preheat oven to 350°F. Spoon filling evenly into croustades. Arrange on baking sheet. Sprinkle cheese over tops. Bake until cheese melts, about 10 minutes.

FLORENTINE APPETIZER PUFFS

Makes 36

  2 **10-ounce packages frozen chopped spinach**
  1 **cup freshly grated Parmesan cheese**
1 1/2 **tablespoons minced onion**
  2 **eggs, beaten to blend**
  2 **cups herb seasoned croutons**
  3 **tablespoons butter, melted**

Preheat oven to 375°F. Lightly grease baking sheets. Cook spinach according to package directions; drain well. Transfer to large bowl. Add Parmesan and onion. Blend in eggs. Stir in croutons and butter. Shape mixture into 1-inch balls. (*Can be prepared 1 week ahead, covered and frozen. Do not thaw before baking. Increase baking time to 20 to 25 minutes.*) Arrange on prepared baking sheets, spacing 1/2 inch apart. Bake until golden brown, about 15 minutes.

PHYLLO-WRAPPED SPINACH ROLLS

Makes 72

  1 **tablespoon olive oil**
1/2 **cup chopped onion**
  1 **10-ounce package frozen chopped spinach, thawed, squeezed dry**
  8 **ounces cottage cheese**
  4 **ounces cream cheese**
  4 **ounces crumbled feta cheese**
  1 **small egg, beaten**

12 **phyllo pastry sheets**
  1 **cup (2 sticks) butter, melted**

Heat oil in large skillet over medium-high heat. Add onion and sauté until translucent, about 3 minutes. Reduce

heat to low and add spinach. Slowly stir in cheeses until well blended. Cook 5 minutes. Remove from heat. Add beaten egg and mix well.

Butter 13x18-inch baking sheet. Stack 3 phyllo sheets on damp towel. Brush each sheet with melted butter. Spoon about 1/2 cup filling into 1 1/2-inch-wide strip down long edge of phyllo. Roll up as for jelly roll, starting at long edge with filling and using towel as aid. Transfer to prepared baking sheet, arranging seam side down. Brush with melted butter. Repeat with remaining phyllo for 3 more rolls. Freeze rolls 15 minutes.

Preheat oven to 350°F. Cut rolls into 1-inch pieces. Bake until golden brown, 15 minutes.

PAKORAS

Serve these Indian vegetable fritters with Tomato Pickle (see page 148) for an unusual first course.

Makes about 2 dozen

3/4 **cup chick-pea flour***
3/4 **cup self-rising flour**
  2 **teaspoons salt**
  1 **teaspoon mild curry powder**
1/2 **teaspoon turmeric**
1/2 **teaspoon chili powder**
  1 **cup (scant) water**
  1 **garlic clove, minced**

    Oil (for deep frying)
  1 **medium potato, peeled and cut into 1/4-inch dice (about 3/4 cup)**
  1 **6-inch zucchini, cut into 1/4-inch dice (about 3/4 cup)**
  1 **small Japanese eggplant, cut into 1/4-inch dice (about 3/4 cup)**
1/4 **head cauliflower, cut into 1/4-inch dice (about 3/4 cup)**
1/2 **medium onion, cut into 1/4-inch dice (about 3/4 cup)**

Sift first 6 ingredients into medium bowl. Gradually stir in water and mix until thickened. Add garlic and beat well. Set batter aside 30 minutes.

Heat oil in deep skillet or wok until hot but not smoking. Add potato, zucchini, eggplant, cauliflower and onion to batter and mix thoroughly. Drop batter into oil by tablespoons in small batches and fry until pale golden, about 40 seconds per side; do not crowd. Remove with slotted spoon and drain on paper towels. (*Can be prepared ahead to this point and stored at room temperature.*) When ready to serve, reheat oil to 400°F and refry fritters in small batches until golden brown, about 30 seconds. Remove with slotted spoon and drain on paper towels. Arrange on platter and serve immediately.

*Available at Middle Eastern, Indian or natural foods markets.

ZUCCHINI APPETIZER SQUARES

Makes about 9 dozen

- 4 cups thinly sliced zucchini
- 1 cup buttermilk baking mix
- 4 eggs, beaten to blend
- 1/2 cup finely chopped onion
- 1/2 cup freshly grated Parmesan cheese
- 1/2 cup vegetable oil
- 2 tablespoons chopped fresh parsley
- 1 garlic clove, minced
- 1/2 teaspoon dried oregano, crumbled
- 1/2 teaspoon seasoned salt
- 1/2 teaspoon salt
  Freshly ground pepper

Preheat oven to 350°F. Butter 9x13-inch ovenproof glass baking dish. Mix all ingredients in large bowl. Spread in prepared dish. Bake until golden brown and tester inserted in center comes out clean, about 30 minutes. Cut into 1-inch squares.

VEGETABLE FRITTERS

Makes 12

- 1 1/2 cups shredded unpeeled baking potatoes
- 3/4 cup shredded unpeeled zucchini
- 1/2 cup shredded peeled carrots
- 1/4 cup grated onions
- 2 eggs, beaten to blend
- 1/4 cup all purpose flour
- 1 tablespoon dried parsley flakes
- 1 teaspoon dried chives
- 1 teaspoon salt
- 1/2 teaspoon freshly ground pepper
- 1/2 teaspoon garlic powder
- 2 tablespoons vegetable oil

Preheat oven to 200°F. Combine potatoes, zucchini, carrots and onions in colander; squeeze dry. Transfer to medium bowl. Stir in next 7 ingredients. Heat oil in heavy medium skillet over medium-high heat. Add vegetable mixture in batches, using 1/4 cup for each fritter and mixing batter frequently. Cook fritters until crisp and browned, 4 to 5 minutes. Turn and cook until browned, 3 to 4 minutes. Drain on paper towels. Serve hot.

CHILI DEVILED EGGS

6 servings

- 6 hard-cooked eggs, halved lengthwise
- 2 tablespoons salsa
- 1 tablespoon mayonnaise
- 1 teaspoon minced onion
- 1 teaspoon finely chopped fresh cilantro
- 1/8 teaspoon freshly ground pepper

Remove yolks from eggs, reserving whites. Mash yolks in small bowl. Stir in remaining ingredients. Fill whites with yolk mixture. Cover and refrigerate overnight. Serve chilled.

BAKED QUESADILLA SQUARES

6 to 8 servings

- 2 cups shredded cheddar cheese
- 2 cups shredded Monterey Jack cheese
- 2 4-ounce cans diced green chilies, drained
- 2 cups milk
- 1 cup buttermilk baking mix
- 4 eggs, beaten to blend
- 1/4 cup salsa
  Sour cream
  Guacamole
  Additional salsa

Preheat oven to 425°F. Spray 9x13-inch ovenproof glass baking dish with non-stick vegetable oil spray. Sprinkle cheeses in bottom. Top with chilies.

Combine milk, baking mix and eggs in large bowl and beat until smooth. Carefully pour over chilies. Top with 1/4 cup salsa. Bake until puffed and golden, 25 to 30 minutes. Cool 10 minutes. Cut into squares and serve. Pass sour cream, guacamole and additional salsa separately.

ORIENTAL CHICKEN WINGS

Makes 32

- 2 cups soy sauce
- 2/3 cup sugar
- 3 tablespoons vegetable oil
- 1 tablespoon ground ginger
- 1 teaspoon five-spice powder
- 2 bunches green onions, thinly sliced
- 32 chicken wings

Blend soy sauce, sugar, oil, ginger and five-spice powder in large bowl until sugar dissolves. Stir in green onions. Add chicken to marinade, turning to coat. Cover and refrigerate overnight.

Preheat oven to 350°F. Drain chicken, reserving marinade. Divide chicken between two heavy large baking sheets. Bake until golden brown and tender, basting occasionally with marinade, 45 to 50 minutes. Serve chicken wings hot or chilled.

THREE-SPICE CHICKEN

Makes about 40 appetizers

- Oil for deep frying
- 1/2 cup all purpose flour
- 1 1/2 teaspoons salt
- 1 teaspoon paprika
- 1 teaspoon onion powder
- 1/2 teaspoon poultry seasoning
- 1 egg, beaten to blend
- 1/2 cup water
- 3 whole boneless chicken breasts, skinned and cut into 1x1 1/2-inch pieces
  Freshly grated Parmesan cheese

Heat oil for deep frying to 375°F. Combine flour and seasonings in shallow bowl. Add egg and water and blend well. Dip chicken into batter, allowing excess to drain back into bowl. Add chicken to oil in small batches and fry until crisp, about 2 to 4 minutes. Drain on paper towels. Transfer chicken to platter. Sprinkle with Parmesan cheese and serve.

STEAMED PORK-FILLED WON TONS

Makes about 50

- 1 pound ground pork
- 1 egg, beaten to blend
- 1 tablespoon soy sauce
- 2 teaspoons minced fresh ginger
- 2 garlic cloves, minced
- 1 teaspoon oriental sesame oil
- 1 10-ounce package gyoza wrappers*

- 1/3 cup chicken broth
- 1/3 cup soy sauce
- 2 tablespoons distilled white vinegar

Combine first 6 ingredients in medium bowl. Place about 1 teaspoon filling in center of 1 wrapper. Bring edges of wrapper up and press into filling at 4 evenly spaced points, leaving some filling exposed at top. Press corners of wrapper into filling. Repeat with remaining filling and wrappers.

Bring water to boil in base of steamer. Oil steamer rack. Arrange won tons on rack, spacing 1 inch apart. Set steamer rack in place, cover and steam until pork is cooked and wrappers are soft, about 20 minutes. (*Can be prepared 1 day ahead. Cool, cover and refrigerate. Resteam 5 minutes.*)

Meanwhile, combine remaining ingredients. Serve won tons immediately, passing dipping sauce separately.

Gyoza wrappers are Japanese won ton wrappers, available at oriental markets.

TANGY SWEET AND SOUR MEATBALLS

8 servings

- 2 pounds ground beef
- 1 1/2 cups finely chopped onions
- 1 cup applesauce
- 1/2 cup finely chopped green bell pepper

- 1/2 cup raisins
- 1/2 cup diced fresh or canned pineapple, drained
- 3 eggs, beaten to blend
- 2 slices day-old bread, crumbled
- 4 bacon strips, cooked and crumbled
- 3 tablespoons steak sauce
- 3 tablespoons barbecue sauce
- 1 tablespoon Worcestershire sauce
  Salt and freshly ground pepper
  Vegetable oil
  Sweet and Sour Sauce (see recipe)

Combine first 12 ingredients with salt and pepper to taste in large bowl and blend well. Shape mixture into 1-inch meatballs. Pour enough oil into large skillet to coat bottom. Warm over medium-high heat. Add meatballs in batches and cook until evenly browned, turning frequently, about 8 minutes. Drain on paper towels. Transfer to large platter. Ladle Sweet and Sour Sauce over meatballs and serve immediately.

Sweet and Sour Sauce

Makes about 3 cups

- 1 tablespoon vegetable oil
- 3/4 cup coarsely chopped onion
- 3/4 cup chopped green bell pepper
- 3/4 cup chopped red bell pepper
- 1 20-ounce can pineapple chunks, drained, juice reserved
- 3 tablespoons soy sauce
- 1 1/2 tablespoons distilled white vinegar
- 3 tablespoons cornstarch
- 2 tablespoons water

Heat oil in medium skillet over medium heat. Add onion and sauté until translucent, 3 to 5 minutes. Add bell peppers and sauté 1 minute. Remove vegetables with slotted spoon; drain on paper towels. Reduce heat to medium-low. Add pineapple juice, soy sauce and vinegar to skillet. Mix cornstarch with water in small bowl, stirring until smooth. Add to skillet and stir until sauce thickens. Return vegetables to skillet. Add pineapple. Cook until heated through, about 5 minutes.

ROAST BEEF TURNOVERS

Makes 6

- 1 10-ounce package frozen puff pastry patty shells, thawed

- 2 tablespoons (1/4 stick) butter
- 1/2 cup thinly sliced celery
- 1/2 cup chopped fresh parsley
- 1/2 cup sliced mushrooms
- 2 shallots, chopped
- 2 cups cubed or shredded cooked roast beef
- 1/4 cup dry breadcrumbs
- 1/2 teaspoon dried basil, crumbled
  Salt and freshly ground pepper
- 1 egg
- 1 tablespoon water
- 1/4 cup sesame seeds

Roll out each patty shell on generously floured surface to 6-inch circle.

Preheat oven to 400°F. Melt butter in medium skillet over medium heat. Add celery, parsley, mushrooms and shallots. Stir until softened, 2 to 3 minutes. Stir in beef, breadcrumbs, basil, salt and pepper. Remove from heat. Spoon 2 heaping tablespoons beef mixture onto center of 1 patty shell. Fold shell in half and seal edges. Transfer to baking sheet. Repeat with remaining beef mixture and shells. Beat egg with water to blend. Brush top of each turnover with egg. Sprinkle with sesame seeds. Bake until golden, about 30 minutes.

SALMON PUFFS

These tasty appetizers are at their best right out of the oven.

Makes 8

- 1/4 cup (1/2 stick) butter
- 1 1/4 cups sliced mushrooms
- 3 tablespoons all purpose flour
- 1 7 1/2-ounce can salmon, drained
- 1/2 cup whipping cream
- 2 tablespoons dry Sherry
- 1 tablespoon fresh lemon juice
- 2 teaspoons snipped fresh chives
  Salt and freshly ground pepper

- 1 17 1/4-ounce package puff pastry
  Whipping cream

Lemon wedges
Fresh parsley
Watercress

Melt butter in heavy medium skillet over medium-high heat. Add mushrooms and cook until softened, about 5 minutes. Add flour, reduce heat to medium-low and stir 2 minutes. Mix in salmon, 1/2 cup cream, Sherry, lemon juice and chives. Season with salt and pepper. Cook until thickened, stirring often, 3 to 4 minutes. Cool.

Preheat oven to 450°F. Cut pastry sheets into eight 4-inch squares. Spoon some of salmon mixture into center of each square. Fold pastry over once to form triangles. Press edges together with fork. Lightly dampen baking sheet with water. Place pastries on sheet. Brush tops with cream. Bake until golden brown, 10 to 15 minutes. Garnish with lemon, parsley and watercress. Serve immediately.

QUICK CRAB CAKES

Makes 8

- 1 pound fresh crabmeat
- 1/2 cup seasoned dry breadcrumbs
- 1 egg, beaten to blend
- 2 tablespoons mayonnaise
- 2 tablespoons whipping cream
- 2 tablespoons minced green onions
- 1 tablespoon chopped fresh parsley
- 1 teaspoon Worcestershire sauce
- 1 teaspoon Dijon mustard
  Dash of hot pepper sauce
  Salt and freshly ground white pepper

  Vegetable oil (for deep frying)
- 2/3 cup all purpose flour
- 1/2 teaspoon paprika
  Lemon wedges

Combine crab, breadcrumbs, egg, mayonnaise, whipping cream, green onions, parsley, Worcestershire sauce, mustard, hot pepper sauce, salt and pepper in large bowl. Toss mixture gently to combine.

Heat oil in large skillet or deep fryer. Mold 1/2 cup crab mixture into

3-inch round cake. Repeat with remaining crab mixture. Combine flour and paprika in shallow dish. Lightly coat crab cakes with flour, shaking off excess. Deep fry until golden brown, about 2 minutes. Drain on paper towels. Serve with lemon wedges.

STUFFED CLAMS

Makes 4 dozen

- 24 whole large clams
- 1 cup (2 sticks) butter or margarine
- 1 large onion, diced
- 1 large green bell pepper, cored, seeded and diced
- 3 celery stalks, diced
- 2 medium carrots, shredded
- 1 large garlic clove, crushed
- 1 tablespoon dried oregano, crumbled
- 1 6-ounce box garlic-onion croutons
- 12 slices bacon, cut into 3-inch pieces

Wash clam shells thoroughly under running water. Pour water into vegetable steamer to depth of 2 inches. Place clams on rack. Cover and steam until shells open, about 5 minutes. Discard any that do not open. Carefully transfer clams to work surface, reserving any liquid; chop clams coarsely. Set aside. Separate shells and clean each half. Let shells drain; pat dry.

Melt butter in heavy large skillet over medium-high heat. Add onion, green bell pepper, celery, carrots, garlic and oregano and sauté until vegetables are tender, stirring frequently, about 10 minutes. Remove vegetables from heat and stir in clams and croutons.

Preheat broiler. Pack 1 tablespoon clam mixture into each half shell. Top with bacon. Broil until bacon is crisp. Serve clams immediately.

CURRIED MUSSELS

4 servings

- 1/4 cup olive oil
- 1 large onion, finely chopped
- 3 garlic cloves, finely chopped
- 1 tablespoon curry powder

- 1/4 cup water
- 1/4 cup dry white wine
- 1 pound (4 cups) mussels, scrubbed and debearded
- 2 tablespoons chopped fresh cilantro
  Pinch of salt
  Sliced French bread

Heat oil in Dutch oven over medium-high heat. Add onion and garlic and sauté until onion is translucent, about 8 minutes. Add curry powder and mix well. Pour in water and wine. Increase heat to high and bring to boil. Add mussels, cover and steam until shells open, 3 to 6 minutes, shaking pan once or twice. Discard any mussels that do not open. Sprinkle with cilantro and salt. Spoon into shallow bowls. Serve mussels with bread.

MUSSELS VINAIGRETTE

4 servings

- 1/4 cup dry white wine
- 2 garlic cloves
- 1 pound mussels, scrubbed and debearded

- 3/4 cup vegetable oil
- 1/4 cup red wine vinegar
- 2 teaspoons Dijon mustard
  Salt and freshly ground pepper
  Butter lettuce leaves
- 1 avocado, chopped
- 1 tomato, seeded and chopped
- 1 bunch green onions, chopped

Combine wine and garlic in large pot or Dutch oven. Set steamer in pot. Add enough water to come just below steamer and bring to boil. Place mussels in steamer, cover and steam 3 minutes. Remove opened mussels. Cook remaining mussels 3 more minutes; discard any that do not open. Transfer mussels to bowl. Cover tightly and refrigerate overnight.

Whisk oil, vinegar, mustard, salt and pepper in small bowl. Line plates with lettuce. Top with mussels. Sprinkle with avocado, tomato and onions. Pour vinaigrette over and serve.

OYSTERS CASINO LOFURNO

4 servings

- 2 tablespoons (1/4 stick) butter
- 1 small onion, minced
- 1/2 medium-size green bell pepper, minced
- 1 medium celery stalk, minced
- 2 slices bacon, chopped and crisply cooked
- 1 2-ounce jar diced pimiento, drained
- 1 teaspoon fresh lemon juice
- 1/2 teaspoon Worcestershire sauce
  Pinch of salt
  Pinch of freshly ground pepper

- 4 slices toast
- 24 oysters, shucked and well drained
  Paprika
  Watercress

Melt butter in medium skillet over medium heat. Add onion, bell pepper and celery and sauté until tender, about 5 minutes. Mix in bacon, pimiento, lemon juice, Worcestershire sauce, salt and pepper. Remove bacon mixture from heat.

Preheat broiler. Arrange toast in shallow baking pan. Top each slice with 6 oysters. Cover oysters with bacon mixture. Sprinkle with paprika. Broil until heated through, 3 to 5 minutes. Garnish with watercress.

BUTTERY STUFFED SHRIMP

8 servings

- 1 cup Italian seasoned breadcrumbs
- 6 tablespoons (3/4 stick) butter, melted
- 2 tablespoons dry vermouth
- 1 tablespoon freshly grated Parmesan cheese
- 1 tablespoon paprika
- 1 1/2 teaspoons minced fresh parsley
- 1 garlic clove, minced
- 8 uncooked jumbo shrimp, shelled, deveined and butterflied
  Clarified butter

Preheat oven to 400°F. Butter large baking pan. Combine first 7 ingredients in large bowl. Arrange shrimp cut side up in prepared pan. Mound filling atop shrimp, pressing to compact. Bake until golden brown, 10 to 12 minutes. Serve immediately with clarified butter for dipping.

CHICKEN NACHO PLATTER

4 to 6 servings

- 8 ounces cheddar cheese, shredded
- 1/2 cup sour cream
- 1 1/2 cups chopped cooked chicken
- 1 4-ounce can diced green chilies, drained
- 1 9-ounce package tortilla chips
- 1 1/2 cups shredded lettuce
- 1/2 cup chopped tomato
  Additional sour cream
  Guacamole
  Salsa

Combine cheese and 1/2 cup sour cream in medium saucepan. Stir over low heat until cheese melts. Add chicken and chilies and stir until heated through. Arrange half of tortilla chips on serving platter and top with half of chicken. Repeat with remaining chips and chicken. Sprinkle with lettuce and tomato. Garnish with sour cream, guacamole and salsa.

RANCH CRACKERS

Makes about 6 cups

- 1 1-ounce envelope ranch salad dressing mix
- 1 teaspoon dried savory, crumbled
- 1/2 teaspoon garlic powder
- 1/2 teaspoon dried dillweed
- 1/4 teaspoon lemon and pepper seasoned salt
- 1/2 cup vegetable oil
- 2 7-ounce boxes small oyster crackers

Preheat oven to 200°F. Combine first 5 ingredients in large bowl. Stir in oil, then crackers. Transfer to 9x13-inch ovenproof glass baking dish. Bake until golden, stirring frequently, about 20 minutes. Cool completely. Store in airtight container. (*Ranch Crackers can be prepared 1 week ahead.*)

PARMESAN DELIGHTS

Preparing this appetizer is a snap.

Makes 48

- 1 cup mayonnaise
- 1 cup freshly grated Parmesan cheese
- 1/2 cup finely chopped green onions

- 12 slices white bread, crusts trimmed, toasted

Combine first 3 ingredients in small bowl. (*Can be prepared 1 day ahead. Cover and refrigerate.*)
Preheat broiler. Cut each bread slice into quarters. Spread 1 heaping teaspoon mayonnaise mixture on each bread square. Place bread squares on baking sheet. Broil just until lightly browned, 2 to 3 minutes. Serve hot.

CHEESE-ALMOND DIAMONDS

Makes about 4 dozen

- 8 ounces finely grated cheddar cheese
- 1 cup (2 sticks) butter, room temperature
- 1 tablespoon caraway seeds
- 1/2 teaspoon salt
- 1/2 teaspoon freshly ground pepper
- 1 3/4 cups plus 3 tablespoons all purpose flour
- 2 tablespoons cornstarch
- 48 (about) blanched almonds

Preheat oven to 325°F. Lightly grease baking sheets. Mix cheese, butter, caraway seeds, salt and pepper in large bowl until light and fluffy. Sift together flour and cornstarch and add to cheese mixture. Shape into 1-inch balls. Transfer to prepared baking sheets. Flatten slightly and press almond into center of each. Pinch corners to form diamond shapes. Bake until lightly browned, 10 to 15 minutes. Cool. Store in airtight container.

CHEDDAR WEDGES

Makes 64

1 1/2 **cups shredded cheddar cheese**
1 **cup chopped ripe olives**
1/2 **cup mayonnaise**
1/2 **cup thinly sliced green onions**
1/2 **teaspoon salt**
1/2 **teaspoon curry powder**
8 **English muffins, split and toasted**

Preheat broiler. Combine first 6 ingredients in medium bowl. Spread about 2 tablespoons cheese mixture over each muffin half. Arrange on broiler pan. Broil until cheese melts, about 3 minutes. Cut muffins into 4 wedges each and arrange on platter.

CHEDDAR CHIP CRISPS

Makes about 20

1/4 **cup (1/2 stick) butter, melted**
3 **ounces cheddar cheese, grated (about 1 1/3 cups)**
1 **cup finely crushed potato chips**
1/2 **cup all purpose flour, sifted**
Pinch of dry mustard
Pinch of freshly ground pepper

Preheat oven to 350°F. Lightly grease baking sheet. Mix all ingredients in medium bowl. Roll heaping teaspoons of mixture into balls. Arrange on prepared baking sheet and flatten with fork or fingers. Bake until crisp and golden brown, 12 to 15 minutes. Serve at room temperature. Store in airtight container. (*Cheddar Chip Crisps can be prepared ahead and frozen.*)

Beverages

SPARKLING APPLE SANGRIA

Makes 2 quarts

2 **medium oranges**
2 **medium lemons**

1/4 **cup sugar**
1/4 **teaspoon cinnamon**
1 **6-ounce can frozen apple juice concentrate, thawed**
1 **750-ml (25.4-ounce) bottle well-chilled sparkling apple cider**
2 **cups (or more) sparkling water**

Using small sharp knife or vegetable peeler, remove peel from 1 orange in 1/2-inch-thick spiral. Squeeze and reserve juice from 1 orange. Cut second orange into thin slices. Squeeze juice from 1 lemon. Add to orange juice. Cut second lemon into thin slices.

Place orange and lemon slices in bottom of large pitcher. Sprinkle with sugar and cinnamon. Using long wooden spoon, crush the fruit and sugar. Blend in reserved citrus juice and apple juice concentrate. Stir in apple cider. Add sparkling water to taste. Drape orange peel over edge of pitcher. Pour sangria into 8 stemmed glasses. Serve immediately.

GRAPEFRUIT AND KUMQUAT SPRITZERS

If you like beverages with the punch of tartness, this is your drink.

Makes 7 cups

13 **preserved kumquats in syrup, drained, 1/4 cup syrup reserved**
1 **large pink grapefruit**
1 **12-ounce can frozen grapefruit juice concentrate, thawed**
1 **liter (33.8 ounces) well-chilled grapefruit-flavored seltzer or sparkling water (about)**

Skewers or thin straws
Ice cubes

Cut 6 kumquats into small pieces.

Using sharp knife, remove peel and white pith from grapefruit. Working over bowl to catch juice, cut between membranes to release sections. Transfer juice and sections to processor. Add cut-up kumquats and puree. Pour into pitcher. Gradually stir in 2 tablespoons reserved kumquat syrup, grapefruit juice and half of seltzer. Add remaining 2 tablespoons reserved kumquat syrup and seltzer to taste.

Thread remaining kumquats on skewers or straws. Fill tall glasses with ice cubes. Pour drink into each. Garnish with skewers. Serve immediately.

PISTARCKLE PUNCH

Makes 12 cups

4 **cups water**
2 **cups sugar**

2 1/2 **cups fresh orange juice**
2 1/2 **cups guava nectar**
1 1/2 **cups minced fresh pineapple**
1 1/4 **cups fresh lemon juice**
1 **tablespoon finely grated orange peel**
2 **teaspoons finely grated lemon peel**
2 **tablespoons grenadine**
Ice cubes
Lemon slices
Mint leaves

Cook water and sugar in heavy medium saucepan over low heat until sugar dissolves, swirling pan occasionally. Increase heat and bring to boil. Cool syrup completely.

Blend orange juice, guava nectar, pineapple, lemon juice and peels in large pitcher. Stir in sugar syrup and grenadine. Pour into large ice-filled glasses. Garnish with lemon and mint.

PEACH PUNCH

Makes 2 1/2 quarts

2 pounds loose-pack frozen sliced peaches, partially thawed
1 12-ounce can well-chilled apricot nectar
1/4 cup fresh lime juice
1/4 teaspoon almond extract
1 liter (33.8 ounces) well-chilled ginger ale (or more)
10 lime slices
10 fresh mint sprigs

Place peaches in processor. With machine running, add nectar through feed tube and puree. Blend in juice and extract. Strain into punch bowl, pressing with back of spoon. Gradually stir in 1 liter ginger ale. Add more to taste if desired. Ladle into 10 stemmed glasses. Garnish with lime and mint.

FRESH STRAWBERRY-CHAMPAGNE SPRITZER

4 servings

1 pint fresh strawberries
1/2 cup fresh orange juice
1/2 cup dry white wine
1/4 cup sugar

1 26-ounce bottle Champagne, chilled

Wash and stem strawberries. Reserve 4 for garnish; halve remaining strawberries. Combine halved strawberries, orange juice, wine and sugar in processor or blender and puree until smooth. Chill 1 hour.

Divide strawberry mixture among 4 large Champagne glasses. Fill with Champagne. Garnish each with 1 reserved whole strawberry and serve.

CARIBBEAN WINE COOLER

1 serving

1/2 teaspoon superfine sugar
Dash of Angostura bitters
1 tablespoon fresh lime juice
1 tablespoon fresh orange juice
2 teaspoons Cognac
Cracked ice

1/2 cup dry white wine
Club soda
Dash of grenadine
1 lime slice
1 strawberry

Stir sugar and bitters in small pitcher until sugar dissolves. Mix in juices and Cognac. Pour mixture into tall glass filled with cracked ice. Stir in white wine. Top up glass with club soda. Blend in grenadine. Garnish with lime slice and strawberry and serve.

SNOWBALL COCKTAIL

Makes about 5 cups

1 6-ounce can frozen limeade concentrate
3/4 cup water
3/4 cup vodka
1 heaping tablespoon coconut snow powder
10 ice cubes, crushed

Combine all ingredients in blender and mix until frothy and smooth. Serve immediately in chilled glasses.

VODKA LIME SLUSH

Makes 3 1/2 quarts

2 quarts lime sherbet, softened
1 32-ounce can pineapple juice
1 32-ounce bottle lemon-lime soda
1 1/2 cups vodka
Lime slices

Combine sherbet and juice in blender or processor in batches and mix well. Transfer to container; cover and freeze until firm, 1 hour or overnight.

Transfer mixture to blender or processor in batches. Add soda and vodka and mix until slushy. Pour into glasses. Garnish with lime slices.

MAD MAGGIES

This tangy drink is a variation on the traditional Margarita.

4 servings

1 cup sweet and sour bar mix
3/4 cup tequila
6 tablespoons Triple Sec

16 ice cubes
1/2 cup fresh orange juice
4 orange slices

Combine first 3 ingredients in blender. Add ice cubes and blend until frothy. Add juice and mix using 1 on/off turn. Pour into chilled glasses. Garnish with orange slices and serve.

RUM SLUSH

Makes 3 quarts

2 cups boiling water
1 cup sugar
3 cups light rum
2 cups strong tea
2 cups water
1 12-ounce can frozen lemonade concentrate
1 6-ounce can frozen orange juice concentrate

Combine boiling water and sugar in large plastic container and stir until sugar is dissolved. Add remaining ingredients and mix thoroughly. Cover and freeze overnight. Spoon mixture into glasses and serve.

PINA BANANA COLADA

2 to 4 servings

1 cup coconut-pineapple juice
6 to 8 ounces (3/4 to 1 cup) light rum
3 tablespoons coconut snow powder
1 ripe banana, sliced into thirds
1 to 1 1/2 cups crushed ice

Combine all ingredients in blender and mix well. Pour into glasses and serve.

FROZEN DAIQUIRI

4 servings

2 cups crushed ice
3/4 cup light rum
1/4 cup fresh lime juice
1/4 cup Triple Sec
2 teaspoons superfine sugar
4 lime slices

Mix all ingredients except lime slices in blender until slushy. Pour into large stemmed glasses. Garnish with lime.

VIRGIN ISLANDS PINA COLADA

For a nonalcoholic version of this classic drink, omit rum and brandy and add 1/4 teaspoon vanilla.

4 servings

> 4 cups ice cubes
> 1 cup pineapple juice
> 3/4 cup dark rum
> 1/2 cup coconut cream
> 1/4 cup brandy
> 4 fresh pineapple wedges
> Mint leaves
> Freshly grated nutmeg

Mix first 5 ingredients in blender until slushy. Pour into tall glasses. Garnish with pineapple, mint and nutmeg.

STRAWBERRY-RUM SLUSH

Makes about 7 cups

> 1 6-ounce can frozen limeade concentrate, thawed
> 6 ounces rum
> 1 pint fresh strawberries, hulled
> 1 to 2 tablespoons sugar (optional)
> 14 ice cubes
> Lime slices

Combine 1/2 can limeade, 3 ounces rum, 1/2 pint strawberries and 1 tablespoon sugar in blender. Mix at medium speed, adding 7 ice cubes 1 at a time until smooth and very thick. Pour into large pitcher. Repeat with remaining ingredients except lime slices. Add to pitcher and stir to blend well. Garnish with lime slices and serve.

SUNBURN

A fresh-tasting tropical drink with two different kinds of rum.

4 servings

> 2 cups pineapple juice
> 1 cup fresh orange juice
> 1/4 cup dark rum
> 1/4 cup light rum
> 2 tablespoons amaretto liqueur
> 2 tablespoons Southern Comfort
> 12 to 16 ice cubes
> Grenadine syrup

Combine first 6 ingredients in large pitcher and shake well. Divide ice cubes among 4 tall glasses. Pour juice mixture over. Add dash of grenadine to each. Stir to blend and serve.

RAMOS FIZZ

2 servings

> 3 ounces gin
> 2 tablespoons plus 1 teaspoon fresh lemon juice
> 1 tablespoon (generous) sugar
> 3/4 cup half and half
> 1 egg white
> 12 drops orange flower water
> 8 ice cubes
> Freshly grated nutmeg

Mix first 3 ingredients in blender on high speed 15 seconds. Add half and half, egg white, orange flower water and 4 ice cubes and blend 30 seconds. Divide remaining ice cubes between 2 brandy snifters. Pour gin mixture over ice. Sprinkle with nutmeg.

JAMAICA FAREWELL

4 servings

> Cracked ice
> 1 cup fresh orange juice
> 3/4 cup tequila
> 1/2 cup Tia Maria
> 3 to 4 tablespoons fresh lime juice
> 4 orange slices

Fill cocktail shaker with cracked ice. Add all ingredients except orange slices. Shake until frosted. Strain into tall glasses filled with cracked ice. Garnish with orange and serve.

CRANBERRY EGGNOG

8 to 12 servings

> 6 eggs, separated
> 4 tablespoons sugar
> 1 1-quart bottle cranberry juice, chilled
> 2 cups whipping cream, chilled
> Dash of ground cloves

Beat yolks in large bowl of electric mixer until light and lemon colored, about 5 minutes. Add 2 tablespoons sugar and beat until slowly dissolving ribbon forms when beaters are lifted. Beat egg whites in another large bowl until soft peaks form. Gradually add remaining 2 tablespoons sugar and beat until stiff and glossy. Fold egg whites into yolk mixture and blend thoroughly. Stir in juice and cream. Sprinkle with cloves. Serve chilled.

SUPER SHAKES

4 servings

> 1 pint (or more) chocolate ice cream
> 2 cups (or more) milk
> 1/4 cup Grand Marnier
> Whipped cream (garnish)
> Grated chocolate (garnish)

Combine ice cream, milk and Grand Marnier in blender and mix 1 to 2 minutes (additional ice cream or milk can be added, depending on desired thickness). Pour into 4 large wine glasses or brandy snifters. Garnish with whipped cream and chocolate.

STRAWBERRY KISS

2 servings

> 1/2 pint strawberry ice cream
> 1 cup crushed ice
> 1/2 cup half and half
> 1/4 cup brandy
> 1/4 cup strawberry liqueur
> 4 fresh strawberries
> 2 small scoops strawberry ice cream (optional)
> 2 fresh strawberries, sliced
> 2 fresh mint sprigs

Chill 2 wide-mouthed stemmed glasses. Combine 1/2 pint ice cream, crushed ice, half and half, brandy, liqueur and 4 strawberries in blender and mix well. Pour into chilled glasses. Float 1 scoop of ice cream in each if desired. Garnish with sliced strawberries and mint sprigs. Serve immediately.

HOT PERKED APPLE CIDER

8 servings

>   8 cups apple cider
> 1/2 cup loosely packed light brown sugar
>   10 3-inch cinnamon sticks
>   6 whole cloves

Pour cider into large percolator. Place remaining ingredients in percolator basket. Perk 10 minutes. Pour into mugs. Garnish each with cinnamon stick from basket and serve.

CITRUS TODDY

Makes 1 quart

> 2 1/2 cups water
>   4 whole cloves
> 1/3 to 1/2 cup honey
>   1 cup fresh orange juice
>   6 tablespoons fresh lemon juice
> 1/4 cup fresh lime juice
>   4 thin lime slices

Bring water and cloves to simmer in heavy medium saucepan. Cover and simmer gently 10 minutes. Add 1/3 cup honey and stir to dissolve. Stir in juices. Cover and heat through; do not boil. Taste and stir in remaining honey if desired. Ladle into 4 mugs. Float lime slice on each and serve.

HOT CURRIED VEGETABLE JUICE

A satisfying drink for winter evenings. Create fanciful green onion "swizzle sticks" for garnish by snipping tops into thin ribbons using scissors, then refrigerating in ice water so they "fan."

Makes 1 quart

>   2 tablespoons (1/4 stick) butter
>   2 tablespoons grated onion
>   1 tablespoon curry powder
>   1 teaspoon ground cumin
>   1 quart vegetable juice
>
> 1/3 cup plain yogurt
>   2 tablespoons whipping cream
> 1/16 teaspoon (or more) cayenne pepper
>
>   4 green onions, trimmed

Melt butter in heavy medium saucepan over medium heat. Add grated onion and stir 1 minute. Add curry powder and cumin and stir 30 seconds. Add vegetable juice and bring to simmer. Cover and simmer 10 minutes.

Meanwhile, blend yogurt, cream and 1/16 teaspoon cayenne in small bowl. Add more cayenne to taste.

Ladle drink into 4 mugs. Top each with spoonful of yogurt mixture. Garnish with green onion and serve.

HOT MULLED CRANBERRY ORANGE JUICE

Makes 2 quarts

>   1 medium orange
>
>   6 cups water (about)
>   20 whole cloves
>   1 3 1/2-inch cinnamon stick
>   1 12-ounce can and one 6-ounce can frozen cranberry juice cocktail concentrate, thawed
> 1/2 cup golden raisins
> 1/2 teaspoon ground cardamom
>   3 tablespoons fresh lemon juice
>   8 thin orange slices

Using small sharp knife, cut eight 3x1/2-inch strips of peel (colored part only) from orange. Cut orange in half; squeeze and reserve juice.

Bring 1 cup water with orange peel strips, 12 cloves and cinnamon stick to simmer in heavy small saucepan. Cover and simmer 20 minutes. Strain liquid into another heavy large saucepan. Add 4 cups water, cranberry juice, raisins and cardamom. Taste and add remaining 1 cup water if desired. Heat over low heat. Stir in reserved orange juice and lemon juice. Pierce rind of each orange slice with one of remaining cloves. Ladle drink into 8 mugs. Garnish each with orange slice.

CAFE BON WEEKEND

2 servings

> 1/2 cup brewed coffee
> 1 1/2 teaspoons sugar

>   2 ounces semisweet chocolate, chopped
>   Pinch of cinnamon
>   1 cup milk, heated
>   2 tablespoons light rum
> 1/4 cup sweetened whipped cream (optional)
>   Cinnamon (optional)

Heat coffee and sugar in heavy small saucepan over low heat until sugar dissolves, swirling pan occasionally. Add chocolate and pinch of cinnamon and stir until chocolate melts. Add milk and whisk until frothy. Pour into hot mugs. Add 1 tablespoon rum to each. Top with whipped cream and dust with more cinnamon if desired.

IRISH COFFEE

Use warmed glasses or mugs with handles for this traditional drink.

8 servings

> 1/4 cup sugar
>   Hot black coffee
>   16 ounces (2 cups) Irish whiskey
> 1/2 cup (generous) whipped cream

Place 1 1/2 teaspoons sugar in each glass. Stir in enough coffee to dissolve sugar. Add 1/4 cup whiskey. Fill to within 1 inch of rim with more coffee. Top with whipped cream (do not stir) and serve immediately.

CAFE BRULOT

12 servings

> 2 1/4 cups Cognac or brandy
> 1/2 cup orange peel julienne
>   36 whole cloves
>   32 sugar cubes
>   12 cinnamon sticks
>   12 cups freshly brewed strong coffee

Heat Cognac with orange peel, cloves, sugar and cinnamon in heavy large saucepan. Tilt pan and ignite Cognac. When flames subside, stir until sugar dissolves. Add fresh coffee and heat through. Ladle into cups.

2 ❖ *Soups*

There's nothing like the enticing and comforting aromas of home-made soup simmering on the stove. And while this image may conjure up thoughts of long hours in the kitchen, nothing could be further from the truth. Soups are a boon to the busy cook, providing endless versatility and exciting variety with a minimum of prep time. Soup-making does not require any difficult or time-consuming techniques, and soups can usually be made several days ahead and reheated just before serving.

Some of the soups included here would set the tone for a fancy dinner party or romantic candlelit dinner for two, while others are a rustic, hearty main dish. For a stunning stage-setter, it would be hard to beat the smooth elegance of Yellow Pepper Soup or shimmering Gingered Chinese Noodle Soup. Or, for a nourishing, soul-satisfying meal for family or friends, try basil-scented Italian Tortellini Soup, chock-full of vegetables and sweet Italian sausage, or San Francisco Cioppino, a fast version of the classic fish soup with crab, scallops and shrimp. Vegetable-Cheese Chowder is a robust vegetarian main course with the tang of freshly grated Parmesan. Serve any of these hearty soups with a crusty loaf of bread, green salad and a light dessert— perhaps poached fruit, purchased sorbet or a creamy custard—and you have a meal perfect for both everyday family dining and casual get-togethers.

Soup provides a welcome respite at any time of year. Some standout warm-weather possibilities are Yogurt-Cucumber Soup, a light and low-calorie refresher; Chilled Ginger-Carrot Soup, which uses fresh orange juice as its base; and Blender Gazpacho with the freshness of summer's best vegetables. Serve these in clear glass bowls for a lovely beginning to either lunch or dinner, or alone—with just a good loaf of bread—as a light lunch entrée.

As further proof of their versatility, many of these soups can be served hot or cold; Apple and Pumpkin Soup spiked with apple brandy, and vivid Cream of Curried Pea Soup are two that are delicious either way.

YOGURT-CUCUMBER SOUP

4 to 6 servings

> 1 32-ounce carton lowfat plain yogurt
> 4 teaspoons vegetable oil
> 1 pound cucumbers, peeled and diced
> 1/2 cup coarsely ground walnuts
> 1 garlic clove, minced
>   Salt and freshly ground pepper
>   Chopped fresh dill

Whisk yogurt in large bowl until smooth. Add oil and whisk until well blended. Mix in cucumbers, walnuts and garlic. Season with salt and pepper. Chill. (*Can be prepared 1 day ahead.*) Ladle into bowls. Garnish with chopped fresh dill.

CHILLED GINGER-CARROT SOUP

8 servings

> 1/2 cup (1 stick) butter
> 2/3 cup chopped green onions
> 6 cups sliced carrots
> 2 teaspoons sugar
> 1 teaspoon ground ginger
> 1/2 teaspoon cinnamon
> 2 tablespoons all purpose flour
> 1 teaspoon salt
> 1/2 teaspoon freshly ground white pepper
> 4 cups water
> 3 cups fresh orange juice
> 1 cup whipping cream
> 2 teaspoons fresh lemon juice
>   Carrot julienne (garnish)

Melt butter in heavy large Dutch oven over medium heat. Add green onions and sauté until tender, about 5 minutes. Stir in carrots, sugar, ginger and cinnamon and sauté 5 more minutes. Blend in flour, salt and pepper and toss until carrots are coated with flour. Cook 1 minute. Add water and orange juice and bring to boil. Reduce heat to medium-low, cover and simmer until carrot is tender, about 20 minutes. Cool slightly. Transfer mixture to processor or blender in batches and puree until smooth. Pour into large bowl. Stir in whipping cream and lemon juice. Taste and adjust seasoning. Cover and refrigerate several hours or overnight. To serve, ladle into bowls and garnish with carrot julienne.

BLENDER GAZPACHO

4 to 6 servings

> 1 cup peeled and diced cucumbers
> 2/3 cup seeded and diced green bell peppers
> 1 4-ounce can diced green chilies, drained
> 1 46-ounce can tomato juice, chilled
> 1 teaspoon seasoned salt
> 1/2 teaspoon Worcestershire sauce
> 3 drops of hot pepper sauce
> 1 1/4 cups diced tomatoes
> 1 cup chopped green onions
>   Salt and freshly ground pepper
>   Lemon slices

Place half of cucumbers, half of bell peppers and half of chilies in blender. Add half of tomato juice and puree on high speed 1 minute. Transfer to large bowl. Repeat with remaining cucumbers, bell peppers, chilies and tomato juice. Add to same bowl. Stir in seasoned salt, Worcestershire and pepper sauce. Add tomatoes and green onions. Season with salt and pepper. Cover and refrigerate at least 1 hour. (*Can be prepared 1 day ahead.*) Ladle soup into bowls. Garnish soup with lemon slices.

TORTILLA CHIP SOUP

4 servings

> 5 1/2 cups chicken broth
> 1/2 cup chopped celery
> 1 teaspoon chili powder
> 1 tablespoon olive oil
> 2 large tomatoes, cored, peeled, seeded and chopped
> 3 small garlic cloves, minced
> 1 teaspoon chopped onion
> 1 teaspoon chopped fresh parsley
> 1 6 3/4-ounce package tortilla chips
> 1 cup grated cheddar cheese

Combine broth (and water if using), celery and chili powder in 3-quart saucepan and bring to boil over medium-high heat. Reduce heat to medium and cook until celery is tender, about 20 minutes. Meanwhile, heat oil in small skillet over medium heat. Add tomatoes, garlic, onion and parsley and sauté until onion is tender, about 5 minutes. Add tomato mixture to broth. Break chips into soup and continue cooking until chips are soft, about 2 minutes. Stir in cheddar cheese and serve immediately.

APPLE AND FENNEL SOUP

8 servings

> 2 tablespoons (1/4 stick) butter
> 1 1/2 cups chopped onions
> 8 cups chicken stock
> 2 large fennel bulbs, trimmed, strings removed, chopped
> 4 large green apples, peeled, cored and chopped
>   Salt and freshly ground pepper

> 1/2 cup crème fraîche
>   Additional crème fraîche
>   Paprika
>   Lime slices

Melt butter in heavy large saucepan over medium heat. Add onions and cook until translucent, about 8 minutes. Add stock and fennel and simmer until fennel is tender, about 20 minutes. Stir in apples and simmer 10 minutes. Season with salt and freshly ground pepper. Cool slightly.

Puree soup in blender or processor in batches. (*Can be prepared 1 day ahead. Cover and refrigerate.*) Return soup to saucepan. Stir in 1/2 cup crème fraîche. Warm gently over low heat until heated through. Ladle into bowls. Garnish with additional crème fraîche, paprika and lime slices. Serve hot.

APPLE AND PUMPKIN SOUP

6 servings

> 1 tart green apple, peeled and cored
>   Fresh lemon juice

3 tablespoons butter
1 medium yellow onion, finely chopped
1 1/2 cups finely chopped celery
2 tablespoons curry powder
1 teaspoon dried thyme, crumbled
3 cups chicken broth
2 cups canned solid pack pumpkin
1 cup applesauce
1/4 cup Calvados
Salt and freshly ground pepper
Sour cream

Shred apple into small bowl. Toss with lemon juice to prevent discoloration.

Melt butter in large saucepan or Dutch oven over medium heat. Add onion and stir until translucent, about 2 minutes. Add celery and cook until tender, about 4 minutes. Stir in curry powder and thyme. Mix in chicken broth, pumpkin and applesauce. Simmer 15 minutes. Add Calvados, salt and pepper and continue simmering 10 minutes. Ladle into bowls. Top with sour cream and shredded apple.

BROCCOLI-SOUR CREAM SOUP

8 servings

3 tablespoons butter
1 large Golden Delicious apple, peeled, cored and diced
1 small onion, thinly sliced
1 bunch broccoli (about 1 1/2 pounds), trimmed, stems peeled and diced, florets separated
4 cups chicken broth
1 teaspoon salt
Freshly ground pepper
1/4 cup sour cream
2 tablespoons snipped fresh chives

Melt butter in heavy large saucepan over low heat. Add apple and onion. Cover and cook until soft, about 10 minutes. Add broccoli, broth and salt. Increase heat and bring to boil. Reduce heat and simmer until broccoli is just tender, about 15 minutes. Puree in blender in batches until smooth. Return soup to saucepan. Warm over low heat. Season with pepper. Ladle soup into bowls. Garnish with sour cream and chives. Serve hot.

CREAMY CARROT SOUP

Makes 4 1/2 cups

3 cups peeled, diced carrots
2 cups (or more) chicken broth
1 medium shallot, quartered
1 teaspoon dried tarragon, crumbled
1 bay leaf
Pinch of freshly grated nutmeg
1 tablespoon butter
1 tablespoon all purpose flour
1 cup whipping cream
Salt and freshly ground pepper

Combine carrots, 2 cups broth, shallot, tarragon, bay leaf and nutmeg in Dutch oven. Cover and cook over medium-high heat until carrots are tender, about 15 minutes. Discard bay leaf. Puree carrot mixture in processor. Return to Dutch oven and bring to boil. Melt butter in heavy small skillet over medium heat. Whisk in flour and cook 2 minutes. Whisk into carrot mixture. Return to boil. Reduce heat to low. Stir in cream. Season with salt and pepper. Mix in additional broth if thinner consistency is desired. Serve hot.

SHERRIED CAULIFLOWER SOUP

4 to 6 servings

1 head cauliflower, cut into florets, steamed until tender
1/4 cup (1/2 stick) unsalted butter
2 medium yellow onions, chopped
4 garlic cloves, pressed
1 14 1/2-ounce can chicken broth
1/2 cup cream Sherry
1/2 teaspoon freshly grated nutmeg
2 cups whipping cream
Salt and freshly ground white pepper
Freshly grated nutmeg

Puree steamed cauliflower in food processor until smooth, about 30 seconds. Melt butter in large saucepan or Dutch oven over medium heat. Add onions and garlic and stir until onions are translucent, about 5 minutes. Add cauliflower puree, broth, Sherry and 1/2 teaspoon nutmeg and simmer 10 minutes. Add cream, salt and pepper. Simmer 10 minutes to blend flavors. Sprinkle with additional nutmeg.

MAUI CORN SOUP

6 servings

2 tablespoons vegetable oil
1/2 cup minced onion
1 garlic clove, minced
6 cups chicken broth
2 cups corn kernels
1 teaspoon ground ginger
1/2 teaspoon sugar
1/4 teaspoon freshly ground pepper
2 tablespoons soy sauce
2 tablespoons water
1 tablespoon cornstarch
2 eggs
2 green onions, thinly sliced
Additional soy sauce (garnish)

Heat oil in large saucepan over medium-high heat until hot. Add onion and garlic and sauté 2 minutes. Pour in broth and bring to boil. Stir in corn, ginger, sugar and pepper. Reduce heat to low, cover and cook until heated through, about 7 minutes. Combine soy sauce, water and cornstarch in small bowl. Slowly blend into soup, stirring constantly until thickened. Beat eggs with green onion in small bowl. Gradually add to soup, stirring until eggs are just set. Ladle into bowls and serve immediately. Pass additional soy sauce separately.

YELLOW PEPPER SOUP

6 servings

1/4 cup olive oil
1 small onion, coarsely chopped
4 large garlic cloves, crushed
2 tablespoons capers, rinsed
1/8 teaspoon dried red pepper flakes
4 large yellow bell peppers (about 1 3/4 pounds), cored, seeded and cut into large pieces
Salt
2 cups beef stock (preferably homemade)

Heat oil in heavy large saucepan over medium-low heat. Add onion and garlic and cook until golden, stirring frequently, about 15 minutes. Add 1 tablespoon capers and red pepper flakes and cook 3 minutes, stirring frequently. Add bell peppers and salt. Cover and cook 10 minutes, stirring frequently. Add stock. Reduce heat, cover and simmer until peppers are soft, stirring often, about 30 minutes.

Puree mixture in blender or processor in batches. Strain back into saucepan, pressing with spoon. (*Can be prepared 2 days ahead. Cover and refrigerate.*) Stir remaining 1 tablespoon capers into soup. Rewarm over low heat. Ladle into bowls and serve.

ESCAROLE AND WHITE BEAN SOUP

4 to 6 servings

- 1/4 **pound lean ground beef**
- 1/4 **pound ground pork**
- 1 **egg, beaten to blend**
- 2 **tablespoons freshly grated Parmesan cheese**
- 2 **tablespoons seasoned dry breadcrumbs**
- 1/4 **teaspoon garlic powder**

- 8 **cups chicken broth**
- 1 **large bunch escarole, chopped**
- 2 **16-ounce cans cannellini beans,* drained**
- 1 **garlic clove, minced**
- 1/2 **teaspoon dried red pepper flakes**
- 1/2 **teaspoon dried basil, crumbled Salt and freshly ground pepper Additional freshly grated Parmesan cheese**

Combine first 6 ingredients in medium bowl. Form into 1-inch balls. Set aside. (*Can be prepared 1 week ahead and frozen. Thaw before continuing.*)

Heat broth in large saucepan over medium heat. Stir in next 5 ingredients. Season with salt and pepper. Add meatballs and cook until firm to touch, about 30 minutes. (*Can be prepared 1 day ahead. Cover and refrigerate. Rewarm before serving.*) Ladle

soup into bowls. Serve immediately, passing additional freshly grated Parmesan cheese separately.

*White kidney beans available at Italian markets. If unavailable, Great Northern or navy beans can be substituted.

MUSHROOM-SHERRY BISQUE

Makes about 4 cups

- 1/2 **pound mushrooms**
- 1 **small onion, quartered**
- 2 **cups chicken broth**

- 3 **tablespoons butter**
- 3 **tablespoons all purpose flour**
- 1/2 **cup milk**
- 1 1/2 **cups half and half Salt and freshly ground pepper**
- 1 **tablespoon dry Sherry Sliced mushrooms**

Finely chop 1/2 pound mushrooms and onion in blender or processor, about 1 minute. Transfer to heavy medium saucepan. Add chicken broth. Cover and simmer 15 minutes.

Meanwhile, melt butter in heavy medium saucepan over medium-low heat. Add flour and stir 2 minutes. Add milk and cook until thickened, stirring occasionally, about 2 minutes. Mix in half and half. Stir into mushroom mixture. Season with salt and pepper. Stir in Sherry. (*Can be prepared 1 day ahead and chilled.*) Ladle into bowls. Garnish with mushrooms.

CREAM OF CURRIED PEA SOUP

This is also refreshing served chilled.

Makes about 4 cups

- 2 **cups chicken broth**
- 1 **cup frozen peas**
- 1 **large celery stalk, leaves included, sliced**
- 1 **medium onion, chopped**
- 1 **medium carrot, peeled and sliced**
- 2 **garlic cloves, minced**
- 1 **teaspoon curry powder**
- 1 **teaspoon salt**

- 1 **cup whipping cream Snipped fresh chives**

Combine 1 cup broth, peas, celery, onion, carrot, garlic, curry powder and salt in large saucepan. Bring to boil. Cover partially, reduce heat and simmer until vegetables are tender, about 15 minutes. Cool slightly.

Puree soup in blender or processor in batches. (*Can be prepared 1 day ahead, covered and refrigerated.*) Return soup to saucepan. Stir in cream and remaining 1 cup broth. Warm gently over low heat until heated through. Ladle into bowls. Garnish with chives. Serve hot.

MINTED PEA SOUP

Makes about 3 1/2 cups

- 1 **10-ounce package frozen peas, thawed, or two cups cooked fresh peas**
- 2 **cups half and half**
- 8 **medium fresh mint leaves Salt and freshly ground pepper Fresh mint leaves**

Puree peas, half and half and 8 mint leaves in blender until smooth. Strain into medium saucepan. Set over medium-low heat and warm through. Season with salt and pepper. Ladle soup into bowls. Garnish with mint leaves. Serve immediately.

CHUNKY CREAM OF POTATO SOUP

Makes 7 cups

- 2 **15-ounce cans whole potatoes, drained**
- 2 1/2 **cups chicken broth**
- 1 **cup chopped onions**
- 2/3 **cup chopped celery**
- 1/2 **teaspoon onion salt**
- 1/2 **teaspoon seasoned salt**
- 1/2 **teaspoon dried dillweed**

- 3 **tablespoons butter**
- 3 **tablespoons all purpose flour**
- 1 **cup milk**
- 1 **cup whipping cream Salt and freshly ground pepper**

Combine half of potatoes with chicken broth, onions, celery, onion salt, seasoned salt and dillweed in large saucepan or Dutch oven. Cover and bring to boil. Reduce heat and simmer until celery is tender, about 15 minutes. Remove from heat and cool slightly. Ladle half of soup into blender or processor and puree. Transfer to large bowl. Repeat procedure with remaining soup. Set aside.

Melt butter in same saucepan over medium-low heat. Whisk in flour. Gradually add milk and cream, whisking until slightly thickened, about 5 minutes. Increase heat to medium. Return pureed soup to pan. Cut remaining potatoes into bite-size pieces. Add to soup. Stir until heated through, about 5 minutes. Season with salt and pepper. Serve hot. (*Can be prepared 1 day ahead. Cover and refrigerate. Rewarm over medium heat.*)

VEGETABLE-CHEESE CHOWDER

4 servings

2 1/2 cups water
  2 cups diced peeled potatoes
3/4 cup minced leeks
1/2 cup diced celery
2 1/2 teaspoons salt

1/4 cup (1/2 stick) butter
1/4 cup all purpose flour
  2 cups milk
1 1/2 teaspoons Worcestershire sauce
1/2 teaspoon dry mustard
1/4 teaspoon freshly ground pepper
  1 12-ounce can cubed tomatoes, drained
  4 ounces freshly grated Parmesan cheese
  1 tablespoon minced fresh parsley

Bring water to boil in large saucepan over high heat. Add potatoes, leeks, celery and 1 teaspoon salt. Return to boil. Reduce heat to medium-low, cover and simmer until vegetables are tender, about 15 minutes.

Melt butter in medium saucepan over medium-low heat. Remove from heat and blend in flour. Add milk, 1 1/2 teaspoons Worcestershire sauce, remaining 1 1/2 teaspoons salt, mustard and pepper. Return to medium-low heat and stir until thickened, about 10 minutes. Stir into potato mixture. Add tomatoes, Parmesan and parsley. Ladle into bowls and serve.

CREAMY GREENS SOUP

8 servings

  1 tablespoon vegetable oil
1/2 medium onion, chopped
  2 celery stalks, diced
  6 to 7 cups vegetable stock
3/4 cup split peas, rinsed
  1 bay leaf

  6 cups diced zucchini
1/2 teaspoon dried basil, crumbled
    Salt and freshly ground pepper
  1 pound spinach, chopped
1/2 cup chopped fresh parsley

Heat oil in heavy large saucepan over medium heat. Add onion and celery and stir until softened, about 5 minutes. Add 4 cups vegetable stock, split peas and bay leaf. Bring soup to boil. Reduce heat, cover partially and simmer for 40 minutes.

Stir zucchini, 2 cups stock and basil into soup. Season with salt and pepper. Simmer 10 minutes. Discard bay leaf. Puree soup in blender or processor in batches. Return to saucepan. Stir in spinach and parsley. Thin soup with remaining stock, if desired. Stir soup over medium heat until warmed through, about 5 minutes. Serve hot.

CURRIED CREAM OF VEGETABLE SOUP

4 to 6 servings

  3 carrots, chopped
1/2 head cauliflower, chopped
  1 medium onion, chopped
  1 medium potato, peeled and chopped
  1 tablespoon chopped fresh parsley
  2 chicken bouillon cubes
  1 cup whipping cream
1/2 teaspoon curry powder
1/4 teaspoon Worcestershire sauce
    Freshly ground white pepper

Bring 3 cups water to boil in 2-quart saucepan over medium-high heat. Add carrot, cauliflower, onion, potato, parsley and bouillon cubes and return to boil. Continue cooking until vegetables are tender, about 15 minutes.

Transfer mixture to blender or processor in batches and puree until smooth. Return to saucepan. Blend in whipping cream. Mix in remaining ingredients. Place over medium heat and cook until heated through. Ladle into bowls. Serve immediately.

CHEESY CREAM OF SPINACH SOUP

6 servings

  3 tablespoons butter
  1 tablespoon vegetable oil
  1 small onion, minced
  2 10-ounce packages frozen chopped spinach, thawed
  2 tablespoons all purpose flour
  1 14 1/2-ounce can chicken broth
  2 cups half and half
1/2 teaspoon freshly ground white pepper
    Freshly grated nutmeg
1/2 pound bacon, chopped and crisply cooked
  1 cup grated cheddar cheese

Melt butter with oil in large saucepan over medium heat. Add onion and cook until translucent, about 5 minutes. Press spinach in large strainer, reserving liquid. Add spinach to onion and mix well. Sprinkle with flour and cook, stirring frequently, 3 minutes. Blend in broth and reserved spinach liquid and bring to simmer. Cook 10 minutes. Stir in half and half, pepper and nutmeg and simmer gently 5 minutes. Add bacon and cheese. Ladle soup into bowls and serve hot.

HERBED CHEESE SOUP

4 servings

1/4 cup (1/2 stick) butter
  3 tablespoons all purpose flour
  1 tablespoon finely chopped chives
  1 teaspoon paprika
  1 teaspoon dry mustard
  1 10 3/4-ounce can chicken broth
  2 cups half and half
  4 ounces semisoft garlic and herb cheese
    Salt and freshly ground white pepper
    Croutons (garnish)

Melt butter in medium saucepan over medium-low heat. Add flour and stir 4 minutes. Blend in chives, paprika and mustard and cook 1 minute. Gradually blend in broth. Add half and half and cheese and bring mixture to boil. Taste and season with salt and white pepper. Ladle soup into bowls. Garnish with croutons and serve immediately.

ITALIAN GARDEN SOUP

8 servings

    2 tablespoons (¼ stick) butter
    1 large onion, coarsely chopped
    1 medium garlic clove, crushed
 1½ cups thinly sliced carrots
 1½ cups thinly sliced celery
    1 medium zucchini, sliced
    1 28-ounce can chicken broth
    1 16-ounce can Italian tomatoes
      (reserve juice)
    1 teaspoon dried oregano,
      crumbled
  ¼ teaspoon dried basil, crumbled
  ⅛ teaspoon freshly ground pepper
      Salt
      Freshly grated Parmesan cheese
      Seasoned croutons

Melt butter in large saucepan over medium-high heat. Add onion and garlic and sauté until onion is soft, about 5 minutes. Add carrots, celery and zucchini and sauté 4 to 5 minutes. Add chicken broth, tomatoes and reserved juice, oregano, basil, pepper and salt. Bring to boil over high heat. Reduce heat, cover and simmer until vegetables are just crisp-tender, 10 to 15 minutes. Ladle into bowls and serve. Pass Parmesan and croutons separately.

CREAMY CHICKEN CORN SOUP

6 to 8 servings

    3 medium russet potatoes, peeled
      and cut into ½-inch dice

    2 tablespoons (¼ stick) butter
    2 tablespoons all purpose flour
    2 cups half and half
    2 cups milk

    4 teaspoons instant chicken
      bouillon powder
    1 teaspoon onion powder
      Salt and freshly ground pepper
 1½ cups cubed cooked chicken
 1½ cups frozen whole kernel corn,
      thawed

Cook potatoes in large saucepan of boiling water until just tender, about 15 minutes. Drain.

Meanwhile, melt butter in heavy large saucepan over medium-low heat. Add flour and stir 2 minutes. Mix in half and half, milk, bouillon and onion powders. Season with salt and pepper. Stir constantly until mixture boils and thickens, about 10 minutes. Reduce heat to low. Stir in chicken, corn and potatoes and cook 15 minutes.

GUAMANIAN HOT AND SOUR SOUP

6 servings

    1 quart chicken stock
  ½ cup canned bamboo shoots,
      rinsed, drained and thinly
      sliced
  ¼ cup cooked shredded pork or
      beef
    1 tablespoon soy sauce
    7 ounces bean curd, rinsed and
      cut into ½-inch dice
    2 tablespoons distilled white
      vinegar
  ¼ teaspoon freshly ground pepper
    3 tablespoons cornstarch
    3 tablespoons water
    1 egg, beaten to blend
    2 teaspoons sesame oil
    1 teaspoon dried red pepper
      flakes
    1 medium-size green onion,
      finely chopped

Combine chicken stock, bamboo shoots, pork and soy sauce in heavy Dutch oven. Bring to boil over high heat. Reduce heat to low, cover and simmer 3 minutes. Add bean curd, vinegar and pepper. Return to boil over low heat. Mix cornstarch and water in small bowl and stir into soup. Slowly stir in egg. Remove from heat and blend in sesame oil and red pepper flakes. Ladle into bowls. Garnish with chopped green onion.

GINGERED CHINESE NOODLE SOUP

Cellophane noodles (also called mung bean threads), oriental sesame oil and rice vinegar are available at oriental markets. Thin spaghetti can be substituted for the noodles.

4 to 6 servings

    3 ounces cellophane noodles*

    2 tablespoons vegetable oil
    1 medium onion, sliced
    2 thin carrots, sliced diagonally
    2 medium garlic cloves, minced
    1 teaspoon minced fresh ginger
    1 medium red bell pepper, thinly
      sliced
    3 cups chicken stock
 1½ cups water
    1 tablespoon soy sauce
    1 cup Smithfield or Black
      Forest ham, cut julienne (about
      4 ounces)
    1 cup shredded watercress leaves
  ½ cup thinly sliced mushrooms
    1 cup (generous) snow peas,
      strings removed
    1 teaspoon oriental sesame oil, or
      to taste
    1 teaspoon rice vinegar, or to
      taste
      Pinch of dried red pepper flakes
    2 green onions, thinly sliced on
      diagonal

Place cellophane noodles in large bowl. Cover with boiling water. Let stand 5 minutes. Drain thoroughly.

Heat oil in wok or deep large skillet over medium-high heat. Add onion and carrots and stir-fry 3 minutes. Add garlic and ginger, then bell pepper. Stir-fry 30 seconds. Add stock, water and soy sauce. Cover and boil 2 minutes. Add ham, watercress, mushrooms and noodles. Return to boil. Cover, turn off heat and let steep 2 minutes. Add snow peas, cover and let steep until vegetables are crisp-tender, about 3 minutes. Stir in sesame oil, rice vinegar and red pepper flakes. Adjust seasoning. Ladle soup into deep bowls. Sprinkle with green onions.

*If unavailable, use 1 generous cup thin spaghetti broken into 3-inch pieces. Cook in boiling water until firm but almost tender to bite. Drain pasta thoroughly.

KIELBASA-SPLIT PEA SOUP

Serve this hearty soup with rye bread.

Makes about 3¹/2 quarts

    2 quarts water
    1 pound split peas, rinsed
 1¹/2 pounds kielbasa sausage, cut
       into bite-size chunks
       Salt and freshly ground pepper
    2 medium boiling potatoes,
       peeled and cubed
  ³/4 cup diced carrots
  ¹/2 cup chopped celery

Combine water and peas in heavy large saucepan or Dutch oven. Bring to boil. Add sausage, salt and pepper. Reduce heat, cover and simmer 30 minutes. Add remaining ingredients and continue simmering until soup is slightly thickened and vegetables are tender, about 15 minutes.

ITALIAN TORTELLINI SOUP

Accompany this hearty soup with crusty garlic bread. The recipe halves easily.

Makes 5 quarts

    4 14¹/2-ounce cans beef broth
    7 cups water
    1 pound sweet Italian sausage,
       cut into ¹/2-inch pieces
    1 9-ounce box tortellini
    1 9-ounce box spinach tortellini
  ¹/2 pound cabbage, shredded
    1 small green bell pepper, cored
       and diced
    1 medium zucchini, sliced
    1 small red onion, chopped
    1 medium tomato, diced
    1 tablespoon chopped fresh basil
       Salt and freshly ground pepper
       Freshly grated Parmesan cheese
       (optional)

Combine first 11 ingredients in large pot. Season with salt and pepper. Bring to slow boil over medium-high heat. Reduce heat and simmer until vegetables are tender, about 15 minutes. Ladle soup into bowls. Serve immediately, passing grated Parmesan separately if desired. (*Soup can be prepared 1 day ahead, covered and refrigerated.*)

SAN FRANCISCO CIOPPINO

A fast version of a classic fish soup.

4 servings

    2 tablespoons olive oil
 3¹/2 cups sliced mushrooms
    2 garlic cloves, minced
 1¹/2 teaspoons dried oregano,
       crumbled
    1 bay leaf, crumbled
    1 teaspoon paprika
  ¹/4 teaspoon dried thyme, crumbled
  ¹/4 teaspoon dried basil, crumbled
  ¹/4 teaspoon chili powder
       Freshly ground pepper
    2 cups dry red wine
    1 28-ounce can crushed tomatoes
       with added puree

    1 cooked crab leg, cut into
       4 pieces
  ¹/2 pound bay scallops
  ¹/2 pound uncooked medium
       shrimp, peeled and deveined
       Chopped fresh parsley

Heat oil in heavy large saucepan over medium heat. Add mushrooms and garlic and cook until softened, stirring occasionally, about 5 minutes. Stir in next 6 ingredients. Season with pepper. Mix in wine and bring to boil. Stir in tomatoes with puree. Reduce heat to medium-low. Cover and simmer 1 hour, stirring occasionally. (*Can be prepared 1 day ahead. Let cool; chill.*)

Increase heat to medium-high. Mix crab, scallops and shrimp into soup. Cook until seafood is tender, about 5 minutes. Ladle into bowls. Sprinkle with parsley and serve immediately.

BRUNSWICK COD CHOWDER

6 to 8 servings

    2 tablespoons (¹/4 stick) butter
  ¹/2 cup chopped onion
    1 garlic clove, minced
    2 cups water
    2 medium potatoes, peeled and
       diced
    1 10-ounce package frozen baby
       lima beans (unthawed)
  ¹/3 cup dry white wine

    1 pound cod fillets, cut into
       1-inch cubes
    1 16-ounce can whole peeled
       tomatoes, drained and chopped
    1 10³/4-ounce can cream of celery
       soup
    1 10-ounce package frozen corn
       (unthawed)
    1 tablespoon chicken bouillon
       granules
    1 teaspoon lemon pepper
       seasoning
    1 teaspoon Worcestershire sauce
    1 teaspoon fresh lemon juice
  ¹/4 teaspoon Old Bay Seasoning
    1 cup half and half

Melt butter in Dutch oven over medium-high heat. Add onion and garlic and stir until soft, 1 to 2 minutes. Add water, potatoes, lima beans and wine. Bring to boil. Reduce heat to low, cover and simmer 15 minutes. Add next 9 ingredients. Cover and continue simmering 15 minutes. Stir in half and half. Cook until heated through, 2 to 3 minutes.

MANHATTAN CLAM CHOWDER

Makes about 6 cups

    3 tablespoons butter or
       margarine
    1 onion, finely chopped
    3 6¹/2-ounce cans chopped clams
    2 8-ounce bottles clam juice
    1 16-ounce can stewed tomatoes
    3 ounces (¹/2 can) tomato paste
    1 medium potato, peeled and
       diced
    3 celery stalks, diced
    3 to 4 bay leaves
       Pinch of dried oregano,
       crumbled
       Minced fresh parsley
       Salt and freshly ground pepper
       Dash of hot pepper sauce

Melt butter or margarine in 2-quart saucepan over medium-high heat. Add onion and sauté until softened, about 10 minutes. Blend in remaining ingredients and bring to boil. Reduce heat and simmer 1 hour. Serve hot.

NEW ENGLAND CLAM CHOWDER

10 to 12 servings

> 5   10³/4-ounce cans cream of potato soup
> 6   cups half and half
> 1   10-ounce can whole baby clams (undrained)
> 1   tablespoon dried minced onion
> 1   tablespoon dried parsley flakes
> 1/2   teaspoon garlic powder
> 1/2   teaspoon seasoned salt
>   Hot pepper sauce
>   Salt and freshly ground pepper
> 1/4   cup (1/2 stick) butter, melted
>   Minced fresh parsley

Heat soup with half and half in heavy large saucepan over medium heat. Add next 6 ingredients. Season with salt and pepper. Reduce heat to low. Simmer gently until thickened, stirring frequently, about 15 minutes. Drizzle butter on top. Ladle soup into bowls. Garnish with parsley.

WEST ISLAND CHOWDER

Makes about 3 quarts

> 1   medium onion, chopped
> 3   bacon strips, chopped
> 4   cups milk
> 4   medium potatoes, peeled and diced
> 2   cups half and half
> 1   12-ounce can whole kernel corn, drained
> 1   8-ounce bottle clam juice
> 1   teaspoon Bon Appétit seasoning
> 1/2   teaspoon dried thyme, crumbled
> 1/2   teaspoon celery salt
> 1/8   teaspoon freshly ground white pepper
> 2   10-ounce cans whole baby clams (undrained)
>   Salt and freshly ground pepper
> 1   tablespoon butter, melted
>   Fresh thyme sprigs

Cook onion and bacon in heavy large saucepan over medium heat until onion is golden and bacon is crisp, stir-ring frequently, about 12 minutes. Add next 9 ingredients and simmer until potatoes are tender, about 15 minutes. Add clams with liquid and simmer until heated through. Season with salt and pepper. (*Can be prepared 1 day ahead. Cover and refrigerate.*) Drizzle butter over soup. Ladle into bowls. Garnish with thyme.

TUNA AND ZUCCHINI CHOWDER

8 servings

> 1   tablespoon butter
> 1   cup peeled and diced potatoes
> 1   medium onion, chopped
> 3   cups chicken stock
> 1   tablespoon snipped fresh chives
> 1   tablespoon chopped fresh parsley
> 1/2   bay leaf
> 1/4   teaspoon chili powder
> 1/4   teaspoon garlic powder
>   Freshly ground pepper
> 2   cups diced unpeeled zucchini
> 1   cup frozen corn
> 1   6¹/2-ounce can water-packed tuna, drained
> 1   teaspoon cornstarch
> 3/4   cup whipping cream
> 1   cup grated cheddar cheese
> 1/4   cup freshly grated Parmesan cheese

Melt butter in heavy medium saucepan over medium heat. Add potatoes and onion and cook until onion softens, stirring frequently, about 8 minutes. Add next 7 ingredients and simmer 10 minutes, stirring occasionally. Mix in zucchini and corn and cook until tender, about 15 minutes, stirring occasionally. Remove bay leaf. Puree 2¹/2 cups soup in blender or processor. Return to saucepan. Mix in tuna. Dissolve cornstarch in cream; add to soup. Bring to simmer, stirring until thickened. Remove from heat. Add grated cheddar and Parmesan and mix until melted. Serve immediately.

BAY SCALLOP SOUP

4 servings

> 2   8-ounce bottles clam juice
> 1   tablespoon unsalted butter
> 1/2   teaspoon Worcestershire sauce
> 1/2   teaspoon dry mustard
> 1/8   teaspoon garlic powder
> 1/8   teaspoon celery salt
> 3/4   pound bay scallops
> 2   egg yolks
> 1   cup whipping cream
>   Snipped fresh chives

Combine first 6 ingredients in medium saucepan and bring to boil. Add scallops and simmer gently 3 minutes. Beat yolks with cream in bowl. Ladle about 1/2 cup hot soup into cream and blend well. Gradually stir cream mixture back into soup. Stir until soup thickens slightly, 1 to 2 minutes. Sprinkle with chives. Serve immediately.

LEMON, CORN AND SHRIMP BROTH

8 servings

> 8   cups chicken stock, preferably homemade
> 1/2   cup saké (Japanese rice wine)
> 3   tablespoons soy sauce
> 1   tablespoon sugar
> 4   thin slices peeled ginger
> 1   cup fresh corn kernels*
> 8   medium uncooked shrimp, peeled and deveined
> 2   tablespoons fresh lemon juice
> 8   green onions, white part only, sliced lengthwise into thin shreds

Bring stock, saké, soy sauce, sugar and ginger to boil in heavy large saucepan. Reduce heat and simmer 5 minutes. Add fresh corn and simmer 5 minutes. Add shrimp and lemon juice and cook until shrimp turn pink, about 30 seconds. Ladle soup into bowls. Garnish with green onions. Serve immediately.

If unavailable, frozen corn can be sub-stituted. Add to soup with shrimp.

3 ◆ Salads

What could be simpler or fresher than an appealing salad? Always a welcome first course or accompaniment to a meal, salads are enjoying a brighter spotlight with today's emphasis on light, healthy and quick-to-prepare food. And busy cooks are taking advantage of the ease and diversity of salads, serving them as first courses, side dishes and even main courses.

The salads in this chapter serve as colorful proof that it's easier than you think to transcend the classic iceberg-lettuce-and-tomatoes-with-vinaigrette combination. All it takes is the freshest of the season's ingredients from the produce section or the garden, and recipes such as the ones included here. We've also included a selection of salad dressings for you to match to your own favorite combinations.

Salads are perfect convenience dishes; the dressing can often be made ahead and the greens washed and chilled, so a quick, last-minute put-together is all that's needed. For a sophisticated starter, try Mushroom-Walnut Salad with Fennel Dressing or Watercress, Pear and Blue Cheese Salad. Any picnic or casual summer menu would be enhanced by Pantry Shelf Bean Salad with a basil-scented vinaigrette, or Sweet Potato Salad, made crunchy with chopped walnuts. Pasta and rice salads provide a hearty change of pace while lending them-selves particularly well to advance preparation: Herbed Pasta and Veg-etable Salad with Pimiento, Tortellini Salad with Feta Cheese and Party Rice Salad are delicious candidates for easy, make-ahead dishes.

Main-course salads are a light, healthful and easy alternative to the multi-course meal—try zesty Green-Chili Chicken Salad; fresh-tasting Shrimp, Avocado and Spinach Salad; or robust Smoked Ham Salad with Mustard Mayonnaise. Add a crusty loaf of bread and bottle of chilled white wine, Beaujolais or rosé for a wonderfully satisfying meal.

First-Course and Side-Dish Salads

WATERCRESS SALAD WITH RASPBERRY DRESSING

2 servings

- 1/2 cup olive oil
- 1/4 cup raspberry vinegar
- 1/2 teaspoon salt
- 1/4 teaspoon freshly ground pepper
- 1/4 teaspoon ground ginger
- 1/4 teaspoon Dijon mustard
- 1 egg yolk

- 1 bunch watercress, stems trimmed
- 1/2 cup peeled, thinly sliced cucumber

Combine oil, vinegar, salt, pepper, ginger, mustard and yolk in jar and shake to blend. Refrigerate until chilled.

Arrange watercress on plates. Top with cucumber. Refrigerate until chilled. Just before serving, shake dressing well and pour over salads. Pass remaining dressing separately.

SHRIMP AND RADICCHIO SALAD

4 servings

- 1/4 cup olive oil
- 2 tablespoons red wine vinegar
- 2 garlic cloves, minced
- 1 shallot, minced
- 1 teaspoon Dijon mustard
- 1/2 pound cooked bay shrimp

- 1 head Boston lettuce, shredded
- 1 head radicchio, shredded

Combine first 5 ingredients in medium bowl. Add shrimp and stir to coat. Cover and chill for 30 minutes.

Just before serving, combine lettuce and radicchio in large bowl. Pour shrimp and vinaigrette over and toss.

STRAWBERRY SPINACH SALAD

6 to 8 servings

- 1/3 cup vegetable oil
- 3 tablespoons red wine vinegar
- 2 teaspoons fresh lemon juice
- 1 teaspoon freshly grated ginger
- 1 pound fresh spinach, stems trimmed
- 2 cups sliced fresh strawberries
- 4 ounces cheddar cheese, shredded

Blend oil, vinegar, lemon juice and ginger in large bowl. Add spinach, berries and cheese and toss.

MUSHROOM-WALNUT SALAD WITH FENNEL DRESSING

8 servings

Dressing
- 1 medium garlic clove
- 1 teaspoon salt
- 1/2 cup olive oil
- 1 egg, beaten to blend
- 3 tablespoons red wine vinegar
- 1/2 teaspoon fennel seeds
  Freshly ground pepper

- 1 medium head romaine lettuce, shredded
- 1 pound mushrooms, thinly sliced
- 4 ounces chopped walnuts (about 3/4 cup)

For dressing: Mash garlic with salt in wooden bowl. Whisk in oil and egg and blend thoroughly. Add remaining dressing ingredients and whisk to blend thoroughly.

Place lettuce in large salad bowl. Arrange mushrooms over and sprinkle with walnuts. Pour dressing over salad and serve immediately.

ROMAINE AND FETA SALAD

6 to 8 servings

- 1/4 cup soy sauce
- 1 teaspoon sesame oil
- 1 teaspoon rice wine vinegar
- 1/2 teaspoon grated fresh ginger
- 1 head romaine lettuce, torn into bite-size pieces
- 1/4 pound feta cheese, finely crumbled
- 1 cup bean sprouts
- 1 tomato, seeded and chopped
  Salt and freshly ground pepper

Mix first 4 ingredients in small bowl. Combine lettuce, feta, sprouts, tomato, salt and pepper in large bowl. Add dressing. Toss well and serve.

RADICCHIO, ENDIVE AND FENNEL SALAD

4 servings

- 1 medium head radicchio, quartered and cut crosswise into 3/4-inch-wide pieces
- 2 large Belgian endives, cut crosswise into 3/4-inch-wide pieces
- 1 medium fennel bulb, trimmed, tough outer leaves removed, cored and cut lengthwise into thin strips
- 1/4 cup minced fresh Italian parsley
- 16 small fresh basil leaves, halved
- 1/4 cup extra-virgin olive oil
  Salt and freshly ground pepper
- 4 teaspoons balsamic vinegar
- 8 slices imported Parmesan cheese (preferably Reggiano)

Combine first 5 ingredients in large bowl. (*Can be prepared 4 hours ahead. Cover with barely damp towel and refrigerate.*) Just before serving, toss salad with oil until well coated. Season with salt and pepper and toss. Add vinegar and toss well. Top with cheese.

Snow Peas with
Lemon-Anchovy
Dipping Sauce,
page 2; Country
Ham with Finger
Biscuits, page 143

Pakoras and Tomato
Pickle, pages 6 and 148

DICK SHARPE

Italian Tortellini Soup, page 21

宴客佳肴

Gingered Chinese Noodle Soup, page 20

Brie and Herb Cheeses
in Pastry, page 5

RICHARD CLARK

West Island Chowder, page 22

From left to right:
Grapefruit and Kumquat Spritzers, page 11;
Sparkling Apple Sangria, page 11;
Citrus Toddy, page 14;
Hot Mulled Cranberry Orange Juice, page 14;
Hot Curried Vegetable Juice, page 14

Clockwise from right: Frozen Daiquiri, page 12;
Pistarckle Punch, page 11; Caribbean Wine Cooler, page 12;
Virgin Islands Piña Colada, page 13; Jamaica Farewell, page 13

CANTALOUPE AND AVOCADO SALAD WITH CHILI DRESSING

6 servings

- 1 small head butter lettuce, torn into pieces
- 1 small head red leaf lettuce, torn into pieces
- 1/2 cup diced celery
  Chili Dressing (see recipe)
- 1 small cantaloupe, seeded, peeled and sliced
- 1 large avocado, pitted, peeled and sliced

Combine first 3 ingredients in large salad bowl. Pour in some of dressing and toss to coat lightly. Add cantaloupe and avocado and toss gently.

Chili Dressing

Makes 1 1/4 cups

- 1/4 cup prepared chili sauce
- 1/4 cup honey
- 3 tablespoons distilled white vinegar
- 2 teaspoons Worcestershire sauce
- 2 teaspoons instant minced onion
  Salt and freshly ground pepper
- 1/2 cup vegetable oil

Combine first 5 ingredients in medium bowl. Season with salt and pepper. Gradually whisk in oil until blended. Cover and chill. Whisk before serving.

SURPRISE SALAD

4 to 6 servings

- 1 head iceberg lettuce, chopped
- 1 red onion, thinly sliced
- 1 pound bacon, cooked and crumbled
- 1 medium head cauliflower, chopped

Creamy Parmesan Dressing
- 3/4 cup mayonnaise
- 3/4 cup freshly grated Parmesan cheese
- 1 tablespoon sugar (optional)

Layer lettuce, onion, bacon and cauliflower in large salad bowl.
For dressing: Combine all ingredients for dressing in small mixing bowl and blend well. Spread evenly over salad. Cover and refrigerate until ready to use. Toss before serving.

POSITIVELY WEST COAST SALAD

6 servings

- 1 pound fresh beets (preferably tiny), steamed until tender when pierced with fork
- 1 9- or 10-ounce package frozen artichoke hearts
- 1 large head red leaf, Boston or romaine lettuce, thoroughly chilled
- 1 ripe avocado, peeled, pitted and cubed
  Mustard Vinaigrette (see recipe)
- 1 cup alfalfa sprouts
- 1/2 cup minced green onions (including tops)

Peel beets under cold running water. Remove stems and root ends. Quarter beets if large. Cover and refrigerate. Bring about 1 inch salted water to boil in medium saucepan. Add artichoke hearts and cook until separated and barely tender, about 1 to 3 minutes. Cool quickly under cold water. Drain and refrigerate until ready to use.

Arrange lettuce leaves on large shallow platter. Mound beets, artichoke hearts and avocado in center. Pour dressing over top. Arrange sprouts in circle around vegetables. Sprinkle green onions over salad and serve.

Mustard Vinaigrette

Makes 3/4 cup

- 9 tablespoons olive oil
- 3 tablespoons white wine vinegar
- 1 tablespoon Dijon mustard
- 1/2 teaspoon minced garlic
- 1/2 teaspoon salt
- 1/4 teaspoon freshly ground pepper

Combine all ingredients in jar with tight-fitting lid and shake well. Shake again just before using. (*Can be prepared up to 1 day ahead and refrigerated.*)

EGYPTIAN SALAD

4 to 6 servings

- 1/2 head romaine lettuce, torn into 1/2-inch strips
- 2 large tomatoes, cut into bite-size pieces
- 1 green bell pepper, cored, seeded and cut into 1/2-inch dice
- 1/2 yellow onion, cut into 1-inch strips
- 1/2 cucumber, quartered and chopped into 1/2-inch pieces
- 2 to 3 tablespoons chopped fresh parsley
- 1 tablespoon fresh lime juice
- 1/2 teaspoon cider vinegar
- 1/2 teaspoon salt
- 1/4 teaspoon ground cumin
- 1/4 teaspoon garlic powder
- 1/8 teaspoon crushed red pepper flakes (optional)

Combine lettuce, tomatoes, green pepper, onion, cucumber and parsley in large bowl. Just before serving, sprinkle remaining ingredients over top of salad and toss thoroughly.

BILTMORE SALAD

Three distinctive mixtures make up this elegant salad course.

8 servings

- 5 medium beets, trimmed
- 10 tablespoons walnut oil
- 6 tablespoons red wine vinegar
- 1/4 cup walnut halves
  Salt and freshly ground pepper

- 2 tablespoons Dijon mustard
- 2 heads limestone (Bibb) or butter lettuce, cut into strips
- 2 Belgian endives, cut julienne

- 24 large radicchio leaves
- 8 limestone (Bibb) or butter lettuce leaves
- 2 14-ounce cans hearts of palm, drained and sliced
- 1 3 1/2-ounce package enoki mushrooms
- 2 tablespoons minced fresh parsley

Cook beets in large pan of boiling salted water until tender, about 35 minutes. Drain. Cool completely. Peel and cut julienne. (*Can be prepared 1 day ahead and refrigerated.*) Transfer to bowl. Add 3 tablespoons oil, 3 tablespoons vinegar and walnuts and toss well. Season with salt and pepper.

Blend remaining vinegar, mustard, salt and pepper in small bowl. Whisk in remaining oil in thin stream. Mix lettuce and endive. Add 3/4 of dressing.

Arrange 3 radicchio leaves on each plate. Press 1 butter lettuce leaf into 1 radicchio leaf on each plate. Spoon beet salad into double leaf, endive salad into second leaf and hearts of palm into third leaf. Sprinkle endive with enoki and parsley. Drizzle remaining dressing over hearts of palm.

SALAD OF WINTER GREENS WITH HAZELNUT VINAIGRETTE

To save time, prepare greens and dressing one day ahead. Wrap greens in paper towels and plastic bags and chill.

8 servings

> 1 small red onion, thinly sliced
> 3 tablespoons distilled white vinegar
> 3 tablespoons water
> 1 small head Boston or green leaf lettuce
> 1 small bunch red leaf lettuce
> 1/2 small bunch Napa cabbage
> 3 cups bite-size pieces escarole, curly endive or Belgian endive
> 1 cup blended chopped fresh herbs (tarragon, basil, mint, cilantro, Italian parsley, arugula and/or watercress)
> 1/4 cup cider vinegar
> 1 garlic clove
> 1/3 cup hazelnut oil
> 1/3 cup vegetable oil
> 1/2 cup toasted and husked hazelnuts
> Salt and freshly ground pepper

Mix onion, distilled vinegar and 3 tablespoons water in medium bowl. Let stand 30 minutes. Drain.

Tear Boston lettuce, red leaf lettuce and cabbage into bite-size pieces.

Combine with escarole, herbs and marinated onion in large bowl.

Combine cider vinegar and garlic in processor or blender. With machine running, gradually add oils through feed tube in thin, steady stream. Add hazelnuts and chop coarsely. Season with salt and pepper. Serve salad, passing dressing separately.

SPINACH AND BUTTER LETTUCE SALAD WITH PIMIENTO DRESSING

6 to 8 servings

Pimiento Dressing
> 1 cup vegetable oil
> 1 4-ounce jar pimientos, drained
> 1/3 cup red wine vinegar
> 3 tablespoons blue cheese
> 1 tablespoon chopped onion
> 1/2 teaspoon sugar *or* honey
> Salt and freshly ground pepper

> 3 cups fresh spinach leaves, torn into bite-size pieces
> 3 cups butter lettuce, torn into bite-size pieces
> 1 avocado, peeled and sliced
> 1 cucumber, thinly sliced
> 1 6-ounce can sliced black olives
> 8 mushrooms, sliced

For dressing: Combine all ingredients in blender and mix until smooth.

Combine remaining ingredients in large bowl. Just before serving, add enough dressing to lightly coat lettuce and toss gently. Reserve remaining dressing for another use.

FETA AND WALNUT SPINACH SALAD WITH BASIL DRESSING

6 servings

> 1 bunch fresh spinach, torn into bite-size pieces
> 1 small avocado, thinly sliced
> 1/2 medium-size red onion, thinly sliced
> 1/2 cup crumbled feta cheese (about 4 ounces)
> 1/2 cup coarsely chopped walnuts
> Basil Dressing (see recipe)

Toss spinach, avocado, onion, feta and walnuts in large bowl. Pour Basil Dressing over and toss.

Basil Dressing
Makes about 3/4 cup

> 1/2 cup olive oil
> 1/4 cup red wine vinegar
> 1 tablespoon dried basil, crumbled
> 2 teaspoons sugar
> 2 large garlic cloves, minced
> 1/2 teaspoon salt
> 1/2 teaspoon freshly ground pepper

Combine all ingredients in blender or processor and mix well. Store in jar with tight-fitting lid in refrigerator. Shake Basil Dressing well before using.

GRAPEFRUIT, RED ONION AND AVOCADO SALAD

4 servings

> 1 1-pound can grapefruit sections, drained, juice reserved
> 2 medium avocados, peeled, pitted and chopped
> 1/4 cup mayonnaise
> 2 teaspoons fresh lemon juice
> Salt and freshly ground pepper
> 1 small head iceberg lettuce
> 1/2 medium red onion, thinly sliced

Cut grapefruit sections into 3 pieces. Toss avocados with all but 2 tablespoons reserved juice from grapefruit. Whisk together mayonnaise, remaining 2 tablespoons grapefruit juice and lemon juice. Season with salt and pepper. Line 4 plates with lettuce. Drain avocados and toss with grapefruit. Divide grapefruit mixture among plates. Top with onion. Drizzle with dressing.

WATERCRESS, PEAR AND BLUE CHEESE SALAD

4 servings

> 1 small head Boston lettuce, torn into bite-size pieces
> 10 ounces watercress leaves

2 Comice pears, cored and cut into 8 pieces each
1/2 cup crumbled blue cheese
1/2 cup walnut halves
1/2 cup walnut oil
2 tablespoons fresh lemon juice
2 tablespoons freshly ground pepper
1 large shallot, minced
1 teaspoon salt

Divide lettuce and watercress among plates. Arrange pear slices in spiral pattern over greens. Top with blue cheese and walnuts. Combine remaining ingredients in jar and shake well. Pour dressing over salad.

SALAD IMPRESARIO

3 to 4 servings

1/2 medium head leaf lettuce, shredded
2 tomatillos,* chopped
3/4 cup peeled and finely chopped cucumber
1/3 cup crumbled feta cheese
3 tablespoons snipped fresh chives
2 tablespoons chopped red bell pepper
1 tablespoon butter
1/3 cup chopped walnuts

1/4 cup hazelnut oil
3 tablespoons fresh lemon juice
2 tablespoons olive oil
2 tablespoons raspberry vinegar
1/2 teaspoon fennel seeds
1/2 teaspoon dry mustard
1/4 teaspoon dried thyme, crumbled
1/4 teaspoon salt
Freshly ground pepper

Combine first 6 ingredients in medium bowl. Melt butter in heavy small skillet over medium heat. Add walnuts and stir 5 minutes. Add to salad.

Combine remaining ingredients in jar with tight-fitting lid and shake well. Pour enough dressing over salad to moisten. Toss thoroughly. Divide salad among plates and serve. Pass remaining dressing separately.

Tomatillos are available at Latin American markets and specialty foods stores.

MANDARIN SPINACH SALAD

6 servings

Dressing

1/4 cup white wine vinegar
4 teaspoons sugar
2/3 teaspoon dry mustard
2/3 teaspoon salt
2 teaspoons fresh lemon juice
2/3 cup vegetable oil
1 tablespoon poppy seeds

1 pound fresh spinach, stemmed and torn into bite-size pieces
1 11-ounce can mandarin oranges, drained
1/4 pound bacon, crisply cooked and crumbled
1 large avocado, sliced
1/4 medium-size red onion, sliced into thin rings

For dressing: Combine vinegar, sugar, mustard and salt in blender or processor and mix well. Add lemon juice. With machine running, gradually add oil. Stir in poppy seeds.

Combine next 5 ingredients in large bowl. Pour dressing over salad and toss gently to coat. Serve immediately.

CAESAR SALAD SUPREME

6 to 8 servings

1 red bell pepper

2 bunches romaine lettuce, torn into bite-size pieces
8 bacon strips, cooked and crumbled
1/2 cup crumbled feta cheese
1/4 cup raw unsalted sunflower seeds
2 tablespoons crumbled blue cheese
1 egg, beaten to blend
1 egg yolk
3 tablespoons fresh lemon juice
1 1/2 teaspoons Salad Supreme seasoning
1 garlic clove, crushed
1/2 teaspoon Worcestershire sauce
1/8 teaspoon hot pepper sauce
1/4 cup olive oil
1/2 cup freshly grated Parmesan cheese

Preheat broiler. Char pepper in broiler until blackened on all sides, about 10 minutes. Wrap in paper bag and let stand 10 minutes to steam. Peel and seed. Rinse pepper if necessary; pat dry. Coarsely chop.

Combine bell pepper and next 5 ingredients in salad bowl and toss. In medium bowl, combine egg, yolk, lemon juice, seasoning, garlic, Worcestershire and hot pepper sauces. Gradually whisk in oil. Pour over salad and toss. Sprinkle with Parmesan and toss. Serve immediately.

TOMATOES IN HERB VINAIGRETTE

6 to 8 servings

1/2 cup fresh parsley
1 tablespoon fresh tarragon or 1 teaspoon dried, crumbled
1 garlic clove
1 egg, room temperature
1/2 cup olive oil
1/4 cup red wine vinegar
1/2 teaspoon salt
Freshly ground pepper
4 large tomatoes, cored and thinly sliced
Crumbled blue cheese

Finely mince parsley, tarragon and garlic in food processor. Add egg, oil, vinegar, salt and pepper and process 5 seconds. Arrange tomato slices on serving platter. Pour dressing over. Sprinkle with cheese and serve.

MINTED TOMATOES

4 to 6 servings

2 tablespoons cider vinegar
1 to 2 tablespoons sugar
Dash of salt
Dash of freshly ground pepper
2 teaspoons minced fresh mint
2 pounds large tomatoes, peeled and sliced

Combine vinegar, sugar, salt and pepper in small saucepan. Bring to boil over high heat. Stir in mint. Let cool slightly. Arrange tomatoes in shallow dish. Pour mixture over. Refrigerate tomatoes before serving.

GREEK-STYLE SALAD

4 to 6 servings

> 2 medium tomatoes, cored and cut into wedges
> 1 medium zucchini, cut into matchstick julienne
> 1 cucumber, sliced
> 1 cup pitted black olives
> 1 medium-size red onion, thinly sliced and separated into rings
> 1/2 pound feta cheese, cubed
> 1 6-ounce jar artichoke hearts with marinade
> 1/4 cup red wine vinegar
> Freshly ground pepper

Combine tomatoes, zucchini and cucumber in large bowl. Add olives, onion rings and feta cheese. Top with artichoke hearts and marinade. Pour red wine vinegar over salad, sprinkle with pepper and toss well. Chill several hours or overnight; toss occasionally. Serve at room temperature.

GREEK CUCUMBER-YOGURT SALAD

4 servings

> 2 medium cucumbers, peeled, seeded and diced
> 1 8-ounce container plain yogurt
> 1 garlic clove, minced
> 1 tablespoon minced fresh dill or 1 1/2 teaspoons dried dillweed
> 2 teaspoons white wine vinegar
> 1/2 teaspoon salt

Combine all ingredients in medium bowl. Mix well. Cover and refrigerate. Serve salad chilled.

MARINATED CUCUMBER SALAD

4 servings

> 2 cucumbers, peeled and sliced
> 4 green onions, chopped into 1/2-inch pieces
> 1/4 cup red wine vinegar
> 1 tablespoon soy sauce
> 1 tablespoon vegetable oil
> Freshly ground pepper

Combine all ingredients in medium bowl. Cover and refrigerate several hours or overnight. Serve salad chilled.

PICKLED BRUSSELS SPROUTS

2 to 4 servings

> 1 8-ounce package frozen brussels sprouts
> 6 tablespoons light olive oil
> 2 tablespoons red wine vinegar
> 2 tablespoons finely chopped onion
> 1 tablespoon chopped fresh parsley
> 1 small garlic clove, finely minced
> 1/2 teaspoon Dijon mustard
> 1/4 teaspoon dried dillweed

Cook brussels sprouts according to package directions. Drain well. Transfer to container with lid. Combine remaining ingredients in medium bowl and mix well. Pour over brussels sprouts, turning to distribute marinade evenly. Seal tightly and refrigerate 1 hour or overnight. Drain mixture well before serving. (*Can be prepared 2 to 3 days ahead and refrigerated.*)

ARTICHOKE AND MUSHROOM SALAD

4 to 6 servings

> 1/3 cup red wine vinegar
> 1/3 cup vegetable oil
> 1/3 cup water
> 2 tablespoons sugar
> 2 tablespoons chopped fresh parsley
> 2 medium garlic cloves, crushed
> 1 teaspoon salt
> 1/4 teaspoon whole black peppercorns
> Hot pepper sauce
> 2 7-ounce cans water-packed artichoke hearts, drained, quartered
> 1 pound large mushrooms, quartered
>
> Parsley sprigs

Whisk first 9 ingredients in large bowl. Add artichoke hearts and mushrooms and mix well. Cover and refrigerate overnight, stirring several times.

Drain salad well. Garnish with parsley. Serve at room temperature.

GREEN BEAN, RED ONION AND BLUE CHEESE SALAD

10 servings

> 2 10-ounce packages frozen cut green beans
> 1 medium red onion, sliced and separated into rings
> 1 2.2-ounce can sliced black olives, drained
> 2 ounces blue cheese, crumbled
> 1/2 cup prepared Italian salad dressing

Bring 1 quart water to boil in medium saucepan. Add beans and cook until just tender, about 2 minutes. Drain well. Transfer to large bowl. Mix in onion, olives and cheese. Stir in dressing and toss thoroughly.

PANTRY SHELF BEAN SALAD

6 servings

Dressing

> 3 tablespoons olive oil
> 1 1/2 tablespoons red wine vinegar
> 1 1/2 teaspoons Dijon mustard
> 1 small garlic clove, crushed
> 1/8 teaspoon freshly ground pepper
> Pinch of dried basil, crumbled
> Pinch of salt

Bean Salad

> 1 20-ounce can kidney beans, drained
> 1 8-ounce can green beans, drained, or 8 ounces fresh green beans, cooked
> 1 medium-size green bell pepper, diced
> 3 medium-size green onions, chopped
> 10 pitted black olives, sliced
> 3 tablespoons minced fresh parsley

For dressing: Combine all ingredients in jar with tight-fitting lid and shake well. Refrigerate until ready to use.

For salad: Mix all ingredients in large bowl. Pour dressing over and toss to coat. Serve chilled.

MARINATED CARROT SALAD

Makes 2 3/4 cups

- 1/2 cup red wine vinegar
- 1/2 cup sugar
- 3 tablespoons vegetable oil
- 1 teaspoon Worcestershire sauce
- 1 teaspoon Dijon mustard
- 1 pound carrots, peeled and shredded

Combine vinegar, sugar, oil, Worcestershire and mustard in medium bowl and mix well. Add carrots and toss to coat. Cover and refrigerate overnight, tossing once or twice. Drain carrots thoroughly before serving.

MARINATED MUSHROOM SALAD

6 to 8 servings

Marinade
- 1 cup olive oil
- 1/2 cup tarragon wine vinegar
- 1 teaspoon dry mustard
- 1 teaspoon mixed dried oregano, thyme and basil, crumbled
- 1/8 teaspoon salt
- 1/8 teaspoon freshly ground pepper

Mushroom Salad
- 1 pound mushrooms, thinly sliced
- 1 medium-size red onion, thinly sliced
- 1 medium celery stalk, finely chopped

For marinade: Combine all ingredients in blender and mix.

For salad: Combine mushrooms, onion and celery in 3-quart dish. Pour marinade over and toss. Cover and refrigerate overnight, stirring twice. Drain mushroom salad before serving.

PEA SALAD WITH TANGY CREAM DRESSING

6 servings

- 1/2 cup sour cream
- 3 tablespoons red wine vinegar
- 4 teaspoons milk
- 1 1/2 teaspoons sugar
- 1/2 teaspoon salt
- 1/4 teaspoon garlic powder

- 1 10-ounce package frozen peas, thawed, patted dry
- 3/4 cup sliced canned water chestnuts, drained
- 1/4 cup thinly sliced green onions
- 6 bacon slices, cooked and crumbled

Combine first 6 ingredients in small bowl. Cover and chill overnight.

Combine remaining ingredients in large bowl. Add dressing and toss.

SAUERKRAUT SALAD

6 servings

- 2 1/2 cups sauerkraut, rinsed and drained
- 1/2 cup chopped celery
- 1/2 cup chopped green bell pepper
- 1/2 cup chopped onion
- 1/2 cup chopped carrots
- 1/2 cup sugar
- 1/2 cup red wine vinegar
- 1/3 cup vegetable oil

Combine first 5 ingredients in large bowl. Whisk sugar, vinegar and oil in small bowl. Pour over vegetables and mix well. Cover and chill overnight.

Drain salad well and serve.

AVOCADO WITH MARINATED VEGETABLES

4 servings

- 1/2 medium-size green bell pepper, seeded and thinly sliced
- 1/2 medium tomato, chopped
- 2 medium-size green onions, sliced
- 6 large green beans, cut into thin strips
- 6 black olives, chopped
- 3/4 cup Sweet Tarragon Dressing (see recipe)

- 2 medium avocados, halved and pitted
- 4 large red leaf lettuce leaves

Combine bell pepper, tomato, green onions, beans and olives in small shallow dish. Marinate in tarragon dressing at room temperature 30 minutes.

Arrange avocado halves on lettuce leaves. Surround avocado with vegetables. Add 1 teaspoon tarragon dressing to each avocado and serve. Pass remaining dressing separately.

Sweet Tarragon Dressing

Makes 3/4 cup

- 6 tablespoons vegetable oil
- 1 tablespoon cider vinegar
- 2 teaspoons fresh lemon juice
- 1 teaspoon sugar
- 1/2 teaspoon dried tarragon, crumbled
- 1/4 teaspoon salt
- Dash of freshly ground pepper

Combine all ingredients in jar with tight-fitting lid and shake well. Chill until ready to serve.

MARINATED VEGETABLE AND TOFU SALAD

12 servings

- 1 pound bean sprouts
- 2 cups sliced mushrooms
- 2 green onions, sliced
- 1 cup sliced cauliflower
- 1 English cucumber, sliced
- 1 carrot, thinly sliced
- 1 green bell pepper, cored, seeded and cut into strips
- 1 cup broccoli florets

Sesame Dressing
- 1 cup white vinegar
- 1/2 cup vegetable oil
- 1/4 cup sugar
- 2 tablespoons sesame oil
- 1 to 2 tablespoons soy sauce
- 1 tablespoon sesame seeds
- 1 large garlic clove, crushed
- 2 teaspoons freshly grated ginger
- Salt and freshly ground pepper
- Hot chili oil

- 1/3 cup minced onion
- 3 tablespoons vegetable oil
- 1/4 teaspoon turmeric
- 1 pound tofu, cubed or mashed
- 1 1/2 teaspoons soy sauce
- Salt

Combine first 8 ingredients in large bowl. Mix next 11 ingredients in processor or blender. Pour dressing over vegetables and toss lightly. Refrigerate several hours or overnight.

Just before serving, drain vegetables thoroughly. Combine onion, oil and turmeric in medium skillet over medium heat and stir until hot. Add tofu, soy sauce and salt and stir until heated through. Spoon over vegetables and serve immediately.

MOTHER'S COLESLAW

Makes 6 cups

- ¾ cup distilled white vinegar
- ½ cup vegetable oil
- 6 tablespoons sugar
- 1 teaspoon celery seeds
  Salt and freshly ground pepper
- 1 medium cabbage, thinly sliced
- 2 medium onions, diced
- 1 green bell pepper, cored and thinly sliced
- 24 pitted green olives, quartered

Combine first 4 ingredients in medium saucepan. Season with salt and pepper. Bring to boil and continue boiling 3 minutes. Remove from heat. Combine cabbage, onions, bell pepper and olives in large bowl. Add hot dressing and toss thoroughly. Cover and refrigerate overnight, stirring occasionally. Drain before serving if desired.

BEER COLESLAW

12 servings

- 8 cups shredded green cabbage (about 2 pounds)
- ½ medium-size green bell pepper
- 1½ tablespoons minced onion
- 1 cup mayonnaise
- ¼ cup beer
- 1 teaspoon celery seeds
- ½ teaspoon salt
- ¼ teaspoon freshly ground pepper

Mix cabbage, bell pepper and onion in large bowl. Combine remaining ingredients in small bowl and mix well. Pour over cabbage and toss to coat. Refrigerate coleslaw at least 30 minutes before serving.

BLUE CHEESE APPLE SLAW

4 to 6 servings

- 2 McIntosh apples, peeled and sliced
- ¼ cup fresh lemon juice
- 1½ cups shredded green cabbage
- ½ cup shredded red cabbage
- 1 cup sour cream
- ¼ cup crumbled blue cheese
- 1 tablespoon grated onion
- 1 tablespoon red wine vinegar

Dip apple slices in lemon juice and combine with green and red cabbage in medium bowl. Mix sour cream, blue cheese, onion and vinegar in small bowl. Pour half of dressing over salad and toss. Add more dressing as desired. Serve chilled.

MIXED CABBAGE COLESLAW

8 servings

- 1 cup mayonnaise
- 6 tablespoons tarragon vinegar
- 2 tablespoons (generous) Dijon mustard
- 1 teaspoon Nature's Seasons seasoning blend
- ¼ teaspoon prepared horseradish
- 1 tablespoon sour cream (optional)
- 1 medium green cabbage head, finely chopped
- ½ medium red cabbage head, finely chopped
- 5 large carrots, peeled and grated
- 6 green onions, sliced

Blend mayonnaise, vinegar, mustard, seasoning blend and horseradish in blender or processor. Cover and refrigerate at least 3 hours. (*Can be prepared 3 days ahead. Stir before using.*) Mix sour cream into dressing to mellow flavors, if desired.

Combine remaining ingredients in large bowl. Pour dressing over and toss thoroughly to coat.

OLD-WORLD POTATO SALAD

6 to 8 servings

- 2 pounds new red potatoes (unpeeled)
- ½ cup chopped green onions
- 1 tablespoon capers, drained and rinsed
- 1 garlic clove, minced
- 3 tablespoons olive oil
- 2 tablespoons red or white wine vinegar
- 1 teaspoon Dijon mustard
  Salt and freshly ground pepper
  Chopped fresh parsley

Place potatoes in large saucepan. Cover with cold water and bring to boil. Reduce heat, cover and simmer until potatoes are tender when pierced with knife, about 25 minutes. Drain; slice.

Transfer potatoes to medium bowl. Add onions, capers and garlic and toss. Bring oil, vinegar and mustard to boil in small saucepan, stirring constantly. Remove from heat. Season with salt and pepper. Pour dressing over potatoes. Toss gently until thoroughly blended. Cool to room temperature. Chill. (*Can be prepared 1 day ahead.*) Garnish with chopped parsley.

GREEK POTATO SALAD

8 to 10 servings

- ½ cup olive oil
- 4 garlic cloves, minced
- 2 pounds red potatoes, peeled and cut into 1½-inch pieces
- 6 carrots, halved lengthwise and cut into 1½-inch pieces
- 1 16-ounce package frozen pearl onions, thawed
- 4 8-ounce cans artichoke bottoms, drained and halved
- 1 cup Kalamata olives, halved and pitted
- ¼ cup fresh lemon juice
- 2 teaspoons dried dillweed
  Salt and freshly ground pepper

Heat oil and garlic in heavy large saucepan over low heat. Add potatoes, carrots and onions and cook until tender, stirring often, about 30 minutes.

Add artichoke bottoms to potato mixture and cook until softened, 2 to 3 minutes. Remove from heat. Stir in olives, lemon juice and dillweed. Season with salt and pepper. Serve potato salad at room temperature.

SWEET POTATO SALAD

6 servings

- 1/4 cup mayonnaise
- 2 tablespoons fresh lemon juice
- 2 tablespoons sugar
- 1/2 teaspoon salt
- 2 large sweet potatoes or yams, cooked in skins
- 1 cup diced celery
- 1 cup chopped tart apple
- 1/3 cup chopped walnuts
- 6 lettuce leaves

Combine mayonnaise, lemon juice, sugar and salt in large bowl and whisk to blend. Peel potatoes and cut into 1/2-inch cubes. Add potatoes, celery, apple and nuts to mayonnaise mixture and toss to coat. Cover and refrigerate. Serve chilled salad on lettuce leaves.

FUSILLI SALAD WITH QUICK AÏOLI DRESSING

8 servings

- 1 pound freshly cooked fusilli pasta
- 2 6 1/2-ounce jars marinated artichoke hearts (undrained)
- 1 1/4 cups Quick Aïoli Dressing (see recipe)
- 3/4 cup frozen peas, cooked
- 3/4 teaspoon salt
- 1/4 teaspoon freshly ground pepper
  Romaine lettuce leaves
  Parsley sprigs
- 1 lemon, cut into 8 wedges
  Sun-dried tomatoes (optional)
  Cayenne pepper

Combine fusilli, artichoke hearts with marinade, dressing, peas, salt and pepper and toss well. Line salad bowl with lettuce. Mound fusilli mixture in center. Garnish with parsley sprigs, lemon wedges and sun-dried tomatoes. Sprinkle lightly with cayenne. Serve immediately.

Quick Aïoli Dressing

Makes 2 1/4 cups

- 10 garlic cloves
- 2 cups mayonnaise
- 1/4 cup fresh lemon juice
- 1 teaspoon Dijon mustard

Mince garlic finely in processor. Add mayonnaise, lemon juice and mustard and process until mixture is smooth, approximately 15 seconds.

SPICY BROCCOLI-ORZO SALAD

4 servings

- 2 1/2 cups steamed broccoli florets
- 8 ounces orzo (rice-shaped pasta), cooked al dente and drained
- 2 large tomatoes, chopped
- 3 medium-size green onions, chopped
- 3 tablespoons chopped fresh parsley
- 1 tablespoon olive oil
- 1 tablespoon red wine vinegar
- 1 teaspoon salt
- 1 teaspoon freshly ground pepper
- 1 teaspoon garlic powder

Combine all ingredients in large bowl and toss. Cover tightly and refrigerate salad overnight. Serve slightly chilled or at room temperature.

TRICOLORED PASTA SALAD WITH MOZZARELLA

4 servings

- 1 garlic clove, crushed
- 1/4 teaspoon salt
- 1/2 cup olive oil
- 1/4 cup red wine or balsamic vinegar
- 1/2 teaspoon dried oregano, crumbled
- 1/4 teaspoon fresh thyme, minced
- 1 cup freshly cooked tricolored pasta
- 1 cup cubed mozzarella cheese
- 1 7 1/2-ounce can baby corn, drained and cut into 1-inch pieces
- 1/2 cup carrots cut julienne, blanched
- 1/2 cup cauliflower florets, cooked until crisp-tender
- 1/2 cup halved stuffed green olives
  Salt and freshly ground pepper

Crush garlic and 1/4 teaspoon salt in mortar with pestle. Transfer to small bowl. Add olive oil, vinegar, oregano and thyme and mix well. Combine pasta, cheese, corn, carrots, cauliflower and olives in large bowl. Pour dressing over and toss to mix well. Season with salt and pepper. Serve immediately.

HERBED PASTA AND VEGETABLE SALAD WITH PIMIENTO

6 to 8 servings

- 1 pound small tricolored pasta shells or rotelle pasta
- 1 cup finely diced celery
- 3/4 cup finely diced peeled carrots
- 1 small zucchini, finely diced
- 1 2-ounce jar pimiento-stuffed green olives, drained and sliced
- 1 2-ounce jar sliced pimientos, drained
- 1/2 cup Champagne salad dressing
- 1 6-ounce jar marinated artichoke hearts, drained (marinade reserved)
- 2 tablespoons balsamic vinegar
- 2 tablespoons fresh basil, finely chopped
- 1 tablespoon fresh rosemary, finely chopped

Cook pasta in large pot of boiling water until just tender but firm to bite. Place celery, carrots and zucchini in colander in sink. Pour cooked pasta with water into colander; drain well. Transfer pasta and vegetables to large serving bowl. Add olives and pimientos. Combine dressing, reserved artichoke marinade, vinegar, basil and rosemary in small bowl and whisk to blend. Pour over pasta mixture. Toss to coat thoroughly. (*Can be prepared 2 days ahead and refrigerated.*) Serve pasta salad at room temperature.

TORTELLINI SALAD WITH FETA CHEESE

6 servings

- 1/2 cup olive oil
- 1/4 cup white wine vinegar
- 1/4 cup chopped green onions
- 3 garlic cloves, chopped
- 1 tablespoon dried basil, crumbled
- 1 teaspoon dried dillweed, crumbled
- 2 12-ounce packages frozen stuffed tortellini, cooked according to package instructions
- 1 8 1/2-ounce can water-packed artichoke hearts, drained and quartered
- 1 large tomato, chopped
- 1/2 cup crumbled feta cheese
- 1/2 cup chopped black olives
- 1/2 cup chopped walnuts

Whisk oil and vinegar in small bowl. Add onions, garlic, basil and dillweed and mix well. Combine remaining ingredients in large bowl. Pour dressing over and toss gently. Refrigerate overnight before serving.

COLD CURRIED RICE

8 to 10 servings

- 4 cups chicken stock
- 2 cups rice
- 1 1/2 tablespoons minced candied ginger
- 2 teaspoons curry powder
- 1/2 teaspoon turmeric
- 1/4 cup vegetable oil
- 1/4 cup fresh lemon juice
  Salt and freshly ground pepper

- 1 cup chopped green bell peppers
- 1/2 cup toasted slivered almonds

- 1/2 cup dark raisins or currants
- 1/2 cup golden raisins
- 2 1/2 tablespoons sour cream
- 2 1/2 tablespoons mayonnaise

Combine first 5 ingredients in large saucepan and bring to boil. Reduce heat to low, cover and simmer until rice is tender and liquid is absorbed, about 30 minutes. Transfer to large bowl. Add oil and lemon juice and toss well. Season with salt and pepper. Cover and chill overnight.

Add green bell peppers, almonds and dark and golden raisins and toss gently. Stir in sour cream and mayonnaise. Refrigerate until ready to serve.

BROWN RICE AND VEGETABLE SALAD

4 to 6 servings

Lemon Herb Dressing

- 1 8-ounce carton plain yogurt
- 1/4 cup fresh lemon juice
- 3 tablespoons olive oil
- 1/4 teaspoon dried marjoram, crumbled
- 1/4 teaspoon dried thyme, crumbled
- 1/4 teaspoon garlic powder
- 1/4 teaspoon freshly ground pepper

- 4 cups cooked brown rice
- 2 medium tomatoes, chopped or 15 cherry tomatoes, halved
- 2 small zucchini, cut into 1/4-inch dice (about 1 1/4 cups)
- 1 red or green bell pepper, cored, seeded and cut into 1/4-inch dice (about 1 cup)
- 2 celery stalks, cut into 1/4-inch dice (about 1 cup)
- 2 carrots, cut into 1/4-inch dice (about 1 cup)

- 1 10-ounce package frozen peas, thawed
- 1 8 3/4-ounce can corn kernels, drained
- 3/4 cup thinly sliced green onions (green part only)
- 3/4 to 1 cup diced pepperoni

For dressing: Combine all ingredients in bowl and mix thoroughly. Refrigerate until ready to use.

Mix remaining ingredients in large bowl. Pour dressing over. Toss lightly.

PARTY RICE SALAD

This is a delicious buffet dish for casual and easy entertaining.

12 to 15 servings

- 8 cups cooked rice (2 1/2 cups uncooked)
- 2 to 3 medium tomatoes, cored and chopped
- 2 cups (scant) diced artichoke hearts
- 1 medium onion, chopped
- 1 cup chopped black olives
- 1 7-ounce jar Italian roasted peppers
- 10 pimiento-stuffed olives, sliced
- 1 teaspoon chopped fresh parsley
- 2/3 cup vegetable oil
- 1/3 cup white wine vinegar
- 2 to 3 garlic cloves, minced
- 1 teaspoon dried oregano, crumbled
- 1 teaspoon dried basil, crumbled
  Salt and freshly ground pepper

Combine first 8 ingredients in large bowl. Whisk oil, vinegar, garlic, oregano, basil, salt and pepper in small bowl. Pour over rice mixture and toss well. Cover and refrigerate overnight.

Main-Dish Salads

❖   ❖   ❖

SPINACH SALAD WITH BULGUR

2 servings

  1 cup boiling water
¹/₂ cup bulgur

  1 bunch fresh spinach, washed
    and patted dry
  1 15¹/₂-ounce can chick-peas
    (garbanzo beans), drained
  1 green bell pepper, cored and
    diced
¹/₃ cup chopped onion
  1 hard-cooked egg, chopped
  1 garlic clove, minced
¹/₄ cup red wine vinegar
  1 tablespoon Dijon mustard
  6 tablespoons olive oil
    Salt and freshly ground pepper

Combine boiling water and bulgur in
small bowl. Soak 1 hour.

   Drain bulgur. Transfer to large
bowl. Add spinach, garbanzo beans,
bell pepper, onion, egg and garlic.
Whisk vinegar and mustard in small
bowl. Add oil in slow stream and mix
well. Season with salt and pepper.
Pour over salad. Toss lightly.

VEGETABLE SALAD WITH FETA CHEESE

4 to 6 servings

  1 garlic clove, halved
  1 head iceberg lettuce, torn into
    bite-size pieces
  3 tomatoes, quartered
  1 cucumber, peeled and sliced
  1 red onion, chopped
  3 celery stalks, diced
  1 green bell pepper, seeded and
    chopped
  6 radishes, sliced
  1 carrot, shredded
  2 tablespoons chopped fresh
    parsley
¹/₂ cup olive oil

¹/₄ cup red wine vinegar
1¹/₂ tablespoons fresh lemon juice
  1 teaspoon dried oregano,
    crumbled
¹/₂ teaspoon salt
¹/₂ teaspoon freshly ground pepper
  1 pound feta cheese, crumbled
 12 to 14 Kalamata olives

Rub interior of large wooden salad
bowl with cut side of garlic. Discard
garlic. Add lettuce, tomatoes, cucumber,
onion, celery, bell pepper, radishes,
carrot and parsley to bowl. Toss lightly.
Combine oil, vinegar, lemon juice,
oregano, salt and pepper in jar with
tight-fitting lid and shake well. Pour
over salad and toss to coat. Add cheese
and olives and toss again.

CHICKEN-APPLE SALAD

This is a perfect filling for pita halves.

Makes 6 ¹/₂ cups

  4 chicken breast halves, skinned
    and boned
  1 cup whipping cream

¹/₂ cup mayonnaise
¹/₂ cup sour cream
¹/₂ cup pecan halves
  1 teaspoon dried tarragon,
    crumbled
¹/₂ teaspoon salt
    Freshly ground pepper
  3 pippin apples, cored and cut
    julienne

Preheat oven to 350°F. Arrange chicken
in single layer in 9x5-inch loaf pan.
Pour cream over. Bake until juices run
clear when pierced with tip of sharp
knife, about 30 minutes. Drain chicken
thoroughly; cool completely.

   Combine mayonnaise, sour cream,
pecans, tarragon, salt and pepper in
large bowl. Shred chicken into 2-inch-
long strips. Add chicken and apples to
dressing and mix well. Cover tightly
and refrigerate overnight.

CURRIED TURKEY SALAD

4 servings

  2 cups cubed cooked turkey or
    chicken
  1 large celery stalk, thinly sliced
¹/₄ cup slivered blanched almonds
¹/₄ cup golden raisins
  1 medium-size green onion,
    thinly sliced
  2 tablespoons mango chutney
  5 tablespoons Curry
    Mayonnaise (see recipe)
    Lettuce
    Mayonnaise

Garnishes
    Hard-cooked eggs (halved)
    Boiled potatoes (halved)
    Cucumber slices
    Fresh pineapple or melon
    chunks
    Tart apple slices
    Mandarin orange sections
    Steamed carrot chunks
    Steamed green beans
    Steamed broccoli

Combine turkey, celery, almonds, raisins, green onion and chutney in medium bowl. Add 2 tablespoons Curry
Mayonnaise and toss to blend. Arrange
lettuce on platter. Spoon turkey mixture atop lettuce. Serve with any or all
of garnishes. Thin remaining 3 tablespoons Curry Mayonnaise with mayonnaise and serve as dip for garnishes.

Curry Mayonnaise

Makes 5 tablespoons

  3 tablespoons mayonnaise
  1 tablespoon curry powder
  1 tablespoon Dijon mustard
  1 teaspoon fresh lemon juice
  1 large garlic clove, minced

Mix all ingredients in small bowl.

CHICKEN AND SNOW PEA SALAD

4 to 6 servings

 3 cups cubed cooked chicken
 1 8-ounce can sliced water chestnuts, drained
 4 hard-cooked eggs, coarsely chopped
 1/2 cup sliced green onions
 1 cup sour cream
 2 teaspoons sugar
 2 teaspoons unsalted curry powder
 2 teaspoons fresh lemon or lime juice
 1/2 teaspoon ground ginger
 1/4 teaspoon freshly ground white pepper

 1/4 pound fresh or thawed frozen snow peas, strings removed Lettuce
 2 hard-cooked eggs, sliced Lemon or lime wedges Parsley sprigs

Mix chicken, water chestnuts, 4 chopped eggs and green onions in large bowl. Combine sour cream, sugar, curry powder, lemon juice, ginger and pepper in small bowl. Pour over salad and toss to combine. Cover salad and refrigerate 24 hours.

Cook snow peas in boiling water until just tender, 1 to 2 minutes. Drain and plunge into ice water to set color. Drain and pat dry. Add peas to salad and toss. Line serving bowl with lettuce. Mound salad in bowl. Garnish with sliced eggs, lemon and parsley. Serve salad chilled.

GREEN CHILI-CHICKEN SALAD

6 servings

Tarragon Vinaigrette
 1/4 cup tarragon vinegar
 1/4 cup vegetable oil
 2 1/2 teaspoons lemon pepper

 2 1/2 cups diced cooked chicken
 1/2 teaspoon lemon pepper
 1 1-pound head iceberg lettuce, cored
 1 cup chopped tomatoes

 1/2 cup grated longhorn cheese (about 2 ounces)
 1/2 cup grated Monterey Jack cheese (about 2 ounces)
 1/2 cup diced green chilies
 1/2 cup pine nuts, toasted

For vinaigrette: Combine vinegar, oil and 2 1/2 teaspoons lemon pepper in small bowl and whisk thoroughly.

Toss chicken with 1/2 teaspoon lemon pepper in medium bowl. Line large serving bowl with 4 or 5 lettuce leaves. Chop remaining lettuce into bite-size pieces. Transfer to serving bowl. Add remaining ingredients and toss lightly. Pour dressing over and toss again. Refrigerate salad for 10 to 15 minutes before serving.

NAPA CABBAGE CHICKEN SALAD

2 servings

 1/2 cup fresh orange juice
 2 tablespoons sliced carrots
 2 tablespoons (1/4 stick) butter
 1 cup chopped red bell peppers
 2 green onions, chopped
 1/4 medium head Napa cabbage, sliced
 2 cups cooked chicken cut into 1 1/2-inch strips
 1/3 cup cubed edam cheese
 20 seedless green grapes
 8 green beans, cut diagonally into 2-inch lengths and parboiled
 1 tomato, peeled and sliced
 5 1/2 tablespoons rice wine vinegar
 1/4 cup hazelnut oil
 1/2 teaspoon paprika
 1/2 teaspoon salt
 1/4 teaspoon dry mustard
 1/8 teaspoon cayenne pepper
 1/8 teaspoon freshly grated nutmeg Dash of freshly ground pepper

Heat orange juice in small saucepan over medium-high heat. Add carrots and cook until crisp-tender; drain. Melt butter in small skillet over medium-low heat. Add red peppers and green onions and sauté until beginning to soften, about 5 minutes. Transfer to bowl. Add carrots, sliced cabbage, chicken, cheese, grapes, beans and tomato. Combine remaining ingredients in jar and shake well. Pour over salad and toss to coat.

JAPANESE CHICKEN SALAD

2 to 3 servings

 1 tablespoon sesame oil
 3 boneless chicken breast halves, skinned and cut into 1/4-inch strips
 1 tablespoon teriyaki sauce
 2 tablespoons mirin (sweet rice wine)
 2 tablespoons soy sauce
 2 tablespoons dashi (Japanese soup stock)
 1 1/2 teaspoons wasabi (Japanese horseradish)
 1 1/2 teaspoons water
 1/4 teaspoon grated fresh ginger Oriental noodles, cooked al dente and chilled

Heat oil in medium skillet over high heat. Add chicken and sauté until opaque, about 2 minutes. Transfer to medium bowl. Drizzle with teriyaki sauce. Mix mirin, soy sauce, dashi, wasabi, water and ginger in small bowl. Pour over chicken and toss. Cover and refrigerate overnight. Serve salad over noodles.

CHICKEN SALAD ORIENTAL

6 to 8 servings

 2 cups peanut oil
 10 won ton skins, cut into 1/2-inch strips
 1 head iceberg lettuce, shredded
 3 cups shredded cooked chicken
 1 cup chopped green onions
 2 tablespoons toasted sesame seeds
 1/4 cup vegetable oil
 3 tablespoons rice vinegar
 2 tablespoons sugar
 1 tablespoon oriental sesame oil
 1 teaspoon salt
 1/2 teaspoon freshly ground pepper

Heat peanut oil in heavy large skillet over medium-high heat. Add won ton skins and fry until golden brown, about 1 minute. Remove using slotted spoon and drain on paper towels. Transfer to large bowl. Add lettuce, chicken, onions and sesame seeds.

Combine remaining ingredients in jar with tight-fitting lid and shake well. Pour dressing over salad and toss to coat. Serve immediately.

CHICKEN-ARTICHOKE SALAD

6 servings

  1 6-ounce package chicken-flavored rice mix
  4 cups diced cooked chicken
  1/2 green bell pepper, seeded and chopped
  8 pimiento-stuffed green olives, sliced
  2 green onions, chopped
  2 6-ounce jars marinated artichoke hearts (undrained)
  1/2 cup mayonnaise
  1/2 teaspoon curry powder
  Salt and freshly ground pepper
  Lettuce leaves
  Cherry tomatoes and toasted slivered almonds (garnish)

Cook rice according to package directions. Transfer to large bowl, fluff with fork and let cool. Add chicken, bell pepper, olives, green onions, artichoke hearts and half of marinade and toss lightly. Mix mayonnaise, curry powder and remaining marinade in small bowl. Pour over salad and toss again. Add salt and pepper. Refrigerate until ready to use. Arrange salad on lettuce leaves. Garnish with tomatoes and almonds.

WARM CHICKEN AND WALNUT SALAD

6 servings

  3 cups chicken stock
  3 whole unskinned chicken breasts, boned
  1 cup walnut halves and pieces
  3 tablespoons light soy sauce
  2 1/2 cups cooked long-grain rice, room temperature
  1/4 cup corn or peanut oil
  2 tablespoons vegetable oil
  2 tablespoons rice vinegar
  Grated peel of 1 lemon
  1 tablespoon freshly grated ginger

  Lettuce leaves
  Seeded red grapes or mandarin orange slices (optional garnish)

Bring chicken stock to boil in medium saucepan. Add chicken, reduce heat and simmer gently until chicken is tender, about 10 to 15 minutes. Transfer chicken to work surface; discard skin. Chop chicken into bite-size pieces. Transfer to large bowl.

  Preheat oven to 400°F. Line baking sheet with foil. Combine nuts and soy sauce in small bowl and toss to coat well. Arrange in single layer on prepared sheet. Bake until crisp, turning once, about 7 to 8 minutes. Reserve 1/4 cup nuts for garnish. Add remainder to chicken. Blend in rice and toss lightly. Combine corn or peanut oil, vegetable oil, rice vinegar and lemon peel in small jar with tight-fitting lid and shake to blend well.

  Just before serving, sprinkle ginger over chicken mixture and toss well. Add dressing and toss gently. Spoon salad onto lettuce-lined plates. Top with remaining nuts and garnish with grapes or mandarin orange slices.

CHICKEN-PASTA SALAD WITH FRUIT

4 servings

  3 whole boneless chicken breasts, cooked and chopped into bite-size pieces
  2 cups seedless green grapes
  1 cup snow peas
 12 fresh spinach leaves, torn into pieces
  1 large celery heart with leaves, chopped
  7 ounces 1-inch cheese raviolini,* cooked, drained and cooled
  1 6-ounce jar artichoke hearts with marinade
  1 kiwi, peeled and sliced
  1/2 large cucumber, sliced
  1/2 cup raisins
  1 green onion, chopped
  2/3 cup mayonnaise
  1/2 cup freshly grated Parmesan cheese
  1/3 cup fresh lemon juice

  Salt and freshly ground white pepper
  Fresh spinach leaves
  Mandarin orange sections (garnish)

Combine first 11 ingredients in large serving bowl and toss gently. Mix mayonnaise, Parmesan cheese, lemon juice, salt and white pepper in small bowl. Pour over salad and toss again. Refrigerate until ready to use. To serve, spoon salad onto spinach-lined plates. Garnish with mandarin orange sections.

*Available at Italian markets.

CALIFORNIA PASTA SALAD WITH PECAN-CILANTRO PESTO

4 to 6 servings

  2 whole boneless chicken breasts
  Garlic powder
  Poultry seasoning
  Salt and freshly ground pepper

  1/2 cup (1 stick) margarine, room temperature
  1/2 cup peanut oil
  1/4 cup Zinfandel
  3 garlic cloves, minced
  1 tablespoon rice wine vinegar
  3 dashes soy sauce
  1/2 teaspoon salt
  Dash of poultry seasoning
  Freshly ground pepper
  3 medium bunches fresh cilantro, washed, stemmed and finely chopped
  1/3 cup pecans
  1/4 pound freshly grated Parmesan cheese

  1 pound freshly cooked rotelle pasta
  1 2-ounce jar pimientos, drained
  Freshly grated Parmesan cheese

Preheat oven to 450°F. Sprinkle chicken with garlic powder, poultry seasoning, salt and pepper. Coat 2 pieces of aluminum foil with nonstick vegetable oil spray. Wrap chicken breasts in foil. Bake 35 minutes.

  Meanwhile, mix margarine, oil, wine, garlic, vinegar, soy sauce, salt, poultry seasoning and pepper in processor until smooth, 2 to 3 minutes. Add cilantro in 3 batches, processing 1 minute after each addition. Add pecans and process until finely ground, using on/off turns. Pour into bowl and stir in 1/4 pound Parmesan. Set aside.

Remove chicken from foil; reserve 1/4 cup cooking juices. Remove skin from chicken. Cut chicken into bite-size pieces. Transfer to large bowl. Add pasta, pimientos, reserved cooking juices and 1/2 cup pesto and mix well. Add more pesto, if desired. Serve immediately. Pass grated Parmesan and remaining pesto separately.

FRESH SPINACH, BROCCOLI AND TUNA SALAD

4 servings

    2 garlic cloves, halved
 1/3 cup olive oil
 1/4 cup freshly grated Parmesan
       cheese
    1 tablespoon plus 1 1/2 teaspoons
       fresh lemon juice
    1 tablespoon plus 1 1/2 teaspoons
       fresh lime juice
       Freshly ground pepper
    1 bunch broccoli, cut into florets,
       blanched
    8 ounces fresh spinach, cut
       julienne
    1 small head red leaf lettuce, torn
       into bite-size pieces
    1 6 1/2-ounce can water-packed
       tuna, drained
    8 cherry tomatoes, halved
    1 ounce alfalfa sprouts (optional)
    2 tablespoons bacon bits

Rub sides of large wooden bowl with cut side of garlic. Discard garlic. Whisk oil, cheese, lemon and lime juices and pepper in same bowl. Add remaining ingredients and toss to coat.

HEAVENLY BLUEFISH SALAD

4 servings

Dressing
 1/2 cup mayonnaise
 1/4 cup plain yogurt
    1 tablespoon half and half

    1 tablespoon fresh lime juice
    1 tablespoon fresh lemon juice
 1/2 teaspoon salt or to taste
 1/8 teaspoon freshly ground pepper

    3 cups cooked flaked bluefish or
       swordfish
 1/2 cup diced celery
 1/4 cup diced green bell pepper
 1/4 cup diced water chestnuts
    2 tablespoons chopped green
       onions, including tops

For dressing: Mix all ingredients in small bowl. Set aside.

Combine remaining ingredients in large bowl and toss gently. Pour half of dressing over salad and toss to coat. Pass remaining dressing separately.

SHRIMP AND RICE SALAD

4 servings

Dressing
 1/4 cup mayonnaise
 1/4 cup sour cream
 1/2 1.7-ounce package French
       dressing mix

    3 cups cooked rice
    1 cup cooked tiny shrimp
 1/4 cup chopped green bell pepper
    2 tablespoons minced onion
    2 tablespoons chopped celery
       Freshly ground pepper

    4 large butter lettuce leaves

For dressing: Combine all ingredients in bowl and mix well.

Toss rice, shrimp, bell pepper, onion and celery in large bowl. Season with pepper. Add dressing and toss to coat. Refrigerate until ready to use.

To serve, arrange lettuce leaves on plates. Top with salad.

SHRIMP, AVOCADO AND SPINACH SALAD

2 to 4 servings

    1 teaspoon sugar
 1/2 teaspoon dried tarragon,
       crumbled
 1/4 teaspoon dry mustard
 1/4 teaspoon seasoned pepper

    5 tablespoons red wine vinegar
    2 tablespoons olive oil

    1 bunch fresh spinach, stemmed,
       torn into bite-size pieces
    1 avocado, cut into 3/4-inch dice
 1/2 pound cooked bay shrimp,
       patted dry
    6 medium mushrooms, sliced
       1/4 inch thick
 1/2 medium Maui, Vidalia or red
       onion, thinly sliced and
       separated into rings
 1 1/2 tablespoons roasted sunflower
       seeds
    1 hard-cooked egg, finely
       chopped

Combine sugar, tarragon, mustard and pepper in small bowl. Add vinegar and oil, whisking until sugar dissolves. Refrigerate until ready to use.

Combine spinach, avocado, shrimp, mushrooms and onion in bowl. Sprinkle with sunflower seeds. Whisk dressing and pour over salad. Toss gently to coat. Sprinkle with egg and serve.

SMOKED HAM SALAD WITH MUSTARD MAYONNAISE

4 servings

 1/2 cup mayonnaise
    2 tablespoons plus 1 teaspoon
       Dijon mustard
    2 tablespoons olive oil
    1 tablespoon plus 1 teaspoon
       white wine vinegar
 1/2 teaspoon dried tarragon,
       crumbled
 1/4 teaspoon sugar
    6 ounces smoked ham, cut into
       1/4-inch-thick julienne
    2 8-ounce cans artichoke
       bottoms, drained, cubed
    1 14-ounce can hearts of palm,
       drained, sliced into 1/2-inch
       rounds

Whisk first 6 ingredients in medium bowl until well blended. Add remaining ingredients and stir to coat well. Refrigerate overnight. Serve chilled.

BEEF SALAD WITH PEPPER DRESSING

A nice starter or luncheon entrée. Accompany with crusty bread.

2 servings

- 1/2 cup soy sauce
- 6 tablespoons sugar
- 1 tablespoon finely grated ginger
- 1 tablespoon minced garlic
- 1 12-ounce New York (top loin) steak, 1 inch thick
- 8 cups bite-size pieces mixed greens (escarole, radicchio, Boston lettuce and red leaf lettuce)
- 1/4 English hothouse cucumber, cut julienne
- 1 1/3 cups thinly sliced red onion
- 1/4 cup soy sauce
- 2 tablespoons fresh lemon juice
- 3/4 teaspoon minced jalapeño chili
- 2 tablespoons peanut oil
- 2 tablespoons olive oil

- 1 teaspoon sesame seeds
- 12 fresh cilantro sprigs

Combine first 4 ingredients in baking dish; stir to dissolve sugar. Add steak, turning to coat. Cover and refrigerate 2 hours, turning occasionally.

Prepare barbecue grill (high heat). Combine greens, cucumber and onion in large bowl. Combine 1/4 cup soy sauce, lemon juice and chili in small bowl. Gradually whisk in both oils.

Grill steak until cooked to desired doneness, about 3 minutes per side for rare. Toss salad with vinaigrette. Divide salad among plates. Slice steak thinly across grain. Arrange atop salad. Sprinkle with sesame seeds. Garnish with cilantro and serve.

Salad Dressings

    ◆

TANGY OIL AND VINEGAR DRESSING

Makes 1 cup

- 3/4 cup vegetable oil
- 5 tablespoons white wine vinegar
- 1/2 teaspoon dry mustard
- 1/2 teaspoon sugar
- 1/2 teaspoon salt
- 1/2 teaspoon freshly ground pepper

Whisk all ingredients in small bowl. Store in jar with tight-fitting lid. Shake dressing well before using.

SAGE COTTAGE VINAIGRETTE

Makes about 1 cup

- 3 tablespoons natural rice vinegar*
- 2 tablespoons Dijon mustard
- 1 large garlic clove
- 1/3 cup olive oil
- 1/4 cup water
  Freshly grated nutmeg
  Freshly ground pepper

Blend vinegar, mustard and garlic in processor or blender. With machine running, add oil in thin stream. Add remaining ingredients and blend thoroughly. (*Can be prepared 1 day ahead and refrigerated.*)

*Available at oriental markets.

CELERY SEED DRESSING

Serve this delicious blend on apple slices or avocado and orange slices.

Makes 1 3/4 cups

- 1 cup safflower oil
- 1/2 cup cider vinegar
- 1/2 cup sugar
- 1 tablespoon whole celery seeds, lightly crushed
- 1 tablespoon dehydrated onion flakes
- 1 teaspoon dry mustard
- 1 teaspoon salt

Combine all ingredients in blender and mix on medium speed 20 seconds. Serve at room temperature or refrigerate and serve chilled. Store in jar with tight-fitting lid. Shake dressing well before using.

ITALIAN SWEET-SOUR SALAD DRESSING

Makes about 2/3 cup

- 1/2 cup vegetable oil
- 1/3 cup red wine vinegar
- 2 tablespoons sugar
- 1 garlic clove, minced
- 1/2 teaspoon salt
- 1/2 teaspoon celery salt
- 1/2 teaspoon coarsely ground pepper
- 1/2 teaspoon dry mustard
- 1/2 teaspoon Worcestershire sauce
- 1/4 teaspoon hot pepper sauce

Combine all ingredients in jar with tight-fitting lid and shake well. (*Can be prepared 1 week ahead and refrigerated. Shake dressing before using.*)

DILLED FETA DRESSING

Delicious over sliced tomatoes.

6 servings

- 1 cup diced feta cheese
- 1/2 cup milk
- 1/2 cup plain yogurt
- 1 tablespoon minced fresh dill or 1 teaspoon dried dillweed

Combine feta, milk, yogurt and dill in processor or blender and mix until smooth. Transfer to small bowl, cover tightly and refrigerate.

TOASTED WALNUT SALAD DRESSING

Makes about 1½ cups

- ¾ cup walnut oil
- ¼ cup tarragon vinegar
- 1 tablespoon chopped fresh parsley
- ½ teaspoon salt
  Freshly ground pepper
- 30 shelled walnut halves, toasted and coarsely chopped
- 1 garlic clove

Combine oil, vinegar, parsley, salt and pepper in jar with tight-fitting lid. Add walnuts and garlic. Cover and refrigerate overnight. Remove garlic clove from dressing when ready to serve.

FRANKFURT GREEN SAUCE

A natural with shellfish or chicken salads.

Makes 2¼ cups

- ⅔ cup mayonnaise, preferably homemade
- ½ cup sour cream
- 1 tablespoon fresh lemon juice
- 1 tablespoon tarragon-flavored white wine vinegar
- 1½ teaspoons Dijon mustard
- 1 teaspoon sugar
  Salt and freshly ground white pepper
- 1 cup minced fresh herbs (parsley, tarragon, chervil, chives, sorrel, dill and watercress)

- 4 hard-cooked eggs, room temperature, finely chopped

Whisk mayonnaise and sour cream in nonaluminum bowl until smooth. Blend in remaining ingredients. Adjust seasoning. Cover with plastic wrap. Refrigerate at least 5 hours. (*Can be prepared 1 day ahead.*)

CREAMY ROQUEFORT DRESSING

Makes about 3 cups

- 1 cup sour cream
- 1 cup mayonnaise
- 6 ounces cream cheese, room temperature
- ½ teaspoon fresh lemon juice
- ¼ teaspoon salt
- ⅛ teaspoon garlic juice
  Freshly ground pepper
- 3 ounces Roquefort cheese, crumbled
  Milk

Combine first 7 ingredients in processor and blend until smooth, about 20 seconds. Transfer to medium bowl. Stir in cheese. Cover and refrigerate overnight. Just before serving, thin dressing with milk to desired consistency.

GREENER GODDESS DRESSING

Also delicious as a dip for crudités.

Makes about 3 cups

- 2 cups mayonnaise
- ½ ripe avocado, mashed
- 2 large green onions, chopped

- ¼ cup chopped fresh parsley
- ¼ cup olive oil
- 3 tablespoons white wine vinegar
- 2 tablespoons anchovy paste
- 1 garlic clove, chopped
- 1 teaspoon dried tarragon, crumbled
  Freshly ground pepper

Combine all ingredients in processor or blender and mix thoroughly. Pour into jar with tight-fitting lid. Refrigerate until ready to serve. Shake well to blend before using.

CHUNKY CUCUMBER SALAD DRESSING

Serve over mixed salad greens or as a dip for fresh vegetables.

Makes about 2 cups

- 1 cup mayonnaise
- 1½ tablespoons fresh lemon juice
- 1 tablespoon cider vinegar
- 1 teaspoon chili powder
- ½ teaspoon seasoned salt
- 1 large cucumber, peeled, seeded and chopped
- 1 large celery stalk, diced
- 5 pimiento-stuffed green olives, diced

Mix first 5 ingredients in blender on low speed or in processor until smooth. Add remaining ingredients and blend 5 seconds. (*Can be prepared 1 day ahead. Cover and refrigerate.*)

4 ❖ *Entrées*

Here in the largest chapter of the book, you'll find an international array of fast and fabulous main courses—choose whatever suits your tastes and the occasion—beef, veal, lamb, pork, poultry, fish, or egg, cheese and vegetable. From light to hearty, casual to elegant, this selection will make preparing either a family dinner or a dinner party seem almost effortless.

Meat entrées are often the centerpieces for elegant dinner parties, and for good reason: In addition to their fine flavor, most cuts, such as steaks, scallops, cutlets and chops, are fast and easy to prepare. We offer a selection of quick and delicious recipes to fit the bill, including Filet Mignon with Oysters and Port Flambé, Herbed Veal with Lemon and Berry-glazed Lamb Chops. You'll also find perfect candidates for more casual fare, such as True Texas Chili, Lamb and Green Bean Stew and Mustard-glazed Spareribs.

Versatile, inexpensive poultry is a universal favorite of busy cooks. The international array that we present here runs the gamut from the zip of Five-Spice Chicken and Vegetable Stir-fry and Chicken Enchiladas to the refined elegance of Chicken with Mustard Cream Sauce and Game Hens in Cognac Sauce.

Another standout is seafood. Fresh fish and shellfish need only brief cooking, and although they are delicious simply grilled or broiled, they're even better when enhanced with a delicate sauce to accent the fresh flavors. For a zesty change of pace, try Sea Bass with Ginger Sauce, Fresh Tuna with Piquant Sauce or the Oriental Hot and Spicy Shrimp with Noodles.

We round out the chapter with a diverse selection of satisfying egg, cheese and vegetable entrées. Both economical and simple to prepare, these dishes are suitable for breakfasts, brunches, lunches and suppers. Sausage and Sour Cream Omelets or Sherried Ham and Mushroom Quiche would make an enticing main dish at any brunch. And many of the entrées here need only a green salad and crusty loaf of bread to become a delightful lunch or supper—try Mexican-style Frittata or Vegetarian Chili for a fast and delicious meal.

Beef

❖ ❖ ❖

PEPPER STEAK

4 servings

- 1 3¹/2-pound sirloin steak (1¹/2 inches thick), edges scored at 2-inch intervals
- 2 tablespoons coarsely ground pepper
- 1 teaspoon salt
- 1 tablespoon butter
- 1 tablespoon olive oil
- ¹/2 cup dry white wine
- ¹/4 cup whipping cream
- ¹/4 cup brandy

Rub both sides of steak with pepper. Sprinkle with salt. Melt butter with oil in heavy large skillet over high heat. Add steak and sear on both sides. Reduce heat to medium-high. Cook 6 to 7 minutes on each side for rare. Transfer steak to serving platter. Add wine to pan and bring to boil, scraping up any browned bits. Add cream and boil sauce until reduced by half. Pour brandy into pan and heat briefly; ignite with match. When flames subside, pour sauce over steak. Serve immediately.

FILET MIGNON WITH OYSTERS AND PORT FLAMBE

2 servings

- 4 ³/4-inch-thick filet mignon steaks
- 2 tablespoons light soy sauce
- 3 tablespoons butter
- 1 medium shallot, minced
- 1 8-ounce jar oysters, drained, liquid reserved
- ¹/4 cup brandy
- 1 tablespoon cornstarch
- ¹/4 teaspoon salt
- ¹/4 cup ruby Port

Brush filets with soy sauce. Melt butter in heavy large skillet over medium heat. Add shallot and stir until soft, about 2 minutes. Increase heat to medium-high. Add filets and cook until browned, about 3 minutes per side for medium-rare. Remove filets; keep warm. Reduce heat to medium. Stir in oysters. Pour brandy into corner of pan and ignite. Stir until edges of oysters begin to curl, about 1 minute. Remove oysters with slotted spoon; set aside. Add enough water to oyster liquid to measure ¹/2 cup. Stir in cornstarch. Add to skillet. Stir until thick and clear, about 2 minutes. Season with salt. Stir in Port. Reduce heat and simmer 2 minutes, stirring constantly. Return oysters to skillet and mix well. Arrange filets on plates. Spoon sauce over. Serve immediately.

ROAST TENDERLOIN WITH PANCETTA, MARJORAM AND RED WINE

4 servings

- 2 tablespoons (¹/4 stick) butter, room temperature
- 1 2-pound beef tenderloin, trimmed of outside fat and sinew
  Coarsely ground pepper
- ¹/4 pound ¹/8-inch-thick slices pancetta* or bacon
- 1 tablespoon butter
- 3 ounces pancetta* or bacon, chopped
- ¹/3 cup minced shallots
- ¹/4 cup Cognac
- 1¹/2 cups dry red wine
- 3 marjoram sprigs
- 3 cups unsalted beef stock (preferably homemade), boiled until reduced to 1¹/2 cups
- 1 teaspoon tomato paste
- ¹/4 cup (¹/2 stick) butter, cut into 4 pieces
  Freshly ground pepper
  Minced fresh marjoram

Preheat oven to 450°F. Spread 2 tablespoons butter over beef. Sprinkle liberally with pepper. Wrap with ¹/4-pound pancetta, securing with toothpicks. Place on rack in roasting pan just large enough to accommodate beef. Bake until thermometer inserted in thickest part of meat registers 120°F, for rare, about 30 minutes. Transfer to platter and tent with foil to keep warm.

Set roasting pan over medium heat. Add 1 tablespoon butter and chopped pancetta and stir 1 minute. Add shallots and stir until tender, about 3 minutes. Pour off all but thin film of fat. Add Cognac and boil until reduced to glaze, scraping up any browned bits, about 1¹/2 minutes. Add ³/4 cup wine and marjoram and boil until reduced to glaze, about 5 minutes. Add remaining wine and boil until reduced to glaze, about 5 minutes. Add stock and tomato paste and boil until reduced to ³/4 cup mixture, adding juices on beef platter, about 8 minutes. Strain into heavy small saucepan, pressing to extract as much liquid as possible. Bring sauce to simmer and whisk in ¹/4 cup butter 1 piece at a time. Season with generous amount of pepper. Cut meat into ¹/2-inch-thick slices, discarding toothpicks. Arrange on heated plates. Spoon sauce over. Sprinkle with minced marjoram and serve.

*Pancetta, unsmoked bacon cured in salt, is available at Italian markets.

RIO GRANDE BEEF BURRITOS WITH CREAMED PEPPERS

4 servings; can be doubled or tripled

- 1 pound skirt or flank steak
- 2 large garlic cloves, crushed
- ¹/2 teaspoon ground cumin
- 1 tablespoon olive oil
- 1 tablespoon fresh lime juice

- 2 tablespoons olive oil
- 2 large onions, thinly sliced

4 Anaheim chilies, roasted, peeled, seeded and cut into thin strips*
2 7-ounce jars roasted red peppers, drained and cut into thin strips
1 cup whipping cream
1 1/2 cups grated Monterey Jack cheese
1 teaspoon dried oregano, crumbled
  Salt and freshly ground pepper

2 tablespoons olive oil

8 8-inch flour tortillas
1 cup grated Monterey Jack cheese

Preheat oven to 450°F. Grease square baking pan. Rub both sides of steak with garlic and cumin, then with 1 tablespoon oil and lime juice. Let stand while preparing peppers.

Heat 2 tablespoons oil in heavy large skillet over medium-high heat. Add onion and cook until beginning to brown, stirring frequently, about 10 minutes. Add chilies and peppers and stir until heated through. Add cream, then 1 1/2 cups cheese and stir until mixture thickens, about 2 minutes. Add oregano. Season with salt and freshly ground pepper.

Heat 2 tablespoons oil in heavy large skillet over high heat. Season steak with salt and pepper. Cook until brown, about 1 1/2 minutes per side for very rare. Transfer meat to work surface. Halve across width, then cut against grain into thin slices.

Hold tortilla over gas burner on low or place on electric burner on low until heated through, about 15 seconds per side. Place on work surface. Spoon 1/8 cup pepper mixture down center. Top with 1/8 of meat. Roll up tortilla, enclosing filling. Arrange in baking pan seam side down. Repeat with remaining tortillas, 3/4 cup pepper mixture and remaining meat. Spoon remaining pepper mixture over tortillas. Sprinkle with 1 cup cheese. (*Can be assembled 2 hours ahead. Cover with foil and refrigerate.*) Bake uncovered (covered if burritos were refrigerated) until cheese melts, 5 to 10 minutes.

*Canned whole mild green chilies can be substituted; do not roast.

ONE-HOUR MIXED GRILL COUSCOUS

6 to 8 servings

3 tablespoons bacon fat
2 large onions, coarsely chopped
3 celery stalks, sliced 1/4 inch thick on diagonal (leaves reserved)
3 10 3/4-ounce cans chicken broth
1 15 1/2-ounce can chick-peas (garbanzo beans), drained
1 15-ounce can lima beans (with liquid)
1 7-ounce bottle pilsner beer
3 carrots, sliced 1/4 inch thick on diagonal
1/4 pound mushrooms, thinly sliced
1 2-ounce jar chopped pimientos, drained
2 large garlic cloves, minced
2 tablespoons soy sauce
3 bay leaves
1 teaspoon sugar
1 teaspoon poultry seasoning
1/2 teaspoon freshly ground white pepper

1 1-pound box couscous, cooked according to package directions
3 1/4 pounds assorted grilled or broiled meats (such as flank steak, filet mignon, kielbasa, lamb chops, pork chops)

Melt bacon fat in Dutch oven over low heat. Add onions and celery and sauté until lightly browned. Add next 13 ingredients. Cover Dutch oven and cook vegetables 30 minutes.

Mound couscous in center of large platter. Arrange grilled meats around couscous. Ladle vegetables and broth over. Garnish with celery leaves.

BURGUNDY BEEF STROGANOFF

6 servings

1/4 cup all purpose flour
1 teaspoon salt
1 teaspoon dried thyme, crumbled
1/2 teaspoon freshly ground pepper
2 pounds round steak, cut into 1 1/2x1/4-inch strips
1/2 cup (1 stick) butter

1 medium onion, finely chopped
1 cup beef broth
1 cup Burgundy

2 tablespoons (1/4 stick) butter
1/2 pound mushrooms, sliced

2 cups sour cream
3 tablespoons tomato paste
1 tablespoon Worcestershire sauce
  Freshly cooked noodles
  Chopped fresh parsley

Combine flour, salt, thyme and pepper in plastic bag. Add meat and shake to coat well. Remove meat, shaking off excess flour. Melt 1/2 cup butter in large skillet over medium heat. Add meat and brown lightly, about 3 minutes. Add onion and stir until tender, about 3 minutes. Pour in broth and wine. Simmer mixture until meat is tender, 30 to 45 minutes.

Melt 2 tablespoons butter in small skillet over medium heat. Add mushrooms and sauté until just tender, 3 to 4 minutes. Stir mushrooms into meat.

Blend sour cream, tomato paste and Worcestershire sauce in small bowl. Slowly stir into meat; do not boil. Transfer noodles to serving dish. Spoon meat over. Top with parsley.

BEEF AND OLIVE STEW

4 to 6 servings

2 tablespoons vegetable oil
1 large onion, chopped
2 garlic cloves, minced
2 pounds flank steak, cut into 1/4x2-inch strips
1 15-ounce can tomato sauce
2 tablespoons red wine vinegar
1 tablespoon dried oregano, crumbled
  Freshly ground pepper
1/2 cup pimiento-stuffed green olives, sliced
1 to 2 marinated jalapeño chilies, diced
  Freshly cooked rice

Heat oil in large skillet over medium heat. Add onion and garlic and stir until translucent, about 6 minutes. Increase heat to medium-high. Add steak and stir until browned, about 3 minutes. Blend in tomato sauce, vinegar, oregano and pepper. Simmer until meat is tender and sauce is thickened, 30 to 40 minutes. Add olives and chilies and stir until heated through. Spoon over rice. Serve immediately.

ZESTY HUNAN BEEF

4 servings

- 1/4 cup soy sauce
- 2 tablespoons dry Sherry
- 2 garlic cloves, minced
- 1 pound lean beef round, sliced into 3x1/4-inch strips

- 1/4 cup vegetable oil
- 4 cups broccoli florets
- 3 1/2 cups sliced mushrooms
- 1 cup thinly sliced carrots
- 5 green onions, cut into 1-inch pieces
- 1/4 cup toasted slivered almonds
- 2 tablespoons finely chopped fresh ginger
- 3/4 teaspoon dried red pepper flakes
- 2 tablespoons cornstarch dissolved in 1 tablespoon water
  Freshly cooked rice

Combine soy sauce, Sherry and garlic in large bowl. Add beef strips. Cover and marinate at room temperature 1 hour or in refrigerator overnight.

Drain beef, reserving marinade. Heat oil in large skillet or wok over high heat. Add beef and stir-fry 2 minutes. Remove from skillet; set aside. Add broccoli, mushrooms, carrots, green onions, almonds, ginger and pepper flakes to skillet and cook 2 minutes. Stir in reserved marinade and cornstarch. Cook until vegetables are crisp-tender and sauce thickens, 4 to 6 minutes. Return beef to skillet and heat through, 1 to 2 minutes. Serve immediately over rice.

MARINATED SESAME BEEF

2 to 4 servings

- 1 1/2 cups chopped green onions
- 1 cup soy sauce
- 1 cup water
- 1/2 cup sugar
- 1/4 cup sesame seeds
- 6 garlic cloves, minced
- 1 teaspoon freshly ground pepper
- 1 pound bottom round of beef, thinly sliced

  Freshly cooked rice
  Chopped green onions

Combine first 7 ingredients in bowl. Place beef in ovenproof glass baking dish. Pour marinade over. Cover and refrigerate overnight, stirring occasionally.

Prepare barbecue (medium-high heat) or preheat broiler. Drain marinade from meat. Grill beef to desired doneness, turning once, about 8 minutes for medium-rare. Mound rice on platter. Top with meat. Garnish with chopped green onions.

BEEF SHISH KEBAB IN ONION MARINADE

4 servings

- 1/2 large onion, grated
- 1/4 teaspoon ground cumin
- 1/4 teaspoon fresh lemon juice
- 1/4 teaspoon cider vinegar
- 1/8 teaspoon garlic powder
  Crushed red pepper flakes (optional)
- 1 pound top sirloin, cut into 12 cubes
  Salt and freshly ground pepper

- 8 cherry tomatoes (optional)
- 1 green bell pepper, cored, seeded and cubed
- 1 large onion, cubed

Combine onion, cumin, lemon juice, vinegar, garlic powder and red pepper flakes in small bowl. Season beef generously with salt and pepper. Rub cumin mixture thoroughly into beef and set aside for 30 minutes.

Preheat broiler or prepare barbecue grill. Alternate meat, tomatoes, green pepper and onion on 4 skewers. Broil or barbecue to desired doneness.

KOREAN-STYLE SHORT RIBS

During barbecue season, cook these tasty ribs on the outdoor grill.

4 servings

- 1 cup soy sauce
- 1/2 cup oriental sesame oil
- 6 large garlic cloves, minced
- 1/4 cup chopped green onions
- 1/4 cup sugar
- 2 teaspoons sesame seeds
- 1/2 teaspoon distilled white vinegar
- 1/2 teaspoon dry mustard
- 1/2 teaspoon freshly ground pepper
- 8 large beef short ribs

Combine first 9 ingredients in medium bowl. Trim excess fat from ribs. Score at 1/2-inch intervals almost to bone. Place ribs in glass baking dish. Pour marinade over. Cover and refrigerate overnight, turning occasionally.

Preheat broiler. Transfer ribs to broiler rack, draining marinade. Broil about 3 inches from heat until ribs are charred, about 8 minutes per side.

ITALIAN GOULASH

4 servings

- 1 pound ground beef
- 1 small onion, chopped
- 1 28-ounce can tomato puree
- 1 garlic clove, minced
- 1 teaspoon dried basil, crumbled
- 1/2 teaspoon sugar

- 1/2 16-ounce package macaroni, freshly cooked
- 1/2 cup freshly grated Parmesan cheese

Cook beef and onion in heavy large saucepan over medium heat until beef is browned, stirring frequently, about 15 minutes. Pour off drippings. Add tomato puree, garlic, basil and sugar. Cover and simmer until thick, stirring occasionally, about 25 minutes. (*Can be prepared 1 day ahead. Cover and refrigerate. Reheat before continuing.*)

Mix in macaroni. Transfer to serving dish. Sprinkle with Parmesan.

SPICY BEEF AND BEAN CASSEROLE

MICROWAVE

6 to 8 servings

    1 pound lean ground beef
    1 medium onion, chopped
    1/2 cup chopped green bell pepper
    1 16-ounce can whole peeled
       tomatoes, drained (liquid
       reserved) and chopped
    1 16-ounce can kidney beans,
       drained
    1 15-ounce can Texas-style beans
       (undrained)
    1 cup tomato sauce
    1 6-ounce can tomato paste
    2 to 2 1/2 teaspoons chili powder
    1 teaspoon seasoned salt
    1/4 teaspoon garlic powder
    1 cup shredded smoked cheddar
       cheese

Combine first 3 ingredients in 8x12-inch glass baking dish. Cover dish and cook on High until onion is translucent, 5 to 6 minutes. Stir to break up meat. Drain well. Add tomatoes, reserved liquid, beans, tomato sauce, tomato paste, chili powder, seasoned salt and garlic powder. Cover and cook on Medium-High until heated through, 16 to 18 minutes. Sprinkle with cheese. Cover and cook on Medium-High 1 minute. Let stand, covered, 5 minutes. Serve immediately.

KEEMA BEEF CURRY MATAR

Accompany this Indian entrée with plain yogurt and freshly cooked rice.

6 servings

    3 tablespoons vegetable oil
    1 large onion, coarsely chopped
    1 tablespoon minced green bell
       pepper
    4 whole cloves
    1 large bay leaf, finely crumbled
 1 1/2 teaspoons chili powder
    1 teaspoon vindaloo curry paste*
       (optional)
    1 teaspoon turmeric
    1/4 teaspoon cinnamon
    1/4 teaspoon freshly ground pepper
    1/8 teaspoon ground cardamom

    Dash of ground coriander
    1 pound lean ground beef
    1 16-ounce can Italian plum
       tomatoes, chopped (reserve
       liquid)
    1 teaspoon salt
    1 cup frozen peas

Heat oil in large heavy skillet over medium heat. Add onion and cook until golden, about 7 minutes. Blend in next 10 ingredients. Reduce heat to medium-low and stir 3 minutes. Add meat and cook until browned, breaking up with wooden spoon. Stir in tomatoes, reserved liquid and salt. Reduce heat to low and simmer until cooked through, about 15 minutes. Add peas and continue cooking until tender, about 3 to 5 minutes. Discard cloves. Serve immediately.

*Available at Middle Eastern or Indian specialty markets.

CINCINNATI "THREE-WAY" CHILI

On its own this chili is great, but it's even better as a "three-way"—over spaghetti and topped with cheddar cheese.

6 to 8 servings

    1 quart hot water
    2 pounds ground beef
    1 12-ounce can tomato paste
    1 large onion, chopped
    3 tablespoons chili powder
    3 bay leaves
    1 tablespoon salt
    1 teaspoon cinnamon
    1 teaspoon freshly ground pepper
    1 teaspoon allspice
    1 teaspoon white wine vinegar
    1/2 teaspoon ground cumin
    1/2 teaspoon Worcestershire sauce
    1/4 teaspoon cayenne pepper
    1/4 teaspoon garlic powder

    1 pound freshly cooked spaghetti
    1 cup grated cheddar cheese

Pour water into large saucepan. Crumble in beef. Add next 13 ingredients. Simmer 3 hours, stirring occasionally. Discard bay leaves. (*Can be prepared 1 month ahead and frozen.*)
   Place spaghetti on serving platter. Pour chili over. Top with cheese.

TRUE TEXAS CHILI

Makes about 8 cups

    2 tablespoons vegetable oil
    2 pounds lean ground beef
    2 medium onions, chopped
       (about 2 cups)
    2 garlic cloves, finely chopped
    1 28-ounce can whole tomatoes
    1 12-ounce can beer
    5 tablespoons chili powder
    2 jalapeño peppers, seeded and
       chopped
    1 tablespoon cumin
    2 teaspoons paprika
    1 teaspoon sugar
       Salt and freshly ground pepper
       Cayenne pepper (optional)
       Shredded cheddar cheese,
       chopped red onion and sliced
       avocado (optional garnishes)

Heat oil in 6-quart saucepan. Add ground beef, onions and garlic and sauté until meat is browned. Stir in next 7 ingredients and bring to boil over medium-high heat. Reduce heat to medium-low and simmer, uncovered, about 45 to 55 minutes. Taste and season with salt, pepper and cayenne pepper, if desired. Ladle into bowls. Garnish with cheese, onion and avocado, if desired.

HEARTLAND CHILI

6 servings

    1 pound ground beef
    1 15-ounce can red kidney beans
       (undrained)
    1 14 1/2-ounce can stewed
       tomatoes, chopped (liquid
       reserved)
    2 medium onions, chopped
    1 small green bell pepper, cored
       and chopped
    1 tablespoon chili powder
    2 small garlic cloves, minced
       Salt and freshly ground pepper

    1 teaspoon all purpose flour
    1 teaspoon caraway seeds, toasted
       and ground

Cook beef in heavy large saucepan over medium heat until brown, stirring frequently, about 15 minutes. Pour off drippings. Reduce heat to low. Add next 6 ingredients. Season with salt and pepper. Simmer 30 minutes, stirring occasionally. Cover and simmer 30 more minutes.

Heat flour in heavy small skillet over low heat until light brown, about 10 minutes. Add ground caraway. Stir into chili. Cook 5 more minutes. Serve hot. (*Chili can be prepared 1 month ahead, covered and frozen.*)

SPICY MEAT LOAF

A delicious way to cool down this spicy dish is to serve it with sour cream.

4 to 6 servings

 1¹/₂ teaspoons salt
 1¹/₂ teaspoons freshly ground
      pepper
   1 teaspoon cayenne pepper
 ¹/₂ teaspoon ground cumin
 ¹/₂ teaspoon freshly grated nutmeg
   1 bay leaf

   2 tablespoons (¹/₄ stick) butter
 ³/₄ cup finely chopped onions
 ¹/₂ cup finely chopped green bell
      pepper
   2 garlic cloves, minced
   1 tablespoon hot pepper sauce
   1 tablespoon Worcestershire
      sauce
 ¹/₂ cup milk
 ¹/₂ cup catsup

 1¹/₂ pounds ground beef
   1 egg, beaten to blend

Combine first 6 ingredients in small bowl. Set seasoning mix aside.

Melt butter in heavy medium skillet over medium heat. Add onions and cook until softened, stirring occasionally, about 5 minutes. Add bell pepper and garlic and cook until onions are translucent and bell pepper softens, stirring occasionally, 5 to 7 minutes. Stir in seasoning mix, hot pepper sauce and Worcestershire sauce and cook until thickened, about 1 minute. Mix in milk and catsup and heat through. Remove from heat and cool slightly.

Preheat oven to 350°F. Remove bay leaf from onion mixture. Combine beef, egg and onion mixture in large bowl. Place on baking sheet and shape into loaf. Cover and bake 30 minutes. Uncover and continue to bake until browned, about 30 minutes.

HEARTY POTATO-BEEF CASSEROLE

4 to 6 servings

 2¹/₂ pounds potatoes, peeled
   2 tablespoons (¹/₄ stick) butter
 ¹/₂ medium green bell pepper,
      chopped
   2 shallots, minced
 ³/₄ pound lean ground beef
   1 large tomato, peeled, seeded
      and chopped
   2 garlic cloves, minced
 1¹/₂ teaspoons salt
 ¹/₂ teaspoon freshly ground pepper
   1 bay leaf
 ¹/₂ cup firmly packed shredded
      Gruyère cheese

Boil potatoes in large amount of salted water until tender, about 25 minutes. Drain and mash well.

Preheat oven to 375°F. Butter 8-inch square baking pan. Melt 2 tablespoons butter in large skillet over medium heat. Add bell pepper and shallots and sauté 3 minutes. Increase heat to medium-high. Add next 6 ingredients. Cook until beef is almost cooked through, stirring frequently, about 10 minutes. Spread ¹/₃ of potatoes over bottom of prepared pan. Cover with half of beef mixture, then ¹/₃ of potatoes and remaining beef. Top with remaining potatoes and sprinkle with cheese. Bake until crusty and golden brown, 10 to 15 minutes.

MEXICAN BEEF CASSEROLE

4 servings

   1 pound ground beef
   1 medium onion, chopped
   1 medium green bell pepper,
      chopped
 1¹/₂ cups chopped carrots
   1 10³/₄-ounce can cream of
      mushroom soup
   1 10-ounce can enchilada sauce
   1 tablespoon chili powder
   1 teaspoon ground cumin
   1 teaspoon cinnamon

   3 8-inch flour tortillas
 1¹/₂ cups grated cheddar cheese
 1¹/₂ cups grated Monterey Jack
      cheese

   1 4-ounce can whole green
      chilies, drained, each sliced into
      3 strips
   1 cup sour cream

Preheat oven to 350°F. Cook ground beef, onion and bell pepper in large skillet over medium heat until beef is browned, about 5 minutes. Drain off fat. Stir carrots, mushroom soup, enchilada sauce, chili powder, cumin and cinnamon into beef and cook 3 minutes.

Place 1 tortilla in bottom of 9-inch round casserole dish. Cover with ¹/₃ of meat mixture, then ¹/₃ of cheeses, then 4 chili strips. Repeat with second layer. For third layer, add remaining tortilla, meat mixture and chilies. Top with remaining cheeses. Bake until bubbly and cheese is melted, about 30 minutes. Serve immediately, passing sour cream separately.

MICROWAVE ENCHILADAS

MICROWAVE

10 servings

   3 tablespoons vegetable oil
   1 garlic clove, minced
   3 tablespoons all purpose flour
 1¹/₂ cups water
   1 10-ounce can enchilada sauce
   1 teaspoon seasoned salt

   1 pound lean ground beef
   2 cups shredded cheddar cheese
 ¹/₂ cup sliced black olives
   1 tablespoon instant onion soup
      mix
 ¹/₂ teaspoon salt
 ¹/₄ teaspoon freshly ground pepper

  10 corn tortillas

Combine oil and garlic in 2-quart ovenproof glass casserole. Cook on High 2 minutes. Whisk in flour until smooth. Blend in water, sauce and seasoned salt. Cook on High 8 minutes, stirring once. Set aside.

Crumble meat into another 2-quart ovenproof glass casserole. Cook on High until no pink remains, stirring occasionally, 5 to 6 minutes. Pour off fat. Blend in 1 cup cheese, olives, instant onion soup, salt and pepper.

Lightly butter 9x13-inch ovenproof glass baking dish. Heat tortillas in package on High 1 minute. Dip 1 tortilla in sauce. Spoon 1 heaping tablespoon meat mixture down center and roll up. Place in prepared dish, seam side down. Repeat with remaining tortillas, sauce and meat. Top with remaining sauce and cheese. Cook on High 10 minutes. Serve immediately.

LIVER, HAM AND BACON SAUTE

2 to 4 servings

  2 bacon slices, cut into ¹/₂-inch-wide strips
  1 medium onion, thinly sliced
 10 mushrooms, sliced
  6 ounces liver, cut into ¹/₂-inch-wide strips
  2 ¹/₈-inch-thick slices baked ham (about 4 ounces), cut into ¹/₂-inch-wide strips
    Freshly cooked rice
¹/₂ cup beef broth
    Salt and freshly ground pepper

Fry bacon in large skillet over medium heat until translucent, about 5 minutes. Add onion and mushrooms. Sauté until onion is translucent and mushrooms release liquid, about 5 minutes. Add liver and cook until browned, about 4 minutes. Mix in ham and stir until heated through. Mound rice on serving platter. Arrange meat and vegetables over rice using slotted spoon; keep warm. Blend broth, salt and pepper into juices remaining in skillet and stir until slightly reduced, 1 to 2 minutes. Pour sauce over meat. Serve immediately.

LIVER WITH TOMATO AND SNOW PEAS

4 servings

  1 tablespoon butter
  6 ounces beef liver, cut into 1-inch-wide strips

 10 mushrooms, sliced
  4 ounces snow peas, trimmed
  3 green onions, cut into 2-inch-long pieces
  1 medium tomato, peeled, seeded and chopped
  2 tablespoons tomato paste
  2 tablespoons beef broth (optional)
    Salt and freshly ground pepper
  1 pound orzo (rice-shaped pasta), freshly cooked

Melt butter in medium skillet over high heat. Add liver and mushrooms and sauté until browned, about 4 minutes. Add snow peas and green onions and toss until crisp-tender, about 1 minute. Add tomato and tomato paste and stir until heated through and well blended, about 2 minutes. Thin with beef broth if desired. Season with salt and pepper. Mound pasta on serving platter. Spoon liver and vegetables over. Serve immediately.

Veal

HERBED VEAL WITH LEMON

4 servings

  8 veal scallops (about 1¹/₃ ounces each)
    Salt and freshly ground pepper
¹/₂ cup all purpose flour
¹/₄ cup (¹/₂ stick) butter
  1 tablespoon oil
  2 tablespoons dry white wine
¹/₂ cup chicken broth
  2 tablespoons fresh lemon juice
  1 tablespoon finely chopped green onion
  1 tablespoon minced fresh parsley
  2 small sprigs fresh rosemary or ¹/₂ teaspoon dried, crumbled
    Freshly cooked rice or pasta
    Lemon wedges (garnish)

Season veal with salt and pepper. Dredge veal in flour to coat well, shaking off excess. Melt butter with oil in heavy skillet over medium-high heat until hot but not smoking. Add veal and brown quickly on both sides, turning frequently. Transfer veal to heated platter. Pour wine into skillet and stir, scraping up any browned bits. Blend in broth, lemon juice, onion, parsley and rosemary. Reduce heat, cover and simmer gently, stirring frequently, 3 to 5 minutes. Return veal to skillet. Cover and simmer gently until tender, about 1 to 2 minutes. Spoon veal over rice or pasta. Serve immediately with lemon.

ROMAN-STYLE VEAL

6 servings

  2 tablespoons olive oil
¹/₄ cup all purpose flour
1¹/₂ pounds ¹/₄-inch-thick veal cutlets
    Freshly ground pepper

  2 tablespoons (¹/₄ stick) butter
¹/₂ cup dry white wine
¹/₂ cup sweet roasted red peppers, drained, cut julienne
  6 to 8 pitted green olives, thinly sliced
  2 tablespoons capers, rinsed and drained

Heat oil in large skillet over high heat. Lightly flour veal, shaking off excess. Add to skillet in batches and sauté until golden, 2 to 3 minutes per side. Transfer to heated platter. Sprinkle with pepper; keep warm.

Melt butter in same skillet over high heat. Add wine, scraping up browned bits. Reduce heat to medium. Add remaining ingredients and stir until heated through. Pour sauce over veal. Serve immediately.

VEAL WITH MUSHROOMS AND ARTICHOKES

4 servings

   1/4 cup all purpose flour
   1/2 teaspoon salt
       Freshly ground pepper
   1 pound veal scallops, pounded
   2 tablespoons (1/4 stick) butter
   1 tablespoon olive oil

   1/2 cup dry white wine
   1/2 cup sliced mushrooms
   1 cup drained water-packed
       canned artichoke hearts
   1 cup whipping cream
   2 tablespoons Dijon mustard
   3 cups freshly cooked white rice

Mix flour, salt and pepper in small dish. Dredge veal in flour. Melt 1 tablespoon butter with oil in heavy large skillet over medium heat. Add veal and sauté until golden brown, 2 to 3 minutes per side. Transfer to heated platter; keep warm.

Stir wine into skillet, scraping up browned bits. Add remaining 1 table-spoon butter to skillet. Add mush-rooms and sauté until tender, 3 to 4 minutes. Blend in artichokes, cream and mustard and cook until heated through. Pour sauce over veal. Serve immediately with rice.

VEAL PARMESAN

6 servings

   1 egg
   1/2 cup freshly grated Parmesan
       cheese
   1/2 cup seasoned dry breadcrumbs
   12 veal scallops, pounded to flatten
       slightly

   1/4 cup plus 3 tablespoons
       vegetable oil
   1 medium onion, minced
   1 medium garlic clove, minced
   1 15-ounce can tomato sauce
   1/4 cup water
   1 tablespoon dried parsley,
       crumbled
   1 teaspoon dried oregano,
       crumbled
   1/8 teaspoon freshly ground pepper

   8 ounces mozzarella cheese, sliced
       or grated
       Freshly grated Parmesan cheese

Beat egg in shallow dish. Combine 1/2 cup Parmesan and breadcrumbs in another shallow dish. Dip veal in egg and then in crumb mixture to coat. Heat 1/4 cup oil in large skillet over medium-high heat. Sauté veal until just browned, about 45 seconds on each side. Drain on paper towels.

Heat remaining 3 tablespoons oil in medium saucepan over medium heat. Sauté onion and garlic until soft, about 7 minutes. Add tomato sauce, water, parsley, oregano and pepper. Reduce heat to low, cover and simmer for 10 minutes, stirring occasionally.

Preheat oven to 350°F. Spoon half of sauce into 9x13-inch oven-proof glass baking dish. Arrange veal over sauce. Top each veal scal-lop with mozzarella. Pour remaining sauce over. Bake until bubbly, about 25 minutes. Serve immediately. Pass Parmesan separately.

VEAL CHOPS WITH TOMATOES AND ARTICHOKE HEARTS

Start the meal with an arugula salad and crusty breadsticks. As a side dish, offer cooked fresh peas tossed with chives. This recipe doubles easily.

2 servings

   3 teaspoons olive oil
   2 tablespoons minced shallots
   1 garlic clove, thinly sliced
   2 tablespoons dry vermouth

   1/4 teaspoon dried thyme,
       crumbled
   1/4 teaspoon dried oregano,
       crumbled
   2/3 cup minced peeled seeded
       Italian plum tomatoes (about
       5 large)
   1/3 cup black Niçoise olives

   1/2 cup chicken broth
   1 small garlic clove, minced
   1 1/2 cups frozen artichoke hearts,
       thawed (about 7 ounces)
       Salt and freshly ground pepper

   2 8-ounce 1-inch-thick veal chops
       (bone in), fat trimmed
   1 garlic clove, flattened

Heat 2 teaspoons oil in heavy small saucepan over medium heat. Add shal-lots and sliced garlic and stir until softened, about 2 minutes. Add dry vermouth, 1/8 teaspoon thyme and 1/8 teaspoon oregano. Increase heat to high and boil until only thin film of liquid remains, stirring constantly, about 1 1/2 minutes. Mix in remaining 1/8 teaspoon thyme and 1/8 teaspoon oregano, tomatoes and olives. Reduce heat and simmer 5 minutes, stirring frequently. (*Can be prepared 1 day ahead. Cover and refrigerate.*)

Bring broth and minced garlic to boil in another heavy medium sauce-pan. Add artichokes and cook until heated through, stirring occasionally. Drain. Season with salt and pepper.

Rub veal with flattened garlic; re-serve garlic. Season veal with salt and pepper. Heat heavy medium nonstick skillet over medium heat until hot. Add remaining 1 teaspoon oil and re-served garlic. Add veal and brown well, about 2 minutes per side. Reduce heat to medium-low. Cover and cook until veal is tender but still pink inside, about 3 minutes for medium. Discard garlic. Arrange veal chops on plates. Tent with foil to keep warm. Pour 2 tablespoons veal pan juices into tomato sauce. Stir sauce over medium heat until heated through. Spoon 3/4 of sauce over veal. Toss artichokes with remaining sauce. Spoon arti-chokes around veal and serve.

Lamb

❖ ❖ ❖

BERRY-GLAZED LAMB CHOPS

4 servings

- 1/2 cup berry jam or jelly
- 2 1/2 tablespoons (or more) coarse-grained mustard
- 8 lamb rib chops

Combine jam and 2 1/2 tablespoons mustard in small bowl. Taste and add more mustard if desired. Place lamb chops on broiler rack. Brush lightly with glaze. Broil until browned, about 5 minutes. Turn and brush other side with glaze. Broil to desired degree of doneness. Serve immediately, passing remaining glaze separately.

FOIL-BAKED LAMB CHOPS

2 servings

- 2 hard-cooked eggs, finely chopped
- 1/2 cup dried breadcrumbs
- 2 tablespoons (1/4 stick) butter, melted
- 1 tablespoon chopped fresh parsley
- 1 garlic clove, minced
- 1 teaspoon salt
- 4 loin lamb chops (about 1 1/2 inches thick), fat trimmed

  Paprika

Preheat oven to 400°F. Combine first 6 ingredients in medium bowl. Press mixture onto top and bottom of each chop. Wrap each chop in foil. Bake 20 to 25 minutes for medium-rare.

Preheat broiler. Open foil; sprinkle chops with paprika. Broil until browned, 2 to 3 minutes.

MEDITERRANEAN LAMB SKEWERS

Serve this colorful main course with Syrian flatbread. The marinade can be doubled and refrigerated for future use.

6 servings

- 1/3 cup olive oil
- 1/3 cup red wine vinegar
- 2 large garlic cloves, minced
- 1 teaspoon dried basil, crumbled
  Salt and freshly ground pepper
- 5 pounds boneless leg of lamb, trimmed and cut into 1 1/2-inch cubes

  Spicy Pepper Sauce (see recipe)

Combine first 4 ingredients in large bowl. Season with salt and pepper. Pierce meat with fork. Add to marinade. Cover tightly and refrigerate 2 days, stirring occasionally.

Prepare barbecue (medium-high heat) or preheat broiler. Drain meat and thread on skewers. Grill to desired doneness, turning once, about 10 minutes for medium. Serve immediately, passing sauce separately.

Spicy Pepper Sauce

Makes about 4 cups

- 1 12 1/4-ounce jar brine-packed red and yellow bell pepper strips, drained (brine reserved) and chopped
- 3 2 1/4-ounce cans sliced black olives, drained
- 1 4-ounce can mushroom stems and pieces, drained
- 3 garlic cloves, minced
- 1 teaspoon dried basil, crumbled
- 1/8 teaspoon dried red pepper flakes
- 1 cup olive oil

  Salt and freshly ground pepper

Combine bell peppers, olives, mushrooms, garlic, basil and red pepper flakes in medium bowl. Add 1 cup reserved brine and olive oil. Season with salt and pepper. Refrigerate in airtight container until ready to use. Serve at room temperature. (*Can be made 5 days ahead.*)

LAMB AND GREEN BEAN STEW

4 to 6 servings

- 2 pounds boneless lamb shoulder, cut into 1-inch cubes
  All purpose flour
  Salt and freshly ground pepper
- 4 tablespoons (1/2 stick) butter
- 4 medium onions, chopped
- 2 pounds green beans, trimmed and cut into bite-size pieces
- 4 cups canned whole tomatoes (undrained)
- 2 cups water
- 1/2 teaspoon ground allspice
  Freshly cooked rice

Pat lamb dry. Dredge in flour, shaking off excess. Season with salt and pepper. Melt butter in large Dutch oven over medium heat. Add lamb in batches and cook until lightly browned, stirring occasionally, about 15 minutes. Return all lamb to Dutch oven. Add onions and cook until lamb is browned and onions are softened, stirring occasionally, about 10 minutes.

Stir green beans into lamb and cook 2 minutes. Stir in tomatoes with juices, water and allspice, breaking up tomatoes with spoon. Season with salt and pepper. Reduce heat and simmer until lamb is tender, about 1 hour 15 minutes. (*Can be made 1 week ahead and frozen in airtight container.*) Serve stew with freshly cooked rice.

HERB- AND GARLIC-MARINATED LEG OF LAMB

6 to 8 servings

- 1 cup olive oil
- 1 onion, sliced
- 1/3 cup dry white wine
- 1/3 cup fresh lemon juice
- 1/3 cup chopped fresh parsley
- 3 garlic cloves, minced
- 1 1/2 tablespoons dried rosemary, crumbled
- 2 teaspoons Dijon mustard
- 1/2 teaspoon salt
- 1/2 teaspoon freshly ground pepper
- 1/4 teaspoon dried red pepper flakes
- 1 5- to 6-pound leg of lamb, boned, butterflied and trimmed

Combine first 11 ingredients. Place lamb in large roasting pan. Pour marinade over. Cover lamb and refrigerate overnight, turning at least once.

Prepare barbecue grill with hot coals. Place lamb on grill and cook 15 minutes per side for rare, basting occasionally with marinade. Let stand 10 minutes before slicing and serving.

CURRIED LAMB

6 servings

- 1/3 cup dehydrated onion flakes
- 1/4 cup warm water
- 3 tablespoons vegetable oil
- 2 tablespoons ground coriander
- 1 1/2 teaspoons ground cumin
- 1 teaspoon ground cardamom
- 1 teaspoon ground ginger
- 1 teaspoon ground turmeric
- 1/2 teaspoon garlic powder
- 1/4 teaspoon freshly ground pepper
- 1/8 teaspoon cayenne pepper
- 2 pounds boneless leg of lamb or lamb stew meat, cut into 1-inch cubes and patted dry
- 2 cups water or stock (lamb or beef)
  Salt
- 1/4 cup plain yogurt
- 1 teaspoon fresh lemon juice
  Cooked rice

Soak onion flakes in water until soft, about 5 minutes. Heat oil in large skillet over medium-high heat. Add onion flakes and sauté until golden, about 4 minutes. Reduce heat to low, add spices and stir 1 minute. Add lamb to skillet. Increase heat to medium-high and cook, stirring frequently, until

meat is evenly browned, 10 to 15 minutes. Add water and salt. Reduce heat to medium, cover and cook until meat is tender, about 20 minutes. Simmer uncovered until sauce thickens, about 20 minutes. Stir in yogurt and lemon juice. Serve over rice.

BASQUE BURGERS

6 servings

- 1 1/2 pounds ground lamb
- 1 large yellow onion, diced
- 1 large red bell pepper, seeded and diced
- 2 tablespoons prepared mint sauce
- 1 tablespoon green peppercorns
- 1 teaspoon freshly ground pepper
- 1/2 teaspoon salt
- 1/2 teaspoon dried tarragon, crumbled
- 6 hamburger buns, toasted

Preheat broiler. Combine all ingredients except hamburger buns in large bowl. Shape into 6 patties. Broil 5 inches from heat source to desired doneness, 5 to 6 minutes per side for rare. Arrange on toasted buns.

Pork

STIR-FRIED PORK WITH CASHEWS

4 servings

- 2 tablespoons peanut oil
- 1 pound boneless pork loin, cut into 1/2-inch strips
- 2 tablespoons soy sauce
- 1 2/3 cups carrot julienne
- 1 1/2 cups diced green bell peppers
- 1/2 cup unsalted dry-roasted cashews
- 1 1/2 tablespoons brown sugar
- 1 tablespoon cornstarch
- 3 tablespoons water
  Salt

Heat oil in wok or heavy large skillet over high heat. Add pork and stir-fry until lightly browned, 2 to 3 minutes. Add soy sauce and stir-fry 1 minute. Reduce heat to medium. Stir in carrot julienne. Cover and cook until crisp-tender, about 3 minutes. Add bell peppers and cashews and stir-fry until bell peppers are crisp-tender, 3 to 4 minutes. Add sugar and stir until dissolved, about 1 minute. Push pork and vegetables to side.

Dissolve cornstarch in water in small bowl and add to wok. Stir until sauce thickens and clears, about 1 minute. Mix pork and vegetables into sauce. Season with salt. Serve immediately.

PORK BOOKLETS

6 servings

- 12 1/2-inch-thick boneless pork loin cutlets
- 6 thick cheddar cheese slices
- 6 ham slices
- 1 egg, beaten to blend
  Salt and freshly ground pepper
- 1/2 cup seasoned breadcrumbs
- 2 tablespoons vegetable oil

Pound pork with mallet until flattened to thickness of 1/4 inch. Top 6 cutlets with 1 cheese slice and 1 ham slice each. Top with remaining 6 cutlets. Pound edges to seal. Season egg with salt and pepper. Dip pork into egg. Coat completely with breadcrumbs. Heat oil in medium skillet over medium-high heat. Add pork and cook until browned, about 5 minutes per side. Serve immediately.

PECAN-CRUSTED PORK CUTLETS WITH GINGER MAYONNAISE

Steamed rice Japanese style is all you need with this creative main course.

8 servings

- **2 pounds boneless pork cutlets, trimmed**
- **1/3 cup Sherry**
- **1/3 cup soy sauce**
- **4 medium green onions, minced**
- **3 tablespoons minced peeled ginger**
- **2 cups fine dry breadcrumbs**
- **1 cup finely chopped pecans (3 ounces)**
  All purpose flour
- **2 eggs, beaten to blend**

  Peanut oil
  Green onion fans
  Ginger Mayonnaise (see recipe)

Pound pork between sheets of waxed paper to 1/4-inch thickness; pat dry. Blend Sherry, soy sauce, green onions and ginger in large nonaluminum bowl. Add pork. Cover and refrigerate at least 2 hours or overnight.

Drain pork; pat dry. Mix breadcrumbs and pecans. Dredge pork in flour, shaking off excess. Dip into eggs. Dredge in breadcrumb mixture, pressing to adhere. Arrange pork on platter. Refrigerate at least 30 minutes.

Heat 1 inch of oil in heavy large skillet over medium-high heat. Cook pork in batches (do not crowd) until crisp and brown, about 3 minutes per side. Arrange on platter. Garnish with green onion fans. Serve immediately. Pass mayonnaise separately.

Ginger Mayonnaise

Makes about 1 1/3 cups

- **1 1-inch piece ginger, peeled**
- **1 large garlic clove**
- **2 egg yolks, room temperature**
- **4 teaspoons cider vinegar**
- **1/4 teaspoon salt**
- **3/4 cup plus 2 1/2 tablespoons peanut oil**
- **1 1/2 tablespoons oriental sesame oil**
- **4 drops hot chili oil***
- **1 Italian plum tomato, seeded and diced**
- **1 small green onion, minced**

Mince ginger and garlic finely in processor. Add yolks, vinegar and salt and blend until smooth. Combine oils. With machine running, add oil mixture through feed tube in slow stream and mix until thickened, about 1 1/2 minutes. Transfer to bowl. Stir in tomato and green onion. Cover and refrigerate at least 1 hour. (*Can be prepared 8 hours ahead.*)

*Hot chili oil is available at oriental foods stores and many supermarkets.

PORK LOIN WITH CREAMY MUSTARD SAUCE

Round off the meal with steamed spinach and red baby new potatoes.

8 servings

- **1 3 1/2-pound boned pork loin, visible fat trimmed, tied**
- **1 1/2 cups dry white wine**
- **1/4 cup Dijon mustard**
- **1 tablespoon plus 1 1/2 teaspoons mustard seeds**
- **2 large garlic cloves, pressed**
  Freshly ground pepper
- **1/4 cup mashed soft silken tofu**
- **1 teaspoon minced fresh rosemary**
- **1/2 teaspoon potato starch dissolved in 1 tablespoon water**
- **8 green onions**
  Fresh rosemary

Preheat oven to 325°F and preheat broiler. Place pork on broiler rack and broil until brown on all sides. Pat pork with paper towels to remove fat.

Transfer pork to heavy Dutch oven. Pour wine over. Mix mustard, mustard seeds and garlic in small bowl. Season with pepper. Rub all but 1 1/2 table-spoons mustard mixture over pork. Cover partially and bake 1 1/4 hours, basting occasionally with pan juices. Uncover, baste and cook about 30 minutes longer for medium.

Transfer pork to platter. Tent loosely with foil to keep warm. Degrease pan juices. Mix tofu and remaining 1 1/2 tablespoons mustard mixture in heavy medium saucepan. Using electric mixer, gradually add pan juices, beating until sauce is smooth. Add rosemary and potato starch mixture. Stir constantly over low heat until sauce thickens, about 2 minutes.

Meanwhile, blanch onions in pot of boiling water until tender, about 3 minutes. Drain well. Cut strings off pork. Slice pork and arrange on platter. Spoon sauce over. Sprinkle with rosemary. Garnish platter with onions.

PORK WITH PRUNES AND MARSALA

4 servings

- **12 extra-large dried prunes**
- **1 cup dry Marsala**
- **1 cup all purpose flour**
- **1 teaspoon salt**
- **1/2 teaspoon freshly ground pepper**
- **2 pounds pork tenderloins, cut into 1/2-inch-wide slices**
- **1/4 cup (1/2 stick) butter**
- **2 tablespoons whipping cream**
- **1 teaspoon red currant jelly**
  Salt and freshly ground pepper

Soak prunes in 1 cup Marsala overnight, stirring occasionally.

Preheat oven to 325°F. Transfer prunes and Marsala to small saucepan. Cover partially and cook over medium heat until tender, about 5 minutes. Strain prunes, reserving Marsala.

Combine flour, 1 teaspoon salt and 1/2 teaspoon pepper in medium bowl. Reserve 1 tablespoon flour mixture. Dredge pork in remaining flour mixture, shaking off excess. Melt butter in heavy large skillet over medium-high heat. Add pork in batches (do not crowd) and cook until lightly browned, turning once, 3 to 4 minutes. Using slotted spoon, transfer pork to ovenproof glass baking dish. Add reserved flour mixture to skillet and stir, scraping up any browned bits. Add reserved Marsala and stir until thickened, about 1 minute. Remove from heat. Add cream and jelly and bring to simmer, stirring. Season with salt and pepper. Pour sauce over pork. Add prunes. Bake until pork is tender, about 25 minutes. Serve immediately.

PORK MEDALLIONS WITH TARRAGON MUSTARD SAUCE

2 servings

>   2 tablespoons (1/4 stick) butter
>   4 1 1/2-inch-thick pork tenderloin medallions, trimmed
>
>   1/2 cup beef broth
>   3/4 teaspoon dried tarragon, crumbled
>   1/2 cup whipping cream
>   1 tablespoon Dijon mustard
>   Salt and freshly ground pepper

Melt butter in medium skillet over medium-high heat. Add pork and sauté until cooked through, 5 to 8 minutes per side. Transfer to serving dish; cover and keep warm.

Pour off fat in skillet. Add broth and tarragon to skillet and cook over high heat until reduced to 1/4 cup, about 10 minutes. Stir in cream and cook until thickened, 3 to 4 minutes. Whisk in mustard. Season with salt and pepper. Spoon sauce over medallions. Serve immediately.

PORK CHOP AND POTATO CASSEROLE

4 servings

>   1 10 3/4-ounce can cream of celery soup
>   3 tablespoons (generous) sour cream
>   4 baking potatoes, peeled and thinly sliced
>   Salt and freshly ground pepper
>
>   4 1-inch-thick pork chops
>   2 tablespoons olive oil

Preheat oven to 350°F. Butter 9x13-inch ovenproof glass baking dish. Combine soup and sour cream in medium bowl.

Arrange half of potatoes in prepared dish. Season with salt and pepper. Pour half of soup mixture over potatoes. Top with remaining potatoes. Pour remaining soup mixture over. Season with salt and pepper. Bake until golden brown, 90 minutes.

Meanwhile, season chops with salt and pepper. Heat oil in heavy large skillet over medium-high heat. Add chops and cook until lightly browned, about 5 minutes per side. Place chops atop potatoes. Cover and bake until potatoes are tender, about 30 minutes. Serve immediately.

ORANGE-GLAZED PORK CHOPS

4 servings

>   4 pork loin chops (about 1 1/2 pounds total)
>   Salt and freshly ground pepper
>   1/2 cup all purpose flour
>   1 tablespoon butter
>   1/2 cup fresh orange juice
>   1/2 cup dry white wine
>   2 tablespoons orange marmalade
>   Orange slices and watercress (garnish)

Season pork chops with salt and pepper. Dredge chops lightly in flour, shaking off excess. Melt butter in heavy large skillet over medium heat. Add chops and cook, turning frequently, until golden brown, about 3 to 5 minutes per side. Stir in orange juice, wine and marmalade. Cover, reduce heat to low and simmer gently 20 to 25 minutes, turning once. Transfer chops to platter and keep warm. Continue cooking sauce until thickened, about 5 minutes. Spoon sauce over chops. Garnish with orange slices and watercress and serve.

FRUIT-STUFFED PORK CHOPS

4 servings

>   1/4 cup (1/2 stick) butter
>   1/3 cup chopped onion

>   2 medium Granny Smith apples, peeled, cored and chopped
>   1/3 cup raisins
>   2 slices firm white bread, torn into small pieces
>   1 egg, beaten to blend
>   1/2 teaspoon poultry seasoning
>   1/8 teaspoon celery salt
>   Salt and freshly ground pepper
>
>   4 1-inch-thick blade end pork loin chops

Melt butter in heavy medium saucepan over medium heat. Add onion and cook until translucent, stirring occasionally, about 8 minutes. Remove from heat. Mix in next 6 ingredients. Season with salt and pepper. Cool mixture completely.

Preheat oven to 350°F. Make slit in edge of each chop opposite rib bone. With knife inserted in slit, cut arc, creating wide pocket with small opening. Divide fruit mixture among pockets. Press to close. Place chops in glass baking dish. Bake until chops are no longer pink, about 35 minutes.

EASY POZOLE

A traditional south of the border one-dish meal made easy with a slow-cooker.

8 to 10 servings

>   1 quart water
>   2 1/2 pounds boneless pork butt steaks, trimmed and cut into 3/4-inch dice
>   1 28-ounce can stewed tomatoes
>   1 medium onion, chopped
>   1 15-ounce can white hominy, drained
>   1 1/4 cups chopped green or red chilies
>   1/2 teaspoon dried oregano, crumbled
>   1/2 teaspoon garlic powder
>   1/2 teaspoon salt
>   1/2 teaspoon freshly ground pepper

Combine all ingredients in 4-quart slow cooker and mix thoroughly. Cover and cook on Low 8 to 9 hours. Ladle into bowls and serve hot.

MUSTARD-GLAZED SPARERIBS

Any leftovers are delicious cold or can be wrapped in foil and reheated.

2 servings; can be doubled or tripled

- 2 teaspoons minced fresh rosemary
- 2 medium garlic cloves, minced
- 1 rack (about 3 pounds) pork spareribs
  Salt and freshly ground pepper

Mustard Glaze
- 1/3 cup firmly packed dark brown sugar
- 1/4 cup coarse-grained Dijon mustard
- 2 tablespoons plus 1 1/2 teaspoons cider vinegar
- 1 tablespoon molasses
- 1 1/2 teaspoons dry mustard

Preheat oven to 350°F. Rub rosemary and garlic into both sides of ribs. Sprinkle with salt and pepper. Arrange meaty side down on baking sheet. Bake 1 hour, turning once. (*Can be prepared 1 day ahead. Cool completely, cover with plastic and refrigerate.*)

Meanwhile, prepare glaze: Combine all ingredients in heavy small saucepan. Bring to simmer, stirring. Cool.

Prepare barbecue grill (medium heat). Place ribs on grill rack, meaty side up. Spread top with 1/3 of glaze. Cook until bottom side is crisp, about 5 minutes. Turn, spread second side with glaze and cook until bottom side is crisp, about 5 minutes. Turn, spread top with glaze and cook until bottom side is glazed, about 5 minutes. Transfer to platter. Cut into individual ribs.

CHINESE RIBS

This marinade is also tasty with chicken.

2 to 4 servings

- 1/2 cup soy sauce
- 1/3 cup sugar
- 1 teaspoon salt
- 1 teaspoon dried grated orange peel
- 1 garlic clove, minced
- 1/4 teaspoon freshly ground pepper
- 3 1/2 pounds baby back pork ribs

Combine first 6 ingredients in small bowl, stirring until sugar dissolves. Transfer to large plastic bag. Add ribs; seal bag and turn several times to coat with marinade. Refrigerate at least 1 hour, turning bag occasionally. (*Can be prepared 1 day ahead.*)

Preheat oven to 350°F. Line baking pan with foil. Drain ribs, discarding marinade. Place ribs on rack. Set in baking pan. Bake until lightly browned, about 30 minutes. Turn ribs over. Bake until dark brown, approximately 30 minutes.

Preheat broiler. Broil ribs until crisp, 2 to 3 minutes.

HEARTY SAUSAGE AND NOODLE CASSEROLE

4 servings

- 1 pound carrots, peeled and thinly sliced
- 3/4 pound bulk pork sausage
- 1 medium onion, diced
- 2 cups egg noodles, cooked and drained
- 1/2 cup water
- 1/3 cup light molasses
- 1/3 cup catsup
- 1 teaspoon Worcestershire sauce

Preheat oven to 350°F. Lightly butter 8-inch square ovenproof glass baking dish. Cook carrots in large saucepan of boiling water until just tender, about 10 minutes. Drain. Cook sausage in medium skillet over medium heat until no pink remains, stirring to crumble, about 10 minutes. Add onion and cook until translucent, about 5 minutes. Pour off fat in skillet. Combine carrots and noodles in prepared baking dish. Top with cooked sausage mixture.

Combine remaining ingredients in medium bowl and mix well. Pour over sausage. Bake until almost all liquid is absorbed, 30 to 40 minutes.

QUICK KIELBASA

2 servings

- 1 tablespoon olive oil
- 1 pound kielbasa sausage
- 2 thick onion slices
- 1 10-ounce can stewed tomatoes, undrained
- 1 teaspoon dried dillweed
- 3/4 teaspoon salt
- 1/2 teaspoon dill seeds
  Dash of cayenne pepper
- 10 snow peas
  Freshly cooked rice or sliced French bread

Heat olive oil in large skillet over medium heat. Add sausage and onion and sauté 5 minutes. Add tomatoes with liquid, dillweed, salt, dill seeds and cayenne; cook 12 minutes. Stir in snow peas and cook 3 minutes. Serve hot with rice or French bread.

SAUSAGE, PEPPERS AND POTATOES

A simple one-dish supper.

6 servings

- 2 1/3 pounds baking potatoes, peeled, cut into 2-inch cubes
- 2 pounds sweet Italian sausage, cut into 2-inch pieces
- 4 large green bell peppers, seeded, cut into 3-inch pieces
- 2 large onions, sliced
- 1 tablespoon olive oil
  Salt and freshly ground pepper

Preheat oven to 350°F. Combine potatoes, sausage, bell peppers and onions in 12x18-inch ovenproof glass baking dish. Drizzle with oil. Season with salt and pepper. Bake until potatoes are tender, stirring occasionally, about 50 minutes. Serve immediately.

Poultry

DOWN-HOME FRIED CHICKEN

4 servings

- 1 3-pound chicken, cut into 8 pieces
- 2 cups milk

- 1 cup all purpose flour
- 1 1/2 teaspoons baking powder
  Salt and freshly ground pepper
- 3/4 cup water

  Vegetable oil (for frying)

Pat chicken dry. Place in medium bowl; add milk. Let stand 1 hour, turning occasionally.

Combine flour, baking powder, salt and pepper in medium bowl. Stir in water. Drain chicken; pat dry. Dip into batter. Place on baking sheet and let stand at room temperature 10 minutes.

Pour enough oil into heavy large skillet to come 1/2 inch up sides of pan. Heat to 375°F. Add chicken to skillet skin side down in batches (do not crowd). Cook until golden brown, about 10 minutes per side for white meat and 12 minutes per side for dark meat. Transfer chicken to paper towels and drain thoroughly.

OVEN-FRIED CHICKEN

This easy version of the traditional southern dish is good hot or cold.

4 servings

- 3 eggs, beaten to blend
- 5 to 6 large garlic cloves, minced
- 2 tablespoons finely chopped fresh parsley
  Salt and freshly ground pepper
- 1 3 1/2-pound chicken, cut into 8 pieces, patted dry

- 2 cups seasoned dry breadcrumbs
- 1 cup freshly grated Parmesan cheese
- 1/2 cup (1 stick) butter

Combine first 3 ingredients in medium bowl. Season with salt and pepper. Add chicken, turning to coat. Cover and chill 3 hours, turning occasionally.

Preheat oven to 350°F. Combine breadcrumbs and cheese in medium bowl. Melt butter in 10x15-inch jelly roll pan in oven. Drain chicken. Pat dry. Dredge in breadcrumb mixture. Add chicken skin side down to pan with butter. Bake until chicken is golden brown, turning occasionally, about 45 minutes.

CHINESE GINGER CHICKEN

4 to 6 servings

- 1 4-pound chicken, cut into 8 pieces
- 3/4 cup ginger brandy
- 1/2 cup honey
- 1/2 cup soy sauce
- 1/2 cup chicken broth
- 1/4 cup fresh lemon juice
- 1/4 teaspoon ground ginger
  Salt and freshly ground pepper

Combine all ingredients in large bowl. Refrigerate for 8 hours or overnight.

Preheat oven to 350°F. Arrange chicken in large shallow baking dish. Brush with brandy mixture. Bake chicken until juices run clear when thigh is pierced with tip of sharp knife, basting frequently, 35 to 40 minutes. Serve chicken immediately.

LEMON-LIME PESTO CHICKEN

4 servings

- 1 3-pound chicken, cut into 8 pieces, patted dry
- 2 tablespoons olive oil
- 2 tablespoons chopped fresh parsley

- 2 tablespoons fresh lemon juice
- 5 teaspoons fresh lime juice
- 3 teaspoons (generous) pesto*
- 1 large garlic clove, minced
  Salt and freshly ground pepper

Pierce chicken with fork and place in glass baking dish. Whisk together next 6 ingredients in medium bowl. Season with salt and pepper. Pour 1/2 cup marinade over chicken, coating well. Cover and refrigerate overnight. Cover and refrigerate extra marinade; bring to room temperature before using.

Preheat oven to 350°F. Uncover chicken and bake in same dish until juices run clear when thigh is pierced, about 45 minutes.

Preheat broiler. Pour off all drippings from chicken. Broil chicken until skin is crisp and brown, turning once, about 15 minutes. Transfer chicken to serving platter. Pour remaining marinade over. Serve hot.

*An Italian basil sauce available at specialty foods stores and many supermarkets.

ORANGE- AND BAY-SCENTED ROASTED CHICKEN WITH NEW POTATOES

Butterflying the chicken increases the area exposed to the marinade, making for a particularly flavorful dish. For a pretty presentation, arrange sautéed snow peas around chicken.

6 servings

- 2/3 cup fresh orange juice
- 1/4 cup olive oil
- 2 tablespoons fresh lemon juice
- 4 large garlic cloves, crushed
- 2 bay leaves, crushed
- 1 tablespoon grated orange peel (orange part only)
- 2 teaspoons sugar
- 1/4 teaspoon cinnamon
- 1/8 teaspoon freshly ground pepper

1/8 teaspoon dried red pepper
flakes
2 3-pound chickens

Salt
18 small new potatoes (1 1/2-to
2-inch diameter)
1/4 cup olive oil
4 fresh sage leaves, chopped

Blend first 10 ingredients in large shallow baking dish. To butterfly chickens, cut out backbones and discard. Open chickens skin side up on work surface and push down on breast bone to flatten, using heel of hand. Turn chickens over and pull back and snap out breastbones. Trim away rib bones. Remove wishbones. Place chickens in marinade, coating thoroughly. Cover and refrigerate overnight.

Position rack in center of oven and preheat to 350°F. Line large shallow baking pan with foil. Top with large rack. Drain chickens, reserving marinade. Season with salt. Arrange skin side up on rack in pan. Baste with marinade. Rub potatoes with 1/4 cup oil and sage. Sprinkle with salt. Place on rack around chickens. Roast until thermometer inserted in thickest part of chicken thighs registers 170°F, basting chickens with marinade, about 1 hour.

Preheat broiler. Transfer potatoes to serving platter. Using poultry shears, quarter chickens. Broil chicken until golden brown, watching carefully. Serve chicken with potatoes.

BAKED CHICKEN WITH SAFFRON AND YOGURT MARINADE

6 servings

3 2 1/2- to 3-pound chickens,
halved
6 tablespoons fresh lime juice
1 1/2 teaspoons salt

3 tablespoons boiling water
1 1/2 teaspoons saffron threads
1 1/2 teaspoons ground coriander
3/4 teaspoon ground cumin
1 medium onion, quartered
1 1 1/2-inch piece fresh ginger,
peeled and quartered
6 medium garlic cloves
1 1/2 teaspoons salt

3/4 teaspoon cayenne pepper
1/2 cup plain yogurt

6 tablespoons (3/4 stick) butter,
melted

Lime wedges
Radishes
Fresh cilantro (optional)

Place chicken in single layer in non-aluminum pan. Combine lime juice and 1 1/2 teaspoons salt. Rub into both sides of chicken. Cover and let stand while preparing marinade.

Combine boiling water and saffron in small bowl. Let stand 5 minutes. Stir coriander and cumin in heavy small skillet over medium-low heat until aromatic, about 30 seconds. Immediately transfer to processor. Add onion, ginger, garlic, 1 1/2 teaspoons salt and cayenne pepper and process to chunky puree. Add yogurt and saffron mixture and just blend. Spread over both sides of chicken. Cover and marinate 8 hours at room temperature or chill overnight, basting occasionally.

Preheat oven to 375°F. Transfer chicken to foil-lined baking pans. Spread any marinade over. Drizzle butter over chicken. Bake until juices run clear when pierced in thigh, basting occasionally, about 45 minutes.

Preheat broiler. Broil chicken until golden brown if necessary. Transfer to plates. Garnish with lime wedges, radishes and cilantro and serve.

SESAME-CRISPED CHICKEN

4 servings

1/4 cup soy sauce
2 1/2 tablespoons dry Sherry
2 tablespoons vegetable oil
2 tablespoons orange marmalade
1 tablespoon honey
1 garlic clove, minced
1 1/2 teaspoons sesame oil
1/4 teaspoon hot pepper sauce
2 chicken breasts, skinned and
halved

6 3 1/2-inch sesame breadsticks,
crushed
2 tablespoons (1/4 stick) butter

Combine first 8 ingredients in blender or processor and mix well. Pour into shallow baking dish. Add chicken and turn several times to coat evenly. Cover and chill several hours or overnight, turning occasionally.

Preheat oven to 375°F. Grease 9x9-inch baking dish. Drain chicken, reserving marinade. Arrange in single layer in prepared dish. Sprinkle with crushed breadsticks and dot with butter. Bake, basting frequently with reserved marinade, until chicken is tender and juices run clear when pricked with fork, about 25 minutes. Serve hot.

TOMATO-CURRY CHICKEN

Rice and steamed green beans are perfect with this tasty main course.

4 to 6 servings

1/2 cup all purpose flour
1/2 teaspoon salt
1/8 teaspoon freshly ground pepper
6 chicken breast halves
1/4 cup (1/2 stick) butter

1 3/4 cups finely chopped onions
3/4 cup finely chopped green bell
peppers
1 1/2 teaspoons curry powder
1 garlic clove, minced
1/2 teaspoon dried thyme,
crumbled
2 cups canned stewed tomatoes

Preheat oven to 350°F. Mix flour, salt and pepper in small bowl. Dredge chicken in flour mixture. Melt butter in heavy large skillet over high heat. Add chicken skin side down and cook until brown, 2 to 3 minutes. Turn chicken over and cook until lightly browned, 1 to 2 minutes. Transfer to 9x13-inch casserole.

Add onions, green peppers, curry, garlic and thyme to skillet and cook over medium heat until onions are soft and golden, stirring occasionally, about 9 minutes. Add stewed tomatoes, increase heat and bring to boil, scraping up any browned bits.

Spoon sauce over chicken. Bake uncovered until juices run clear when meat is pierced, about 30 minutes.

GOLDEN CURRIED CHICKEN

8 servings

> 8 chicken breast halves, skinned and boned
>
> 1/4 cup (1/2 stick) butter
> 1/3 cup honey
> 1/4 cup Dijon mustard
> 2 tablespoons prepared mustard
> 1 small garlic clove, crushed
> 2 teaspoons fresh lemon juice
> 2 teaspoons curry powder
> 1 teaspoon salt
> Freshly cooked rice

Preheat oven to 350°F. Butter 9x13-inch ovenproof glass baking dish. Arrange chicken in prepared dish. Set aside.

Melt butter in medium saucepan over medium heat. Add next 7 ingredients and whisk until smooth. Pour over chicken. Cover with foil and bake 10 minutes. Uncover and baste with sauce. Continue baking, uncovered, basting occasionally, until chicken is opaque and juices run clear when pierced with tip of sharp knife, 10 to 15 minutes. Serve with rice.

CHICKEN WITH ROSEMARY SAUCE

2 servings

> 4 small boneless chicken breast halves, skinned
> All purpose flour
> 3 tablespoons butter
>
> 3/4 cup chopped onions
> 1 garlic clove, minced
> 1 teaspoon dried rosemary, crumbled
> 1 tablespoon all purpose flour
> 1/2 cup chicken broth
> 1/2 cup milk

Preheat oven to 325°F. Pat chicken dry. Dredge in flour. Melt butter in heavy medium skillet over medium heat. Add chicken and cook until light brown, about 3 minutes per side. Transfer chicken to small glass baking dish.

Add onions, garlic and rosemary to same skillet and cook until onions soften, stirring frequently, about 5 minutes. Add 1 tablespoon flour and stir 2 minutes. Combine broth and milk and mix into onion mixture. Cook until sauce thickens, stirring frequently, about 8 minutes. Pour over chicken. Cover and bake until chicken is springy to touch, about 20 minutes.

ITALIAN CHICKEN BAKE

4 servings

> 2 tablespoons olive oil
> 1/2 pound mushrooms, sliced
> 3/4 cup chopped onions
> 2 garlic cloves, minced
> 4 to 6 boneless chicken breast halves, skinned
> Freshly ground pepper
> 2/3 cup dry white wine
> 1/2 teaspoon dried Italian herb seasoning, crumbled
> 1/2 teaspoon dried basil, crumbled
> 1/2 teaspoon dried parsley flakes, crumbled
>
> 2/3 cup prepared spaghetti sauce
> 1/4 cup freshly grated Parmesan cheese
> 1/4 teaspoon dried red pepper flakes
> Additional freshly grated Parmesan cheese

Preheat oven to 350°F. Heat oil in heavy large skillet over medium heat. Add mushrooms, onions and garlic and cook until softened, about 5 minutes, stirring occasionally. Transfer to bowl using slotted spoon. Add chicken to skillet (in batches if necessary). Season with pepper. Cook until light brown, 2 to 3 minutes per side. Stir in mushroom mixture. Add wine, Italian herb seasoning, basil and parsley. Reduce heat to low. Cover and simmer gently 5 minutes.

Transfer chicken and mushroom mixture to 9x11-inch ovenproof glass baking dish. Spoon spaghetti sauce over chicken. Sprinkle with 1/4 cup Parmesan and red pepper flakes. Cover with foil and bake until juices run clear when chicken is pierced with sharp knife, about 15 minutes. Serve immediately, passing additional Parmesan.

PARMESAN CHICKEN ROLLS

4 servings

> 2 chicken breasts, split, skinned and boned
> 1/4 teaspoon salt
> 1/4 teaspoon freshly ground pepper
> 1/2 cup dry white wine
> 3/4 teaspoon dried tarragon, crumbled
> 1 large garlic clove, crushed
>
> 1/4 cup freshly grated Parmesan cheese
> Additional freshly grated Parmesan cheese
> Dash of paprika
> Chopped fresh parsley

Cut fillets from chicken breasts and set aside. Pound chicken breasts to thickness of 1/4 inch. Season with salt and pepper. Combine wine, tarragon and garlic in shallow dish. Add chicken breasts, turning to coat. Marinate at room temperature 30 minutes.

Preheat oven to 350°F. Grease 9x9-inch baking dish. Finely chop fillets in processor. Mix in 1/4 cup Parmesan. Remove chicken from dish, reserving marinade. Spread Parmesan mixture over 1 side of each chicken breast. Roll up and secure with toothpicks. Transfer to baking dish. Pour marinade over. Sprinkle with additional Parmesan and paprika. Bake until tender, basting frequently, 25 to 30 minutes. Garnish with chopped parsley and serve.

RICOTTA-STUFFED CHICKEN BREASTS

4 servings

> 2 cups ricotta cheese
> 1 10-ounce package frozen chopped spinach, thawed, drained and squeezed dry
> 1 egg
> 1/2 cup freshly grated Parmesan cheese
> 1/2 cup grated Swiss cheese
> 2 garlic cloves, minced
> 1/2 teaspoon salt
> 1/4 teaspoon freshly ground pepper
> 4 chicken breast halves, boned (skin intact)

Butter
Freshly cooked rice or spinach
pasta

Preheat oven to 350°F. Combine first 8 ingredients in medium bowl and mix thoroughly. Rinse chicken breasts and pat dry. Pound slightly to even thickness. Carefully separate skin from chicken using fingers or small paring knife, leaving skin attached on one long side to form pocket. Divide stuffing among pockets, patting gently to distribute evenly. Secure with toothpicks. Arrange chicken skin side up in baking dish. Dot with butter. Bake until juices run clear when pierced with fork, basting with pan drippings every 10 minutes, about 30 to 35 minutes. Serve immediately over rice or pasta.

CHICKEN WITH HOMEMADE HERB CHEESE

The herb cheese is good on its own with crackers, and makes a great gift when packed in an earthenware crock.

4 servings

   1 8-ounce package cream cheese, room temperature
1/4 cup (1/2 stick) butter, room temperature
1 1/2 tablespoons whipping cream
1/4 teaspoon garlic powder
1/8 teaspoon dried oregano, crumbled
1/8 teaspoon dried thyme, crumbled
1/8 teaspoon dried marjoram, crumbled
1/8 teaspoon dried dillweed
1/8 teaspoon dried basil, crumbled
1/8 teaspoon freshly ground pepper

   4 whole chicken breasts, skinned and boned (left whole)
     Salt and freshly ground pepper

Mix first 10 ingredients in medium bowl until smooth. Cover tightly and refrigerate at least 1 hour. (*Can be prepared 1 week ahead.*)

   Preheat oven to 350°F. Pat chicken dry. Place chicken between sheets of plastic wrap and flatten to thickness of 1/4 inch using meat mallet or rolling pin. Place 2 generous tablespoons of

cheese in center of each breast. (Reserve remainder for another use.) Fold chicken over and secure with toothpicks. Place in glass baking dish. Season with salt and pepper. Bake until springy to touch, about 30 minutes. Drizzle melted cheese in baking dish over chicken. Serve hot.

CHICKEN WITH IRISH WHISKEY SAUCE

4 servings

   2 tablespoons (1/4 stick) unsalted butter
   1 tablespoon all purpose flour
   1 cup half and half
1/4 cup chicken broth
   1 tablespoon Irish whiskey
   1 bay leaf
   1 teaspoon freshly ground pepper
1/2 teaspoon dried basil, crumbled
1/2 teaspoon dried chervil, crumbled
1/2 teaspoon dried thyme, crumbled
1/4 teaspoon dried rosemary, crumbled

16 asparagus spears, freshly cooked
   4 boneless chicken breast halves, skinned and pounded to thickness of 1/4 inch
   8 tablespoons grated Swiss cheese

Preheat oven to 350°F. Melt butter in heavy medium saucepan over medium heat. Add flour and stir 2 minutes. Gradually whisk in half and half, broth and whiskey. Reduce heat to low. Add bay leaf, pepper, basil, chervil, thyme and rosemary and stir until thickened, approximately 8 minutes.

   Meanwhile, arrange 4 asparagus spears lengthwise over each chicken breast. Top each with 2 tablespoons sauce and 1 tablespoon cheese. Roll chicken up lengthwise and arrange seam side down in ovenproof glass baking dish. Bake chicken until opaque, 20 to 25 minutes.

   Rewarm remaining sauce. Discard bay leaf. Transfer chicken to serving platter. Pour sauce over. Sprinkle with remaining cheese. Serve immediately.

FIVE-SPICE CHICKEN AND VEGETABLE STIR-FRY

4 servings

1/2 cup apple juice
1/4 cup soy sauce
1/4 cup plum wine*
   5 garlic cloves, minced
1/2 teaspoon five-spice powder
   4 boneless chicken breast halves, skinned, cut into bite-size pieces

   6 tablespoons oriental sesame oil
   3 small dried red chilies, halved and seeded
1/2 teaspoon cayenne pepper
   1 cup peeled and chopped carrots
3/4 cup chopped unsalted dry-roasted peanuts
   2 cups sliced celery
1 1/3 cups sliced mushrooms

   1 teaspoon cornstarch
     Freshly cooked rice

Combine 1/4 cup apple juice, soy sauce, plum wine, garlic and spice powder in medium bowl. Add chicken and stir to coat. Marinate 30 minutes.

   Meanwhile, heat 3 tablespoons oil in wok or heavy large skillet over high heat. Add 1 1/2 chilies and cayenne pepper and stir until lightly sizzling. Remove chilies with slotted spoon and discard. Add carrots and peanuts and stir-fry 1 minute. Add celery and stir-fry until vegetables are crisp-tender, about 1 minute. Add mushrooms and stir-fry until softened slightly, about 30 seconds. Remove from wok.

   Drain chicken, discarding marinade. Add remaining oil and chilies to wok and heat until sizzling. Remove chilies with slotted spoon and discard. Add chicken and stir-fry until opaque, about 3 minutes. Dissolve cornstarch in remaining 1/4 cup apple juice and add to wok. Return vegetable mixture to wok and stir-fry until sauce thickens, 3 to 5 minutes. Serve stir-fry immediately with rice.

Available at oriental markets.

CASHEW CHICKEN STIR-FRY

2 servings

- 1/2 cup raw, unsalted cashews

- 2 tablespoons cream Sherry
- 3 teaspoons cornstarch
- 2 teaspoons dark soy sauce
- 1/4 teaspoon dried red pepper flakes
- 1 large boneless chicken breast half, skinned and cut into 3/4-inch cubes
- 1/2 cup chicken broth

- 2 tablespoons vegetable oil
- 1 8-ounce can whole peeled water chestnuts, drained and quartered
- 1 tablespoon oyster sauce Freshly cooked rice

Preheat oven to 350°F. Place cashews on baking sheet. Toast until lightly browned, stirring occasionally, about 20 minutes. Set aside.

Combine Sherry, 1 teaspoon cornstarch, 1 teaspoon soy sauce and red pepper flakes in medium bowl. Add chicken and stir to coat. Cover and marinate 15 minutes. Combine chicken broth, remaining 2 teaspoons cornstarch and remaining 1 teaspoon soy sauce in cup. Set aside.

Heat oil in wok or heavy large skillet over high heat. Add chicken mixture and stir-fry 2 minutes. Add water chestnuts to wok and stir-fry until chicken is just opaque, about 1 minute. Stir broth mixture and add to wok. Stir until sauce boils and thickens, 1 to 2 minutes. Mix in oyster sauce and cashews. Serve immediately over rice.

STIR-FRIED CHICKEN WITH SHALLOTS

4 servings

- 1 pound skinned and boned chicken breasts, cut into bite-size pieces
- 1 egg, beaten to blend
- 2 tablespoons dry Sherry
- 1 tablespoon soy sauce
- 1/8 teaspoon salt

- 1/4 cup cornstarch
- 3 tablespoons peanut oil

- 3 tablespoons fermented black beans,* minced
- 3 garlic cloves, minced
- 1 tablespoon minced fresh ginger
- 12 medium shallots, chopped
- 1 tablespoon soy sauce
- 1 tablespoon sugar Freshly cooked rice

Combine first 5 ingredients in medium bowl. Cover and refrigerate at least 8 hours or overnight.

Remove chicken from marinade. Discard marinade. Place cornstarch in bowl. Add chicken and stir to coat. Heat oil in wok or heavy large skillet over high heat. Add beans, garlic and ginger and stir-fry until fragrant, about 30 seconds. Add chicken and stir-fry until browned, about 3 minutes. Add shallots and stir-fry until translucent, about 3 minutes. Add 1 tablespoon soy sauce and sugar and stir-fry until sugar dissolves and pan juices thicken, 1 to 2 minutes. Serve immediately over rice.

*Available at oriental markets.

PEANUT BUTTER CHICKEN

Serve this African-style main course with rice, fried bananas and cold beer.

4 to 6 servings

- 1/2 cup peanut oil
- 1 3 1/2-pound chicken, cut into 8 pieces
- 2 cups chopped onions
- 1/2 cup creamy peanut butter
- 1/4 teaspoon cayenne pepper Salt
- 2 cups water Chopped peanuts

Heat oil in heavy large skillet over medium-high heat. Add chicken and cook until browned and tender, turning occasionally, about 25 minutes. Transfer chicken to platter. Pour off all but 2 tablespoons drippings. Add onions to same skillet and cook until soft, about 5 minutes. Stir in peanut butter, cayenne pepper and salt. Gradually mix in water. Return chicken to pan. Simmer until sauce thickens slightly. Transfer to serving platter. Garnish with chopped peanuts.

LEMON-SHERRY CHICKEN

6 servings

- 6 boneless chicken breast halves, skinned Salt and freshly ground pepper
- 1/2 cup (1 stick) butter, melted

- 2 tablespoons dry Sherry
- 2 tablespoons fresh lemon juice
- 2 teaspoons grated lemon peel
- 1 cup whipping cream
- 2 tablespoons (1/4 stick) butter, cut into 6 slices Freshly grated Parmesan cheese

Flatten chicken using meat mallet or rolling pin. Season with salt and pepper. Melt 1/2 cup butter in heavy large skillet over medium-high heat. Add chicken and cook until browned, about 5 minutes per side. Transfer to ovenproof glass baking dish.

Preheat broiler. Add Sherry, lemon juice and peel to skillet and bring to boil, scraping up any browned bits. Slowly stir in cream. Season with salt and pepper. Pour sauce over chicken. Place slice of butter on each piece of chicken; sprinkle with cheese. Broil chicken until top is golden brown, approximately 1 minute.

TRIPLE CITRUS CHICKEN

2 servings

- 2 whole chicken breasts, boned and split
- 1/4 teaspoon salt
- 1/8 teaspoon freshly ground pepper
- 1 medium orange, halved
- 1 medium lemon, halved
- 1 medium lime, halved

Season chicken with salt and pepper. Squeeze juice from fruits into shallow dish. Add chicken and marinate overnight in refrigerator, turning twice.

Preheat broiler. Using tongs, transfer chicken to broiler pan; reserve marinade. Broil chicken until lightly browned, 5 to 7 minutes on each side, basting frequently with marinade. Discard marinade. Serve chicken hot.

Greek-style Salad, page 36

Grapefruit, Red Onion and
Avocado Salad, page 34

JOHN REED FORSMAN

Watercress, Pear and Blue Cheese Salad, page 34

Beef Salad with Pepper Dressing, page 45

Cantaloupe and Avocado Salad
with Chili Dressing, page 33

Mixed Cabbage Coleslaw, page 38

Curried Turkey Salad, page 41

ALAN KROSNICK

Mixed Lettuces, Vegetables and Shrimp
with Frankfurt Green Sauce, page 46

CHICKEN BREASTS WITH CHIPOTLE SAUCE

This hot, spicy dish goes well with herbed rice and braised leeks.

6 servings

> 3 whole chicken breasts, skinned and halved
> 1 small onion
> 1 small carrot
> 1 small celery stalk with leaves
> 6 whole black peppercorns
> Pinch of freshly grated nutmeg
> 4 cups (about) chicken stock
>
> Chipotle Sauce (see recipe)
> 4 tomatoes, peeled and diced
> 3 green onions (green part only), minced

Combine first 6 ingredients in large pot. Add enough stock to cover. Cover and bring to boil. Skim surface. Remove pan from heat. Cover and let stand until chicken is just springy to touch, 15 to 18 minutes.

Carefully cut chicken breasts from bones in single pieces. Slice breasts diagonally and fan on plates. Spoon sauce over. Sprinkle with tomatoes and green onions and serve.

Chipotle Sauce

Makes about 3/4 cup

> 3/4 cup (or more) chicken stock
> 3/4 cup mashed soft silken tofu
> 1/4 cup plus 1 1/2 teaspoons minced white onion
> 3 tablespoons canned chipotle chilies in adobo sauce, drained and seeded*
> 3 tablespoons creamy peanut butter
> 1/4 teaspoon salt

Blend 3/4 cup stock, tofu, onion, chilies, peanut butter and salt in processor until smooth. Transfer sauce to heavy medium saucepan. Stir 5 minutes over low heat to blend flavors. Strain into heavy small saucepan, pressing with back of spoon. (*Can be prepared 1 day ahead. Cover and refrigerate. Rewarm over low heat before con-*

tinuing.) Thin sauce with additional stock if desired. Adjust seasoning.

*Available at Latin American markets and some specialty foods stores.

MARMALADE-GLAZED CHICKEN

Serve this sweet chicken dish with wild rice and steamed green beans.

2 servings

> 1 tablespoon olive oil
> 3 boneless chicken breast halves, skinned and pounded to thickness of 1/4 inch
> 1 egg, beaten to blend
> 1/2 cup dry breadcrumbs
>
> 1/4 cup Grand Marnier
> 1/4 cup orange marmalade
> 1 teaspoon fresh lemon juice
> 1/4 teaspoon Worcestershire sauce
> 1/4 teaspoon Dijon mustard
> 1/4 teaspoon garlic powder

Heat oil in medium skillet over medium-high heat. Dip chicken in egg, then in crumbs to coat well. Shake off excess. Cook until browned, about 1 1/2 minutes per side. Remove from skillet; keep warm.

Add Grand Marnier to skillet. Bring to boil, scraping up browned bits. Blend in marmalade. Mix in remaining ingredients. Reduce heat to low. Return chicken to skillet. Cover and simmer 10 minutes. Baste chicken with glaze and continue cooking until juices run clear when pierced with tip of sharp knife, about 5 minutes; check frequently to avoid burning glaze.

CHICKEN STROGANOFF

4 to 6 servings

> 5 boneless chicken breast halves, skinned and cut into 1-inch pieces
> Salt and freshly ground pepper
> 3 tablespoons butter
> 1 medium onion, sliced
> 1/2 pound mushrooms, sliced
>
> 1 tablespoon all purpose flour
> 1 cup chicken broth, heated

> 1/2 cup sour cream
> 1 tablespoon Dijon mustard
> Chopped fresh parsley
> Freshly cooked rice

Season chicken with salt and pepper. Melt 2 tablespoons butter in heavy large skillet over medium-high heat. Add chicken and cook until opaque, stirring occasionally, about 5 minutes. Transfer to serving dish. Cover and keep warm. Add onion and mushrooms to skillet and cook until light brown, stirring frequently, 6 to 8 minutes. Add to chicken in dish.

Melt remaining butter in small saucepan over medium-low heat. Add flour and stir 3 minutes. Whisk in broth and stir vigorously until sauce is thickened and smooth, about 5 minutes. Stir in sour cream and mustard. Heat sauce until warmed through, about 3 minutes; do not boil. Pour over chicken. Top with parsley. Serve immediately with rice.

CHICKEN WITH MUSTARD CREAM SAUCE

4 to 6 servings

> 1/3 cup all purpose flour
> Salt and freshly ground pepper
> 6 boneless chicken breast halves, pounded flat
> 4 tablespoons (1/2 stick) unsalted butter
>
> 3 tablespoons chopped shallots
> 1/2 cup dry white wine
> 2 cups whipping cream
> 1/2 cup Dijon mustard
> Fresh parsley sprigs
> Freshly cooked rice

Mix flour, salt and pepper on plate. Pat chicken dry. Dredge in flour mixture. Melt 2 tablespoons butter in heavy large skillet over medium-high heat. Add chicken skin side down and cook until just springy to touch, about 3 minutes per side. Transfer chicken to platter. Keep warm.

Melt remaining butter in same skillet over medium heat. Add shallots and cook until translucent, stirring occasionally, about 1 minute. Increase heat to high. Add wine and bring to boil, scraping up any browned bits. Reduce heat to medium. Simmer until wine is reduced by half, about 4 minutes. Stir in cream. Continue simmering until sauce is reduced to 1 1/2 cups. Stir in mustard. Pour sauce over chicken. Garnish with parsley. Serve with rice.

CHICKEN SHANGHAI

4 servings

- 1/3 **cup soy sauce**
- 1/3 **cup water**
- 2 **tablespoons light brown sugar**
- 1 **tablespoon dry Sherry**
- 1 **teaspoon ground ginger**
- 3 **pounds chicken legs**
  Orange wedges

Combine first 5 ingredients in medium bowl. Place chicken in heavy large skillet. Pour sauce over. Bring to boil. Reduce heat to low, cover and simmer 30 minutes, turning chicken occasionally. Uncover and increase heat to medium-low. Simmer until chicken is cooked through and sauce thickens to glaze, turning chicken occasionally, about 15 minutes. Alternate chicken and orange wedges on platter.

CHICKEN NORMANDY

4 servings

- 1 **tablespoon butter**
- 1 **medium apple, peeled, cored and sliced**
- 1 **teaspoon sugar**
- 4 **whole chicken breasts, skinned, boned and halved**
- 1/4 **cup apple juice**
- 2 **tablespoons brandy**
- 1/3 **cup whipping cream**

Melt butter in heavy large skillet over medium heat. Add apple and sugar and cook until apple is just tender, 2 to 3 minutes. Remove with slotted spoon. Add chicken to skillet and cook until golden, turning once, about 5 minutes. Add apple juice and brandy. Reduce heat to medium-low, cover and cook until chicken is tender, about 10 minutes. Set chicken aside. Return apple to skillet with cream. Increase heat to

medium-high and stir until slightly thickened, 5 to 8 minutes. Return chicken to skillet and spoon sauce over. Serve chicken immediately.

CINNAMON CHICKEN

2 to 4 servings

- 4 **boneless chicken breast halves**
- 1/4 **teaspoon cinnamon**
- 1/4 **teaspoon ground cloves**
  Salt and freshly ground pepper
- 2 **tablespoons vegetable oil**
- 3/4 **cup chopped onions**
- 2 **garlic cloves, minced**
- 3/4 **cup fresh orange juice**
- 2 **tablespoons raisins**
- 1 **tablespoon capers, drained and rinsed**

Pat chicken dry. Season with cinnamon, cloves, salt and pepper. Heat oil in heavy large skillet over medium-high heat. Add chicken skin side down and cook until browned, 3 to 4 minutes. Add onions and garlic. Turn chicken and cook until second side is brown, stirring onions and garlic frequently, 3 to 4 minutes. Pour off oil in skillet. Add orange juice, raisins and capers to skillet. Reduce heat to low. Cover and cook until juices run clear when chicken is pierced with sharp knife, about 10 minutes.

CHICKEN BREASTS WITH CHUNKY TOMATO-SHERRY CREAM SAUCE

2 servings

- 1 1/2 **tablespoons butter**
- 4 **boneless chicken breast halves, skinned**
  Seasoned salt
  Freshly ground pepper
  Freshly grated nutmeg
- 1/2 **pound mushrooms, sliced**
- 1/4 **cup finely chopped onion**
- 1/4 **cup chopped fresh parsley**
- 1/4 **teaspoon dried basil, crumbled**
- 1/2 **cup dry Sherry**
- 1 **teaspoon Dijon mustard**
- 2 **medium tomatoes, seeded and chopped**
- 3/4 **cup half and half**

Melt butter in heavy large skillet over medium-high heat. Pat chicken dry. Season chicken with seasoned salt, pepper and nutmeg. Add chicken to skillet and cook until browned on one side, about 3 minutes. Add mushrooms and onion. Turn chicken and cook until browned, stirring mushrooms and onion occasionally, about 3 minutes. Sprinkle with parsley and basil. Reduce heat to medium-low. Stir in Sherry. Cover and simmer until chicken is springy to touch, about 10 minutes. Transfer chicken to serving platter using slotted spatula.

Stir mustard into mushroom mixture. Mix in tomatoes and half and half. Increase heat and boil until thickened, stirring occasionally, about 8 minutes. Pour sauce over chicken.

CHICKEN BUDAPEST WITH EASY HOMEMADE NOODLES

6 servings

- 1 **tablespoon vegetable oil**
- 3 **whole chicken breasts, skinned, boned and cut into chunks**
- 1 **cup chicken broth**
- 1/3 **cup minced onion**
- 2 **tablespoons Hungarian sweet paprika**
- 2 **tablespoons minced fresh parsley**
- 1 **teaspoon garlic salt**
- 1/2 **teaspoon Italian herb seasoning**

- 1 **cup all purpose flour**
- 2 **eggs, beaten to blend**

- 3 **tablespoons all purpose flour**
- 1 **cup sour cream**
- 1 **tablespoon Hungarian hot paprika**

Heat oil in large skillet over medium-high heat. Add chicken and stir until no longer pink, about 4 minutes. Stir in broth, onion, sweet paprika, parsley, garlic salt and Italian seasoning. Reduce heat, cover skillet and simmer chicken for 20 minutes.

Meanwhile, bring large saucepan of water to boil. Beat 1 cup flour and eggs to form thick dough. Pinch off small pieces of dough and drop into boiling water 3 or 4 at a time. Boil until noodles rise to top. Remove with slotted spoon; drain well.

Using slotted spoon, transfer cooked chicken to plate. Whisk 3 tablespoons flour into skillet and cook over medium heat until thickened, about 3 minutes. Reduce heat to low. Blend in sour cream and hot paprika. Add chicken and noodles. Stir until heated through.

CHICKEN MOGHLAI

4 servings

 3 tablespoons butter
 2 medium onions, sliced
 3 garlic cloves, minced
 1 teaspoon ground cumin
 1/2 teaspoon ground ginger
 1/2 teaspoon ground turmeric
 1/2 teaspoon caraway seeds
 1/4 teaspoon cayenne pepper
 1 16-ounce can whole tomatoes (undrained)
 1/2 cup chicken stock
 4 chicken breast halves, skinned
 1 1/2 cups sour cream
 1 teaspoon brown sugar
 1/2 teaspoon ground cardamom
 1/4 teaspoon ground cloves
 1/4 teaspoon freshly grated nutmeg
   Pinch of salt
   Freshly cooked rice
   Chopped fresh cilantro

Melt butter in large deep skillet over medium heat. Add onions and sauté until translucent. Add garlic, cumin, ginger, turmeric, caraway seeds and cayenne. Stir in tomatoes with liquid, crushing with wooden spoon. Blend in stock. Add chicken and bring to boil. Reduce heat to low and simmer 10 minutes. Stir in sour cream, brown sugar, cardamom, cloves, nutmeg and salt. Cover and simmer 20 minutes, stirring occasionally. Uncover and continue cooking 20 more minutes, stirring frequently. Mound rice on platter. Spoon chicken mixture over. Garnish with cilantro and serve immediately.

COQ AU VIN

4 to 6 servings

 6 bacon slices, chopped
 4 whole chicken breasts, split
 1 teaspoon salt
 1/4 teaspoon freshly ground pepper
 1/4 cup brandy
 2 cups dry white wine
 1 cup chicken broth
 1 garlic clove, minced
 1 bay leaf

 3 tablespoons butter
 6 small onions, peeled and quartered
 1/2 pound mushrooms, quartered
 1/4 cup all purpose flour
 2 tablespoons (1/4 stick) butter, melted
   Fresh parsley sprigs
   Freshly cooked rice

Cook bacon in heavy large skillet over medium heat until done but not crisp, about 8 minutes. Remove with slotted spoon. Add chicken to same skillet and cook until browned, about 6 minutes per side. Season with salt and pepper. Return bacon to skillet. Pour brandy into pan and heat briefly; ignite with match. When flames subside, add dry white wine, broth, garlic and bay leaf. Reduce heat, cover and simmer 30 minutes.

Meanwhile, melt 3 tablespoons butter in medium skillet over medium heat. Add onions and mushrooms and cook until softened, stirring occasionally, about 6 minutes. Add to chicken. Discard bay leaf. Mix flour and 2 tablespoons melted butter in small bowl until paste forms. Stir into chicken and simmer until sauce thickens. Transfer to serving platter. Garnish with parsley sprigs. Serve with rice.

CHICKEN WITH MUSHROOM-BACON SAUCE

Crusty rounds of garlic toast make a perfect accompaniment.

4 servings

 1 cup all purpose flour
 1 teaspoon salt
 1/2 teaspoon freshly ground pepper
 1 3 1/2-pound chicken, cut into 8 pieces
 2 tablespoons (1/4 stick) butter
 2 tablespoons vegetable oil
 3 bacon slices, cut into 1-inch pieces
 12 small mushrooms
 12 pearl onions, peeled
 2 shallots, chopped
 6 fresh tarragon leaves
 1/4 teaspoon freshly grated nutmeg
 1 cup dry red wine
 2 tablespoons brandy

Combine flour, salt and pepper on plate. Pat chicken dry. Dredge in seasoned flour. Melt butter with oil in heavy large skillet over medium-high heat. Add chicken skin side down (in batches if necessary) and brown well, about 4 minutes per side. Remove chicken from skillet.

Fry bacon in same large skillet over medium-high heat until browned, 2 to 3 minutes. Reduce heat to medium-low. Stir in mushrooms, onions, shallots, tarragon and nutmeg. Cover and cook until mushrooms soften, about 3 minutes. Return chicken to skillet. Add wine and brandy. Cover and simmer until juices run clear when thigh is pierced with knife, about 25 minutes. Transfer chicken to platter; keep warm. Continue cooking sauce until slightly thickened, about 5 minutes. Adjust seasoning. Pour sauce over chicken. Serve immediately.

CHICKEN BREASTS WITH WALNUT SAUCE

2 servings

 1/4 cup all purpose flour
   Salt and freshly ground pepper
 2 whole chicken breasts
 1 tablespoon butter
 1 tablespoon vegetable oil
 1/2 cup sliced mushrooms
 1/2 cup water
 1/4 cup chopped green onions
 1 tablespoon chopped fresh parsley
 1/2 cup ground walnuts
 1/2 cup plain yogurt, room temperature
 2 tablespoons brandy
   Freshly cooked rice or rice pilaf

Mix flour, salt and pepper on plate. Pat chicken dry. Dredge in flour mixture. Melt butter with oil in heavy large skillet over high heat. Add chicken skin side down and brown well on both sides. Stir in mushrooms, 1/2 cup water, green onions and parsley and bring to boil. Reduce heat to low, cover and cook until chicken is tender, 15 to 20 minutes. Remove chicken from skillet; keep warm. Degrease sauce. Add walnuts, yogurt and brandy to skillet. Mound rice on platter. Arrange chicken on top. Pour sauce over.

CHICKEN TERIYAKI WITH PINEAPPLE

4 servings

   3/4 cup soy sauce
   1/2 cup sugar
   1/4 cup salad oil
   1/4 cup saké
   1 medium garlic clove, crushed
   1/4 teaspoon ground ginger
   1 pound boneless chicken breasts, skinned and cut into 1-inch cubes

   8 large mushrooms
   8 cherry tomatoes
   1 large onion, cut into large chunks
   1 large green bell pepper, seeded and cut into large chunks
   1/4 fresh pineapple, peeled and cut into large chunks

Combine first 6 ingredients in large bowl and stir until sugar dissolves. Add chicken to marinade and refrigerate for 45 minutes.

Prepare barbecue grill. Remove chicken from marinade, reserving marinade. Divide chicken pieces and remaining ingredients among four 12-inch skewers. Grill until chicken is browned, turning frequently and brushing with reserved marinade, about 10 minutes. Serve immediately.

ITALIAN SKEWERED CHICKEN

8 servings

   3 tablespoons olive oil
   2 large garlic cloves, minced
   1/2 to 1 teaspoon dried rosemary, crumbled
   1/4 to 1/2 teaspoon freshly ground pepper

   Juice of 1 large lemon
   2 whole chicken breasts, boned and cut into 1-inch pieces
   1 medium onion, cut into eighths
   4 whole pita breads, halved and warmed

Combine first 5 ingredients in large shallow dish. Add chicken pieces and onion to marinade and stir to coat. Cover and refrigerate overnight, stirring once or twice.

Preheat broiler. Thread alternating pieces of chicken and onion on four 10-inch skewers. Reserve marinade. Broil until browned, basting frequently with marinade and turning skewers occasionally, about 10 minutes. Remove from skewers. Spoon into pita bread halves and serve immediately.

BROILED CHICKEN WITH GARLIC PESTO

4 servings

Garlic Pesto Butter Sauce
   1/2 cup (1 stick) butter, room temperature
   1 medium-size green onion, chopped
   2 teaspoons Garlic Pesto (see recipe)
   1 teaspoon fresh lemon juice
   1 teaspoon sage
   1/4 teaspoon freshly ground pepper
   Pinch of salt

   2 whole chicken breasts, boned and halved

For sauce: Mix all ingredients in processor; sauce will be thick.

Preheat broiler. Top chicken with sauce. Broil until chicken is tender, 5 minutes on each side, basting occasionally with sauce. Serve immediately.

Garlic Pesto

Makes 3/4 cup

   1/2 cup unpeeled garlic cloves (about 24 medium)
   1/2 cup safflower oil

Soak garlic in warm water to loosen skin, about 5 minutes; peel. Puree in processor. With machine running, add

oil through feed tube in slow steady stream. Spoon paste into jar with tight-fitting lid. Store pesto in freezer.

SOFT CHICKEN TACOS

6 servings

   2 tablespoons vegetable oil
   1 medium onion, finely chopped
   1 large garlic clove
   2 cups chopped cooked chicken
   2 cups fresh tomato puree (about 4 large tomatoes)
   1 4-ounce can diced green chilies, drained
   Salt and freshly ground pepper

   Vegetable oil (for deep frying)
   6 medium corn tortillas
   2 cups shredded Monterey Jack cheese
   1 large avocado, thinly sliced
   Shredded lettuce
   Hot salsa

Heat 2 tablespoons oil in heavy large skillet over medium-high heat. Add onion and garlic and sauté until onion is translucent, about 5 minutes. Discard garlic. Add chicken, tomato puree and chilies. Season with salt and pepper. Reduce heat to medium-low and simmer 10 minutes. Set mixture aside.

Heat oil in deep fryer or heavy large skillet to 375°F. Cook 1 tortilla 45 seconds. Remove and fold in half using tongs. Cook 15 seconds. (If using skillet, cook 45 seconds, then fold in half and cook 15 seconds per side.) Drain on paper towels. Repeat with remaining tortillas. Spoon some chicken mixture into each shell. Fill each with some cheese, avocado, lettuce and salsa. Serve immediately.

CORNMEAL CREPES WITH CHICKEN-CHEESE FILLING

Makes 6

   1/2 cup all purpose flour
   1/4 cup cornmeal
   1/2 teaspoon baking powder
   1/2 teaspoon salt
   2/3 cup milk

2 eggs, beaten to blend

1/3 cup water

2 tablespoons snipped fresh chives

1/8 teaspoon chili powder
Vegetable oil

1 10 1/2-ounce can condensed cream of chicken soup

1 cup shredded cooked chicken

1/2 cup grated Swiss or Gruyère cheese

1/8 teaspoon freshly grated nutmeg

Combine first 4 ingredients in medium bowl. Add milk, eggs, water, 1 tablespoon chives and chili powder, stirring until smooth. Heat heavy 6-inch skillet over medium-high heat. Brush lightly with oil. Add 1/4 cup batter, tilting to spread evenly. Cook until golden and bubbly, about 2 minutes. Turn and cook second side until just set. Transfer to plate. Repeat with remaining batter, stirring occasionally. Adjust heat and brush skillet lightly with oil as necessary. (*Can be prepared 1 day ahead. Cover and refrigerate.*)

Preheat oven to 350°F. Grease 9x13-inch ovenproof glass baking dish. Combine soup, chicken, cheese, 1 tablespoon chives and nutmeg in bowl. Place 1/4 cup filling in center of each crepe. Fold sides over filling to form tube shape. Place seam side down in prepared pan. Bake until heated through, about 20 minutes. Serve hot.

CHICKEN ENCHILADAS

4 servings

8 corn tortillas

1 3-ounce package cream cheese, room temperature

2 cups chopped cooked chicken (white meat only), lightly seasoned with salt and freshly ground pepper

1/4 cup mild green chile salsa

3 1/2 cups grated Monterey Jack cheese

1/2 cup freshly grated Parmesan cheese

1/2 cup grated cheddar cheese

1 cup half and half

1/2 cup sour cream

4 large green onions, finely chopped (garnish)

1 large tomato, finely chopped (garnish)

Preheat oven to 375°F. Grease 8x12-inch baking dish. Spread tortillas with cream cheese. Top each with some of chicken, salsa and 3 cups Monterey Jack cheese. Roll tortillas up and arrange seam side down in prepared baking dish. Sprinkle with remaining 1/2 cup Monterey Jack, Parmesan and cheddar. Pour half and half over top. Cover enchiladas loosely with foil and bake until heated through, 35 to 40 minutes.

Top each enchilada with 1 tablespoon sour cream. Continue baking, uncovered, 5 minutes. Garnish with green onion and tomato and serve.

MUSHROOM-CHICKEN LIVER SAUTE

2 to 4 servings

5 tablespoons butter

1 pound chicken livers, patted dry

1 large onion, sliced

1/2 pound mushrooms, sliced

2 tablespoons wine vinegar

1 teaspoon Worcestershire sauce

1 teaspoon salt

1/2 teaspoon freshly ground pepper

1/8 teaspoon dried oregano, crumbled

1/8 teaspoon hot pepper sauce

2 tablespoons sweet vermouth
Freshly cooked rice or noodles

Melt 3 tablespoons butter in large skillet over medium-high heat. Add chicken livers and sauté until browned outside but still pink inside, about 2 to 3 minutes. Remove from skillet with slotted spoon and set aside. Melt 2 more tablespoons butter in same skillet over medium heat. Add onion and mushrooms and sauté until mushrooms are tender, about 5 minutes. Stir in vinegar, Worcestershire sauce, salt, pepper, oregano and hot pepper sauce and cook 5 minutes. Add vermouth and chicken livers and cook until heated through, about 2 minutes. Serve over rice or noodles.

CHICKEN LIVERS STROGANOFF

4 to 6 servings

1/4 cup (1/2 stick) butter or margarine

1 large onion, chopped (about 2 cups)

1/4 pound mushrooms, sliced

1 pound chicken livers

1 tablespoon paprika

1/2 teaspoon salt

1 cup sour cream, room temperature

1 to 2 tablespoons dry Sherry
Freshly cooked noodles or rice

Melt butter in heavy large skillet over medium-high heat. Add onion and sauté until tender, about 5 minutes. Add mushrooms and continue cooking 3 minutes. Stir in livers, paprika and salt and cook until livers are browned outside but still pink inside, about 7 to 9 minutes. Remove from heat and slowly stir in sour cream and Sherry, blending well. Serve hot over freshly cooked noodles or rice.

CHICKEN LIVERS WITH APPLE

4 servings

2 to 3 tablespoons butter

1 large Spanish onion, diced

1 pound chicken livers

2 medium McIntosh apples, peeled, cored and chopped
Salt and freshly ground pepper
Freshly cooked rice

6 slices bacon, crisply cooked and crumbled

Heat butter in large skillet over medium-high heat. Add onion and sauté until translucent, about 5 minutes. Add chicken livers and sauté 2 minutes. Reduce heat to medium-low and cook until livers are slightly pink in centers, 4 to 5 minutes. Stir in chopped apple. Cover and cook 1 minute. Season with salt and pepper. Spoon mixture over rice. Sprinkle with crumbled bacon and serve.

GAME HENS IN COGNAC SAUCE

4 servings

>   2 Cornish hens, split in half
>   Salt and freshly ground pepper
> 1/4 cup (1/2 stick) butter
>   1 tablespoon oil
> 1/2 pound mushrooms, sliced
>   2 small sprigs rosemary or
> 1/2 teaspoon dried, crumbled
>   Freshly cooked wild or
>   herb rice
>   2 tablespoons Cognac
> 1/2 cup whipping cream

Season hens with salt and pepper. Melt butter with oil in heavy large skillet over medium-high heat until hot but not smoking. Add hens and brown well on all sides. Add mushrooms and rosemary. Reduce heat to low, cover and cook until hens are tender, about 20 minutes. Spread rice on heated platter. Warm Cognac in small saucepan over low heat. Sprinkle Cognac over hens and ignite, shaking pan gently until flame subsides. Set hens over rice. Add cream to skillet and cook gently about 5 minutes, whisking often. Spoon sauce over hens and rice.

ORIENTAL CORNISH HEN

MICROWAVE

2 servings

> 1/2 cup soy sauce
> 1/2 cup Sherry
> 1/4 cup honey
>   1 garlic clove, finely minced
>   1 teaspoon grated fresh ginger
>   1 Cornish game hen (about
>   1 1/2 pounds), split lengthwise
>   Chopped fresh parsley
>   (garnish)
>   Freshly cooked wild rice

Combine first 5 ingredients in shallow 1 1/2-quart glass baking dish. Cover and cook on High 3 minutes. Arrange hen halves in dish breast side down and baste with sauce. Cover and cook on High 4 minutes. Turn halves over and baste with sauce. Cover and cook on High 4 minutes. Let stand until juices run clear when pricked with fork, about 5 to 8 minutes. Garnish with parsley and serve immediately. Accompany with wild rice and sauce.

DUCK WITH HONEY-CURRY GLAZE

Serve this impressive dish on a large platter surrounded by carrot and celery root julienne sautéed quickly in butter.

4 servings

>   1 4 1/2-pound duck
>   Salt and freshly ground pepper

> 1/4 cup honey
>   2 tablespoons (1/4 stick) butter
>   2 tablespoons light brown sugar
>   1 teaspoon curry powder
>   1 teaspoon Dijon mustard
>   2 tablespoons dark rum

Preheat oven to 350°F. Pat duck dry; trim excess fat. Pierce skin all over with fork. Sprinkle duck inside and out with salt and pepper. Arrange duck breast side up on rack in roasting pan. Roast 1 1/2 hours, draining off drippings as they accumulate.

Combine all remaining ingredients except rum in heavy small saucepan. Heat over medium-low heat, stirring until sugar dissolves. Increase oven temperature to 400°F. Brush duck with curry glaze. Roast until skin is brown and crisp, about 30 minutes. Place duck on warmed serving platter. Heat rum in heavy small saucepan; do not boil. Ignite with match. Pour over duck. Serve immediately.

Fish and Shellfish

SEA BASS WITH GINGER SAUCE

2 servings

>   2 1-pound sea bass fillets

> 1/4 cup peanut oil
>   2 tablespoons minced peeled
>   fresh ginger
> 1/3 cup chopped green onions
> 1/4 cup soy sauce
>   4 teaspoons chopped fresh
>   cilantro

Bring water to boil in base of steamer. Place fish on plate and arrange on steamer rack. Cover and cook until fish is just opaque, about 9 minutes per inch of thickness.

Meanwhile, heat oil in small skillet over medium-high heat. Add ginger and cook until crisp, 2 to 3 minutes. Transfer fish to serving platter. Pour ginger and oil over. Top with green onions, soy sauce and cilantro.

CRISPY CHEESE-TOPPED FISH

6 servings

>   2 pounds fresh or frozen, thawed
>   white fish fillets, such as cod or
>   sole (about 1 1/2 inches thick)
> 1/2 teaspoon salt
> 1/8 teaspoon freshly ground pepper

>   6 tablespoons (3/4 stick) butter
>   1 medium onion, chopped
>   3 cups fresh breadcrumbs

1 cup grated cheddar cheese
1/4 cup chopped fresh parsley
1 teaspoon dry mustard

Preheat oven to 350°F. Lightly grease 9x12-inch ovenproof glass baking dish. Season fillets with salt and pepper. Arrange fillets in prepared baking dish.

Melt butter in large skillet over medium-low heat. Add onion and stir until tender, about 5 minutes. Add remaining ingredients and mix well. Spread topping over fillets. Bake until fish is opaque and flakes easily and topping is golden brown, 20 to 25 minutes. Serve immediately.

BAKED COD CASSEROLE

4 servings

1 1/2 pounds fresh or frozen, thawed cod (1 to 1 1/2 inches thick)
1/4 cup chopped onion
1 tablespoon fresh lemon juice

1/4 cup (1/2 stick) butter
2 tablespoons all purpose flour
1 teaspoon salt
1/2 teaspoon freshly ground white pepper
2 cups warm milk
1 cup shredded cheddar cheese

2 tablespoons (1/4 stick) butter
1/3 cup dry breadcrumbs
1/4 cup freshly grated Parmesan cheese
1/4 teaspoon paprika

Preheat oven to 400°F. Lightly grease 1-quart ovenproof glass casserole. Arrange fish in prepared dish. Sprinkle with onion and lemon juice. Bake until fish flakes easily and is opaque, about 20 minutes. Cool slightly. Discard onion and juices. Flake fish with fork.

Melt 1/4 cup butter in medium saucepan over medium heat. Stir in flour, salt and pepper. Cook until thickened slightly, stirring constantly, 2 to 3 minutes. Gradually blend in milk, stirring until smooth and thickened, about 10 minutes. Add cheese and cook until melted, 2 to 3 minutes. Mix in fish. Return to casserole and spread evenly. (*Can be prepared 1 day ahead, covered and refrigerated.*)

Preheat oven to 375°F. Melt 2 tablespoons butter in small skillet over low heat. Stir in breadcrumbs, Parmesan and paprika and mix well. Sprinkle over casserole. Bake until heated through and golden brown, 20 to 30 minutes. Serve hot.

FLOUNDER IN FRESH TOMATO SAUCE

2 servings

1 tablespoon vegetable oil
1 small onion, chopped
1 garlic clove, minced
2 medium tomatoes, seeded and chopped
1 tablespoon chopped fresh basil
1/2 teaspoon salt
1/8 teaspoon freshly ground pepper
2 4-ounce flounder fillets
1 tablespoon whipping cream

Heat oil in medium skillet over medium heat. Add onion and sauté until tender, about 7 minutes. Add garlic and sauté until golden, 2 to 3 minutes. Stir in tomatoes, basil, salt and pepper. Tuck ends of fillets under. Transfer to skillet and spoon some of tomato mixture over. Reduce heat to low, cover and cook until fish is tender, 10 to 12 minutes. Transfer fish to serving platter using slotted spoon and keep warm. Increase heat to medium and cook sauce until thickened, about 5 minutes. Stir in cream. Pour sauce over fish and serve immediately.

FLOUNDER ROLLS WITH PECAN-RICE FILLING

6 servings

1 cup freshly cooked rice
1/3 cup chopped pecans
1 10 1/2-ounce can cream of celery soup
3/4 teaspoon dried tarragon, crumbled
2 pounds flounder or sole fillets
1/4 cup sour cream
2 tablespoons chopped fresh parsley
Paprika
Fresh lemon juice

Preheat oven to 375°F. Combine rice, pecans, 1/4 cup soup and tarragon in small bowl. Place 2 tablespoons rice mixture on each fillet. Gently roll up lengthwise, securing with toothpicks. Combine sour cream, parsley and remaining soup in flameproof baking dish and bring to simmer over medium heat. Arrange fillets in dish. Cover and bake until fish is opaque, about 8 to 10 minutes. Sprinkle with paprika and lemon juice and serve immediately.

BAKED HALIBUT WITH ONION-TOMATO SAUCE

4 servings

2 tablespoons olive oil
1 1/4 cups chopped onions
2 cups chopped green onions
1 cup chopped fresh parsley
2 garlic cloves, minced
1 8-ounce can tomato sauce
4 8-ounce 1-inch-thick halibut steaks
Salt and freshly ground pepper

Preheat oven to 375°F. Grease 9x13-inch ovenproof glass baking dish. Heat oil in heavy medium skillet over medium heat. Add onions and cook until translucent, stirring frequently, about 8 minutes. Stir in green onions, parsley and garlic. Add tomato sauce and simmer until slightly thickened, about 5 minutes. Place halibut in prepared dish. Season with salt and pepper. Pour onion mixture over. Bake until fish is tender, 20 to 25 minutes.

SALMON BONNE FEMME

2 servings

1 to 2 tablespoons butter
2 salmon steaks, cut 1 inch thick
2 tablespoons white wine vinegar
3 tablespoons green peppercorn mustard
1/2 cup whipping cream
Salt and freshly ground pepper

Melt butter in large skillet over low heat. Add salmon and sauté until lightly brown, about 5 minutes. Turn salmon over and continue cooking 5 to 6 more minutes. Transfer to platter and set aside. Add vinegar to skillet, scraping up any browned bits. Reduce liquid slightly. Whisk in mustard until well blended. Add cream, salt and pepper and whisk again. Reduce heat and cook until warmed through, about 1 minute; *do not boil*. Return steaks to skillet, spooning some of sauce over top. Cook until heated through, about 2 to 3 minutes. Serve immediately.

SALMON IN SORREL SAUCE

2 servings

   2 1/2-pound salmon steaks

   2 tablespoons (1/4 stick) butter
   2 shallots, finely minced
   3/4 cup dry white wine
   1 cup chicken broth
   2 cups whipping cream
   6 tablespoons finely chopped
      sorrel leaves
      Salt and freshly ground pepper

Preheat broiler. Broil salmon until opaque, about 4 minutes per side. Transfer to platter. Keep warm.

   Melt butter in medium skillet over medium heat. Add shallots and sauté until tender, 1 to 2 minutes. Add wine, increase heat to high and boil until reduced to glaze, about 3 minutes. Add broth and boil until reduced to 1/3 cup, about 4 minutes. Reduce heat to medium. Stir in cream and sorrel. Cook until thickened, about 8 minutes. Season with salt and pepper. Serve salmon, passing sorrel sauce separately.

GRILLED SALMON WITH TARRAGON MAYONNAISE

6 servings

   2 cups mayonnaise
   1/4 cup chopped fresh tarragon *or*
   1/4 cup chopped fresh parsley
      and 2 teaspoons dried
      tarragon, crumbled
   3 tablespoons finely minced green
      or red onion
   2 tablespoons fresh lemon juice
   2 tablespoons chopped capers
   1/4 teaspoon freshly ground pepper
      Salt

      Vegetable oil
   6 salmon steaks (about
      1/2 pound each), cut 1 inch
      thick
      Lemon or lime slices, halved
      (garnish)
      Fresh tarragon sprigs (garnish)

Combine mayonnaise, tarragon, onion, lemon juice, capers and pepper in large bowl and blend well. Season with salt. Cover and chill 2 to 24 hours.

   Arrange rack over grill or broiler pan about 5 inches from heat source. Brush rack with oil. Preheat coals or broiler. Place salmon steaks on rack and spread top of each with 2 to 2 1/2 tablespoons tarragon mayonnaise. Broil 6 minutes. Turn fish over and spread with another 2 to 2 1/2 tablespoons sauce. Broil until tip of knife pierced into middle of steak near center bone meets little resistance, 4 to 6 more minutes. (Fish should be barely opaque with touch of deeper pink color remaining.) Arrange on serving platter. Garnish with lemon or lime slices and tarragon sprigs. Pass remaining tarragon mayonnaise.

SHARK STEAKS IN OYSTER SAUCE

4 servings

   4 1-inch-thick shark steaks
      (1/2 to 3/4 pound each)
      Freshly ground pepper

   1 tablespoon sesame oil
   1 cup sliced mushrooms
   1/2 cup diced green onion tops
   1 small garlic clove, minced
   1/2 cup oyster sauce
   1/2 cup soy sauce
   1 medium tomato, thinly sliced

Season fish with pepper. Place on elevated rack in Dutch oven or wok. Pour in enough water to come just below rack. Cover and bring to boil over high heat. Steam fish until tender, about 5 minutes, turning once.

   Meanwhile, heat oil in large skillet over medium heat. Add mushrooms, onion and garlic and sauté until mushrooms release their liquid, 3 to 5 minutes. Stir in oyster and soy sauces. Add fish to skillet and cook 1 minute per side. Transfer fish to serving platter. Remove mushrooms using slotted spoon and mound atop fish. Garnish with tomato. Pass sauce separately.

BAKED SAND DABS WITH GRAPEFRUIT

2 servings

   1 pound sand dabs or other thin
      fish fillets
      Butter
      Juice of 1 grapefruit
   1 tablespoon soy sauce
   1 tablespoon chopped fresh
      parsley
      Freshly cooked rice

Preheat oven to 350°F. Arrange fish in shallow baking dish and dot with butter. Combine grapefruit juice, soy sauce and parsley in small bowl. Pour over fish. Bake until fish is opaque, about 7 to 10 minutes. Serve over rice.

SPICY RED SNAPPER

4 servings

   4 6-ounce red snapper fillets
   1 1/2 teaspoons fresh lemon juice
   1 tablespoon vegetable oil
   1/2 cup chopped green bell pepper
   1/2 cup chopped onion
   1/2 cup dry white wine
   1 tablespoon chopped fresh
      parsley
   1/2 teaspoon dried basil, crumbled
   1/2 teaspoon cayenne pepper
      Freshly ground pepper
   1 cup chopped tomatoes
   1/4 cup freshly grated Parmesan
      cheese
   1/8 teaspoon hot pepper sauce
      Freshly cooked rice

Preheat oven to 350°F. Sprinkle fish with lemon juice. Heat oil in heavy medium skillet over medium-low heat. Stir in bell pepper and onion and cook until softened, about 5 minutes. Add fish and cook 1 minute per side. Add wine, parsley, basil, cayenne and pepper. Cover and simmer 2 minutes. Transfer to ovenproof glass baking dish. Spoon tomatoes over fish. Sprinkle with Parmesan and hot pepper sauce. Bake until fish is opaque, about 8 minutes. Serve immediately with rice.

CAJUN CALAMARI

4 servings

1/4 cup vegetable oil
1 cup chopped green onions
2 tablespoons soy sauce
1/2 teaspoon sugar
1 garlic clove, minced
1 pound squid, cleaned and sliced into 1/4-inch-thick rings

Salt and freshly ground white pepper
Freshly cooked rice

Heat oil in heavy medium skillet over medium-low heat. Stir in green onions, soy sauce, sugar and garlic. Add squid and simmer until tender, stirring occasionally, about 25 minutes.

Season squid with salt and white pepper. Serve with rice.

SOLE ALMONDINE

2 to 4 servings

5 tablespoons butter
1 tablespoon olive oil
4 sole fillets (about 1 pound)
All purpose flour
2 eggs, beaten to blend
1/4 cup slivered almonds, toasted
1/4 cup dry white wine
2 tablespoons fresh lemon juice
Lemon wedges

Melt 4 tablespoons butter with oil in large skillet over medium-high heat. Dip fillets in flour, then in beaten eggs. Add to skillet and cook until browned and just cooked through, 2 to 3 minutes per side. Transfer to serving platter; keep warm. Melt remaining 1 tablespoon butter in same skillet, scraping up browned bits. Add almonds and cook until heated through, about 1 minute. Add wine and lemon juice and simmer until slightly thickened, stirring constantly. Pour over fish. Garnish with lemon wedges.

SOLE IN MUSTARD CREAM

4 servings

2 tablespoons (1/4 stick) butter
1 1/2 tablespoons diced onion
2 tablespoons red wine vinegar
3/4 cup whipping cream

1 pound sole fillets
1 1/2 tablespoons Dijon mustard
Freshly cooked rice

Melt butter in heavy large skillet over medium-low heat. Add onion and sauté until very soft, 10 to 15 minutes. Increase heat to medium-high. Add vinegar and boil until almost evaporated, about 2 minutes. Add cream and boil until reduced by half, about 5 minutes. Add fish and cook until opaque, turning once, about 5 minutes. Gently remove fish; keep warm. Add mustard to skillet and heat briefly; do not boil. Return fish to skillet and spoon sauce over. Serve immediately over freshly cooked rice.

CUCUMBER SOLE

4 servings

1 cup peeled, seeded and coarsely chopped cucumber
1/2 cup sliced green onions
1/4 cup coarsely chopped celery
1 tablespoon chopped fresh parsley
1 teaspoon dried dillweed, crumbled
1 cup dry white wine
4 6-ounce sole fillets
1 cup whipping cream
2 teaspoons prepared horseradish
Salt and freshly ground pepper

Combine cucumber, green onions, celery, parsley and dillweed in 12-inch skillet. Pour wine over. Set fish fillets atop vegetables. Cover and bring to boil. Reduce heat and simmer gently until fish is opaque, about 5 minutes. Transfer fish to heated serving platter; keep warm. Add cream and horseradish to vegetable mixture. Season with salt and pepper. Simmer over high heat until thickened, stirring frequently, 3 to 5 minutes. Pour off any juices from fish. Ladle sauce over.

SWORDFISH STEAKS WITH MUSHROOM SAUCE

4 to 6 servings

3 tablespoons white wine or water

3 tablespoons fresh lemon juice
1 garlic clove, minced
1/2 teaspoon salt
1/2 teaspoon freshly ground pepper
1/2 teaspoon dried thyme, crumbled
1/2 teaspoon dried oregano, crumbled
2 pounds swordfish steaks

3 tablespoons olive oil
1/2 pound mushrooms, sliced
Fresh parsley sprigs

Combine wine, lemon juice, garlic, salt, pepper, thyme and oregano in small bowl. Place fish in plastic bag. Add wine mixture and seal bag tightly. Refrigerate at least 2 hours, or overnight, turning bag occasionally.

Preheat broiler or prepare barbecue grill. Remove fish from bag, reserving marinade. Broil or barbecue until fish turns opaque, about 4 to 6 minutes on each side. (Allow about 9 minutes per inch of thickness.) Meanwhile, heat olive oil in medium skillet over medium-high heat. Add mushrooms and sauté until tender, about 5 minutes. Stir in marinade and continue cooking until sauce is heated through, about 1 to 2 minutes. Transfer fish to platter. Pour mushroom sauce over top. Garnish with parsley.

LIME-MARINATED SWORDFISH WITH CILANTRO BUTTER

4 servings

4 6-ounce 1-inch-thick swordfish steaks
2 1/2 tablespoons lime juice
Salt and freshly ground pepper

1/2 cup (1 stick) butter
1 garlic clove, minced
3/4 cup fresh cilantro, finely chopped
1/2 teaspoon dried red pepper flakes
Lime wedges

Place swordfish in nonaluminum dish. Pour lime juice over. Season with salt and freshly ground pepper. Marinate swordfish 20 minutes, turning once.

Prepare barbecue (medium heat) or preheat broiler. Melt butter in heavy small saucepan over medium heat. Add garlic and cook 30 seconds. Mix in cilantro and pepper flakes and cook until cilantro is heated through, about 1 minute. Grill swordfish until just opaque, about 7 minutes per side, basting frequently with cilantro butter. Serve with lime wedges.

BARBECUED SWORDFISH IN HERB MARINADE

2 servings

- 1/4 cup plus 2 tablespoons oil
- 1/4 cup chopped onion
- 2 tablespoons red wine vinegar
- 1 small garlic clove, minced
- 1 teaspoon Dijon mustard
- 1/4 teaspoon dried basil, crumbled
- 1/2 bay leaf, crushed
- 1 pound swordfish steaks, about 1 inch thick

Combine first 7 ingredients in shallow dish. Add swordfish, turning several times to coat with marinade. Let stand at least 1 hour, turning occasionally.

Prepare barbecue. Grill swordfish until opaque, about 5 minutes per side, basting frequently. Serve hot.

FRESH TUNA WITH PIQUANT SAUCE

Serve with lots of crusty Italian bread to soak up the zesty sauce.

6 servings

Sauce
- 1/2 cup olive oil (preferably extra-virgin)
- 1/2 cup minced fresh Italian parsley
- 1/2 cup pickled red bell pepper strips, drained and diced
- 1/3 cup thinly sliced green onions
- 2 to 3 tablespoons fresh lemon juice
- 2 tablespoons minced fresh oregano or 2 teaspoons dried, crumbled
- 1 to 2 tablespoons capers, drained and rinsed
  Salt

- 6 3/4-inch-thick 8-ounce tuna steaks

- 1/4 cup olive oil
- 2 tablespoons fresh lemon juice
  Freshly ground pepper
- 4 fresh oregano sprigs

For sauce: Combine oil, parsley, bell pepper strips, onions, 2 tablespoons lemon juice, oregano, 1 tablespoon capers and salt in heavy medium saucepan over low heat. Cook 5 minutes to blend flavors, stirring occasionally. Taste, adding more lemon juice and capers if desired. (*Can be prepared 2 weeks ahead. Cover and chill. Bring to room temperature before serving.*)

Place fish in nonaluminum dish just large enough to accommodate in single layer. Drizzle with 1/4 cup oil and 2 tablespoons lemon juice. Sprinkle with pepper. Turn to coat both sides. Place oregano sprigs under and over fish. Cover and let stand 30 minutes.

Prepare barbecue grill (high heat) or preheat broiler. Set fish on rack and cook to desired doneness, about 4 minutes per side for medium. Transfer fish to plates. Top with sauce.

SAUTEED BLUE TUNA WITH VEGETABLES

4 servings

- 1/4 cup (1/2 stick) unsalted butter
- 1/4 cup water
- 1 medium-size white onion, cut crosswise into thin rings, then rings halved
- 4 ounces snow peas, strings discarded, cut into thin strips (2 cups)
- 7 ounces enoki mushrooms, trimmed (2 cups)
- 4 large fresh shiitake mushrooms, sliced (3/4 cup)
- 4 medium radishes, sliced thinly into rounds (3/4 cup)
- 1 tablespoon chopped fresh thyme leaves or 1/2 teaspoon dried, crumbled
  Salt and freshly ground pepper
  Fresh lemon juice

- 1 pound fresh tuna,* skinned, boned and cut into 1-inch cubes
  Vegetable oil

Bring butter and water to simmer in large skillet over high heat. Add onion, peas, mushrooms and radishes and cook until peas are crisp-tender, about 3 minutes, stirring occasionally. Remove from heat. Stir in thyme. Blend in salt, freshly ground pepper and lemon juice. Cover and keep warm.

Pat fish dry. Pour enough oil into another large skillet just to cover bottom. Place over medium-high heat and bring almost to smoking point. Season fish with salt and pepper. Add fish to skillet and sauté until outside is crisp, about 1 minute. Remove fish from skillet using slotted spoon. Divide vegetable mixture among individual plates. Top evenly with fish and serve.

*Swordfish can be substituted for tuna.

SCALLOPS WITH RED CHILI CREAM SAUCE

4 servings

- 1 small dried red chili, seeded and chopped
- 1 1/2 cups hot water
- 1 large red bell pepper, cored and cut into pieces
- 1/2 cup diced onion
- 1 to 2 small fresh red chilies, seeded and diced
- 1 1/2 teaspoons ground toasted coriander seeds
- 1 garlic clove, minced
- 1/2 cup whipping cream
  Salt

- 2 pounds sea scallops
- 3 tablespoons vegetable oil
- 2 tablespoons fresh lime juice
  Fresh cilantro leaves

Place dried chili in small bowl. Pour hot water over. Let soak 30 minutes. Transfer mixture to heavy medium skillet over medium heat. Add bell pepper, onion, red chilies, coriander and garlic and simmer until bell pepper is tender, about 20 minutes. Purée sauce in blender or processor until smooth. Return to skillet. Stir in cream. Cook over medium-high heat until sauce is reduced by half, about 2 minutes. Season sauce with salt.

Pat scallops dry. Cut any large ones in half. Heat oil in heavy large skillet over high heat. Add scallops and stir until opaque, about 2 minutes. Remove from skillet using slotted spoon. Sprinkle with lime juice. Season with salt. Boil pan juices until reduced to 3 tablespoons, about 30 seconds. Stir pan juices into sauce. Heat until warmed through, 1 to 2 minutes. Spoon most of sauce onto platter. Arrange scallops on top. Spoon remaining sauce over. Garnish with cilantro.

SHERRIED SCALLOPS AND MUSHROOMS

2 servings

> 2 tablespoons (1/4 stick) unsalted butter
> 2 tablespoons vegetable oil
> 1/3 teaspoon dry mustard
> Dash of Worcestershire sauce
> 2 large shallots, thinly sliced
> 1 garlic clove, minced
> 6 large mushrooms, thinly sliced
> 12 ounces fresh or thawed frozen scallops
> 2 tablespoons fresh lemon juice
> 1 tablespoon dry Sherry (optional)
> 1 teaspoon chopped fresh parsley
> Salt and freshly ground pepper
> Freshly cooked rice
> Fresh parsley sprigs

Melt butter with oil in large skillet over low heat. Stir in mustard and Worcestershire sauce. Increase heat to medium-high. Add shallots and garlic and sauté 2 minutes. Add mushrooms and sauté until liquid is released, about 5 minutes. Add scallops and sauté until opaque, about 5 minutes. Mix in lemon juice, Sherry and chopped parsley. Season with salt and pepper. Reduce heat and simmer gently 2 minutes. Spoon over rice. Garnish with parsley sprigs and serve.

SATIN SCALLOPS

2 servings

> 6 large dried shiitake mushrooms
> 1 tablespoon light soy sauce
> 1 tablespoon cornstarch
> 1 tablespoon gin

> 1/2 pound bay scallops, rinsed and patted dry
> 3 tablespoons peanut oil
> 6 dried red chilies
> 1 tablespoon minced fresh ginger
> 1 teaspoon minced garlic
> 1/2 cup red bell pepper julienne
> 1/2 cup bamboo shoot julienne
> 2 tablespoons hoisin sauce
> 2 tablespoons thinly sliced green onions

Cover dried mushrooms with warm water and let stand until softened, about 30 minutes. Drain mushrooms and squeeze dry. Cut julienne; set aside. Combine soy sauce, cornstarch and gin in small bowl. Add scallops and let stand 5 minutes. Drain scallops, discarding soy sauce mixture.

Heat oil in wok or heavy large skillet over medium-high heat. Add chilies and stir until darkened, about 30 seconds. Discard chilies. Add ginger and garlic and stir until garlic is golden. Add scallops and stir 2 minutes. Remove scallops with slotted spoon. Add mushrooms, bell pepper, bamboo shoots and hoisin sauce and stir until vegetables are crisp-tender, about 1 minute. Return scallops to wok, add green onions and stir 30 seconds.

SESAME SHRIMP ON SKEWERS

4 servings

> 2 pounds uncooked medium shrimp, peeled and deveined
> 1/2 cup soy sauce
> 1/3 cup chopped green onions
> 1/4 cup oriental sesame oil
> 1/4 cup water
> 3 garlic cloves, minced
> 1 1/2 teaspoons ground ginger
> 1/2 teaspoon freshly grated nutmeg

Combine all ingredients in large bowl. Cover and let marinate in refrigerator at least 8 hours or overnight.

Preheat broiler. Drain shrimp, discarding marinade. Thread shrimp on skewers. Broil 4 inches from heat source until opaque, 1 to 2 minutes per side. Serve immediately.

SHRIMP WITH LIME BUTTER SAUCE

6 servings

> 1/3 cup fresh lime juice
> 1/2 cup (1 stick) well-chilled butter, cut into 8 pieces
> 4 tablespoons chopped fresh cilantro
> 3 tablespoons corn oil
> 2 pounds uncooked medium shrimp, peeled and deveined

Boil lime juice in heavy small saucepan over medium-high heat until reduced to 2 1/2 tablespoons, about 2 minutes. Remove from heat and whisk in 2 butter pieces 1 at a time. Set pan over low heat and whisk in remaining butter 1 piece at a time. (If sauce breaks down at any time, remove from heat and whisk in 2 butter pieces.) Remove sauce from heat. Whisk in 3 tablespoons chopped cilantro.

Heat oil in wok or heavy large skillet over medium-high heat. Add shrimp (in batches if necessary) and stir-fry until just opaque, about 3 minutes. Transfer shrimp to serving platter. Pour sauce over. Sprinkle with remaining cilantro and serve.

MEDITERRANEAN STIR-FRY

2 servings

> 1 tablespoon olive oil
> 4 large garlic cloves, finely diced
> 2 sweet red peppers, seeded and cut julienne
> 1 large onion, thinly sliced
> 3 cups broccoli (about 1 pound), cut into bite-size pieces and steamed until crisp-tender
> 2 tablespoons toasted unsalted pine nuts
> 1 tablespoon raisins
> 8 ounces medium shrimp, cooked, shelled and deveined
> Salt and freshly ground pepper

Heat oil in wok or large skillet over medium heat. Add garlic and cook, stirring constantly, until golden, about 1 minute (be careful not to burn). Remove garlic using slotted spoon and set aside. Increase heat to high. When oil is very hot, add pepper and onion and stir-fry until slightly softened, about 2 minutes. Mix in broccoli, nuts and raisins and stir-fry until broccoli is heated through, about 1 minute. Return garlic to wok with shrimp and stir-fry just until heated through. Season with salt and pepper.

SIMPLE GREEK SHRIMP

4 servings

- 1/4 cup (1/2 stick) butter
- 1 large green bell pepper, seeded and chopped
- 1 large onion, chopped
- 1 28-ounce can stewed tomatoes
- 2 cups clam juice
- 1 1/2 cups dry white wine
- 1 cup white or brown rice
- 1 pound medium-size shelled shrimp, cooked just until pink
- 2 6 1/2-ounce cans minced clams, drained
- 1 cup feta cheese, crumbled

Melt butter in large skillet over low heat. Add green pepper and onion and sauté until crisp-tender, about 5 minutes. Add tomatoes, clam juice, wine and rice. Increase heat to medium-high and boil 25 to 30 minutes. Add shrimp and clams. Reduce heat to medium and simmer 3 minutes. Transfer to serving dish and sprinkle with cheese.

SHRIMP IN GARLIC

2 servings

- 16 uncooked large shrimp, peeled and deveined (tails intact)
- 5 tablespoons dry white wine
- 3 tablespoons olive oil
- 4 garlic cloves, minced

- 1/4 cup (1/2 stick) butter
- 1/4 teaspoon dried basil, crumbled
- 1/4 teaspoon dried oregano, crumbled
- 1/8 teaspoon ground cumin
  Salt and freshly ground pepper
  Freshly cooked rice

Cut each shrimp in half lengthwise. Combine wine, oil and garlic in medium bowl. Add shrimp, stirring to coat. Cover and let shrimp marinate in refrigerator 2 to 24 hours.

Melt butter in heavy large skillet over medium heat. Add shrimp with marinade, basil, oregano and cumin. Season with salt and pepper. Stir until shrimp are pink, about 4 minutes. Serve immediately with rice.

CORIANDER SHRIMP SAUTE

Serve with steamed rice.

4 servings

- 1/4 cup (1/2 stick) butter
- 16 uncooked large shrimp, peeled and deveined
- 1 1/2 teaspoons coriander seeds, crushed
  Salt and freshly ground pepper
- 1/4 cup dry white wine
  Fresh parsley sprigs

Melt butter in heavy large skillet over medium heat. Add shrimp, coriander, salt and pepper and stir until shrimp are just opaque, about 2 minutes. Add wine. Increase heat to high and boil 1 minute. Transfer to platter. Garnish with parsley and serve.

LEMON-PEPPER SEAFOOD KEBABS

Serve with herbed rice pilaf.

4 servings

- 1/2 cup olive oil
- 1/2 cup fresh lemon juice
- 1 tablespoon minced fresh parsley
- 1 tablespoon minced fresh thyme
- 1 tablespoon grated lemon peel
- 1 tablespoon freshly ground pepper
- 8 sea scallops
- 4 thin prosciutto slices, halved lengthwise
- 8 large shrimp, peeled (tails left on)

- 4 small pattypan squash, trimmed
- 4 large pearl onions, peeled
- 6 large mushrooms
- 1 medium red bell pepper, quartered and seeded
- 1 medium yellow bell pepper, quartered and seeded
- 1 long Japanese eggplant, cut crosswise into 4 pieces
- 1 medium green bell pepper, quartered and seeded

Combine first 6 ingredients in small bowl. Wrap each scallop with prosciutto; secure with toothpick. Place scallops and shrimp in shallow dish. Pour oil mixture over. Cover; marinate in refrigerator 2 hours.

Cook squash in large pot of boiling salted water until just beginning to soften in center, about 6 minutes. Transfer to colander, using slotted spoon. Add onions to water and boil until just beginning to soften in center, about 5 minutes. Drain thoroughly. Thread all vegetables on 2 skewers.

Prepare barbecue grill with white coals. Alternate scallops and shrimp on 2 skewers; reserve marinade. Oil grill rack. Place vegetable and seafood skewers on rack and cook until seafood just turns opaque and vegetables begin to brown, basting with marinade, about 12 minutes, turning once.

HOT AND SPICY SHRIMP WITH NOODLES

2 servings; can be doubled

- 1 cup fresh orange juice
- 2/3 cup chicken broth
- 1/4 cup soy sauce
- 2 tablespoons grated orange peel
- 2 teaspoons sugar

- 3 tablespoons peanut oil
- 2 small carrots, peeled and cut into 2x1/2x1/4-inch strips
- 2 Anaheim chilies, seeded and cut into 2x1/2-inch strips
- 1 large red bell pepper, seeded and cut into 2x1/2-inch strips

- 1 8-ounce package soba noodles or spaghetti
- 1 tablespoon oriental sesame oil

- 6 quarter-size slices peeled fresh ginger, minced
- 4 garlic cloves, minced
- 3 green onions, minced
- 3/4 teaspoon dried red pepper flakes

3/4 pound uncooked unpeeled large shrimp, legs removed
2 1/2 teaspoons cornstarch dissolved in 2 tablespoons chicken broth
Orange peel julienne
Green onion fans (optional)

Combine first 5 ingredients in small bowl; stir to dissolve sugar.

Heat 1 tablespoon peanut oil in wok or heavy large skillet over high heat. Add carrots, Anaheim chilies and bell pepper and stir-fry until beginning to soften, 4 minutes. Transfer vegetables to bowl.

Cook noodles in large pot of rapidly boiling water until just tender but still firm to bite, about 3 minutes. Drain well. Toss with sesame oil. Return to hot pot. Cover to keep warm.

Heat remaining 2 tablespoons peanut oil in wok over high heat. Mix in ginger, garlic, minced green onions and pepper flakes. Add shrimp and stir until beginning to turn pink, about 1 minute. Add orange juice mixture and cook until shrimp are almost cooked through, stirring occasionally, about 3 minutes. Return vegetables to wok and stir until heated through. Pour cornstarch mixture into center of wok. Stir until sauce thickens. Transfer noodles to heated platter. Spoon shrimp mixture over. Garnish with orange peel julienne and green onion fans. Serve immediately, or cool and serve at room temperature.

GINGER SHRIMP WITH PEA PODS

4 servings

2 tablespoons vegetable or peanut oil
1/4 teaspoon sesame oil or to taste
3/4 pound medium shrimp, shelled and deveined
1 garlic clove, crushed
1 1/2 cups fresh or frozen snow peas (about 1/4 pound)
1 8-ounce can sliced water chestnuts, drained
1/2 cup chicken broth
2 tablespoons soy sauce or to taste
1 tablespoon cornstarch
1 tablespoon cold water

1 tablespoon grated fresh ginger
Chow mein noodles or freshly cooked rice

Heat oils in wok or heavy skillet until hot but not smoking. Add shrimp and stir-fry 2 minutes. Transfer to plate and set aside. Add garlic to wok and stir 15 to 20 seconds. Add snow peas, water chestnuts, broth and soy sauce and stir-fry 2 minutes. Combine cornstarch and water in small cup and blend until smooth. Add to wok. Return shrimp to wok with ginger and stir until sauce thickens and mixture is heated through. Serve immediately over chow mein noodles or rice.

SZECHWAN SHRIMP

4 servings

6 green onions, split lengthwise and cut into 1-inch pieces
1/2 cup canned sliced bamboo shoots
1 tablespoon minced fresh ginger
3 large garlic cloves, minced
1/2 cup catsup
3 tablespoons Sherry
1 tablespoon soy sauce
3 drops of hot pepper sauce
1 tablespoon cornstarch
2 tablespoons water

1 tablespoon peanut oil
1 pound uncooked peeled and deveined medium shrimp, cut into bite-size pieces
1 tablespoon toasted sesame seeds
Freshly cooked rice

Combine green onions, bamboo shoots, ginger and garlic in small bowl. Set aside. Combine catsup, Sherry, soy sauce and hot pepper sauce in another bowl. Set aside. Dissolve cornstarch in water in another bowl.

Heat oil in wok or heavy large skillet over high heat. Add onion mixture and stir-fry until softened, about 1 minute. Add shrimp and stir-fry until just opaque, about 2 minutes. Pour in catsup mixture and stir 30 seconds. Stir cornstarch mixture; add to wok and cook until sauce thickens slightly. Transfer to platter. Sprinkle with sesame seeds. Serve with rice.

SHRIMP HURRY CURRY

4 servings

1/4 cup (1/2 stick) butter
3/4 cup finely chopped onions
2 garlic cloves, minced
3 tablespoons all purpose flour
2 tablespoons curry powder
1/2 teaspoon ground ginger
1 cup chicken broth
1 cup whipping cream
1 pound cooked medium shrimp
2 tablespoons fresh lemon juice
Freshly cooked rice
Chopped peanuts
Toasted shredded coconut
Dried currants
Chutney

Melt butter in large skillet over medium heat. Add onions and garlic and sauté until soft and translucent. Stir in flour, curry powder and ginger and cook 3 minutes. Slowly add broth and cream. Stir until thickened, about 5 minutes. Add shrimp and lemon juice and cook until heated through, about 2 minutes. Serve shrimp over rice, passing remaining ingredients separately to garnish.

PARADISE PRAWNS CREOLE

4 servings

4 tablespoons (1/2 stick) butter
2 tablespoons all purpose flour
1 1/3 cups fish stock or clam juice
1 cup seeded and diced green bell peppers
3/4 cup chopped onions
1 1/2 cups diced tomatoes
1 4 1/2-ounce can chopped olives, drained
1/2 cup catsup
1 1/2 teaspoons fines herbes seasoning
1 teaspoon paprika
3/4 teaspoon cayenne pepper
Salt
24 medium shrimp, peeled and deveined
Freshly cooked rice

Melt 2 tablespoons butter in heavy medium saucepan over medium heat until lightly browned. Add flour and stir 2 minutes. Slowly add stock and cook until sauce is smooth and thickened, stirring often, about 8 minutes.

Meanwhile, melt remaining 2 tablespoons butter in heavy large saucepan over medium heat. Add bell peppers and onions and cook until tender, stirring frequently, about 8 minutes. Add tomatoes and cook until softened, about 5 minutes. Stir in sauce. Add olives, catsup, fines herbes, paprika, cayenne pepper and salt and stir until well blended. Reduce heat to medium-low. Add shrimp. Cover and simmer until shrimp are just pink, about 7 minutes. Place rice on platter. Top with shrimp and sauce.

SEAFOOD FETA CASSEROLE

Serve this flavorful dish over orzo (rice-shaped pasta) for a hearty one-dish meal.

6 servings

- 2 tablespoons olive oil
- 1 pound pearl onions
- 2 large garlic cloves, minced
- 1 28-ounce can stewed tomatoes (undrained)
- 1/2 cup dry white wine
- 3 tablespoons chopped fresh parsley
- 3/4 teaspoon dried oregano, crumbled
  Freshly ground pepper

- 1 pound fresh cod, scrod, haddock or halibut, cut into 3/4-inch pieces
- 1/4 pound medium raw shrimp, peeled and deveined, room temperature
- 1/2 pound feta cheese, cut into chunks

Heat oil in 3-quart saucepan over medium-high heat. Add onions and sauté until browned, about 5 minutes.

Add garlic and sauté 10 seconds. Increase heat to high and stir in tomatoes with liquid, wine, 2 tablespoons parsley, oregano and pepper. Bring to boil. Reduce heat, cover and simmer 10 minutes, stirring occasionally. (*Can be prepared up to this point 1 day ahead and refrigerated. Bring to room temperature before using.*)

Preheat oven to 400°F. Pour tomato mixture into 2 1/2-quart casserole. Top with fish. Cover and bake 10 minutes. Add shrimp to casserole. Sprinkle with feta cheese. Continue baking until fish flakes easily and shrimp are cooked through, about 10 minutes. Sprinkle with remaining 1 tablespoon parsley.

SEAFOOD JAMBALAYA

4 to 6 servings

- 2 tablespoons (1/4 stick) butter
- 2 large yellow onions, chopped
- 2 garlic cloves, chopped
- 2 28-ounce cans Italian plum tomatoes, drained (1/2 cup liquid reserved)
- 2 1/2 cups chicken broth
- 1 medium green bell pepper, seeded and chopped
- 1/2 teaspoon dried thyme, crumbled
- 1/2 teaspoon dried red pepper flakes, crushed
- 1 bay leaf
  Salt and freshly ground pepper
- 2 cups uncooked rice

- 1 pound large shrimp, peeled and deveined
- 1 pound sea scallops

Melt butter in Dutch oven over low heat. Add onions and garlic and stir until translucent, about 3 minutes. Add tomatoes with reserved liquid, broth, bell pepper, thyme, pepper flakes, bay leaf, salt and pepper. Bring to boil. Stir in rice. Cover and simmer until liquid is completely absorbed, about 30 minutes.

Add shrimp and scallops to rice mixture. Continue cooking until seafood is just opaque, about 2 minutes. Discard bay leaf. Taste and adjust seasoning. Serve immediately.

ONE-HOUR PAELLA

4 servings

- 4 Italian sausages (about 12 ounces total), cut into 1-inch pieces
- 1 medium onion, chopped
- 1 small red bell pepper, chopped
- 1 small green bell pepper, chopped
- 2 large garlic cloves, crushed
- 2 boneless chicken breast halves, skinned and cut into 1-inch pieces
- 1 1/2 cups long-grain rice
- 2 1/4 cups chicken broth
  Salt and freshly ground pepper

- 12 medium prawns in shells
- 2 medium tomatoes, peeled, quartered and seeded
  Pinch of ground saffron
  French bread

Sauté sausage in heavy Dutch oven over medium-high heat until cooked through, 5 to 6 minutes. Reduce heat to medium. Add onion, bell peppers and garlic and sauté until onion is soft, about 5 minutes. Add chicken and sauté until lightly browned, 6 to 8 minutes. Add rice and sauté until translucent, about 2 minutes. Add broth. Season with salt and pepper. Bring to boil. Reduce heat to low, cover and simmer until almost all liquid is absorbed, about 20 minutes.

Stir rice mixture with fork. Add prawns, tomatoes and saffron. Cover and cook until all liquid is absorbed and prawns are pink, 8 to 10 minutes. Serve paella with French bread.

Egg, Cheese and Vegetable

❖ ❖ ❖

EGGS A LA SUISSE

4 servings

- 2 ounces Swiss cheese, thinly sliced
- 4 eggs, room temperature
- 4 teaspoons freshly grated Parmesan cheese
  Salt
  Cayenne pepper
- 1/4 cup half and half
- 1/2 cup shredded Swiss cheese
  Freshly grated nutmeg

Preheat oven to 350°F. Fill roasting pan with 1/2 inch water and place in oven. Divide sliced cheese among 4 custard cups. Break 1 egg into each cup. Sprinkle with Parmesan, salt and cayenne. Spoon 1 tablespoon half and half over each. Sprinkle with Swiss cheese and nutmeg. Place cups in roasting pan. Bake until cheese melts and eggs are set, 15 to 18 minutes. Remove cups from water and dry carefully. Serve immediately.

EGGS MEXICANOS

4 servings

- 1 tablespoon vegetable oil
- 3 corn tortillas, cut into wedges
- 1/4 cup chopped onion
- 4 eggs, beaten to blend
- 1/4 teaspoon salt
- 1/2 cup shredded Monterey Jack cheese
  Salsa

Heat oil in large skillet over high heat. Add tortilla wedges and fry until crisp, about 2 minutes. Add onion and stir 1 minute. Reduce heat to medium. Add eggs and salt and stir until eggs begin to set. Add cheese. Continue stirring until cheese melts and eggs are set. Serve hot, passing salsa separately.

HUEVOS RANCHEROS, KIDS' STYLE

6 servings

- 1 pound cheddar cheese, grated
- 2 4-ounce cans diced green chilies, drained, liquid reserved
- 12 eggs, beaten to blend
  Salt and freshly ground pepper
  Corn tortillas
  Salsa

Preheat oven to 350°F. Butter 9x13-inch glass baking dish. Spread cheese over bottom of prepared dish. Sprinkle with chilies. Blend liquid reserved from chilies into eggs. Season with salt and pepper. Pour over cheese and chilies. Bake until eggs are set, about 40 minutes. Cut into squares. Serve immediately with tortillas and salsa.

CHEESY EGGS

6 servings

- 1 1/2 tablespoons butter
- 1 tablespoon all purpose flour
- 1/2 teaspoon Dijon mustard
- 1/4 teaspoon salt
- 1/4 teaspoon freshly ground pepper
- 3/4 cup milk
- 1/4 cup grated sharp cheddar cheese
- 6 eggs
- 3 English muffins, halved and toasted

Preheat oven to 325°F. Lightly grease 7x11-inch baking dish. Melt butter in small saucepan over medium-low heat. Stir in flour, mustard, salt and pepper. Gradually add milk. Continue cooking until smooth and thick, stirring frequently, about 5 minutes. Add cheese and stir until melted. Pour cheese sauce into prepared dish. Carefully break eggs into sauce. Bake until eggs are set, 10 to 15 minutes. Slice into 6 squares. Serve eggs immediately on toasted English muffin halves.

SCRAMBLED BRUNCH EGGS

4 servings

- 6 slices thick-cut bacon
- 6 tablespoons (3/4 stick) butter, room temperature
- 1 medium onion, cut into 1/4-inch dice
- 1 tablespoon all purpose flour
- 1 cup whipping cream
  Salt and freshly ground pepper
- 8 eggs
- 3 tablespoons chopped fresh parsley
- 4 English muffin halves, toasted
  Fresh parsley sprigs

Fry bacon in heavy large skillet until crisp. Drain thoroughly, crumble into small bowl and set aside. Melt 2 tablespoons butter in medium skillet over medium heat. Add onion and sauté until transparent, about 5 minutes. Stir in flour, blending well. Pour in whipping cream and mix thoroughly. Increase heat and bring to boil, stirring constantly. Reduce heat to low and simmer gently until thickened, about 2 to 3 minutes, stirring occasionally. Taste and season with salt and pepper. Keep sauce warm.

Mix eggs and 2 tablespoons butter in processor or blender until smooth. Melt remaining 2 tablespoons butter in large skillet over medium heat. Add egg mixture and scramble until creamy (not set). Blend bacon and chopped parsley into sauce. Arrange muffins on plates. Divide eggs evenly over muffins. Spoon sauce atop eggs. Garnish with parsley and serve immediately.

ITALIAN EGG TOASTS

4 servings

- 4 slices white or wheat bread
- 1/4 cup (1/2 stick) butter
- 4 eggs
- 4 thin sandwich-size slices pastrami or ham, or 8 slices capocollo or salami
- 1 cup grated Swiss, Monterey Jack, provolone or mozzarella cheese

Cut holes in centers of bread slices with 1-inch round cutter. Melt butter in large skillet over medium-high heat. Add bread slices (reserve cut rounds for use as croutons) and cook until crisp and lightly browned on 1 side, about 2 minutes. Flip bread over; break eggs into centers. Reduce heat to medium-low. Cover and cook until eggs are almost done, about 2 minutes. Arrange meat slices over eggs and sprinkle with cheese. Cover and cook until cheese melts, 1 to 2 minutes.

CHILI PUFFED EGGS

10 to 12 servings

- 10 eggs, beaten to blend
- 1 pound Monterey Jack cheese, grated
- 2 cups cottage cheese
- 1/2 cup (1 stick) butter, melted
- 1/2 cup all purpose flour
- 1 teaspoon baking powder
- 1/2 teaspoon salt
- 2 4-ounce cans diced green chilies, drained

Preheat oven to 350°F. Lightly butter 9x13-inch ovenproof glass baking dish. Combine first 7 ingredients in large bowl. Stir in chilies. Pour egg mixture into prepared pan. Bake until lightly browned and tester inserted in center comes out clean, about 35 minutes.

EGG, SAUSAGE AND APPLE BRUNCH

4 to 6 servings

- 1 pound pork sausage
- 6 large pippin apples, peeled, cored and thickly sliced
- 2 tablespoons sugar
- 1/4 teaspoon cinnamon
- 2 tablespoons (1/4 stick) butter
- 6 eggs, beaten to blend

Shape sausage into 3-inch patties. Cook in large dry skillet over medium-high heat until browned, 7 minutes per side. Pour off fat in skillet. Reduce heat to medium. Add apples, sprinkle with sugar and cinnamon and cook until softened, stirring frequently, about 10 minutes. Transfer mixture to serving platter and keep warm.

Melt butter in medium skillet over low heat. Add eggs and scramble to desired firmness. Add to platter and serve immediately.

BACON-CHEESE OVEN OMELET

6 servings

- 4 ounces Swiss cheese, thinly sliced
- 7 bacon slices
- 8 eggs, beaten to blend
- 1 cup milk
  Salt and freshly ground pepper
  Italian parsley

Preheat oven to 350°F. Lightly butter 9-inch round baking dish. Arrange cheese slices in bottom. Cook bacon in large skillet over low heat until done but still flexible. Drain well on paper towels. Chop 4 slices; halve remaining 3 slices crosswise and curl each into spiral. Whisk eggs and milk. Season with salt and pepper. Stir in chopped bacon. Pour over cheese. Bake 25 minutes. Place parsley in center of omelet. Arrange bacon curls around edge. Bake 5 more minutes. Cool 5 minutes.

SAUSAGE AND SOUR CREAM OMELETS

2 servings

- 8 ounces hot Italian sausage (casings removed), cut into bite-size pieces
- 2 tablespoons chopped green onions
- 1/2 cup sour cream
- 4 eggs, beaten to blend
- 2 tablespoons water
- 1/2 teaspoon celery salt
- 1 tablespoon vegetable oil

Cook sausage and onions in heavy medium skillet over medium-high heat until meat is browned, stirring frequently, 8 to 10 minutes. Remove sausage mixture using slotted spoon and drain on paper towels. Transfer to medium bowl. Mix in sour cream. Do not wash skillet.

Whisk eggs with water and celery salt until well blended. Heat sausage drippings over medium-high heat. Pour half of egg mixture into skillet. Using spatula, lift eggs as they cook, letting uncooked part run underneath until omelet is cooked but still creamy. Spoon half of sausage mixture over half of omelet. Slide out onto plate, folding omelet over filling. Keep warm. Heat oil in same skillet over medium-high heat. Repeat process for second omelet. Serve immediately.

CUSTOM OMELET

6 to 8 servings

- 3 tablespoons butter
- 8 bacon slices, diced
- 1 medium green bell pepper, seeded and diced
- 1 small onion, diced
- 4 ounces cooked ham or chicken, diced
- 1/2 cup cooked fresh artichoke hearts or canned, drained
- 1/4 cup halved black olives
- 1/4 cup halved green olives
- 8 eggs
- 1/2 can beer, room temperature
  Pinch of paprika
  Salt and freshly ground pepper
- 1 1/2 cups grated mozzarella cheese
  Sliced tomatoes

Melt butter in large cast-iron skillet over medium heat. Add bacon and fry until just cooked but not crisp, about 5 minutes. Add bell pepper and onion and sauté until onion is translucent, about 10 minutes. Remove from heat; cool mixture slightly.

Preheat oven to 450°F. Spread bell pepper mixture evenly over bottom of skillet. Sprinkle ham, artichoke hearts and olives over bell pepper mixture. Beat eggs with beer, paprika, salt and pepper. Pour into skillet. Sprinkle with cheese. Bake until center is firm, about 25 minutes. Cut into wedges, garnish with tomato slices and serve.

OMELET PIE

6 servings

- **2 pounds red new potatoes, peeled and halved**

- **2 tablespoons (1/4 stick) butter**
- **2 tablespoons vegetable oil**
- **1 medium onion, sliced**
- **5 eggs, beaten to blend**
  Salt and freshly ground pepper

- **1 10-ounce package frozen chopped spinach, cooked and drained**
- **3 garlic cloves, minced**
- **3 eggs, beaten to blend**
- **4 tablespoons tomato sauce, heated**
  Freshly grated Parmesan cheese

Cook potatoes in large saucepan of boiling water until tender. Drain well in colander. Cool slightly; slice.

Melt 1 tablespoon butter with 1 tablespoon oil in heavy large skillet over medium heat. Add onion and cook until softened, stirring occasionally, about 5 minutes. Add potatoes and cook 2 minutes, stirring frequently. Mix in 5 eggs. Season with salt and pepper. Pierce holes in egg mixture and lift up edges with spatula, tipping pan to allow uncooked egg to flow under until new edge forms, 1 to 2 minutes; do not stir. Slide omelet onto large plate. Invert into same skillet and cook until set, about 2 minutes. Transfer to serving plate; keep warm.

Melt remaining 1 tablespoon butter with remaining 1 tablespoon oil in same skillet over medium heat. Add spinach and garlic and cook until spinach is dry, stirring occasionally, about 3 minutes. Add remaining 3 eggs. Season with salt and pepper. Pierce holes in egg mixture and lift up edges with spatula, tipping pan to allow uncooked egg to flow until new edge forms, about 2 minutes; do not stir. Slide omelet onto large plate. Invert into same skillet and cook until eggs are set, about 2 minutes. Place atop first omelet. Top with tomato sauce. Sprinkle with Parmesan. Serve Omelet Pie warm or at room temperature.

POTATO AND GREEN ONION FRITTATA WITH SOUR CREAM AND CAVIAR

This is especially good with salmon caviar or golden whitefish caviar.

2 servings; can be doubled

- **3 tablespoons butter**
- **10 ounces new potatoes (2 medium), quartered lengthwise and thinly sliced crosswise**
  Freshly ground pepper
- **4 green onions, sliced**

- **6 eggs**
  Salt

  Sour cream
  Minced green onion tops
  Caviar

Melt 1 tablespoon butter in heavy broilerproof 9-inch skillet (if doubling recipe use heavy 12-inch skillet) over medium-high heat. Add potatoes and sprinkle generously with pepper. Cook until crusty and just tender, stirring frequently and reducing heat if necessary to prevent burning, about 8 minutes. Add 4 sliced green onions and stir 2 minutes. Cool potatoes slightly.

Beat eggs lightly in medium bowl to blend. Stir in potatoes. Season with salt. Wipe out skillet. Add 2 tablespoons butter and melt over medium heat. Add egg mixture. Pierce egg mixture with fork and lift up edges with spatula, tipping pan to allow raw egg to flow under until edge forms, about 1 minute; do not stir. Reduce heat to low. Cover skillet and cook until eggs are almost set, about 5 minutes.

Meanwhile, preheat broiler. Uncover skillet and broil frittata until eggs are set, watching carefully. Garnish with sour cream, minced green onion tops and caviar.

FRIDAY SPECIAL POTATO FRITTATA

4 servings

- **2 tablespoons (1/4 stick) butter**
- **2 tablespoons olive oil**
- **3 medium russet potatoes, peeled and cut into 1/2-inch dice**
- **3 tablespoons all purpose flour**
- **3/4 teaspoon paprika**
- **1/2 teaspoon garlic powder**
- **1/4 teaspoon Italian seasoning**

- **8 eggs, beaten to blend**
- **1/4 cup freshly grated Parmesan cheese**
  Salt and freshly ground pepper

Melt butter with oil in heavy 10-inch skillet over medium heat. Mix potatoes and flour. Add potatoes, paprika, garlic powder and Italian seasoning to skillet and cook until potatoes are just tender, stirring often, 10 minutes.

Combine eggs with Parmesan in medium bowl. Season with salt and pepper. Pour egg mixture over potatoes. Pierce holes in egg mixture and lift edges with spatula, tipping pan to allow uncooked egg to flow under, until edge forms, about 1 minute; do not stir. Reduce heat to low, cover skillet and continue cooking until eggs are set, 10 to 12 minutes. Invert onto platter. Serve immediately.

MEXICAN-STYLE FRITTATA

2 servings

- **1 tablespoon butter**
- **1/2 cup minced onion**
- **2 to 3 jalapeño chilies, seeded and finely chopped**
- **2 large tomatoes, diced**

- **5 eggs, beaten to blend**
- **6 ounces cheddar cheese, grated**
- **1/4 cup chopped fresh cilantro**
  Salt and freshly ground pepper
- **2 tablespoons (1/4 stick) butter**

  Fresh cilantro sprigs

Melt 1 tablespoon butter in heavy small skillet over medium-low heat. Add onion and chilies and cook until tender, stirring occasionally, about 5 minutes. Stir in tomatoes and cook until softened, stirring occasionally, about 3 minutes. Cool slightly.

Transfer tomato mixture to medium bowl. Add eggs, cheese, 1/4 cup cilantro and salt and pepper. Melt 2 tablespoons butter in heavy 9-inch ovenproof skillet over medium heat. Add egg mixture. Pierce holes in egg mixture and lift edges with spatula, tipping pan to allow uncooked egg to flow under, until edge forms, about 1 minute; do not stir. Reduce heat to low. Cover and cook until eggs are almost set, about 5 minutes.

Meanwhile, preheat broiler. Uncover skillet and broil frittata until eggs are set and top is golden brown, watching carefully. Garnish with cilantro.

HASH FRITTATA

4 servings

- 2 tablespoons vegetable oil
- 1 medium potato, peeled and cut julienne
- 1 medium onion, thinly sliced
- 1/4 cup finely chopped green bell pepper
- 3/4 cup chopped, cooked steak, roast beef, turkey or chicken
- 8 eggs, beaten to blend

Heat oil in large nonstick skillet over medium heat. Add potato, onion and bell pepper. Cover and cook until tender, stirring occasionally, about 10 minutes. Sprinkle meat evenly over vegetables. Pour eggs over. Cook until eggs are set on bottom and beginning to firm on top, 4 to 5 minutes. Place lightly greased rimless baking sheet over skillet. Holding firmly, quickly flip skillet to invert frittata onto sheet. Slide frittata back into skillet. Continue cooking until set on bottom, about 3 minutes. Serve immediately.

HEARTY BREAKFAST HASH

To save cooking time, prepare the potatoes the day before, cover and chill.

2 to 4 servings

- 1/4 cup (1/2 stick) butter
- 5 medium boiling potatoes, cooked, peeled and cut into 1-inch cubes
- 1/2 teaspoon seasoned salt
  Salt and freshly ground pepper
- 2 4-ounce packages sliced smoked ham, cut into 1/2-inch-wide strips
- 4 eggs, beaten with 1 tablespoon milk
- 2 tablespoons chopped fresh parsley

Melt butter in heavy large skillet over medium-high heat. Add potatoes, seasoned salt, salt and pepper. Cook until lightly browned, about 15 minutes. Add ham. Cook 3 minutes, tossing gently. Reduce heat to low. Pour eggs over potato mixture. Turn hash with spatula until egg is well incorporated and cooked through, 3 to 4 minutes. Garnish hash with parsley.

PORTUGUESE PANCAKE

6 servings

- 5 tablespoons olive oil
- 4 medium zucchini, diced
- 1 large onion, chopped
- 1 medium-size green bell pepper, chopped
- 3 celery tops with leaves, chopped
- 3 fresh parsley sprigs, chopped
- 1 garlic clove, minced
- 1 8-ounce can tomato sauce
- 1 1/2 teaspoons dried basil, crumbled
- 1 1/2 teaspoons dried oregano, crumbled
  Salt and freshly ground pepper

- 5 eggs
- 1/2 cup milk
- 1 cup grated sharp cheddar cheese
  Paprika

Heat oil in large cast-iron skillet over medium heat. Stir in zucchini, onion, bell pepper, celery, parsley and garlic. Cook until zucchini is crisp-tender, stirring frequently, about 5 minutes. Mix in tomato sauce, basil, oregano, salt and pepper. Simmer until mixture thickens slightly, about 2 to 3 minutes. Remove from heat. Spread mixture evenly in bottom of skillet.

Preheat broiler. Beat eggs with milk. Season with salt and pepper. Pour over zucchini mixture in skillet. Cover and cook over low heat until eggs begin to set, about 10 minutes; *do not stir.* Sprinkle with cheese and paprika. Broil until lightly browned and cheese is melted. Cut Portuguese Pancake into wedges and serve.

MAKE-AHEAD BREAKFAST CASSEROLE

Assemble this the night before and pop it into the oven the next morning.

6 servings

- 6 to 8 slices egg bread, crusts trimmed
- 2 pounds link sausages, cooked and drained
- 1 tablespoon vegetable oil
- 1 large onion, sliced
- 8 ounces mushrooms, sliced
- 5 eggs, beaten to blend
- 1 cup milk
- 1 10 3/4-ounce can cream of mushroom soup
- 1 cup shredded sharp cheddar cheese

Butter 9x13-inch ovenproof glass dish. Line bottom with bread. Arrange cooked sausages on top. Heat oil in medium skillet over medium heat. Add onion and stir until translucent, about 2 minutes. Add mushrooms and sauté until limp, about 5 minutes. Sprinkle onion mixture over sausages. Whisk eggs, milk and soup. Pour over onion mixture. Top with shredded cheese. Cover and refrigerate overnight.

Preheat oven to 350°F. Bake uncovered, until heated, 40 minutes.

MUSHROOM CRUST QUICHE

Chop and shred the ingredients for this tasty dish in the food processor to make everything ready for quick assembly.

6 to 8 servings

Butter
5 tablespoons butter
1/2 **pound mushrooms, coarsely chopped**
1/2 **cup finely crushed soda crackers**
3/4 **cup chopped green onions**
2 **cups shredded Monterey Jack cheese**
1 **cup creamed cottage cheese**
3 **eggs, beaten to blend**
1/4 **teaspoon cayenne pepper**
1/4 **teaspoon paprika**

Preheat oven to 350°F. Lightly butter 9-inch pie plate. Melt 3 tablespoons butter in heavy medium skillet over medium heat. Add mushrooms and stir until tender, about 4 minutes. Remove from heat. Stir in crushed crackers. Press into bottom and sides of prepared pie plate. Melt 2 tablespoons butter in same skillet. Add onions and stir until softened, about 3 minutes. Sprinkle over crust. Top with Monterey Jack cheese. Blend cottage cheese, eggs and cayenne in processor. Pour over cheese. Sprinkle with paprika. Bake until tester inserted in center comes out clean, about 35 minutes. Cool 10 minutes.

SHERRIED HAM AND MUSHROOM QUICHE

6 to 8 servings

1 **unbaked 9-inch pie shell**
1 **egg white, lightly beaten**
2 **tablespoons (1/4 stick) butter**
4 **ounces mushrooms, sliced**
3 **green onions, sliced**
3 **ounces boiled ham, sliced into 1/4-inch strips**
3 **tablespoons Sherry**
Salt and freshly ground pepper
1/4 **cup freshly grated Parmesan cheese**
4 **ounces grated Swiss or Gruyère cheese**
3 **eggs**

1 1/2 **cups whipping cream**
Freshly grated nutmeg

Preheat oven to 450°F. Prick pie shell with fork; brush with egg white. Bake until golden, about 5 minutes. Remove from oven and set aside. (Retain oven temperature at 450°F.) Melt butter in large skillet over medium-high heat. Add mushrooms and onions and sauté until mushrooms are tender, about 4 minutes. Drain excess liquid, if necessary. Add ham and Sherry to skillet and continue cooking until Sherry evaporates, about 3 to 4 minutes. Transfer mixture to large strainer and drain, pressing gently with back of spoon. Arrange in pie shell. Season with salt and pepper and sprinkle with cheeses. Beat eggs lightly in small bowl. Gradually beat in cream. Gently pour mixture over cheeses. Sprinkle with nutmeg. Transfer pie shell to baking sheet. Bake 15 minutes. Reduce oven temperature to 350°F and continue baking until knife inserted near center comes out clean, about 10 to 15 minutes. Serve quiche hot.

HAM AND GRITS QUICHE WITH TWO CHEESES

Delicious for breakfast or brunch.

6 to 8 servings

1 **tablespoon butter**
1/2 **cup chopped mushrooms**
1/4 **cup chopped onion**

2 **cups whipping cream**
4 **eggs, beaten to blend**
1/2 **teaspoon dry mustard**
1/4 **teaspoon cayenne pepper**
1/4 **teaspoon freshly grated nutmeg**
1/2 **cup grated Swiss cheese**
1/2 **cup grated cheddar cheese**

1 **9-inch baked pie crust**
1/2 **cup cooked ham, chopped**
3 **sausage links, cooked and chopped**
3 **bacon slices, chopped and cooked**
1/2 **cup cooked quick-cooking grits**

Melt butter in heavy medium skillet over medium heat. Add mushrooms and onion and cook until softened, stirring frequently, about 5 minutes.

Combine next 5 ingredients in medium bowl. Set aside. Combine cheeses in another bowl.

Preheat oven to 375°F. Place crust on baking sheet. Sprinkle ham and sausage over bottom of crust. Top with half of cheese and all of bacon. Spoon mushroom mixture over. Top with grits. Sprinkle with remaining cheese. Pour cream mixture over. Bake quiche until top is puffed and browned, about 40 minutes. (*Can be prepared 1 day ahead. Cover and refrigerate. Rewarm quiche before serving.*)

EASY MEXICAN QUICHE

Makes 2

3/4 **pound chorizo sausage, casings removed**
1/2 **pound ground beef**
1 1/2 **cups finely chopped onions**
1 **package taco seasoning**

1 **16-ounce can refried beans**
2 **baked 9-inch deep-dish pie crusts**
1 **4-ounce can diced mild green chilies, drained**
2 **cups shredded Monterey Jack cheese**
2 **cups shredded sharp cheddar cheese**

8 **eggs, beaten to blend**
1 **cup sour cream**
1 **cup guacamole**
15 **to 20 corn chips**
1/2 **cup shredded sharp cheddar cheese**
Pitted black olives

Combine sausage, ground beef and onions in medium skillet over medium heat. Cook until onion is translucent and meats are cooked through, about 12 minutes. Pour off fat. Add taco seasoning and mix well. Set aside.

Spread refried beans evenly over bottom of each crust. Sprinkle chilies over beans. Combine Monterey Jack and 2 cups cheddar cheese. Sprinkle 1/2 cup over each crust. Divide sausage mixture between each, spreading evenly. Cover with remaining 3 cups mixed cheese, adding 1½ cups to each. (*Can be prepared 1 day ahead and refrigerated, or 1 month ahead and frozen.*)

Preheat oven to 350°F. Carefully pour half of beaten eggs into each quiche. Bake until toothpick inserted in centers comes out clean, about 30 minutes, covering edges of crust with foil if browning too quickly. Cool 10 minutes. Spread ½ cup sour cream evenly over top of each quiche. Spoon guacamole around inside edges of crusts. Stand corn chips in guacamole. Sprinkle ¼ cup shredded cheddar over top of each quiche. Garnish with olives.

QUICK SPINACH-SAUSAGE QUICHE

6 servings

 1 tablespoon butter
1¾ cups sliced mushrooms
 1 12-ounce package frozen spinach soufflé, thawed
 ½ pound sweet Italian sausage, casings removed, cooked and crumbled
 ¾ cup shredded Swiss cheese
 2 eggs, beaten to blend
 3 tablespoons milk
 1 baked 9-inch deep-dish pie crust

Preheat oven to 400°F. Melt butter in heavy large skillet over medium-high heat. Add mushrooms and cook until softened, stirring occasionally, about 7 minutes. Remove from heat. Mix in spinach soufflé, sausage, cheese, eggs and milk. Spoon into crust. Bake until tester inserted in center comes out clean, 30 to 35 minutes. (Wrap edges of crust in aluminum foil if browning too quickly.) Let quiche stand at room temperature 5 to 10 minutes to firm before serving.

BACON, GREEN ONION AND PORT-SALUT TART

2 to 4 servings

 6 slices meaty bacon, cut into ⅓-inch-wide pieces
 1 9-inch deep-dish pie crust, baked

 1 tablespoon butter (optional)
 1 bunch green onions, sliced
   Freshly ground pepper
 3 eggs
1½ cups half and half
 ½ teaspoon salt
   Freshly grated nutmeg
 ½ pound Port-Salut or Muenster cheese, trimmed and grated

Preheat oven to 375°F. Cook bacon in heavy medium skillet over medium-low heat until crisp. Transfer to paper towels using slotted spoon. Sprinkle bacon over crust. Add enough butter to skillet to measure 1 tablespoon fat if necessary. Add green onions and sprinkle with pepper. Cook over medium heat until tender, stirring frequently, about 2 minutes. Transfer to medium bowl. Add eggs, half and half, salt and nutmeg; mix to blend. Sprinkle cheese over crust. Pour in egg mixture. Sprinkle top liberally with pepper. Place tart on baking sheet. Cook until beginning to puff and knife inserted in center comes out clean, about 40 minutes (cover edges with foil if browning too quickly). Serve tart immediately.

GOAT CHEESE TART

2 to 4 servings

 3 ounces goat cheese (such as Montrachet), crumbled
 1 tablespoon olive oil
 1 teaspoon minced fresh thyme or ¼ teaspoon dried, crumbled
 1 9-inch baked pie crust
 ¾ cup half and half
 1 egg
 1 egg yolk
 ¼ teaspoon salt
   Freshly ground pepper

Preheat oven to 375°F. Toss cheese with oil and thyme in small bowl. Spread in pie crust. Mix all remaining ingredients in medium bowl to blend. Pour over cheese. Place tart on baking sheet and bake until filling is puffed and brown, covering edges with foil if browning too quickly, about 35 minutes. Cut into wedges and serve hot.

CHEESE AND SHRIMP QUICHE WITH MUSHROOMS

6 servings

 5 slices bacon
 ⅔ cup sliced mushrooms (about 4 large)
 2 teaspoons finely chopped onion
 1 unbaked 9-inch deep-dish pie shell
 1 cup shredded Swiss cheese (about 3 ounces)
 1 4½-ounce can small shrimp, drained
 4 eggs, beaten to blend
 1 7½-ounce can cream of mushroom with wine soup *or* 7½ ounces cream of mushroom soup and 2 tablespoons Sherry
 ¼ teaspoon freshly grated nutmeg
 ¼ teaspoon freshly ground pepper

Preheat oven to 350°F. Cook bacon in medium skillet over medium-high heat until crisp. Remove from skillet using slotted spoon; drain on paper towels and set aside. Discard all but 2 tablespoons drippings. Add mushrooms and onion to skillet and sauté until tender, about 4 minutes. Crumble bacon into pie shell. Sprinkle mushrooms, onion, cheese and shrimp evenly over bacon. Combine eggs, soup, nutmeg and pepper in medium bowl and beat well. Pour into pie shell. Bake until tester inserted in center comes out clean, about 35 to 40 minutes.

TOMATO-CHEESE TART

8 servings

 2 cups buttermilk baking mix
 ⅓ cup unsalted margarine
 1 egg, beaten to blend

 2 medium tomatoes, sliced
 8 ounces ricotta cheese
 ½ cup grated Monterey Jack cheese
 ½ cup grated mozzarella cheese
 2 eggs, beaten to blend
 1 teaspoon dried basil, crumbled
 1 teaspoon dried oregano, crumbled
 ½ teaspoon garlic powder

½ teaspoon onion powder
¼ teaspoon freshly ground pepper
2 tablespoons freshly grated
   Parmesan cheese

Preheat oven to 350°F. Place baking mix in large bowl. Cut in margarine until crumbly. Add 1 egg and stir until soft dough forms. Press into 9-inch glass pie plate. Line with parchment or foil. Fill with dried beans or pie weights. Bake until pastry is set, about 10 minutes. Remove beans and parchment. Bake until crust is golden brown, about 5 minutes. Cool.

Layer half of tomatoes in bottom of crust. Combine next 9 ingredients in large bowl. Spoon into crust. Top with remaining tomatoes. Sprinkle with Parmesan. Bake until filling is set and golden brown, about 30 minutes. Cool tart slightly in pan.

EGGPLANT PIE

2 to 4 servings

1 medium eggplant, peeled and
   cut lengthwise into
   ¼-inch-thick slices
2 tablespoons olive oil

½ cup chopped tomato
½ cup chopped green bell pepper
½ cup chopped onion
½ cup sliced mushrooms
1 teaspoon dried oregano,
   crumbled
½ teaspoon garlic powder
½ cup grated mozzarella cheese
½ cup grated sharp cheddar
   cheese
2 teaspoons freshly grated
   Parmesan cheese

Preheat broiler. Brush eggplant slices on both sides with oil. Place on baking sheet or broiler pan. Broil until browned, 3 to 5 minutes per side.

Preheat oven to 350°F. Arrange eggplant slices in 9-inch pie plate, overlapping slices in spoke pattern. Press edges together to form a crust. Combine tomato, bell pepper, onion and mushrooms in medium bowl. Spoon vegetable mixture over eggplant. Sprinkle with oregano and garlic powder. Combine grated mozzarella and cheddar cheeses and sprinkle over

vegetables. Top with Parmesan. Bake until cheese is melted and golden, 20 to 25 minutes.

EGGPLANT ROLLATINI

A savory vegetarian main course.

4 servings

⅔ cup vegetable oil
1 medium eggplant, peeled and
   cut lengthwise into ¼-inch-
   thick slices
2 eggs, beaten to blend
1¼ cups dried breadcrumbs

1 cup ricotta cheese
1 cup grated mozzarella cheese
4 cups Quick Tomato Sauce (see
   recipe)
   Additional grated mozzarella
   cheese

Heat oil in heavy large skillet over medium-high heat. Dip 1 eggplant slice into eggs. Dip into breadcrumbs, coating thoroughly. Add to skillet and cook until browned, about 3 minutes per side. Drain on paper towels. Repeat with remaining eggplant.

Preheat oven to 350°F. Spread ricotta over each eggplant slice. Sprinkle with mozzarella. Roll up jelly roll fashion, starting at one short end. Secure each with toothpick. Spread 2 cups tomato sauce in bottom of 9x13-inch ovenproof glass baking dish. Place rolls atop sauce. Pour remaining 2 cups sauce over. Sprinkle with additional mozzarella. Bake until cheese is golden, about 30 minutes.

Quick Tomato Sauce

This tangy sauce is also delicious over freshly cooked pasta.

Makes about 4 cups

1 16-ounce can crushed plum
   tomatoes (undrained)
1 8-ounce can tomato sauce
½ cup tomato paste
¼ cup dry red wine
2 teaspoons freshly grated
   Parmesan cheese
1 bay leaf
½ teaspoon dried basil, crumbled
½ teaspoon dried oregano,
   crumbled

Combine all ingredients in heavy medium saucepan. Bring to boil, stirring occasionally. Reduce heat and simmer until thickened, stirring occasionally, about 20 minutes. Serve hot. (*Can be prepared up to 1 month ahead and frozen in airtight container.*)

ALMOND SPINACH ROULADE

6 servings

Pancake
2 tablespoons (¼ stick) butter,
   melted
1 cup sifted all purpose flour
1 teaspoon baking powder
½ teaspoon salt
2 cups milk
2 eggs

Herbed Spinach Filling
5 tablespoons butter
½ cup chopped almonds
¼ cup chopped onion
1 tablespoon all purpose flour
¼ teaspoon dried thyme,
   crumbled
¼ teaspoon salt
⅛ teaspoon freshly grated nutmeg
   Pinch of freshly ground pepper
1 10-ounce package frozen
   chopped spinach, thawed and
   drained

2 cups shredded cheddar cheese

1 cup sour cream
½ to 1 tablespoon Dijon mustard

For pancake: Preheat oven to 375°F. Line 10x15-inch jelly roll pan with foil, allowing overlap on sides and ends. Brush 2 tablespoons butter evenly over foil, including overlap. Sift flour, baking powder and salt into large bowl of electric mixer. Add milk and eggs and beat until smooth. Pour batter into prepared pan, spreading evenly. Bake pancake until barely brown, about 23 to 25 minutes.

Meanwhile, prepare filling: Melt 2 tablespoons butter in medium skillet over medium-high heat. Add almonds and onion and sauté until nuts are lightly toasted, about 10 minutes. Stir in flour, thyme, salt, nutmeg and pepper and cook 1 minute. Add spinach and continue cooking 5 minutes, stirring constantly. Remove from heat.

Remove pancake from oven. Cover pan with towel, then top with large cutting board, if desired. Invert pancake onto towel and board or other flat surface. Remove pan and gently peel off foil. Spread filling evenly over pancake. Sprinkle cheese over top. Carefully roll up pancake lengthwise. Let stand 10 minutes. (*Roulade can be prepared ahead to this point, cooled, wrapped and refrigerated, or frozen.*)

Combine sour cream and mustard in small serving bowl. Set aside. Slice roulade evenly into 6 pieces. Melt remaining 3 tablespoons butter in large skillet over medium-high heat. Add sliced roulade and sauté until lightly browned. Serve immediately. Pass sour cream separately.

GOAT CHEESE CREPES WITH HERBED SQUASH SAUCE

4 servings

    1/2 cup all purpose flour, sifted
      2 small eggs, beaten to blend
    1/3 cup milk
    1/3 cup water
  1 1/2 tablespoons safflower oil
    1/2 teaspoon fines herbes seasoning
    1/8 teaspoon salt

  1 1/2 tablespoons olive oil
      2 large pattypan squash, chopped
      1 small yellow crookneck squash, chopped
    1/4 cup chopped onion
      1 small garlic clove, minced
      1 teaspoon dried dillweed, crumbled
    1/2 teaspoon dried tarragon, crumbled
        Salt and freshly ground pepper
      2 tablespoons sour cream
   2 to 4 tablespoons whipping cream

        Melted butter

      1 cup goat cheese

Combine first 7 ingredients in bowl and mix. Set batter aside.

Heat olive oil in medium skillet over medium heat. Add next 6 ingredients with salt and pepper to taste and sauté until vegetables are soft, about 12 minutes. Transfer to blender. Add sour cream and puree until smooth. Thin to saucelike consistency with whipping cream. Pour into saucepan and keep warm over low heat.

Heat 5- to 6-inch skillet over medium-high heat. Lightly brush bottom of skillet with melted butter. Add 2 to 3 tablespoons batter, tilting to spread evenly. Cook crepe until bottom is just done, but not browned. Turn or flip and cook second side until just done. Turn out onto plate. Repeat with remaining batter.

Spread about 2 tablespoons goat cheese across middle third of each crepe. Fold top and bottom thirds over to enclose filling. Transfer to serving dish. Ladle sauce over.

CHILE RELLENO BURRITOS

12 servings

      5 tablespoons butter
      1 medium onion, finely chopped
      2 cups sour cream
    1/4 teaspoon cayenne pepper
        Dash of salt
        Dash of freshly ground pepper
      1 15-ounce can refried beans

      4 eggs, beaten to blend
     12 whole green chilies
      3 cups grated Monterey Jack cheese

     12 8-inch flour tortillas
     12 avocado slices
        Mild or hot salsa

Heat 2 tablespoons butter in medium skillet over medium heat. Add onion and sauté until soft, 5 to 7 minutes. Stir in 2 tablespoons sour cream, cayenne pepper, salt and pepper. Mix in refried beans. Remove from heat, cover skillet and keep warm.

Melt 1 tablespoon butter in another medium skillet over medium heat. Pour 1/3 of eggs into skillet. Arrange 4 chilies over eggs in half of pan. Sprinkle with 1 cup cheese. Cook until just set, about 2 minutes. Fold other half over (as for omelet) and cook until firmly set, about 1 minute. Slice into 4 pieces, cutting between chilies. Keep warm. Repeat twice.

Warm tortillas in dry skillet over medium heat, 1 minute per side. Fill each with egg strip, bean mixture, sour cream and avocado slice. Add salsa to taste. Roll up, then fold in edges. Serve burritos immediately.

VEGETARIAN CHILI

6 servings

    1/4 cup vegetable oil
      2 cups chopped onions
  3 3/4 cups chopped tomatoes
  3 2/3 cups sliced mushrooms
      2 cups broccoli florets
      2 cups sliced zucchini
      1 cup chopped green bell peppers
      3 tablespoons chili powder
    1/2 teaspoon garlic powder
    1/8 teaspoon freshly ground pepper
    1/4 cup water
      2 teaspoons all purpose flour
      2 8 3/4-ounce cans red kidney beans, drained
      3 cups freshly cooked rice
        Sour cream
        Chopped green onions
        Shredded cheddar cheese

Heat oil in Dutch oven over medium-high heat. Add onions and sauté until translucent and slightly softened. Reduce heat to medium and add tomatoes, mushrooms, broccoli, zucchini, bell peppers, chili powder, garlic powder and pepper. Cover and simmer until vegetables are crisp-tender, about 10 minutes. Combine water and flour and stir into vegetable mixture. Add beans and cook until chili thickens, stirring frequently, about 5 minutes. Divide rice among bowls. Spoon chili over rice. Top with sour cream, green onions and cheese. Serve hot.

5 ❖ *Pasta, Pizza and Sandwiches*

Pastas and pizzas are familiar standbys that have recently taken on star status, as American cooks rediscover the joys of these simple, satisfying foods. Sandwiches have long been a popular meal-in-one. This chapter includes all three for a convenient selection of fast, delicious recipes that are sure to become favorites.

It's a well-known and much-appreciated fact that pasta is easy to prepare, requiring only a few minutes of boiling time and a quick toss with a zesty sauce. There is no limit to the combinations you can create with store-bought pasta—use the recipes on the following pages to start, then use your imagination to try new combinations with different shapes of pasta and innovative sauces. And its wonderful versatility allows pasta to be served either as a first course or main dish. Try Pasta with Creamy Ricotta Pesto or Spaghetti with Asparagus, Almonds and Mushrooms as an appetizing first course before a simple, grilled fish, chicken or meat entrée. Or, for a hearty main dish, try Cheesy Skillet Lasagne or Linguine with Garlic-Clam Sauce.

Although you may not think of pizza as being in the quick-to-prepare category, it can be made in a snap using the recipes included here. Toppings (use the ones suggested in the recipes, or experiment with your own favorites) can be assembled ahead, the cheese grated, and the dough can even be made one day ahead. You may want to make a batch or two of dough to keep in the freezer, ready for impromptu lunches, snacks or suppers. As an alternative to homemade dough, three of the recipes here use tortillas for a light, easy "crust," along with both traditional and out-of-the-ordinary toppings such as ground lamb, tomatoes, chilies, olives, onions, mushrooms, bell peppers, and of course, cheese.

Imaginative toppings and fillings also highlight the selection of sandwich recipes. Such tempting combinations as Sausage and Bell Pepper Sandwich, spiced with oregano and served hot, Bourbon and Beef Sandwiches, served on French rolls and doused with a rich sauce, and Chicken and Mustard Green Sandwiches, dressed with a tangy mixture of mayonnaise and chutney, will make you want to elevate these creations from brown-bag status to the lunch or dinner table.

Pasta

❖   ❖   ❖

FETTUCCINE WITH BLUE CHEESE SAUCE

2 to 4 servings

- 1/4 cup (1/2 stick) butter
- 1 shallot, finely minced
- 1/2 cup dry white wine
- 1 cup whipping cream
- 1 cup crumbled blue cheese
- 2 tablespoons chopped fresh parsley
  Fresh ground pepper
- 8 ounces freshly cooked spinach fettuccine

Melt butter in large skillet over medium-high heat. Add minced shallot and sauté until just tender, about 2 minutes. Add wine and simmer until reduced to about 2 tablespoons. Stir in cream and simmer until heated through and slightly thickened, 2 to 3 minutes. Add 1/2 cup cheese and parsley and blend until smooth. Season with pepper. Place fettuccine in serving dish. Pour sauce over and toss. Sprinkle with remaining cheese.

PASTA WITH CREAMY RICOTTA PESTO

6 to 8 servings

- 3/4 cup fresh basil
- 1/4 cup fresh parsley
- 1 garlic clove
- 1/4 cup olive oil
- 1 cup ricotta cheese
- 1 pound fettuccine, freshly cooked
- 1 pint cherry tomatoes, stemmed and halved
  Freshly grated Parmesan or Romano cheese

Mince basil, parsley and garlic in food processor or blender. Add oil and process until thick, about 10 seconds. Add ricotta and process until well

blended. Arrange pasta on serving platter. Pour pesto over and toss to coat well. Top with tomatoes. Serve immediately, passing grated cheese separately.

PASTA WITH WALNUT SAUCE

All the chopping and grating for this tasty pasta sauce can be done in a snap with a food processor.

MICROWAVE

4 servings

- 2 cups milk
- 6 tablespoons (3/4 stick) butter
- 1/4 cup grated Swiss cheese
- 1/4 cup freshly grated Parmesan cheese
- 1/4 cup all purpose flour
- 1 teaspoon salt
- 1/4 teaspoon freshly ground white pepper
- 2 tablespoons coarsely chopped walnuts
  Freshly grated nutmeg
- 1 pound freshly cooked fusilli pasta
  Additional freshly grated Parmesan cheese

Heat milk in large ovenproof glass bowl on High 2 minutes. Stir in butter, cheeses, flour, salt and pepper. Cook on High, stirring frequently, until slightly thickened, 4 to 5 minutes. Add walnuts and nutmeg and mix well. Add sauce to pasta and toss. Serve, passing Parmesan separately.

EVEN QUICKER CARBONARA

4 first- or 2 main-course servings

- 8 bacon slices, cut into 1-inch pieces
- 1/2 cup whipping cream

- 1 teaspoon dried red pepper flakes
- 3 eggs, beaten to blend
- 1 cup freshly grated Parmesan cheese
- 1/2 pound dried linguine, freshly cooked
- 1/4 cup (1/2 stick) butter, melted
  Salt and freshly ground pepper

Cook bacon in heavy small skillet over medium heat until crisp. Remove using slotted spoon; drain on paper towels. Pour off all but 1 tablespoon drippings. Add cream and pepper flakes to skillet and heat until warm, 3 to 4 minutes. Whisk 3 eggs and 1/2 cup Parmesan in small bowl. Place pasta in serving bowl. Add butter and toss. Stir in egg mixture. Add cream mixture and toss thoroughly. Mix in bacon. Season with salt and pepper. Sprinkle with remaining 1/2 cup Parmesan. Serve immediately.

FETTUCCINE WITH PROSCIUTTO, ROSEMARY AND PEAS

4 servings

- 2 tablespoons olive oil
- 1/2 cup chopped onion
- 3 rosemary sprigs
- 2 garlic cloves, crushed
- 2 cups whipping cream
- 1/2 pound thinly sliced prosciutto, cut julienne
- 5 ounces tiny frozen peas, thawed
- 1 pound fettuccine, freshly cooked
- 1/4 cup freshly grated Parmesan cheese
  Additional freshly grated Parmesan cheese

Heat oil in heavy large skillet over medium-high heat. Add onion, rosemary and garlic and cook until onions are translucent and garlic is brown, about 2 minutes. Discard garlic. Stir in cream. Increase heat and bring to boil. Reduce heat and simmer until sauce thickens, 6 minutes. Discard rosemary. Add prosciutto and peas to sauce and cook until heated through, about 1 minute. Place pasta in large bowl. Pour sauce over. Add 1/4 cup Parmesan and toss. Serve, passing Parmesan.

PASTA WITH SUN-DRIED TOMATOES

2 servings

- 1/2 **pound linguine**
- 1/4 **cup plus 2 tablespoons extra-virgin olive oil**
- 1/3 **cup chopped fresh parsley**
- 1/4 **cup finely chopped sun-dried tomatoes**
- 1 **tablespoon tomato paste**
- 1 **garlic clove, minced**
- 1/4 **teaspoon dried red pepper flakes**
  Salt and freshly ground pepper
  Parsley sprigs
  Whole sun-dried tomatoes
  Freshly grated Parmesan cheese

Cook pasta in large saucepan of boiling salted water until just tender but still firm to bite, about 8 minutes. Drain. Return to same pan. Add next 6 ingredients. Season with salt and pepper. Toss over medium-low heat until warmed through. Transfer to plates. Garnish with parsley sprigs and whole sun-dried tomatoes. Sprinkle with freshly grated Parmesan.

PASTA WITH SUN-DRIED TOMATOES, CREAM AND WALNUTS

2 to 4 servings

- 2/3 **cup whipping cream**
- 1/2 **cup sun-dried tomatoes in oil, drained and cut julienne**
- 6 **tablespoons Port**
- 5 **tablespoons olivada***
- 3 **tablespoons minced fresh parsley**
- 2 **teaspoons fresh lemon juice**
- 3/4 **pound fettuccine, freshly cooked**

- 2 **tablespoons olive oil**
- 1/4 **pound prosciutto, cut julienne**
- 1/4 **cup chopped walnuts**
  Freshly grated Parmesan cheese

Combine cream, tomatoes, Port, olivada, parsley and lemon juice in medium saucepan. Simmer until sauce thickens slightly, stirring often, 10 minutes.

Place pasta in bowl. Add olive oil and toss well. Pour sauce over. Top with prosciutto and walnuts. Sprinkle with freshly grated Parmesan.

*Olivada, or olive paste, is available at Italian markets as well as some supermarkets.

PENNE WITH SPICY RED SAUCE

6 appetizer servings

- 2/3 **cup olive oil**
- 12 **garlic cloves, slightly crushed**
- 2 **16-ounce cans whole tomatoes (undrained)**
- 2 **cups chopped fresh parsley**
- 1/2 **teaspoon dried red pepper flakes**
  Salt and freshly ground pepper
- 1 **pound penne pasta, freshly cooked**
  Freshly grated Parmesan cheese

Cook oil and garlic in heavy large skillet over medium-high heat until garlic begins to sizzle. Stir in tomatoes with liquid, 1 1/2 cups parsley and red pepper flakes, breaking up tomatoes with spoon. Season with salt and pepper. Reduce heat to medium-low. Cover partially and cook until tomatoes are thick and pulpy, stirring occasionally, about 1 hour 15 minutes.

Discard garlic. Mix in remaining parsley. Pour sauce over pasta and toss well. Sprinkle with Parmesan cheese.

PASTA WITH TOMATO-MUSHROOM SAUCE

MICROWAVE

4 to 6 servings

- 1 **28-ounce can Italian-style tomatoes, undrained**
- 1 **cup sliced mushrooms**
- 1/4 **cup olive oil**

- 2 **large garlic cloves, crushed**
- 2 **tablespoons minced fresh basil or 1 tablespoon dried, crumbled**
- 1 **tablespoon minced fresh parsley**
  Pinch of dried red pepper flakes
  Salt and freshly ground pepper
- 3/4 **pound fettuccine, freshly cooked**
  Freshly grated Parmesan cheese

Coarsely chop tomatoes in processor or blender. Set aside.

Combine mushrooms, olive oil, garlic, basil, parsley and pepper flakes in shallow 10-inch round microwave-safe dish. Cover with plastic. Cook on High 3 minutes; stir. Mix in tomatoes, salt and pepper. Cook uncovered on High 3 minutes; stir. Continue cooking on High until thickened, about 3 more minutes. Ladle over freshly cooked pasta and sprinkle with Parmesan. Serve immediately.

LINGUINE WITH BELL PEPPER JULIENNE AND TOMATO AND BASIL SAUCE

6 servings

- 1/2 **cup olive oil**
- 1/2 **cup minced onions**
- 4 **small garlic cloves, minced**
- 3 **pounds tomatoes, peeled, seeded and coarsely chopped**
- 1/4 **cup chopped fresh basil with stems**
- 2 **teaspoons salt**
- 1/4 **teaspoon freshly ground pepper**
- 1 1/2 **pounds red bell peppers, seeded and cut into 1/8-inch julienne**
- 1/2 **pound yellow bell peppers, seeded and cut into 1/8-inch julienne**
- 2 **tablespoons fresh basil leaf julienne**
- 1 1/2 **pounds spinach linguine and/or egg linguine**
  Fresh basil julienne

Heat 1/4 cup oil in heavy large skillet over low heat. Add onions and cook until translucent, stirring occasionally, about 8 minutes. Add half of garlic and stir 30 seconds. Increase heat to medium. Add tomatoes, chopped basil, salt and pepper and bring to boil. Reduce heat and simmer until almost all liquid evaporates, stirring occasionally, about 25 minutes. (*Can be prepared 4 hours ahead. Reheat before using.*)

Heat remaining 1/4 cup oil in another heavy large skillet over medium-high heat. Add bell peppers and cook until tender and edges begin to brown, stirring occasionally, about 10 minutes. Add remaining garlic and stir 30 seconds. Stir in 2 tablespoons basil.

Meanwhile, add pasta to large pot of rapidly boiling salted water, stirring to prevent sticking. Cook until just tender but still firm to bite. Drain well. Toss with peppers.

Transfer pasta to large bowl. Top with tomato sauce. Garnish with basil.

SPAGHETTI WITH ASPARAGUS, ALMONDS AND MUSHROOMS

6 to 8 servings

- 1/4 cup (1/2 stick) unsalted butter
- 2 large garlic cloves, minced
- 1 cup olive oil
- 1 1/2 pounds asparagus, cut into 1-inch pieces
- 1 1/2 cups sliced mushrooms
- 1/2 cup slivered almonds
- 1 teaspoon chopped fresh basil or 1/2 teaspoon dried, crumbled
- 1 teaspoon chopped fresh oregano or 1/2 teaspoon dried, crumbled
- 1 teaspoon chopped fresh thyme or 1/2 teaspoon dried, crumbled
- 1/2 teaspoon chopped fresh rosemary or 1/4 teaspoon dried, crumbled
- 2 large tomatoes, peeled, seeded and diced
  Salt and freshly ground pepper
- 1 pound spaghetti, freshly cooked
- 1/4 cup freshly grated Parmesan cheese
- 1/4 cup freshly grated Romano cheese

Melt butter in heavy large skillet over medium-low heat. Add garlic and cook until translucent, about 5 minutes. Add oil, asparagus, mushrooms, almonds, basil, oregano, thyme and rosemary and cook until asparagus is crisp-tender, stirring frequently, about 5 minutes. Mix in tomatoes. Season with salt and pepper. Remove from heat. Place pasta in large bowl. Pour vegetable mixture over and toss thoroughly. Sprinkle with freshly grated Parmesan and Romano cheeses.

VEGETABLE FETTUCCINE CARBONARA

6 servings

- 4 eggs
- 1/4 cup whipping cream
- 8 slices bacon, chopped
- 1/2 cup sliced mushrooms
- 1/2 cup sliced carrots
- 1/2 cup sliced cauliflower
- 1/2 cup frozen peas, thawed
- 1/2 cup sliced zucchini
- 1/2 red bell pepper, seeded and cut into 1-inch strips
- 1/4 cup sliced green onions
- 1 garlic clove, chopped

- 1 1-pound package fettuccine
- 1/4 cup (1/2 stick) butter, cut into pieces
- 1 cup freshly grated Parmesan cheese
  Salt and freshly ground pepper

Beat eggs with cream in small bowl and set aside. Cook bacon in heavy large skillet until crisp. Remove with slotted spoon and set aside. Add mushrooms, carrots, cauliflower, peas, zucchini, red bell pepper, onions and garlic to skillet and sauté until crisp-tender, about 5 to 7 minutes.

Meanwhile, cook fettuccine in large amount of boiling salted water until al dente. Drain well. Transfer to large serving bowl. Add butter and toss thoroughly. Add egg mixture and toss lightly. Add vegetables, bacon and cheese and toss again. Season with salt and pepper. Serve hot.

SPRINGTIME SPAGHETTINI

6 appetizer servings

- 2 tablespoons salt
- 1 pound very thin egg noodles*
- 1/4 cup (1/2 stick) butter
- 2 teaspoons minced garlic
- 2 large carrots, cut julienne
- 1 medium zucchini, cut julienne
- 1 small sweet red or green pepper, seeded and cut julienne

- 1 cup whipping cream
- 1/2 cup freshly grated Parmesan cheese
- 1/4 cup chopped fresh dill or 1 1/3 tablespoons dried dillweed
- 1/2 teaspoon salt
- 1/4 teaspoon freshly ground pepper
  Fresh dill sprigs (garnish)
  Additional Parmesan cheese

Bring water to rapid boil in large saucepan over high heat. Add salt and pasta and cook to al dente. Meanwhile, melt butter in large skillet over medium-high heat. Add garlic and sauté until garlic just begins to color, about 1 minute. Add vegetables and toss over high heat for 2 minutes. Remove skillet from heat.

Drain pasta well. Place vegetables over high heat. Stir in cream, 1/2 cup Parmesan, dill, salt and pepper. Add pasta to skillet and toss gently to blend well. Divide pasta evenly among 6 heated plates. Garnish each with dill. Serve immediately. Pass additional Parmesan cheese separately.

If egg noodles are not available, capellini or very thin spaghetti can be substituted.

PASTA AND VEGETABLES WITH THREE CHEESES

4 servings

- 1 cup part skim milk ricotta cheese
- 1/2 cup grated mozzarella cheese
- 1/2 cup freshly grated Romano cheese
- 2 egg yolks
- 1/2 teaspoon dried thyme, crumbled

1/2 teaspoon dried basil, crumbled
1/2 teaspoon dried oregano, crumbled
1/8 teaspoon garlic powder
    Salt and freshly ground pepper

2 cups broccoli florets
1 cup minced onions
3 medium carrots, peeled and sliced
2 celery stalks, sliced

1/2 pound spaghetti
1 tablespoon vegetable oil
1 cup diced fresh tomatoes
1/2 cup chopped fresh parsley

Combine first 8 ingredients in medium bowl. Season with salt and pepper.

Steam broccoli, onions, carrots and celery until broccoli is crisp-tender, about 5 minutes.

Add pasta and oil to large pot of boiling water and cook until pasta is just tender but still firm to bite, about 5 minutes. Drain. Return to pot. Add steamed vegetables and toss. Add cheese mixture and toss. Transfer to serving bowl. Spoon tomatoes in center of pasta. Garnish edges with parsley. Serve immediately.

HAY AND STRAW FETTUCCINE

The combination of green and yellow pasta gives this dish its name.

4 servings

1 cup broccoli florets
1 cup cauliflower florets

5 tablespoons butter
2 boneless chicken breast halves, skinned and cut into thin strips
1 cup sliced mushrooms
1 garlic clove, minced

1/4 pound fettuccine, freshly cooked
1/4 pound spinach fettuccine, freshly cooked
2 cups whipping cream
1/4 cup freshly grated Parmesan cheese
    Salt and freshly ground pepper
    Additional freshly grated Parmesan cheese

Cook broccoli and cauliflower in salted boiling water until crisp-tender, 3 to 4 minutes. Drain.

Melt 3 tablespoons butter in heavy large skillet over medium-high heat. Add chicken, mushrooms and garlic and stir until chicken is opaque, 3 to 4 minutes. Remove from heat.

Place pasta in heavy large saucepan. Add remaining 2 tablespoons butter and toss over low heat until melted. Add cream and stir until heated through. Mix in 1/4 cup Parmesan. Season with salt and pepper. Add broccoli, cauliflower and chicken mixture and toss until heated through, 1 to 2 minutes. Transfer to serving platter. Sprinkle with additional Parmesan. Serve immediately.

SPAGHETTINI PRIMAVERA

4 to 6 servings

4 tablespoons fruity olive oil
1 pound sweet Italian sausage

2 dried hot chili peppers

1 28-ounce can Italian plum tomatoes, drained and chopped
1 cup finely minced fresh parsley (preferably Italian)
2 large garlic cloves, minced
3 red bell peppers, roasted, peeled and thinly sliced
1 sprig fresh oregano or 1 teaspoon dried, crumbled
    Salt and freshly ground pepper

3/4 pound imported spaghettini
3 tablespoons finely minced fresh parsley
3 tablespoons freshly grated Parmesan cheese
    Additional Parmesan

Heat 2 tablespoons oil in heavy large skillet over medium heat. Add sausage, cover partially and cook until browned on all sides, about 20 minutes. Remove sausage with slotted spoon.

Discard all but 1 tablespoon fat from skillet. Increase heat to medium-high and add remaining 2 tablespoons

oil. Add chili peppers and sauté until skins turn black. Discard peppers.

Add tomatoes, parsley and garlic to skillet and bring to simmer. Reduce heat and add red pepper, oregano, salt and pepper. Cover and simmer gently, stirring occasionally, about 15 minutes.

Thinly slice sausage and add to skillet. Cover partially and keep warm.

Bring large quantity of salted water to boil. Add spaghettini and cook until al dente (firm to the bite). Immediately add 2 cups cold water to stop cooking process. Drain well. Add to skillet and toss thoroughly with sauce. Sprinkle with parsley and Parmesan. Serve immediately. Pass additional Parmesan cheese and serve with French bread.

CHEESY SKILLET LASAGNE

10 servings

1 pound ground beef
1 medium onion, chopped
1 15-ounce can tomato sauce
1 tablespoon dried oregano, crumbled
    Dash of garlic powder
1 15-ounce container ricotta cheese
1 egg
    Salt and freshly ground pepper
10 freshly cooked lasagne noodles
14 ounces mozzarella cheese, grated

Sauté beef and onion in large deep skillet over medium-high heat until beef is browned and onion is translucent, about 8 minutes. Pour off fat. Add 2/3 of tomato sauce, oregano and garlic powder and heat through. Remove from heat. Set half of beef-tomato mixture aside. Combine ricotta, egg, salt and pepper in medium bowl. Spoon half of cheese mixture over beef in skillet. Top with 5 noodles, half of mozzarella, reserved beef-tomato mixture, remaining cheese mixture, 5 noodles and remaining tomato sauce. Sprinkle with remaining mozzarella. Cook over low heat until warmed through completely and cheese melts, about 5 minutes.

FETTUCCINE MILANO

6 servings

- 1 pound spicy Italian bulk sausage
- 1/2 cup (1 stick) butter
- 1/2 cup olive oil
- 3 cups sliced mushrooms
- 1 large green bell pepper, seeded and cut into chunks
- 1 cup minced green onions
- 1 cup chopped fresh parsley
- 2 garlic cloves, minced
- 1 teaspoon dried basil, crumbled
- 1 teaspoon dried oregano, crumbled
- 1/2 teaspoon dried rosemary, crumbled
- 1 pound fettuccine, freshly cooked
  Freshly grated Parmesan cheese

Cook sausage in large skillet over medium-high heat until browned, crumbling with fork, about 10 minutes. Remove with slotted spoon; drain on paper towels. Pour off fat. Melt butter with oil in same skillet. Add mushrooms, bell pepper, green onions, parsley, garlic, basil, oregano and rosemary and sauté until vegetables are tender, about 12 minutes. Remove from heat; stir in sausage. Mound pasta on serving platter. Top with sausage mixture and sprinkle with freshly grated Parmesan.

CAPELLINI WITH ZESTY CRAB SAUCE

2 servings

- 1 tablespoon butter
- 1/2 cup chopped green onions
- 1 garlic clove, minced
- 2 medium tomatoes, peeled, seeded and chopped
- 1/4 cup chicken broth
- 1/2 pound cooked crabmeat, shredded
- 1 tablespoon lemon juice
- 1/2 teaspoon celery salt
  Freshly ground pepper
- 1/4 cup chopped fresh parsley
- 4 ounces capellini, freshly cooked
  Parsley sprigs

Melt butter in large skillet over medium heat. Add green onions and garlic. Stir until onions are tender, about 3 minutes. Add tomatoes and broth. Increase heat and bring to boil, stirring constantly. Reduce heat and simmer 2 minutes. Stir in crab, lemon juice, celery salt and pepper. Cook until heated through, about 2 minutes. Stir in chopped parsley. Mound pasta on serving platter. Stir in crab mixture. Garnish with parsley sprigs.

LINGUINE WITH GARLIC-CLAM SAUCE

Monterey Jack cheese lifts this entrée out of the ordinary.

4 servings

- 5 tablespoons butter
- 1/4 cup vegetable oil
- 3 garlic cloves, minced
- 2 6 1/2-ounce cans minced clams, drained, juice reserved
- 1/4 cup chopped fresh parsley
- 1 cup grated Monterey Jack cheese
- 1 8-ounce package linguine, freshly cooked

Melt butter with oil in medium skillet over medium heat. Add garlic and stir until golden, 4 to 5 minutes. Remove from heat and mix in clam juice and parsley. Return to heat and bring to boil. Reduce heat and simmer 10 minutes. Stir in clams and cheese and cook until cheese melts, about 3 minutes. Arrange pasta on serving platter. Pour clam sauce over pasta and serve.

RED CLAM SPAGHETTI

Fresh clams can be used.

2 to 3 servings

- 1 tablespoon butter
- 3 tablespoons vegetable oil
- 8 garlic cloves, minced
- 1 1/2 cups tomato sauce
- 2 teaspoons Worcestershire sauce
- 1 teaspoon sugar
- 1/2 teaspoon dried basil, crumbled
- 1/2 teaspoon dried oregano, crumbled
- 1/2 teaspoon dried rosemary, crumbled
- 1 10-ounce can whole baby clams, drained
  Salt and freshly ground pepper

- 1/2 pound spaghetti, freshly cooked

Melt butter with oil in heavy medium saucepan over low heat. Add garlic and cook until beginning to color, stirring occasionally, about 3 minutes. Add tomato sauce, Worcestershire sauce, sugar, basil, oregano and rosemary. Simmer until thickened, stirring occasionally, about 15 minutes. Stir in clams. Season with salt and pepper. Simmer 3 more minutes. (*Can be prepared 1 month ahead and frozen.*)

Place pasta in bowl and pour sauce over. Serve immediately.

TARRAGON SHRIMP FETTUCCINE

4 to 6 servings

- 1/2 cup (1 stick) butter
- 2 pounds medium shrimp, peeled and deveined
- 4 medium garlic cloves, minced
- 1 teaspoon dried tarragon, crumbled
- 2 cups whipping cream
- 1 1/2 cups freshly grated Parmesan cheese
  Pinch of cayenne pepper
- 2 tablespoons dry white wine
- 1 pound fettuccine, freshly cooked
- 3 tablespoons minced fresh parsley

Melt butter in large skillet over medium heat. Add shrimp, garlic and tarragon and stir until opaque and just pink, about 1 minute. Remove shrimp using slotted spoon; set aside. Add cream, cheese and cayenne to skillet and stir until bubbly, about 2 minutes. Mix in wine. Return shrimp to skillet. Toss gently until heated through, about 1 minute. Pour shrimp mixture over pasta. Toss to mix well. Sprinkle with minced fresh parsley.

FAST MACARONI CASSEROLE

6 servings

- 1 tablespoon butter
- 1 1/2 cups uncooked macaroni
- 1 pound lean ground beef
- 2 cups tomato juice

1 medium onion, chopped
1/2 teaspoon garlic powder
1/2 teaspoon dried oregano, crumbled
1/2 teaspoon chili powder
   Salt and freshly ground pepper
1 1/2 cups grated cheddar cheese

Preheat oven to 350°F. Melt butter in heavy large skillet over medium-high heat. Add macaroni and stir to coat. Add beef and cook until browned, stirring occasionally, about 10 minutes. Pour off drippings. Stir in tomato juice. Bring to boil. Mix in next 4 ingredients. Season with salt and pepper. Transfer to 9x13-inch ovenproof glass baking dish. (*Can be prepared 1 month ahead and frozen.*) Cover and bake until macaroni is tender, about 20 minutes. Top with cheese. Bake uncovered until cheese melts, about 10 minutes.

PASTA SHELLS WITH SAVORY STUFFING

MICROWAVE

6 servings

3/4 pound Italian sweet sausage, casings removed, coarsely chopped
1 pound ground veal

1 1/4 cups chopped green onions
3 medium garlic cloves, crushed
1/4 cup freshly grated Parmesan cheese
1/4 cup freshly grated Romano cheese
1 egg, beaten to blend
   Salt and freshly ground pepper
1 12-ounce box jumbo pasta shells, freshly cooked
2 1/2 cups Microwave Mornay Sauce (see page 150)
2 tablespoons chopped fresh parsley

Place sausage in 2-quart microwave-safe casserole. Cook uncovered on High 3 minutes; stir. Cook on High 3 more minutes. Break veal into small pieces and add to sausage. Cook on High 3 minutes; stir. Cook on High 3 more minutes. Remove sausage and veal with slotted spoon and set aside.

Discard all but 1 tablespoon drippings from casserole. Add green onions and garlic and cook on High 2 minutes; stir. Continue cooking until wilted, about 30 seconds. Add veal mixture, cheeses, egg, salt and pepper and blend well. Carefully stuff each cooked shell with about 1 tablespoon veal mixture. Arrange shells in microwave-safe 9x14-inch oval baking dish. Top with sauce. Cover tightly with plastic. Cook on High 3 minutes. Turn dish 1/4 turn. Continue cooking on High until heated through, 2 to 3 minutes. Garnish with parsley.

FLORENTINE LASAGNE ROLLS WITH SHRIMP SAUCE

4 servings

   Olive oil
2 10-ounce packages frozen chopped spinach, cooked and cooled
2 eggs
1/2 cup freshly grated Parmesan cheese
1 garlic clove, minced
1/2 teaspoon freshly grated nutmeg
1/2 teaspoon salt
1/4 teaspoon freshly ground pepper
1 cup ricotta cheese
8 lasagne noodles, cooked
1 1/2 tablespoons olive oil
9 ounces cooked bay shrimp
   Leaf lettuce
4 large cooked shrimp, halved
2 cups Shrimp Sauce (see recipe)
   Freshly grated Parmesan cheese

Preheat oven to 350°F. Lightly coat 9x13-inch baking dish with olive oil. Combine spinach, 1 egg, 1/2 cup Parmesan, garlic, nutmeg, salt and pepper in large bowl. Mix ricotta with remaining egg in medium bowl. Pat 1 lasagne noodle dry with paper towel. Set on waxed paper. Brush with about 1/2 teaspoon olive oil. Spread about 3 tablespoons spinach mixture over noodle. Spread 2 tablespoons ricotta mixture over spinach. Pat about 12 bay shrimp onto ricotta. Carefully roll up noodle, starting at 1 short end, to enclose filling. Secure with toothpick. Transfer to prepared baking dish. Repeat with re-

maining noodles. (*Can be prepared 1 day ahead, covered tightly and refrigerated. Bring to room temperature before continuing.*) Bake 35 minutes. Garnish with lettuce and shrimp halves. Serve hot. Pass Shrimp Sauce and Parmesan separately.

Shrimp Sauce

Makes about 2 cups

2 tablespoons (1/4 stick) butter
1 teaspoon minced shallot
1/2 cup half and half
1 10 3/4-ounce can cream of shrimp soup
1/2 cup sour cream
3 ounces cooked bay shrimp
3 tablespoons cream Sherry

Melt butter over medium heat in medium saucepan. Add shallot and sauté until limp. Pour in half and half and stir until bubbling. Add remaining ingredients. Stir until hot; do not boil.

MEXICAN LASAGNE

8 to 10 servings

1 tablespoon vegetable oil
2 pounds lean ground beef
4 cups tomato juice
1 15-ounce can kidney beans, drained
1 6-ounce can tomato paste
1 15/8-ounce package chili mix

10 uncooked lasagne noodles
2 cups cottage cheese
2 cups shredded cheddar cheese

Heat oil in large skillet over medium-high heat. Add beef and stir until just browned, crumbling with fork, about 5 minutes. Pour off fat. Add next 4 ingredients. Reduce heat, cover partially and simmer 30 minutes.

Preheat oven to 375°F. Lightly grease 9x13-inch ovenproof glass baking dish. Arrange 5 noodles in dish. Cover with 2 cups meat mixture, then 1 cup cottage cheese and 1/3 of cheddar. Repeat with noodles, meat mixture, cottage cheese and cheddar. Top with remaining meat mixture and cheddar. Cover with foil. Bake until bubbly and noodles are cooked through, about 30 minutes. Let stand 15 minutes.

Pizza

❖ ❖ ❖

FIESTA PIZZAS

4 servings

- 1 large tomato, seeded and chopped
- 1/2 cup diced green chilies
- 1/2 cup sliced black olives
- 1/4 cup minced green onions
  Butter, room temperature
- 4 10-inch flour tortillas
- 2 cups shredded cheddar cheese
- 2 cups shredded Monterey Jack cheese
- 1 cup sliced mushrooms
  Hot salsa (optional)

Toss tomato, chilies, olives and green onions in medium bowl. Heat large skillet over medium-high heat. Butter both sides of 1 tortilla. Cook until underside is lightly browned and crisp, 1 to 2 minutes. Turn tortilla and reduce heat to low. Sprinkle with 1/2 cup cheddar and 1/2 cup Monterey Jack. Top with 1/4 cup mushrooms. Spoon 1/4 tomato mixture over. Drizzle with salsa if desired. Cover and cook until cheese melts, checking frequently, about 5 minutes. Remove and keep warm. Repeat with remaining ingredients. Serve pizzas immediately.

SPECIAL ARMENIAN PIZZAS

The traditional lahamagine *recipe with a southwestern twist—a flour tortilla is used for each crust.*

Makes 6

- 1 pound ground lamb
- 1 tablespoon dried minced onion
- 1 teaspoon dried oregano, crumbled
- 1 teaspoon freshly grated nutmeg
- 1 teaspoon dried mint, crumbled
- 1/2 teaspoon freshly ground pepper
- 6 8-inch flour tortillas
- 6 tablespoons crumbled feta cheese

- 1/4 cup freshly grated Parmesan cheese
- 1 yellow bell pepper, cut julienne

Preheat broiler. Cook lamb in medium skillet over medium heat until brown and crumbly, about 7 minutes. Drain well. Stir in next 5 ingredients. Arrange tortillas on 2 large baking sheets. Divide meat among tortillas, spreading to within 1/2 inch of edges. Sprinkle 1 tablespoon feta and 2 teaspoons Parmesan over each. Top each with bell pepper. Broil until cheese melts and browns, about 4 minutes.

SPA PIZZAS

Use any combination of the toppings here. Sautéed eggplant and squash, artichoke hearts, tomatoes and onions are some other delicious possibilities.

Makes 4 individual pizzas

- 3 tablespoons olive oil
- 1/2 cup minced onions
- 1 cup tomato sauce
- 2 garlic cloves, minced
- 1/2 teaspoon dried oregano, crumbled
- 1/4 teaspoon Italian herb seasoning

- 3/4 cup sliced mushrooms
- 1/2 medium zucchini, thinly sliced

- 4 8-inch flour or 6-inch corn tortillas
- 1 cup grated mozzarella cheese
- 1/2 cup diced green bell pepper
- 1/2 cup diced red bell pepper
- 1/2 cup sliced black olives

Heat 2 tablespoons oil in heavy medium saucepan over medium heat. Add onions and cook until golden, stirring occasionally, about 5 minutes. Stir in tomato sauce, garlic, oregano and Italian seasoning. Simmer until thickened, about 5 minutes.

Heat remaining 1 tablespoon oil in heavy medium skillet over medium

heat. Add mushrooms and zucchini and cook until tender, stirring occasionally, about 5 minutes. Set aside.

Preheat oven to 350°F. Place tortillas on baking sheet and bake until crisp, about 4 minutes. Spread about 1/4 cup sauce over each. Sprinkle each with 1/4 cup cheese. Top pizzas with mushrooms, zucchini, bell peppers and olives. Bake until cheese melts, about 5 minutes.

UPSIDE-DOWN PIZZA

4 servings

- 1/4 cup chopped onion
- 1/4 cup chopped green bell pepper
- 10 small mushrooms, sliced
- 1/4 pound pepperoni, thinly sliced
- 1 cup grated mozzarella cheese
- 1 8-ounce can tomato sauce
- 1 small garlic clove, minced
- 1/2 teaspoon dried oregano, crumbled
- 1 3/4 cups Homemade Baking Mix (see recipe) *or* buttermilk baking mix
- 3/4 cup water
- 1 egg, beaten to blend
- 2 tablespoons freshly grated Parmesan cheese

Preheat oven to 350°F. Grease 9-inch round cake pan. Sprinkle onion and green pepper over bottom of pan. Layer with mushrooms. Arrange pepperoni over vegetables and top with mozzarella. Combine tomato sauce, garlic and oregano in small bowl. Spoon over cheese, spreading evenly. Combine 1 3/4 cups baking mix, water, egg and Parmesan in medium bowl and stir briefly to moisten. Spoon over sauce, spreading gently. Bake until top is golden brown, about 30 minutes. Immediately turn out onto platter. Cool 5 minutes. Slice into wedges.

Homemade Baking Mix

Makes 2 1/3 cups

   2 cups all purpose flour
   1 tablespoon baking powder
   1 tablespoon sugar
   1 teaspoon salt
   1/3 cup solid vegetable shortening

Combine dry ingredients in large bowl. Cut in shortening using 2 knives or pastry blender until mixture resembles coarse meal. Store baking mix in tightly covered jar.

SPICY SAUSAGE PIZZA

4 to 6 servings

   1/2 pound hot Italian sausage, linguiça (Portuguese garlic sausage) or chorizo, casings removed, sliced
   1 16-ounce jar pizza sauce
   1 tablespoon sugar
   1 teaspoon dried oregano, crumbled
   1 garlic clove, minced
   1/2 teaspoon paprika
      Salt and freshly ground pepper

   1 envelope dry yeast
   1 cup warm water (105°F to 115°F)
   2 1/2 cups all purpose flour
   1 tablespoon vegetable oil
   1 teaspoon sugar
   1 teaspoon salt
   6 ounces mozzarella cheese, shredded
   6 ounces Muenster cheese, shredded
      Grated Parmesan cheese

Generously grease 12x17-inch baking sheet. Cook sausage in medium skillet over medium-high heat until well browned, 8 to 10 minutes. Drain sausage on paper towels; set aside.

Combine pizza sauce, 1 tablespoon sugar, oregano, minced garlic, paprika, salt and pepper in medium saucepan and simmer over medium heat.

Preheat oven to 450°F. Sprinkle yeast over warm water in small bowl; stir to dissolve. Let stand 5 minutes. Blend flour, oil, yeast mixture, 1 tea-spoon sugar and 1 teaspoon salt in medium bowl with fork. Dust hands with flour. Gather dough into ball and place in center of prepared baking sheet. Gently flatten dough, spreading out to edges of sheet. Let stand 2 to 3 minutes. Spread sauce over crust, leaving 1/2-inch border. Sprinkle mozzarella and Muenster over sauce. Dot with sausage slices. Sprinkle with Parmesan. Bake 8 minutes. Reduce temperature to 425°F and continue baking until bubbly and crust is golden brown, about 20 minutes. Let stand 5 minutes. Serve immediately.

QUICK TOMATO, CHEESE AND MUSHROOM PIZZA

The easy dough makes preparing this lunch or supper dish a snap.

Makes one 16-inch pizza

   5 to 6 medium tomatoes, peeled, seeded and chopped, drained well
   1 pound mozzarella cheese, diced
   3/4 cup olive oil
   1/2 cup fresh basil, chopped
   4 garlic cloves, minced
      Salt and freshly ground pepper

   1 envelope dry yeast
   1 teaspoon sugar
   1 cup warm water (105°F to 115°F)
   1 tablespoon safflower oil
   1 teaspoon salt
   3 cups (about) all purpose flour

   2 1/2 cups sliced mushrooms

Combine tomatoes, mozzarella, oil, basil and garlic in large bowl. Season with salt and pepper. Let stand at least 1 hour. (*Can be prepared 1 day ahead. Cover with plastic and refrigerate.*)

Oil 16-inch pizza pan. Sprinkle yeast and sugar over warm water in medium bowl; stir to dissolve. Let stand until foamy, about 5 minutes. Stir in oil and salt. Mix in enough flour 1/2 cup at a time to form soft dough. Knead on floured surface until smooth and elastic, adding more flour if sticky, about 8 minutes. (*Can be pre-pared 1 day ahead. Seal in plastic bag and refrigerate. Bring to room tempera-ture before rolling.*)

Preheat oven to 400°F. Roll dough out to fit prepared pan. Cover and let rise in warm draft-free area 20 minutes. Bake dough 5 minutes. Remove crust from oven and cool 5 minutes. (Retain oven temperature.)

Arrange tomato mixture and sliced mushrooms over crust. Bake until edges are light golden brown and crisp, 20 to 25 minutes.

STROMBOLI

Serve this "pizza turnover" with a salad for a casual Sunday supper, or slice it for a delicious appetizer.

4 main-course servings

   1 tablespoon olive oil
   1/3 3-pound package frozen pizza dough, thawed
   8 thin slices hard salami
   8 thin slices provolone cheese
   8 thin slices capocollo*
   1 1/2 teaspoons Dijon mustard
   1/4 cup freshly grated Parmesan cheese
   1/2 teaspoon garlic salt
   1/2 teaspoon dried oregano, crumbled
   1/2 teaspoon seasoned salt
   3/4 cup shredded mozzarella cheese

Preheat oven to 375°F. Brush 11x17-inch baking sheet with oil. Roll dough out on prepared sheet to edges. Arrange salami slices in lengthwise row down center of dough, leaving 1/2-inch space at ends. Top with provolone, then capocollo. Spread with mustard. Sprinkle with Parmesan, garlic salt, oregano and seasoned salt. Cover with mozzarella. Bring long sides of dough together atop filling and brush with water. Pinch and fold over to close. Brush short ends with water and pinch closed. Bake until golden brown, about 25 minutes. Serve warm.

An Italian sausage available at Italian delis and specialty foods stores.

GOLDEN CALZONE

6 servings

1 1-pound loaf frozen white bread dough, thawed
3 tablespoons margarine, room temperature
1/4 teaspoon garlic powder
8 slices provolone cheese
8 slices hard salami
6 slices mortadella

4 thin slices boiled ham
2 green onions, sliced
Sesame seeds

Preheat oven to 350°F. Grease baking sheet. Roll dough out on lightly floured surface to 12x18-inch rectangle. Combine margarine and garlic powder. Spread 2 tablespoons margarine over top of dough. Arrange provolone, salami, mortadella and ham over margarine. Sprinkle with green onions. Fold top 1/3 of dough over middle, then fold bottom 1/3 up over top, as for business letter, enclosing filling. Transfer to prepared sheet. Pinch ends to seal filling. Spread remaining 1 tablespoon margarine over top of calzone and sprinkle with sesame seeds. Bake until golden brown, about 30 minutes. Cool 5 minutes. Serve hot.

Sandwiches

SUPER SUBMARINE SANDWICH

6 to 10 servings

1/4 cup (1/2 stick) butter or margarine, room temperature
1 tablespoon Dijon mustard
1 tablespoon minced fresh parsley
1 garlic clove, crushed
1/4 teaspoon red pepper flakes, crushed
1 14-inch loaf unsliced Italian or French bread
2 medium-size firm tomatoes, cored and thinly sliced
1 medium onion, thinly sliced
6 ounces mozzarella cheese, thinly sliced
6 ounces Italian dry salami or pepperoni, thinly sliced
3 pickled sweet peppers (stems removed), seeded and diced

Preheat oven to 400°F. Combine first 5 ingredients in small bowl and mix thoroughly. Divide bread into 1 1/2- to 2-inch slices; do not cut through to bottom. Spread 1 teaspoon butter mixture on every other slice. Arrange tomatoes, onion, cheese, salami and peppers in every slice. Wrap loaf tightly in foil. Transfer to baking sheet. Bake until cheese is melted, about 20 minutes.

REUBEN SALAD SANDWICH

4 servings

1/2 pound corned beef, thinly sliced lengthwise
1 medium tomato, diced
2/3 cup sauerkraut, drained
1/3 red onion, sliced and separated into rings
1/2 cup Italian dressing

1 cup shredded iceberg lettuce
8 rye bread slices, toasted
Coarse-grained mustard
1/2 cup shredded Swiss cheese

Combine corned beef, tomato, sauerkraut, onion and dressing in medium bowl and mix well. Cover with plastic and refrigerate 1 hour.

Preheat broiler. Drain corned beef mixture. Add lettuce and toss to combine. Spread 4 slices of toast with mustard. Top each with some of corned beef salad. Sprinkle with shredded cheese. Broil until cheese melts. Top with remaining toast.

BACON, PIMIENTO AND CHEDDAR CHEESE SANDWICHES

6 servings

2 1/2 cups shredded cheddar cheese
12 bacon slices, cooked and crumbled

1 4-ounce jar pimientos, drained
3 green onions, chopped
1/4 cup mayonnaise
6 6-inch French bread rolls, split lengthwise
Freshly ground pepper

Preheat oven to 350°F. Combine first 4 ingredients in medium bowl. Spread mayonnaise on rolls. Spread 3/4 cup cheese mixture on 1 side of rolls. Season with pepper. Top with other half of rolls. Wrap sandwiches in foil. Bake until cheese melts, about 15 minutes.

SAUSAGE AND BELL PEPPER SANDWICH

6 servings

1 1/2 pounds sweet Italian sausages, cut into 1/2-inch slices
1/2 cup water

2 large green bell peppers, seeded and cut into 1-inch pieces
2 medium onions, cut into 1-inch pieces
2 teaspoons dried oregano, crumbled
6 crusty French bread rolls, halved

Cook sausage in large skillet over medium heat until browned, about 10 minutes. Reduce heat to low, add water, cover and simmer 10 minutes.

Add bell peppers, onions and oregano to skillet and sauté until tender, about 10 minutes. Pour off liquid. Spoon sausage mixture into rolls and serve.

Rio Grande Beef Burritos
with Creamed Peppers, page 48

Roast Tenderloin with Pancetta,
Marjoram and Red Wine, page 48;
Herbed Turnips Dauphinois, page 124

True Texas Chili, page 51

Pecan-crusted Pork Cutlets
with Ginger Mayonnaise, page 57;
Stir-fried Romaine, Sugar Snaps
and Green Onions, page 121;
Steamed Rice

Mediterranean Lamb Skewers, page 55

Veal Chops with Tomatoes
and Artichoke Hearts, page 54

Orange- and Bay-scented Roasted Chicken
with New Potatoes, page 60;
Sautéed Snow Peas

IRWIN HOROWITZ

BOURBON BEEF SANDWICHES

3 to 4 servings

    1 cup catsup
    5 tablespoons Worcestershire
      sauce
    6 tablespoons steak sauce
    3/4 cup chutney
    3/4 cup chili sauce
    1/4 teaspoon hot pepper sauce
    1/2 cup bourbon

    1 tablespoon butter
    1 tablespoon vegetable oil
    1 pound thinly sliced round steak
    3 or 4 French bread rolls, halved

Combine first 7 ingredients in large bowl. Cover and chill overnight.

Pour sauce into saucepan. Cover and simmer 30 minutes.

Melt butter with oil in large skillet over high heat. Add meat in batches and brown well. Add meat to sauce and stir until heated through. Spoon onto rolls. Serve immediately. Pass remaining sauce separately.

PEPPERONI PIZZA BREAD

Makes 2 loaves

    1 tablespoon olive oil
    2 pounds pizza dough or one
      2-pound package frozen bread
      dough, thawed
    1/2 pound pepperoni, sliced
    1 pound mozzarella cheese,
      grated
    1 tablespoon garlic powder
    1 teaspoon dried basil, crumbled
    1 teaspoon dried oregano,
      crumbled
    1 teaspoon dehydrated onion
      flakes
    1/2 cup grated Parmesan cheese
      Salt and freshly ground pepper
    1 egg, beaten to blend
      Sesame seeds

Brush two 11x17-inch baking sheets with olive oil. Divide dough in half. Roll 1 dough piece out to edges of 1 prepared sheet. Place half of pepperoni slices in crosswise rows on dough, leaving 1/2-inch borders at ends. Sprinkle with half of mozzarella, half of garlic powder, half of basil, half of oregano and half of onion. Top with half of Parmesan. Season with salt and pepper. Starting at short end, roll up jelly roll fashion and turn seam side down on baking sheet. Brush with egg. Slice crosswise slits in top of dough. Sprinkle with sesame seeds. Repeat with remaining ingredients. (*Can be prepared 1 week ahead. Wrap tightly and freeze. Thaw before baking.*)

Preheat oven to 400°F. Bake until golden brown, about 25 minutes. Slice loaves. Serve immediately.

CHICKEN AND MUSTARD GREEN SANDWICHES

If you're a fan of well-dressed sandwiches, add a little more mayonnaise and/or chutney if desired.

2 servings; can be doubled or tripled

    5 tablespoons mayonnaise
    1/4 cup Major Grey's chutney
    1 baguette, ends trimmed, halved
      lengthwise and crosswise

    1 tablespoon butter
    2 large boneless chicken breast
      halves, skinned
      Salt and freshly ground pepper
    1 bunch mustard greens or other
      bitter greens, stemmed

Preheat broiler. Mix mayonnaise and chutney. Spread some on cut sides of bread. Broil cut sides up until golden.

Melt butter in heavy large skillet over medium heat. Season chicken with salt and pepper. Sauté until springy to touch, about 5 minutes per side. Transfer to plate. Add greens to skillet. Season with salt and pepper. Stir until wilted, about 1 1/2 minutes. Arrange on bottom bread pieces. Slice chicken across grain on diagonal and arrange over greens. Spread with remaining mayonnaise mixture. Top with bread.

TOASTED MUSHROOM SANDWICHES

Makes 8

    2 tablespoons (1/4 stick) butter
    1 pound mushrooms, finely
      chopped
    1 teaspoon minced onion
    1 cup sour cream
    1/4 teaspoon garlic powder
    1/4 teaspoon dried thyme,
      crumbled
    1/4 teaspoon fresh lemon juice
      Salt and freshly ground pepper

    16 whole wheat or rye bread slices
      Butter, room temperature

Melt 2 tablespoons butter in heavy large skillet over medium heat. Add mushrooms and onion and cook until liquid evaporates, stirring frequently, about 15 minutes. Remove from heat. Stir in next 4 ingredients. Season with salt and pepper.

Spread 1/4 cup mushroom mixture on each of 8 bread slices. Top with remaining 8 slices. Spread butter on outside of sandwiches. Heat another heavy large skillet over medium heat. Add sandwiches (in batches, if necessary) and cook until bread is toasted, about 2 minutes per side. Serve hot.

TUNA PITAS WITH YOGURT AND MUSTARD

2 servings

    1 6 1/2-ounce can solid white tuna
      in water, drained and flaked
    1/2 cup plain lowfat yogurt
    1 celery stalk, diced
    1 teaspoon coarse-grained
      mustard
    1/4 teaspoon dried dillweed
      Salt and freshly ground pepper
    2 pita breads, halved crosswise
    8 lettuce leaves
    2 tomatoes, sliced thickly

Combine first 5 ingredients in medium bowl. Season with salt and pepper. (*Can be prepared 1 day ahead. Cover and refrigerate.*) Line bread halves with lettuce leaves and tomatoes. Divide tuna mixture among bread pockets. Serve immediately.

CRAB- AND CHEESE-STUFFED FRENCH BREAD

Present this either as a main course or, cut into thinner slices, as an appetizer.

4 main-course servings

   1 16-inch loaf French bread, cut in half lengthwise and hollowed out
   12 ounces cheddar cheese, grated
   8 ounces cooked fresh crabmeat, flaked
   6 tablespoons chopped green onions
   1/4 cup mayonnaise
   1/8 teaspoon hot pepper sauce

Preheat oven to 350°F. Place bread on ungreased baking sheet. Sprinkle cheese over bread halves. Combine remaining ingredients in small bowl. Spoon crab mixture over cheese. Bake until cheese bubbles, about 20 minutes. Cut each piece in half crosswise.

AVOCADO-STUFFED PITA BREAD

4 to 6 servings

   4 or 5 pita breads, halved
   1 large firm ripe avocado, peeled and sliced
   1 tablespoon fresh lemon juice
   2 hard-cooked eggs, chopped
   1 large tomato, peeled, cored, seeded and chopped
   1/2 cup thinly sliced green onions
   1/2 cup shredded cheddar cheese
   1/2 cup diced celery
   1 2 1/4-ounce can sliced ripe olives, drained
   1/2 teaspoon garlic salt
   3 drops hot pepper sauce
   1 to 1 1/2 cups shredded iceberg lettuce
      Alfalfa sprouts

Preheat oven to 350°F. Wrap pita tightly in foil. Bake until heated through, 10 minutes.

   Meanwhile, combine avocado and lemon juice in medium bowl and mash well. Add eggs, tomato, onions, cheese, celery, olives, garlic salt and hot pepper sauce, stirring to blend. Fill each pita half with lettuce and avocado mixture. Top with alfalfa sprouts.

NUTTY NUT SANDWICHES

These are easy enough for kids to make for their own lunchboxes. They are also excellent when grilled.

Makes 8

   1 cup grated cheddar cheese
   1/2 cup shredded zucchini
   1 Granny Smith apple, cored and chopped
   1 3-ounce package cream cheese, room temperature
   1/4 cup unsalted peanuts, chopped
   2 tablespoons honey
   16 whole wheat bread slices

Combine first 6 ingredients in medium bowl. Spread cheese mixture on 8 bread slices. Top with remaining 8 bread slices. (*Can be prepared 8 hours ahead. Wrap and refrigerate.*)

VEGETARIAN DELIGHT

An unusual open-face hot sandwich.

10 to 12 servings

   2 cups grated cheddar cheese
   1 8-ounce can tomato sauce
   1 4.2-ounce can chopped black olives
   1/3 cup olive oil
   2 ounces diced green chilies
   3 medium-size green onions, chopped
   1/2 teaspoon minced garlic
   1 loaf French bread, cut into 1/2-inch slices

Preheat broiler. Mix all ingredients except bread in large bowl. Arrange bread slices on broiler pan. Spread each with some of cheese mixture. Broil until bubbly, about 1 minute. Serve sandwiches immediately.

6 ❖ *Vegetables, Rice and Grains*

Well-chosen side dishes complement an entrée and show it off—they also provide delicious flavor on their own. It's easier than you think to achieve the perfect balance when matching these vegetable, rice and grain dishes to your entrée. You might want to pair a main course that includes a rich sauce with a lighter accompaniment such as Spinach with Caramelized Onions or Vegetable-Rice Medley. To complement an elegant entrée, try either Butternut Squash and Shallots with Cumin and Turmeric or Pecan Pilaf, or serve them both. A more casual meal calls for something comforting like Corn Bread Casserole, Double Cheese and Zucchini Bake or Homestyle Sage Potatoes.

Many of the dishes here would be equally delicious as a first course, and some are hearty enough to serve as a main dish. Timbales of Fresh Asparagus, garnished with asparagus tips, diced tomato and chopped parsley make a light and pretty first course, and zesty Mustard-Dill Artichokes, served hot with melted Parmesan cheese are a welcome beginning to any meal. For a satisfying vegetarian lunch or dinner, you need only add a salad to Stuffed Eggplant with Wild Rice or Corn Soufflé-filled Peppers.

Vegetables

❖ ❖ ❖

MUSTARD-DILL ARTICHOKES

4 servings

4 medium artichokes

2 1/4-inch-thick lemon slices
2 tablespoons olive oil

1/2 cup Champagne mustard or Dijon mustard
1 teaspoon dried dillweed, crumbled
2 tablespoons (1/4 stick) butter
1/4 cup freshly grated Parmesan cheese

Cut off artichoke stems. Discard tough outer leaves at base. Using scissors, carefully trim leaf points and trim 1/2 inch from top of each artichoke.

Combine enough water to cover artichokes with lemon slices and oil in large saucepan and bring to boil. Add artichokes. Reduce heat, cover partially and simmer until artichoke bottoms are tender, 35 to 40 minutes. Drain well. Arrange artichokes in ovenproof glass baking dish.

Preheat oven to 350°F. Blend mustard and dillweed in small saucepan. Add butter and whisk over medium heat until blended. Spoon mustard sauce over artichokes. Sprinkle with Parmesan. Bake until cheese melts, about 15 minutes.

TIMBALES OF FRESH ASPARAGUS

4 servings

2 pounds fresh asparagus spears, tough ends discarded
2 eggs
1 egg yolk
1 teaspoon salt
1/4 teaspoon freshly grated nutmeg
Dash of freshly ground pepper

1/2 medium tomato, peeled, seeded and diced
1 tablespoon chopped fresh parsley

Preheat oven to 400°F. Lightly grease four 6-ounce custard cups. Cook asparagus in enough boiling water to cover until tender, about 5 to 8 minutes. Drain well. Cut off 12 tips and set aside. Chop remaining asparagus; transfer to blender or processor and puree until smooth. Beat eggs and yolk in medium bowl. Add salt, nutmeg and pepper. Stir in asparagus puree and mix thoroughly. Spoon into prepared cups. Arrange in 9x9-inch baking pan. Pour in boiling water to depth of 1 inch. Bake timbales until set, about 30 minutes.

Just before serving, warm reserved asparagus tips in simmering water until heated through. Invert timbales onto serving plates. Top each with reserved tips. Arrange diced tomato on tips; sprinkle with chopped parsley.

GREEN BEANS WITH ONION AND GARLIC

4 servings

1 pound green beans, trimmed and cut into 2-inch pieces
2 tablespoons olive oil
1 small onion, chopped
1 large garlic clove, minced
6 tablespoons freshly grated Parmesan cheese
1/4 cup white wine vinegar
Salt and freshly ground pepper

Steam beans until tender, about 10 minutes; keep warm. Heat oil in large skillet over low heat. Add onion and garlic and sauté until translucent, about 8 minutes. Transfer beans to serving dish. Add onion mixture and remaining ingredients. Toss well.

GREEN BEANS PARMESAN

6 servings

1/4 cup vegetable oil
1 small green bell pepper, seeded and diced
1 small red bell pepper, seeded and diced
1/4 cup chopped onion
1 garlic clove, minced
1 1/2 pounds green beans, cut into 1-inch pieces
1 teaspoon dried basil, crumbled
1 teaspoon salt

3/4 cup freshly grated Parmesan cheese

Heat oil in heavy medium skillet over medium heat. Add bell peppers, onion and garlic and cook until onions are translucent, about 3 minutes. Add beans, basil and salt. Cover and steam until tender, about 7 minutes.

Remove from heat. Stir in 1/2 cup Parmesan. Transfer to serving dish. Sprinkle with remaining Parmesan.

SPICY KIDNEY BEANS WITH RICE

4 servings

1 tablespoon olive oil
1 2-ounce piece salt pork, scored around edges and rinsed completely
1 large onion, chopped
1 green bell pepper, cored, seeded and chopped
2 small garlic cloves, minced

2 15-ounce cans kidney beans (undrained)
1/2 cup tomato sauce
1/3 cup water
1 chicken bouillon cube
Freshly ground pepper
Freshly cooked rice

Heat oil in heavy large saucepan over low heat. Add salt pork and cook until lightly browned, about 10 minutes. Increase heat to medium. Add onion, bell pepper and garlic and cook until soft, stirring often, about 10 minutes.

Add beans with liquid, tomato sauce, water and bouillon to onion mixture. Season with pepper. Reduce heat to low. Cover and simmer 1 hour. Remove salt pork. Serve beans over rice.

COWBOY BEAN BAKE

Terrific with barbecued meats.

6 to 8 servings

 6 bacon slices
 1 medium onion, chopped
 1/2 cup catsup
 3 tablespoons dark brown sugar
 1 tablespoon cider vinegar
 1 teaspoon salt
 1 teaspoon dry mustard
 1 16-ounce can pork and beans
 1 16-ounce can kidney beans, drained
 1 16-ounce can lima beans or butter beans, drained

Preheat oven to 350°F. Cook bacon in heavy medium skillet over medium heat until crisp, about 5 minutes. Transfer bacon to paper towels; reserve drippings. Add onion to skillet with drippings and cook until translucent, stirring occasionally, about 7 minutes. Transfer onion with drippings to large bowl. Add next 5 ingredients to bowl. Crumble bacon; add to onion mixture. Mix in pork and beans, kidney beans and lima beans. Transfer to 9x13-inch glass baking dish. (*Can be prepared 1 day ahead. Cover and refrigerate.*) Bake until bean mixture bubbles, 30 to 35 minutes. Serve immediately.

BROCCOLI PARMESAN

6 to 8 servings

 2 pounds broccoli, cut into 3-inch-long florets
  Salt

 2 egg whites, room temperature
 1/2 cup mayonnaise
 1/3 cup freshly grated Parmesan cheese

 1/4 cup dried parsley flakes, crumbled
  Grated peel of 1 lemon
 2 tablespoons (1/4 stick) butter, melted

Cook broccoli in 5- to 6-quart saucepan of lightly salted boiling water until crisp-tender, 3 to 4 minutes. Drain; rinse under cold water and drain again.

Preheat oven to 425°F. Beat egg whites until soft peaks form. Gently fold in mayonnaise, cheese, parsley flakes and grated peel. Arrange broccoli in 1 1/2- to 2-quart oval ovenproof glass baking dish. Drizzle with melted butter. Spread egg white mixture over top. Bake until top is puffy and golden brown, about 5 minutes.

CABBAGE AND ZUCCHINI STIR-FRY

MICROWAVE

6 servings

 1/2 large cabbage head, shredded (about 6 cups)
 1 medium onion, thinly sliced (about 2 cups)
 3 tablespoons butter or margarine
 3 medium zucchini, sliced (about 3 cups)
 1/4 teaspoon crushed red pepper flakes
 1 tablespoon soy sauce
 1/2 teaspoon salt or to taste
 1/8 teaspoon freshly ground pepper
  Toasted sesame seeds (garnish)

Combine cabbage, onion and butter in 2-quart glass baking dish. Cover and cook on High, stirring once, until cabbage is tender, about 6 minutes. Stir in zucchini and red pepper flakes. Cover and cook on High, stirring twice, until zucchini is tender, about 7 to 8 minutes. Blend in soy sauce, salt and pepper. Sprinkle with sesame seeds.

GOLDEN CARROT CRUNCH

4 to 6 servings

 6 cups carrot julienne
 1 1/2 tablespoons butter, melted

 1/4 cup blanched slivered almonds, toasted
 1 1/2 tablespoons brown sugar
 1 1/2 teaspoons grated orange peel
  Salt and freshly ground pepper

Cook carrots in large saucepan of boiling water until crisp-tender, about 8 minutes. Drain. Melt butter in heavy large skillet over medium-low heat. Stir in almonds, sugar, orange peel and salt and pepper. Add carrots and cook until just tender, stirring occasionally, about 5 minutes. Serve immediately.

CARROT-ONION STIR-FRY

6 servings

 6 tablespoons (3/4 stick) butter
 1 medium onion, thinly sliced
 6 medium carrots, peeled and cut julienne
 1 tablespoon sugar
 1 1/2 teaspoons dried tarragon, crumbled
  Salt and freshly ground pepper

Melt butter in wok or heavy large skillet over medium heat. Add onion and stir until softened, about 3 minutes. Increase heat to medium-high. Add carrots and stir until just crisp-tender, about 5 minutes. Stir in sugar and tarragon and cook 2 more minutes. Season with salt and pepper and serve.

SHAKER CORN PUDDING

8 servings

  Butter
 3 tablespoons butter, room temperature
 2 tablespoons all purpose flour
 2 tablespoons sugar
 1 teaspoon salt
 3 eggs, beaten to blend
 2 cups fresh or frozen corn
 1 3/4 cups milk
  Freshly ground white pepper

Preheat oven to 325°F. Butter deep 1 1/2-quart baking dish. Mix 3 tablespoons butter, flour, sugar and salt with fork in large bowl until blended. Add eggs and beat well. Stir in corn and milk. Season with pepper. Pour into prepared dish. Bake 20 minutes. Stir through. Continue baking until pudding is golden and knife inserted in center comes out clean, about 25 minutes. Serve immediately.

CORN BREAD CASSEROLE

10 to 12 servings

> Butter
> 6 tablespoons (³/4 stick) butter
> 2 large onions, chopped
> 1 7-ounce can diced green chilies, well drained
> 2 17-ounce cans creamed corn
> 1 1-pound package cornmeal muffin mix
> 2 eggs, beaten to blend
> 2 tablespoons milk
> 1 cup sour cream
> 3 cups grated sharp cheddar cheese

Preheat oven to 425°F. Lightly butter 9x13-inch ovenproof glass baking dish. Melt 6 tablespoons butter in heavy medium skillet over medium-high heat. Add onions and chilies and cook until onions are light brown, stirring frequently, about 8 minutes. Combine corn, cornmeal mix, eggs and milk in large bowl and blend well. Pour into prepared pan. Spoon onion mixture over. Top with sour cream and then cheese. Swirl through layered mixture with knife. Bake until puffed and golden, about 35 minutes. Cool 10 minutes and serve.

SAUTEED CUCUMBERS

4 servings

> 2 large cucumbers, peeled, seeded and cut julienne
> 2 teaspoons salt
> 1 cup whipping cream
> 2 tablespoons chopped fresh dill
> Freshly ground pepper
> 2 tablespoons (¹/4 stick) butter

Toss cucumber with salt in colander and let drain 20 minutes. Rinse under cold running water and let drain again. Pat dry with paper towel. Meanwhile, boil cream, dill and pepper in small saucepan until mixture is reduced by half, about 20 minutes. Set aside. Melt butter in large skillet over medium-high heat. Add cucumber and sauté until crisp-tender, about 3 to 5 minutes. Stir in cream mixture. Cook until heated through, about 2 to 3 minutes.

SAUTE OF EGGPLANT AND BELL PEPPERS

A traditional Catalan side dish.

6 servings

> ¹/4 cup olive oil
> 1 small eggplant, chopped
> 1 small onion, sliced
> 1 cup chopped green bell peppers
> 1 cup chopped red bell peppers
> 1 cup chopped tomatoes
> Salt and freshly ground pepper

Heat oil in heavy large skillet over medium heat. Add eggplant and cook until softened, stirring occasionally, about 5 minutes. Add onion and cook until translucent, stirring frequently, about 5 minutes. Mix in bell peppers and cook until crisp-tender, about 2 minutes. Add tomatoes and stir until heated through, about 2 minutes. Season with salt and pepper.

EGGPLANT PROVENCAL

2 to 3 servings

> Butter
> 2 tablespoons (¹/4 stick) butter
> 2 tablespoons olive oil
> 1 small eggplant (³/4 to 1 pound), sliced ¹/2 inch thick
> 4 small tomatoes, peeled and chopped
> 2 garlic cloves, minced
> 1 teaspoon salt
> ³/4 teaspoon herbes de Provence
> ¹/2 teaspoon freshly ground pepper
> ¹/2 cup fresh breadcrumbs

Butter 6-inch square ovenproof glass baking dish. Melt 1 tablespoon butter with 1 tablespoon oil in large skillet over medium heat. Add eggplant and sauté until soft and browned, 5 to 10 minutes. Transfer to plate. Remove skin and discard. Mash eggplant with fork until slightly chunky. Set aside.

Preheat oven to 350°F. Melt remaining 1 tablespoon butter with remaining 1 tablespoon oil in skillet. Add tomatoes, garlic, salt, herbes de Provence and pepper. Sauté until juices begin to bubble. Add eggplant to tomato mixture. Turn into prepared dish. Stir in breadcrumbs. Bake until golden, 15 to 20 minutes. Serve hot.

STUFFED EGGPLANT WITH WILD RICE

MICROWAVE

6 servings

> 3 medium eggplants (about 1 pound each)
> ¹/3 cup olive oil
> 1 medium onion, finely chopped
> ¹/2 pound mushrooms, thinly sliced
> 2 garlic cloves, pressed
> 1 8-ounce can tomato paste
> 1 cup dry white wine
> 2 tablespoons chopped fresh parsley
> 1¹/2 teaspoons dried oregano, crumbled
> 1¹/2 teaspoons dried basil, crumbled
> 1 teaspoon dried marjoram, crumbled
> 1 teaspoon dried mint, crumbled (optional)
> ¹/2 teaspoon dried chervil, crumbled (optional)
> ¹/2 teaspoon freshly grated nutmeg
> ¹/2 teaspoon cinnamon
> 2 cups freshly cooked wild rice
> ¹/2 cup chopped walnuts (optional)
> Freshly grated Parmesan cheese

Lightly grease large glass or ceramic baking dish. Prick eggplants with fork and place in another large glass dish. Cook on High until tender, 6 to 8 minutes. Cut in half lengthwise and remove pulp, leaving ¹/4- to ¹/2-inch shells. Chop reserved pulp. Heat oil in large skillet over medium heat. Add chopped pulp, onion, mushrooms and garlic and sauté until vegetables are softened, 3 to 5 minutes. Add tomato paste, wine, herbs, nutmeg and cinnamon. Stir 3 minutes. Remove from heat and add rice. Stir in nuts if desired. Spoon mixture into reserved shells. Sprinkle with cheese. Transfer to prepared baking dish. Cook on High until heated through, 12 to 14 minutes. Serve immediately.

EGGPLANT AND MUSHROOM PARMESAN

4 servings

- 1/2 cup olive oil
- 1 medium eggplant (about 1 1/2 pounds), sliced 1/2 inch thick
- 2 eggs, beaten to blend
- 1 cup Italian seasoned breadcrumbs
- 1/2 pound mushrooms, sliced
- 1 1/2 cups freshly grated Parmesan cheese
- 1 15-ounce jar pizza sauce
- 1/2 pound mozzarella cheese, thinly sliced

Butter 9x13-inch baking dish. Heat 1/4 cup oil in medium skillet over medium-high heat. Dip 1 eggplant slice in eggs, then breadcrumbs. Add to skillet and cook until golden brown, about 2 minutes per side. Remove with slotted spoon; drain eggplant thoroughly on paper towels. Repeat with remaining eggplant, eggs and crumbs, adding remaining 1/4 cup oil to skillet as necessary.

Preheat oven to 350°F. Arrange half of eggplant slices in bottom of prepared baking dish. Cover eggplant with sliced mushrooms and 1/2 cup freshly grated Parmesan. Top with remaining eggplant. Pour pizza sauce over eggplant. Sprinkle with remaining 1 cup Parmesan. Bake 20 minutes. Layer mozzarella slices over top. Continue baking until cheese is bubbly and beginning to brown, about 10 minutes. Serve immediately.

MUSTARD MUSHROOMS

2 to 3 servings

- 1/4 cup (1/2 stick) butter
- 1/2 small onion, chopped
- 1 pound mushrooms, sliced
- 1/3 cup dry vermouth
- 1 tablespoon Dijon mustard
  Salt and freshly ground pepper

Melt butter in heavy skillet over low heat. Add onion. Cover and cook until translucent, about 10 minutes. Increase heat to medium-high, add mushrooms and sauté until tender, about 5 minutes. Add vermouth and cook, stirring occasionally, until liquid is almost evaporated, about 2 minutes. Blend in mustard; do not boil. Season with salt and pepper to taste. Serve hot.

CREAMED MUSHROOMS

Delicious over toast points as a side dish with roast chicken.

4 servings

- 3 tablespoons butter
- 1/3 cup chopped green onions
- 1/2 pound mushrooms, thinly sliced
- 1 1/2 teaspoons soy sauce
  Salt and freshly ground pepper
- 1 cup whipping cream

Melt butter in heavy medium skillet over medium heat. Add onions and cook until softened, stirring occasionally, about 5 minutes. Stir in mushrooms and soy sauce. Season with salt and pepper. Cook 3 minutes, stirring occasionally. Reduce heat to low. Add cream and cook until thickened, stirring occasionally, about 10 minutes.

GOLDEN BAKED ONIONS

This can be served either as a side dish or with a salad to make a complete meal.

6 servings

- Butter
- 1/2 cup (1 stick) butter
- 6 medium onions, sliced
- 1 10 3/4-ounce can cream of chicken soup
- 1 cup milk
  Salt and freshly ground pepper
- 3/4 pound Gruyère or Swiss cheese, grated
- French bread slices
  Melted butter

Preheat oven to 350°F. Butter 2-quart shallow oval baking dish. Melt 1/2 cup butter in large skillet over medium heat. Add onions and cook until tender and translucent, stirring frequently, about 15 minutes. Transfer onions to prepared dish. Combine soup, milk, salt and pepper in bowl. Pour over onions. Sprinkle with grated cheese. Dip bread slices in melted butter on 1 side. Arrange buttered side up over onion mixture to cover completely. Bake until bread is browned, about 30 minutes. Serve hot.

CALIFORNIA-STYLE STUFFED PEPPERS

4 servings

- 4 green bell peppers, tops cut off, cored and seeded
- 1 large carrot, peeled and grated
- 1 1/4 cups corn kernels
- 1/4 cup chopped walnuts
- 1/4 cup raisins
- 4 tablespoons (1/2 stick) butter, room temperature
- 3 tablespoons dry breadcrumbs
- 2 tablespoons unsalted shelled sunflower seeds
- 2 tablespoons grated onion
  Salt and freshly ground pepper
- 2 tablespoons shredded cheddar cheese

Cook peppers in large saucepan of boiling water 5 minutes. Rinse under cold water; drain.

Preheat oven to 350°F. Lightly butter 8-inch square ovenproof glass baking dish. Combine carrot, corn, walnuts, raisins, 2 tablespoons butter, 1 tablespoon breadcrumbs, sunflower seeds, onion, salt and pepper in large bowl and mix well. Arrange peppers in prepared dish. Divide mixture among peppers. Top each with cheese and remaining breadcrumbs. Dot with remaining butter. Bake until heated through, about 30 minutes.

CORN SOUFFLE-FILLED PEPPERS

6 servings

6 red or green bell peppers, tops cut off and reserved, cored and seeded
1/4 cup (1/2 stick) butter
1/2 cup chopped onion
1/4 cup chopped fresh parsley
2 garlic cloves, minced
1 tablespoon all purpose flour
1/3 cup whipping cream
3 eggs, separated
1 cup fresh corn kernels or 1 cup canned, drained
1/3 cup freshly grated Parmesan cheese
Salt and freshly ground pepper

Preheat oven to 375°F. Place peppers in glass baking dish. Stem and chop pepper tops. Melt 1/4 cup butter in heavy large skillet over medium heat. Add chopped pepper tops and onion and cook until softened, stirring frequently, about 5 minutes. Add parsley and garlic and stir until onions are translucent, about 3 minutes. Stir in flour. Slowly add cream and stir until thickened, about 1 minute. Remove from heat. Whisk in yolks. Stir in corn and Parmesan. Season with salt and pepper. Transfer mixture to large bowl and cool for 5 minutes.

In another bowl, beat egg whites until stiff but not dry. Gently fold whites into corn mixture. Divide evenly among peppers. Bake until browned, 25 to 30 minutes.

RANCH-STYLE POTATO SLICES

4 to 6 servings

6 medium baking potatoes, unpeeled, cut into 1/2-inch-thick slices
1 cup water
1 cup prepared cheese sauce, heated
1 cup prepared ranch salad dressing
1/4 cup chopped green onions
1/2 cup crumbled cooked bacon

Preheat oven to 400°F. Place potato slices in nonstick 8-inch square baking pan. Pour water over. Cover and bake until potatoes are tender but not crumbly, about 40 minutes. Drain off water. Pour cheese sauce and ranch dressing over potatoes. Sprinkle with green onions and bacon. Serve immediately.

HOMESTYLE SAGE POTATOES

3 to 4 servings

2 tablespoons (1/4 stick) butter
1 small onion, thinly sliced
1 garlic clove, minced
2 small unpeeled potatoes, sliced in half lengthwise, then paper-thin crosswise, to form half circles
1 tablespoon coarsely chopped fresh sage or 1 teaspoon dried, crumbled

Melt butter in large nonstick skillet over medium-low heat. Add onion and garlic and stir until translucent, 2 to 3 minutes. Add potatoes and sage. Cover and cook 10 minutes, stirring occasionally. Turn potatoes over using spatula. Continue cooking until bottom is golden brown, about 5 minutes.

GRUYERE POTATOES

8 to 10 servings

2 1/2 pounds red new potatoes, peeled

2 1/2 cups shredded Gruyère cheese
Salt and freshly ground pepper
1 cup half and half

Boil potatoes until almost tender, about 20 minutes. Drain. Slice thinly.
Preheat oven to 350°F. Lightly butter 2-quart baking dish. Layer half of potatoes in prepared dish. Top with half of cheese and salt and pepper. Add remaining potatoes. Pour half and half over. Top with remaining cheese. Bake until lightly browned and potatoes are tender, about 35 minutes.

CONFETTI MASHED POTATOES

6 to 8 servings

7 medium russet potatoes, peeled
1/2 cup milk
1/4 cup (1/2 stick) butter, room temperature
1 8-ounce package cream cheese, cut into chunks, room temperature
1/2 cup chopped green onions
1 2-ounce jar chopped pimientos, well drained
Salt and freshly ground pepper
1 egg, beaten to blend

Place potatoes in large saucepan. Cover with cold water and boil until tender. Drain. Mash potatoes with milk and butter in large bowl. Mix in cream cheese, green onions and pimientos. Season with salt and pepper. Stir in egg. Transfer potatoes to 9x13-inch glass baking dish. (*Can be prepared 1 day ahead. Cover and refrigerate.*)
Preheat oven to 350°F. Bake potatoes until puffed and light brown, about 25 minutes.

GOLDEN CREAMY MASHED POTATOES

6 servings

8 medium potatoes, peeled and cut into 1-inch cubes
12 tablespoons (1 1/2 sticks) margarine
2 medium onions, finely chopped
1 1/2 cups sour cream
Salt and freshly ground pepper
1 tablespoon paprika

Grease 10-inch pie pan. Place potatoes in large saucepan or Dutch oven. Add water to cover. Bring to boil. Reduce heat and simmer until potatoes are tender, about 15 minutes.
Meanwhile, melt 4 tablespoons margarine in heavy small skillet over medium heat. Add onions and stir until golden, about 5 minutes. Set aside.
Preheat oven to 350°F. Drain potatoes well. Transfer to large bowl. Lightly mash with potato masher. Add remaining 8 tablespoons margarine,

sour cream, salt and pepper. Using electric mixer, beat on high speed until smooth and creamy. Spoon mixture into prepared pie pan. Spread sautéed onions evenly over top. Sprinkle with paprika. (*Can be prepared 1 day ahead, covered and refrigerated.*)

Bake uncovered until golden brown, 30 minutes. Serve hot.

MICROWAVE POTATOES ROMANOFF

MICROWAVE

6 to 8 servings

- 4 medium potatoes (about 2¹/₂ pounds)
- 2 tablespoons (¹/₄ stick) butter
- 3 medium onions (about 1¹/₂ pounds), grated
- 1¹/₄ cups grated cheddar cheese
- 1 cup sour cream
- 1 teaspoon salt
- ¹/₄ teaspoon freshly ground pepper
- ¹/₄ teaspoon paprika

Pierce potatoes with fork. Arrange in circle in microwave. Cook on High until tender, 12 to 15 minutes. Cool slightly. Peel; shred in food processor.

Melt butter on High in 1¹/₂-quart casserole. Add grated onion and stir to coat. Cover and cook on High until translucent, about 5 minutes, stirring once or twice. Blend in potatoes, ³/₄ cup cheese, sour cream, salt, pepper and paprika. Sprinkle with remaining ¹/₂ cup cheese. Cook, uncovered, on High until heated through, 12 to 15 minutes.

HASH BROWN BAKE

8 to 10 servings

- 1 2-pound package frozen hash browns, thawed
- 2¹/₂ cups grated sharp cheddar cheese
- 2 cups sour cream
- 1 10³/₄-ounce can cream of chicken soup
- ¹/₂ cup chopped onion
- ¹/₄ cup (¹/₂ stick) butter, melted
  Salt and freshly ground pepper

- 2 cups cornflakes cereal, crushed
- ¹/₂ cup (1 stick) butter, melted

Preheat oven to 350°F. Lightly butter 7x10-inch ovenproof glass baking dish. Combine first 6 ingredients in large bowl. Season with salt and pepper. Transfer to prepared baking dish. Mix cornflakes and ¹/₂ cup butter and sprinkle over potato mixture. Bake until browned, about 45 minutes.

DILLED POTATO PANCAKES

Makes about six 4-inch pancakes

- 1 large baking potato, peeled and grated
- 1 egg, beaten to blend
- 1¹/₂ teaspoons minced fresh dill or ¹/₂ teaspoon dried dillweed
  Salt and freshly ground pepper

  Vegetable oil (for frying)

Place potato in medium bowl. Cover with cold water. Let stand 10 minutes. Drain. Pat dry with paper towels. Combine potato, egg and dill in medium bowl. Season with salt and freshly ground pepper.

Pour enough oil into heavy large skillet to come ¹/₄ inch up sides. Heat to 350°F. Spoon batter into skillet by 2 heaping tablespoonfuls; flatten with spatula to 4-inch cakes. Cook until golden brown, 3 to 4 minutes per side. Transfer to paper towels and drain well. Serve immediately.

ROSEMARY ROSTI

This is an especially easy version of the famous Swiss potato pancake.

2 to 4 servings

- 1¹/₄ pounds baking potatoes, peeled and shredded
- 2 tablespoons (¹/₄ stick) butter
- 2 tablespoons olive oil
- 2 teaspoons chopped fresh rosemary
  Salt and freshly ground pepper
  Fresh rosemary sprig

Pat potatoes dry with paper towels. Melt butter with oil in heavy 12-inch skillet over medium heat. Add potatoes to skillet and press to form

cake. Sprinkle with chopped rosemary, salt and pepper. Cook until crisp, about 6 minutes per side. Garnish with rosemary sprig. Serve hot.

STIR-FRIED ROMAINE, SUGAR SNAPS AND GREEN ONIONS

8 servings

- 2 tablespoons soy sauce
- 2 tablespoons oriental sesame oil
- 2 teaspoons white wine vinegar
- 1 teaspoon sugar
- 1 tablespoon vegetable oil
- 2 large heads romaine lettuce, sliced crosswise into 1-inch strips
- 1 pound sugar-snap or snow peas, trimmed
- ¹/₂ cup minced green onions
- 2 tablespoons toasted sesame seeds

Blend soy sauce, sesame oil, vinegar and sugar. Heat vegetable oil in wok or heavy deep skillet over medium-high heat. Add lettuce and peas and toss 2 minutes. Pour in soy sauce mixture.

Remove from heat. Cover and let stand until lettuce wilts, about 2 minutes. Sprinkle with green onions and sesame seeds. Serve immediately.

SPINACH WITH CARAMELIZED ONIONS

2 to 4 servings

- 3 tablespoons olive oil
- 1 large red onion, thinly sliced
- 1 pound fresh spinach leaves, stemmed
- 1 tablespoon fresh lemon juice
  Freshly ground pepper

Heat oil in heavy large skillet over medium-high heat until hot but not smoking. Add onion and sauté, stirring constantly, until onion is caramelized, about 15 minutes. Continue cooking until some of onion is dark and crisp, about 3 minutes. Quickly add spinach and stir until just wilted but still bright green. Remove from heat. Add lemon juice and pepper. Toss gently. Serve immediately.

SPINACH-FETA STRUDEL

8 to 10 servings

Butter
1 1/2 cups (3 sticks) butter
3 tablespoons olive oil
1 1/2 cups minced onions
3 10-ounce packages frozen chopped spinach, thawed and drained
1/2 pound feta cheese, chopped
5 eggs, beaten to blend
1/2 cup chopped green onions
1 1/2 teaspoons dried dillweed

1 pound phyllo pastry sheets

Preheat oven to 375°F. Butter 9x13-inch baking dish. Melt 1/2 cup butter with oil in medium skillet over medium heat. Add onion and sauté until golden, about 10 minutes. Transfer to large bowl with slotted spoon. Mix in spinach, cheese, eggs, green onions and dried dillweed.

Melt remaining 1 cup butter in same skillet. Layer half of phyllo in prepared dish, brushing with melted butter between each sheet; stagger sheets or fold edges under to fit. Top with filling, spreading evenly. Layer remaining phyllo over filling, brushing with melted butter between each sheet. Using sharp knife, cut through top layers to mark 2-inch squares. Bake until top is puffy and golden brown, 30 to 35 minutes. Cut strudel into squares and serve.

SPINACH AND LENTIL PILAF

4 servings

3 tablespoons butter
1 large bunch spinach, chopped
1 garlic clove, minced
1 cup cooked lentils
1 tablespoon chopped fresh parsley
1/4 teaspoon ground cumin
1/4 teaspoon ground coriander
Salt and freshly ground pepper
1 tablespoon butter, melted

Melt 3 tablespoons butter in heavy large skillet over medium-high heat. Add spinach and garlic and stir until spinach is wilted, about 3 minutes. Add lentils, parsley, cumin, coriander, salt and pepper and stir until just heated through; do not overcook. Top with melted butter.

BUTTERNUT SQUASH AND SHALLOTS WITH CUMIN AND TURMERIC

6 servings

1/4 cup (1/2 stick) butter
1 teaspoon cumin seeds
1/2 teaspoon turmeric
1 1 3/4-pound butternut squash, peeled, seeded and cut into 1-inch pieces
12 shallots, peeled
Salt and freshly ground pepper
2 teaspoons sugar

Melt butter in heavy large skillet over medium-low heat. Add cumin and turmeric and stir 1 minute. Add squash and shallots. Season with salt and pepper; stir to coat with butter. Cover and cook until squash is just tender, stirring occasionally, about 25 minutes. (*Can be prepared 4 hours ahead. Reheat before continuing, stirring occasionally.*) Just before serving, sprinkle with sugar and stir gently to blend.

CINNAMON CARROT-STUFFED SQUASH

8 servings

4 large crookneck squash

4 large carrots, peeled and cut into 1-inch pieces
2 tablespoons (1/4 stick) butter
1 cup chopped onions

1 teaspoon honey
1/2 teaspoon cinnamon
Salt
Freshly grated Parmesan cheese

Cook squash in large saucepan of boiling water until tender, about 8 minutes. Remove using slotted spoon and drain. Halve lengthwise and scoop seeds from centers. Place halves on broiler pan; set aside.

Cook carrots in same saucepan of boiling water until soft, about 15 minutes. Meanwhile, melt 1 tablespoon butter in medium skillet over medium heat. Add onions and stir until golden and beginning to brown, about 10 minutes. Set aside.

Preheat broiler. Drain carrots. Transfer to food processor or blender. Add onion, remaining butter, honey, cinnamon and salt; puree. Mound mixture in squash. Top with Parmesan. Broil until golden, 5 minutes.

ITALIAN SPAGHETTI SQUASH

MICROWAVE

4 to 6 servings

1 2-pound spaghetti squash
1/4 cup water
1 small zucchini, thinly sliced
6 medium mushrooms, thinly sliced
2 tablespoons (1/4 stick) butter or margarine
1 large garlic clove, minced
Dash of salt
1/2 teaspoon dried basil, crumbled
1/4 teaspoon dried oregano, crumbled
1/4 teaspoon salt
1/8 teaspoon freshly ground pepper
1 large tomato, seeded and diced
1/3 cup freshly grated Parmesan cheese

Cut squash in half lengthwise and discard seeds and loose strings. Place squash cut side up in large shallow dish. Add 1/4 cup water to dish. Cover with plastic wrap. Cook on High until tender, 7 to 8 minutes. Loosen spaghettilike strands with fork and scrape out. Set aside. Combine zucchini, mushrooms, butter, garlic and dash of salt in large glass bowl. Cook on High 2 minutes, stirring twice. Add squash, basil, oregano, 1/4 teaspoon salt and pepper and toss well. Mix in tomato. Sprinkle Parmesan over top. Cook on High until Parmesan melts, about 2 minutes. Serve hot.

NO-EGGPLANT RATATOUILLE

6 servings

- 1/2 teaspoon dried oregano, crumbled
- 1/2 teaspoon dried marjoram, crumbled
- 1/8 teaspoon dried sage, crumbled
  Salt and freshly ground pepper
- 1/2 cup (1 stick) butter, cut into 8 pieces
- 2 medium yellow onions, coarsely chopped
- 1/4 pound mushrooms, thickly sliced
- 5 green onions, white parts sliced, green tops finely chopped
- 2 large garlic cloves, minced
- 1 yellow chili* (optional), seeded and sliced
- 2 yellow crookneck squash, sliced 1/4 inch thick
- 2 small zucchini, sliced 1/4 inch thick
- 1 green bell pepper, seeded and cut into chunks
- 1 red bell pepper, seeded and cut into chunks
- 2 medium tomatoes, seeded and coarsely chopped
- 2 tablespoons soy sauce

- 1 tablespoon cornstarch
- 1/4 cup water
- 1 cup broccoli florets

Mix oregano, marjoram, sage, salt and pepper in small bowl. Place 4 pieces of butter in Dutch oven. Top with onions, mushrooms, sliced onions, half of garlic, chili (if desired), squash, zucchini, bell peppers, remaining garlic, tomatoes, soy sauce and remaining 4 pieces butter, sprinkling herb mixture between layers. Cook over high heat until vegetables begin sizzling, about 1 minute. Cover and cook 1 minute. Do not stir. Reduce heat to low and continue cooking ratatouille for 20 minutes without stirring.

Dissolve cornstarch in water. Add cornstarch and broccoli to vegetables. Increase heat to medium. Stir rata-touille until thickened and broccoli is crisp-tender. Garnish with chopped green onion tops. Serve hot.

*Also known as a guero chili.

DEEP-FRIED SWEET POTATOES

8 servings

- 3 cups peanut oil
- 6 small to medium sweet potatoes, scrubbed, quartered lengthwise and patted dry
- 1 cup sugar
- 2 teaspoons cinnamon
- 1/2 teaspoon freshly grated nutmeg

Heat oil in deep fryer to 375°F. Add potatoes and fry until golden brown, 6 to 8 minutes. Drain briefly on paper towels. Combine remaining ingredients in shallow plate. Roll potato pieces in sugar mixture.

SWEET POTATO-APPLE CASSEROLE

MICROWAVE

4 to 6 servings

- 6 medium-size sweet potatoes (about 5 pounds)
- 4 medium apples, cored and thinly sliced (about 1 pound)
- 1/2 cup firmly packed brown sugar
- 1/2 cup chopped walnuts or pecans
- 1/4 cup (1/2 stick) butter or margarine, melted
- 1/4 cup fresh orange juice
- 1 tablespoon freshly grated orange peel
- 1 teaspoon cinnamon
- 1/4 teaspoon mace

Pierce potatoes with fork. Arrange on microwave-safe rack. Cook on High 20 minutes, turning halfway through cooking time. Peel potatoes and slice thinly. Arrange apples in shallow glass or ceramic baking dish. Sprinkle with sugar. Layer potato slices evenly over apples. Sprinkle nuts over potatoes. Combine remaining ingredients in small bowl. Pour over top. Cover and cook on High until apples are tender, 5 to 7 minutes. Serve warm.

SAUTEED CHERRY TOMATOES

4 servings

- 2 tablespoons butter
- 1 pint cherry tomatoes
- 2 medium-size green onions, sliced diagonally
- 1 tablespoon chopped fresh parsley
- 1 teaspoon dried basil, crumbled
- 1 small garlic clove, minced
  Pinch of onion powder

Melt butter in large skillet over high heat. Add remaining ingredients and sauté 1 minute. Serve immediately.

MUSHROOM-STUFFED TOMATOES

6 servings

- 1 tablespoon butter
- 1 tablespoon vegetable oil
- 1 pound mushrooms, thinly sliced
- 1/2 cup minced fresh parsley
- 1/4 cup dry white wine
- 2 garlic cloves, minced

- 1/3 cup seasoned breadcrumbs
- 1/4 cup freshly grated Parmesan cheese
  Olive oil
- 6 large tomatoes, tops sliced off, pulp removed and shells drained

Melt butter with oil in large skillet over medium heat. Add mushrooms and cook until soft, stirring occasionally, about 10 minutes. Mix in parsley, wine and garlic. Increase heat to medium-high and simmer until almost all liquid evaporates, about 5 minutes. Remove from heat. Cool slightly.

Position rack in upper third of oven and preheat to 400°F. Combine breadcrumbs and cheese with enough olive oil to moisten. Divide mushroom mixture among tomato shells. Sprinkle with breadcrumbs. Arrange in 8-inch square baking dish. Bake until crumbs are golden brown, 10 to 15 minutes.

HERBED TURNIPS DAUPHINOIS

4 servings

    1 large garlic clove
      Butter
    1 pound young turnips, peeled
      and thinly sliced
    2 tablespoons all purpose flour
  1/4 cup snipped fresh chives
 1 1/4 cups whipping cream
  1/2 teaspoon (or more) salt
  1/2 teaspoon freshly ground pepper
  1/4 teaspoon freshly grated nutmeg

Preheat oven to 350°F. Rub 7x10-inch porcelain or glass baking dish with garlic. Butter generously. Add 1/3 of turnips. Sprinkle with 1 tablespoon flour, then 1/3 of chives. Add 1/3 of turnips, sprinkle with 1 tablespoon flour and 1/3 of chives. Top with remaining turnips and sprinkle with remaining chives. Scald cream with 1/2 teaspoon salt, pepper and nutmeg. Taste cream mixture, adding more salt if desired. Pour over turnips. Cover with foil and bake 30 minutes. Remove foil and continue baking until turnips are tender, top browns and cream thickens, about 20 minutes. Serve hot.

ZUCCHINI AU GRATIN

6 to 8 servings

      Butter
 1 1/2 tablespoons butter
 1 1/2 tablespoons all purpose flour
  3/4 cup milk
    1 tablespoon fresh lemon juice
  1/4 teaspoon freshly grated nutmeg
  1/8 teaspoon hot pepper sauce
    3 medium zucchini, grated
    1 egg, beaten to blend
      Salt and freshly ground pepper
    3 tablespoons fresh breadcrumbs
    3 tablespoons freshly grated
      Parmesan cheese

Preheat oven to 425°F. Lightly butter 8-inch glass pie pan. Melt 1 1/2 tablespoons butter in heavy medium skillet over medium heat. Add flour and stir 1 minute. Add milk and stir until thickened and smooth, 1 to 2 minutes. Mix in lemon juice, nutmeg and hot pepper sauce. Remove from heat. Stir in zucchini and egg. Season with salt and pepper. Transfer mixture to prepared pie pan. Combine breadcrumbs and Parmesan. Sprinkle over zucchini. Bake until set and golden brown, about 35 minutes. Serve immediately.

ZUCCHINI ANISETTE

4 to 6 servings

    2 tablespoons vegetable oil
    6 medium zucchini, peeled,
      quartered and cut into 1/2-inch
      pieces
      Salt and freshly ground pepper
 7 1/2 teaspoons white wine vinegar
    2 tablespoons anisette

Heat oil in heavy medium skillet over high heat. Add zucchini and cook until tender, stirring frequently, 4 to 5 minutes. Transfer to platter using slotted spoon. Do not wash skillet. Season zucchini with salt and pepper. Stir vinegar and anisette into skillet. Bring to boil. Reduce heat and simmer 2 minutes. Pour over zucchini. Serve hot.

DOUBLE CHEESE AND ZUCCHINI BAKE

10 to 12 servings

      Butter
  1/2 cup (1 stick) butter
    1 medium onion, chopped
    2 garlic cloves, minced
    8 medium zucchini, sliced
    2 cups shredded Monterey Jack
      cheese
    1 cup freshly grated Parmesan
      cheese
  1/2 cup dry breadcrumbs
    1 teaspoon Italian seasoning
      Salt and freshly ground pepper

    3 eggs, beaten to blend
  1/2 cup whipping cream

Preheat oven to 350°F. Butter 9x13-inch glass baking dish. Melt 1/4 cup butter in heavy large skillet over medium-high heat. Add onion and garlic and cook until softened, stirring occasionally, 4 to 5 minutes. Add zucchini and cook until just tender, stirring frequently, about 10 minutes. Remove from heat. Stir in 1 cup Monterey Jack cheese, 1/2 cup Parmesan, 1/4 cup breadcrumbs and Italian seasoning. Season with salt and pepper.

Transfer mixture to prepared dish. Sprinkle remaining Monterey Jack cheese over. Combine eggs and cream. Pour over zucchini. Sprinkle remaining Parmesan and breadcrumbs over. Dot with remaining 1/4 cup butter. Bake until golden brown, about 35 minutes. (*Can be prepared 1 day ahead. Cover and chill. Rewarm before serving.*)

QUICK ZUCCHINI PANCAKES

Makes about 6 pancakes

    2 cups grated unpeeled zucchini
      (about 2 large)
  1/3 cup buttermilk baking mix
  1/4 cup freshly grated Parmesan
      cheese
    1 egg, lightly beaten
    1 teaspoon finely chopped onion
  1/8 teaspoon freshly ground pepper
    2 tablespoons (1/4 stick) butter
    6 tablespoons shredded cheddar
      cheese

Combine first 6 ingredients in medium bowl. Melt butter in heavy large skillet over medium heat. Drop batter into skillet by tablespoons and cook until golden brown, about 3 to 4 minutes per side. Sprinkle 1 tablespoon cheese over each pancake and serve hot.

PLUM TOMATO AND ZUCCHINI MEDLEY

MICROWAVE

6 to 8 servings

    5 Italian plum tomatoes,
      1 1/2 inches in diameter, sliced
      1/4 inch thick
    2 medium zucchini, 1 1/2 inches in
      diameter, sliced 1/4 inch thick
    2 small white onions, 1 1/2 inches
      in diameter, thinly sliced

    3 tablespoons butter, melted
    1 tablespoon tomato paste
  1/2 teaspoon dried basil, crumbled
  1/2 teaspoon dried oregano,
      crumbled
  1/8 teaspoon salt
  1/8 teaspoon freshly ground pepper

Arrange tomatoes, zucchini and onions, alternating slices, in concentric rings in 2-quart round glass baking dish.

Whisk remaining ingredients in small bowl. Pour over vegetables. Cover and cook on High until vegetables are crisp-tender, about 6 minutes.

SUMMER VEGETABLE SKEWERS WITH CUMIN BUTTER

2 servings; can be doubled or tripled

- 1 small red bell pepper, seeded and cut into 1¹/2-inch squares
- 1 small yellow bell pepper, seeded and cut into 1¹/2-inch squares
- 2 small ears fresh corn, husked and cut into 1-inch-thick rounds

Cumin Butter
- 6 tablespoons (³/4 stick) butter
- ³/8 teaspoon ground cumin
- ¹/4 teaspoon dried red pepper flakes
  Salt and freshly ground pepper

1¹/2 tablespoons chopped fresh cilantro

Prepare barbecue grill (medium heat). Alternate vegetables on 4 skewers.

For butter: Melt butter with cumin, red pepper flakes, salt and pepper in heavy small saucepan. Remove from heat and stir in chopped cilantro.

Arrange skewers on barbecue rack. Brush with some of butter. Grill until vegetables are just crisp-tender and beginning to char, turning and basting occasionally, about 15 minutes. Remove from grill. Brush with butter.

VEGETABLES AU GRATIN

4 to 6 servings

- ¹/4 cup (¹/2 stick) butter
- ³/4 cup diced green bell peppers
- 1 garlic clove, crushed
- ¹/4 cup all purpose flour
- ²/3 cup milk
- ³/4 teaspoon salt

- ¹/4 teaspoon sugar
- ¹/8 teaspoon freshly ground pepper
- ¹/8 teaspoon dried basil, crumbled
- ¹/8 teaspoon dried oregano, crumbled
- 1 cup grated cheddar cheese
- 1 1-pound can stewed tomatoes, drained
- 1 1-pound can whole onions, drained
- 1 10-ounce package frozen corn, thawed

Preheat oven to 350°F. Melt butter in 10-inch skillet over medium heat. Add green bell peppers and garlic and sauté 2 to 3 minutes. Add flour and stir 2 minutes. Blend in milk, salt, sugar, pepper, basil and oregano and stir until thickened, about 2 minutes. Remove from heat. Add ¹/2 cup cheese with tomatoes, onions and corn. Turn mixture into 2-quart baking dish. Sprinkle with remaining cheese. Bake until vegetable mixture is heated through and cheese is melted, approximately 35 minutes. Serve warm.

Rice and Grains

PARMESAN-WINE RICE

2 to 4 servings

- 1 tablespoon butter
- 1 medium onion, chopped
- 1 garlic clove, minced
- 1 cup chicken broth
- ³/4 cup rice
- ¹/2 cup dry white wine
- ¹/2 cup freshly grated Parmesan cheese

Melt butter in heavy medium skillet over medium heat. Add onion and garlic and cook until translucent, stirring occasionally, about 8 minutes. Stir in broth, rice and wine. Bring to boil. Reduce heat to low. Cover and cook until liquid is absorbed, about 25 minutes. Mix in Parmesan.

MEXICAN RICE

This would make a tasty accompaniment to any south-of-the-border main dish.

4 servings

- 2 cups freshly cooked white rice
- 1 cup shredded Monterey Jack cheese
- 1 cup sour cream
- ¹/2 cup diced green chilies

Preheat oven to 350°F. Butter 1-quart baking dish. Mix all ingredients in bowl. Turn into dish. Cover and bake until cheese melts and rice is heated through, about 20 minutes.

HERBED RICE

MICROWAVE

4 to 6 servings

- 2 cups water
- 1 cup long-grain rice
- 6 medium mushrooms, sliced
- 2 tablespoons (¹/4 stick) butter
- 2 tablespoons chopped chives
- 2 beef bouillon cubes
- ¹/2 teaspoon dried basil, crumbled
- ¹/2 teaspoon dried marjoram, crumbled
  Freshly ground pepper

Combine all ingredients in 3-quart glass baking dish. Cover and cook on High 15 minutes. Let stand 8 to 10 minutes. Fluff rice with fork and serve.

FRESH CILANTRO PILAF

6 to 8 servings

> 1 tablespoon vegetable oil
> 1/2 cup unsalted cashews
>
> 1/4 cup (1/2 stick) butter
> 1 small cinnamon stick
> 6 to 8 whole black peppercorns
> 5 whole cloves
> 4 cardamom pods
> 2 cups long-grain rice
> 1 cup finely chopped fresh cilantro
> Salt and freshly ground pepper
> 3 1/2 cups water

Heat oil in heavy small saucepan over medium heat. Add cashews and cook until golden, stirring frequently, about 5 minutes. Set cashews aside.

Melt butter in heavy medium saucepan over medium-high heat. Stir in cinnamon, peppercorns, cloves and cardamom. Add rice and cook until beginning to brown, stirring frequently, about 9 minutes. Stir in cilantro. Season with salt and pepper. Add water. Bring to boil. Reduce heat, cover and simmer until rice is tender, about 15 minutes. Discard cinnamon stick. Garnish rice with cashews.

ORZO-RICE PILAF WITH LEMON SAUCE

Serve this as a side dish with quickly sautéed chicken breasts.

8 servings

Pilaf
> 1/2 cup (1 stick) butter
> 1 cup orzo (rice-shaped pasta)
> 4 cups water
> 1 cup long-grain rice
> 3 chicken bouillon cubes

Lemon Sauce
> 5 egg yolks
> 1 tablespoon cornstarch
> 1/8 teaspoon cayenne pepper
> 1 1/2 cups water
> 1 chicken bouillon cube
> 1/4 cup fresh lemon juice

For pilaf: Melt butter in 2-quart saucepan over medium-high heat. Add orzo and cook until golden, stirring constantly, about 10 minutes. Add 4 cups water, rice and 3 bouillon cubes and bring to boil. Reduce heat to low, cover and simmer until liquid is absorbed and orzo and rice are tender, about 30 minutes.

Meanwhile, prepare Lemon Sauce: Whisk yolks, cornstarch and cayenne pepper in 1-quart saucepan until well blended. Stir in 1 1/2 cups water and 1 bouillon cube. Cook over medium-low heat, stirring constantly, until thickened; *do not boil.* Stir in lemon juice. Serve; pass sauce separately.

PECAN PILAF

6 to 8 servings

> 1/2 cup (1 stick) butter or margarine
> 1 cup chopped pecans
> 1/2 cup chopped onion
> 2 cups long-grain rice
>
> 2 cups canned chicken broth
> 2 cups water
> 1/2 teaspoon salt (optional)
> 1/4 teaspoon dried thyme, crumbled
> 1/8 teaspoon freshly ground pepper
> 3 tablespoons chopped fresh parsley

Melt 3 tablespoons butter in large skillet over medium-high heat. Add pecans and sauté until lightly browned, about 2 to 3 minutes. Transfer pecans to small bowl using slotted spoon. Cover and set aside. Melt remaining butter in same skillet. Add onion and sauté until tender, about 5 minutes. Add rice and stir until evenly coated, about 2 minutes.

Meanwhile, bring broth, water, salt, thyme, pepper and 2 tablespoons parsley to boil in medium saucepan over medium-high heat. Add to rice. Cover, reduce heat to low and simmer until liquid is absorbed, about 20 minutes. Add pecans and remaining parsley. Fluff with fork and serve.

VEGETABLE-RICE MEDLEY

2 servings

> 1 cup broccoli florets
> 3/4 cup sliced peeled carrots
> 3/4 cup red bell pepper julienne
> 1/2 cup sliced onions
> 1 tablespoon bacon bits
> 1 1/2 cups brown rice, freshly cooked
> 2 tablespoons (1/4 stick) butter, room temperature
> 1 tablespoon chopped fresh basil
> 1/4 cup freshly grated Parmesan cheese

Combine first 4 ingredients in steamer over boiling water. Steam until tender, about 4 minutes. Add bacon bits and steam until heated through, about 1 minute. Toss hot rice with butter and basil. Mound on platter. Top with vegetables. Sprinkle with Parmesan.

ITALIAN FRIED RICE

4 servings

> 2 tablespoons vegetable oil
> 2 medium onions, chopped
> 6 Italian sweet or hot sausages, casings removed
> 2 carrots, diced (about 1 cup)
> 1 bunch broccoli florets
> 4 cups cooked brown rice
> 1 tablespoon tamari sauce
> 3 eggs, beaten
> 1 teaspoon Worcestershire sauce
> Hot pepper sauce

Heat 1 tablespoon oil in heavy large skillet or wok over medium-high heat until hot but not smoking. Add onions and sauté until golden, stirring frequently, about 10 to 12 minutes. Remove from skillet and set aside. Add sausage and cook until no longer pink, breaking into chunks with fork, about 7 to 8 minutes. Remove mixture to plate; drain fat from skillet. Add 1 tablespoon oil and heat over medium heat until hot but not smoking. Add carrots and broccoli and cook until crisp-tender. Stir in sausage, onions and rice. Whisk tamari sauce into beaten eggs and add to skillet, mixing thoroughly. Blend in Worcestershire and hot pepper sauces to taste.

SAUSAGE AND WILD RICE CASSEROLE

Delicious with roast chicken.

6 to 8 servings

    1 pound bulk sausage
    1/2 cup chopped celery
    1/2 cup chopped onion
    1/2 cup sliced mushrooms

    2 cups water
    1 10³/4-ounce can cream of
      mushroom soup
    1 cup wild rice
    1 cup grated cheddar cheese
      Salt and freshly ground pepper

Preheat oven to 325°F. Cook sausage in heavy large skillet over medium-high heat until browned, breaking up with spoon, about 5 minutes. Add celery, onion and mushrooms and cook until tender, stirring occasionally, about 5 minutes.

Pour off drippings from skillet. Mix in water, soup, rice and cheese. Season with salt and pepper. Transfer mixture to 9x13-inch glass baking dish. Bake until rice is tender and top of casserole is browned, about 1½ hours.

GARDEN RICE

4 servings

    3 tablespoons butter
    3/4 cup chopped onions
    1 pound zucchini, thinly sliced
      (about 3½ cups)
    3 cups cooked rice
    1 cup chopped canned tomatoes,
      drained
    1 cup fresh or thawed frozen
      corn kernels
    1½ teaspoons salt
    1/4 teaspoon freshly ground pepper
    1/4 teaspoon ground coriander
    1/8 to 1/4 teaspoon dried oregano,
      crumbled

Melt butter in heavy large skillet or wok over medium-high heat. Add onions and cook until tender, about 3 to 4 minutes. Add remaining ingredients, increase heat to high and stir-fry until heated through, about 3 minutes. Serve immediately.

SONORAN RICE

6 to 8 servings

    1 28-ounce can whole peeled
      tomatoes, drained and chopped
    2 cups tomato juice
    1½ cups finely chopped onions
    1 cup water
    1 cup canned diced mild green
      chilies, drained
    2 tablespoons (1/4 stick) butter
    1 small jalapeño chili, seeded and
      finely chopped
    2 teaspoons chopped fresh basil
      or 3/4 teaspoon dried, crumbled
    2 teaspoons garlic powder
    1½ teaspoons ground cumin
    1 teaspoon freshly ground white
      pepper
    3/4 teaspoon ground coriander
      Salt
    1½ cups uncooked rice

Preheat oven to 375°F. Combine all ingredients except rice in 5-quart flame-proof casserole. Stir over high heat until butter melts, about 4 minutes. Reduce heat to medium. Add rice. Cover, transfer to oven and bake until liquid is absorbed, about 35 minutes.

BARLEY AND MUSHROOM PILAF

4 to 6 servings

    3 tablespoons butter
    1½ cups barley
    1 small onion, chopped
    2 4-ounce cans sliced
      mushrooms, drained
    2½ cups chicken broth

Preheat oven to 350°F. Melt butter in large skillet over medium heat. Add barley and sauté until golden and toasted, 6 to 8 minutes. Add onion and cook until soft, 3 to 5 minutes. Stir in mushrooms. Transfer to 2-quart baking dish. Add chicken broth. Cover and bake until all liquid is absorbed, about 1 hour. Serve hot.

MEDITERRANEAN PILAF

4 servings

    6 tablespoons (3/4 stick) butter
    1 ounce uncooked dry vermicelli
    1 cup coarse-ground bulgur
    1 mushroom bouillon cube
      dissolved in 1½ cups water
    1 tablespoon dried parsley,
      crumbled
    1 tablespoon minced onion flakes
    1 teaspoon dried mint, crumbled
    1 teaspoon salt (optional)

Melt butter in heavy 2-quart saucepan over medium heat. Break vermicelli into butter. Cook until golden, stirring frequently, about 4 minutes. Add bulgur and sauté until white specks appear, about 2 minutes. Add dissolved bouillon, parsley, onion, mint and salt. Reduce heat to low, cover and cook until bulgur is tender and liquid is absorbed, about 25 minutes. Fluff with fork and serve immediately. (*Can be prepared 6 hours ahead. Cool and cover. Reheat in double boiler.*)

SPICED COUSCOUS

6 servings

    1/4 cup (1/2 stick) butter
    1/4 teaspoon cinnamon
    1/4 teaspoon ground cardamom
    1/8 teaspoon ground cloves
    2¼ cups chicken stock or one
      14½-ounce can chicken broth
      plus enough water to measure
      2¼ cups
    1/2 cup dried currants
    1½ cups couscous
    2 tablespoons (1/4 stick) unsalted
      butter, room temperature
      Salt
    1/4 cup chopped toasted cashews or
      toasted pistachios

Melt 1/4 cup butter in heavy medium saucepan over low heat. Add spices and cook 2 minutes, stirring occasionally. Add stock and currants. (*Can be prepared 4 hours ahead.*) Bring to boil. Mix in couscous and 2 tablespoons butter. Cover and remove from heat. Let stand 5 minutes. Fluff with fork; season with salt. Transfer couscous to bowl, add nuts and toss well.

SPRING VEGETABLE COUSCOUS

4 servings

1½ cups chicken stock
  1 cup couscous

½ cup finely diced radishes
¼ cup thinly sliced green onion
    tops
  1 plum tomato, seeded and diced
  1 tablespoon olive oil
    Salt and freshly ground pepper

Bring stock to boil in heavy small saucepan. Pour over couscous in medium bowl; do not stir. Cover couscous and let stand 10 minutes.

Add radishes, green onions, tomato and oil to couscous and fluff with chopstick or fork to combine. Season with salt and pepper. Serve warm.

VEGETABLE AND CHICK-PEA COUSCOUS

2 servings; can be doubled or tripled

  2 tablespoons olive oil
  1 onion, sliced
¼ teaspoon (scant) turmeric
¼ teaspoon (scant) ground cumin
¼ teaspoon (scant) cinnamon
¼ teaspoon (scant) cayenne
    pepper
    Freshly ground pepper
  2 carrots, peeled and cut on
    diagonal into 1-inch pieces
  1 turnip or rutabaga, peeled,
    quartered lengthwise and cut
    crosswise into ½-inch-thick
    slices
4½ cups chicken broth
  1 zucchini, quartered lengthwise
    and cut into 1-inch-long pieces

  1 8¾-ounce can chick-peas
    (garbanzo beans), rinsed and
    drained
  1 tablespoon butter
  1 cup couscous
    Minced fresh cilantro

Heat oil in heavy medium saucepan over medium heat. Add onion and cook until softened, stirring occasionally, about 8 minutes. Add spices and stir 30 seconds. Mix in carrots and turnip. Add 3 cups broth and bring to boil. Reduce heat and simmer until vegetables are almost tender, stirring occasionally, about 30 minutes. Add zucchini and chick-peas and simmer until zucchini is crisp-tender, about 12 minutes. Adjust seasoning.

Meanwhile, bring remaining chicken broth and butter to boil in small saucepan. Mix in couscous. Cover pan and remove from heat. Let stand 5 minutes. Fluff with fork.

Spoon couscous onto plates. Top with vegetable mixture and broth. Sprinkle with cilantro and serve.

KASHA WITH MUSHROOMS AND SWISS CHARD

2 servings; can be doubled or tripled

  4 large Swiss chard stalks,
    trimmed
  4 tablespoons (½ stick) butter
½ medium onion, chopped
½ pound mushrooms, sliced
    Freshly ground pepper
  1 cup chicken broth
    Salt

½ cup whole kasha
  1 egg, beaten to blend

Remove ribs from chard leaves. Halve ribs lengthwise and slice thinly crosswise. Shred leaves. Melt 2 tablespoons butter in heavy medium saucepan over medium-low heat. Add onion and chard ribs and cook until onion is tender, stirring occasionally, about 10 minutes. Add mushrooms and shredded chard leaves. Season generously with pepper. Stir until mushrooms soften, about 5 minutes. Add broth and salt and bring to boil.

Meanwhile, combine kasha and ½ of egg (reserve remainder for another use) in medium bowl. Heat heavy large skillet over high heat. Add kasha and stir until egg dries and kasha kernels separate, about 3 minutes. Reduce heat to low. Add stock and vegetable mixture. Cover and cook until kasha is tender and liquid is absorbed, about 20 minutes. Add remaining 2 tablespoons butter and toss well. Serve immediately.

CRACKED WHEAT WITH TOASTED NUTS

4 to 6 servings

  2 cups water
  1 cup cracked wheat

¼ cup (½ stick) butter
¾ cup chopped walnuts or
    slivered almonds
  2 tablespoons tamari or soy sauce

Bring water to boil in heavy medium saucepan. Stir in cracked wheat. Reduce heat to low, cover and simmer (without lifting lid) until wheat is tender, about 25 to 30 minutes.

Meanwhile, melt butter in medium skillet over medium-low heat. Add nuts and sauté until browned, about 4 minutes. Stir in tamari or soy sauce.

Turn wheat into dish. Fluff with fork and pour nut mixture over.

ANDRE GILLARDIN

Lemon-Pepper Seafood Kebabs, page 84

Sautéed Blue Tuna
with Vegetables, page 82

Grilled Salmon with Tarragon
Mayonnaise, page 80

IRWIN HOROWITZ

Ginger Shrimp with Pea Pods, page 85

Fresh Tuna with Piquant Sauce, page 82

Scallops with Red Chili
Cream Sauce, page 82

PETER A. HÖGG

Satin Scallops, page 83

Hot and Spicy Shrimp
with Noodles, page 84

7 ❖ *Breads*

Nothing beats the wholesome, old-fashioned goodness of home-baked bread fresh from the oven. The satisfaction of baking—and eating—homemade bread is one that you don't have to pass up for lack of time. The recipes here will show you shortcuts and time-savers to perfect loaves, both savory and sweet. You'll also find an assortment of muffins, rolls, biscuits, scones and popovers, along with breakfast puffs, pancakes and waffles.

Quick breads and muffins fit nicely into a busy schedule: They freeze beautifully, and most can be refrigerated for a few days before serving. Apricot-Coconut Bread, with the added zest of orange, can be prepared two days ahead; Walnut-Raisin Zucchini Bread, drizzled with a sweet glaze and chopped walnuts, can be made three days ahead. Fragrant Herb-Cheese Popovers and pretzel-like Pepper Wreaths can both be made two days in advance. And for ultimate convenience in muffin-baking, try Raisin Bran Muffins—the batter keeps in the refrigerator for several weeks, allowing you to bake just the right amount of fresh muffins in a snap.

In addition to the generous selection of fruit, nut and whole-grain muffins, we offer a tempting assortment of simple-to-make breakfast and brunch breads: Easy Cinammon Puff and Lemon Pancakes would add a new twist to any morning menu, as would Almond French Toast and Bacon-Cheese Waffles. And our easy scone recipes may prompt you to serve an afternoon tea featuring trays of each variety— ginger-cream, yogurt and currant-Marsala.

To many of us, dinner seems incomplete without some kind of bread. The breads here offer tremendous possibilities for accompanying all sorts of main dishes. Country ham would be perfect with Mini Caraway Biscuits, or try Buttermilk Biscuits with fried chicken or barbecued ribs. Herbed breads and rolls are wonderful partners for robust stews, while Garlic-Chive Bread is a natural with pasta.

Next time you want to add a touch of homemade goodness to dining, whip up some of these recipes. A basket of warm, fragrant breads turns any meal into a celebration.

TOMATO BRUSCHETTA

4 servings

8 1/2-inch-thick slices French bread
Extra-virgin olive oil
2 garlic cloves, halved
Salt and freshly ground pepper

2 large tomatoes, cut into 1/3-inch-thick slices
8 fresh Italian parsley sprigs

Preheat broiler. Place bread slices on baking sheet and cook until brown on both sides. Brush one side with oil; rub with garlic. Sprinkle with salt and pepper. (*Can be prepared 4 hours ahead. Let stand at room temperature.*)

Place tomato slice atop each bread slice. Brush with oil; sprinkle with salt and pepper. Broil until heated through. Top with parsley and serve.

HERB TOAST

Great with a salad for lunch.

Makes about 50

1 cup (2 sticks) butter, room temperature
2 tablespoons dried parsley, crumbled
2 teaspoons dried tarragon, crumbled
2 teaspoons dried marjoram, crumbled
3/4 teaspoon garlic salt
1 16-ounce loaf thinly sliced white bread
Sesame seeds

Preheat oven to 300°F. Combine first 5 ingredients in blender or processor and mix until smooth. Spread bread slices with butter mixture. Halve each. (*Can be prepared 8 hours ahead. Wrap tightly and refrigerate.*) Place on baking sheet. Sprinkle with sesame seeds. Bake until lightly browned, 20 to 25 minutes. Serve warm or at room temperature. (*Can be prepared 3 days ahead. Store in airtight container.*)

GARLIC-CHIVE BREAD

4 to 6 servings

1 loaf Italian or French bread, cut into 3/4-inch-thick slices

6 tablespoons (3/4 stick) unsalted butter
6 tablespoons olive oil
2 large garlic cloves, minced
1/2 cup snipped fresh chives
1/3 cup freshly grated Parmesan cheese
Freshly ground pepper

Preheat oven to 400°F. Arrange bread cut side down on foil-lined baking sheet. Melt butter with oil in heavy small saucepan over medium-low heat. Add garlic and cook 2 minutes, stirring occasionally. Remove from heat. Mix in chives, Parmesan and pepper. Using slotted spoon, sprinkle chives and cheese over bread. Brush sides with butter-oil mixture; drizzle over tops. Bake until golden brown, 12 to 15 minutes. Serve hot or warm.

CRUSTY SAUSAGE-PEPPER BREAD

Serve this spicy bread with tossed green salad for a delicious midday meal.

Makes 2 loaves

1 pound hot Italian sausage, casings removed

2 1/2 cups grated cheddar cheese
1/2 cup finely chopped onion
1/4 cup seeded and finely chopped green bell pepper
1/4 cup finely chopped celery
2 jalapeño chilies, finely chopped
2 16-ounce loaves frozen bread dough, thawed
2 tablespoons (1/4 stick) butter, melted

Cook sausage in heavy medium skillet over medium-high heat until browned, about 5 minutes. Remove sausage with slotted spoon; drain on paper towels.

Preheat oven to 350°F. Grease 2 baking sheets. Combine sausage, cheese, onion, bell pepper, celery and chilies in medium bowl. Roll each dough piece out on lightly floured surface to 9x16-inch rectangle. Transfer to prepared sheets. Spread half of sausage mixture evenly over each piece of dough, leaving 1/2-inch border. Roll up as for jelly roll starting at 1 long side. Brush each with butter. Bake until golden brown, about 40 minutes.

MIXED FLOUR FLATBREAD

Makes about 18

2 cups rice flour*
1 1/2 cups whole wheat flour
1/2 cup graham flour*
1 large onion, finely chopped
2 to 3 jalapeño chilies, seeded and finely chopped
2 tablespoons finely chopped fresh cilantro
2 teaspoons cumin seeds
Salt and freshly ground pepper
2 1/2 cups water
Vegetable oil

Combine first 7 ingredients in large bowl. Season with salt and pepper. Add water and stir until smooth. Heat heavy large skillet over medium-high heat. Brush lightly with oil. Stir batter and pour 1/3 cup into skillet, spreading to 5-inch round. Cook until light brown, about 2 minutes per side. Transfer to heated plate. Repeat with remaining batter, stirring occasionally and adding oil to skillet as necessary.

Available at natural foods stores.

MUSHROOM BREAD

MICROWAVE

Makes 1 loaf

1 cup (2 sticks) butter or margarine
1/2 pound mushrooms, finely diced
1/4 cup minced onion
3 garlic cloves, minced
2 teaspoons chopped fresh parsley

1 1-pound loaf French or sourdough bread, sliced 1 to 1 1/2 inches thick
1/2 cup freshly grated Parmesan or Romano cheese

Combine butter, mushrooms, onion, garlic and parsley in 8-inch square ovenproof glass baking dish. Transfer to microwave. Cook on Medium 3 minutes. Remove from microwave and stir to mix thoroughly.

Preheat oven to 350°F. Spread mushroom mixture on both sides of each slice of bread. Sprinkle cheese over mushroom mixture. Reassemble loaf and wrap in foil. Bake until heated through, 25 to 30 minutes.

MEXICAN CORN BREAD

12 servings

- 1¼ cups yellow cornmeal
- ½ cup all purpose flour
- 1 tablespoon baking powder
- 1 teaspoon salt
- 2 eggs, beaten to blend
- 1¼ cups milk
- ¾ cup shredded sharp cheddar cheese
- ½ cup vegetable oil
- ½ cup canned cream-style corn
- 1 medium onion, minced
- 3 strips crisply cooked bacon, crumbled
- 2 tablespoons finely chopped jalapeño peppers

Preheat oven to 350°F. Lightly butter 10-inch cast-iron skillet. Place in oven until hot. Mix cornmeal, flour, baking powder and salt in medium bowl. Mix remaining ingredients in large bowl. Stir in dry ingredients just until blended. Spoon into prepared skillet. Bake until golden and tester inserted in center comes out clean, about 30 minutes. Serve immediately.

GREEN CHILI CORN BREAD

8 servings

- 2 eggs
- ¼ cup sugar
- 1 cup plain yogurt
- 1 cup all purpose flour
- 1 cup cornmeal
- 2 teaspoons baking powder
- 1 teaspoon baking soda
- ½ cup frozen whole kernel corn, thawed and drained
- 1 4-ounce can chopped mild green chilies, drained
- ¼ cup (½ stick) butter, cut into 4 pieces, room temperature
- 1 tablespoon finely chopped red bell pepper

Preheat oven to 425°F. Butter 9-inch square baking dish. Beat eggs and sugar in large bowl. Stir in yogurt. Combine flour, cornmeal, baking powder and baking soda in medium bowl. Blend into yogurt mixture. Add corn, chilies and butter and mix well. Turn into baking dish. Sprinkle with red pepper. Bake until bread is golden and toothpick inserted in center comes out clean, 15 to 20 minutes. Serve bread immediately.

ONION CHEESE CUSTARD BREAD

6 to 8 servings

- 1 tablespoon vegetable oil
- ½ cup sliced onions
- 1½ cups milk
- 1 egg, beaten to blend
- 1½ cups buttermilk baking mix
- 1 cup grated sharp cheddar cheese
- 1 tablespoon poppy seeds
- 2 tablespoons (¼ stick) butter, melted

Preheat oven to 400°F. Grease 9-inch pie pan. Heat 1 tablespoon oil in heavy medium skillet over medium-low heat. Add onions and cook until golden brown, stirring occasionally, about 10 minutes. Set aside. Combine milk and egg in medium bowl. Blend in baking mix. Add onions and ½ cup cheese. Pour into prepared pan. Sprinkle with remaining ½ cup cheese and poppy seeds. Drizzle with butter. Bake until golden brown, about 35 minutes. Cool slightly in pan. Cut into wedges. Serve warm. (*Can be prepared 1 month ahead and frozen.*)

APPLE SPICE BREAD

Makes 2 loaves

- 1 cup milk
- 1½ tablespoons fresh lemon juice
- ½ cup (1 stick) butter, room temperature
- 1½ cups firmly packed dark brown sugar
- 2 eggs, beaten to blend
- 1 teaspoon vanilla
- 2¼ cups all purpose flour
- 2 teaspoons baking soda
- 1 teaspoon cinnamon
- ½ teaspoon freshly grated nutmeg
- ¼ teaspoon salt
- 2 cups peeled, cored and chopped Granny Smith apples

Preheat oven to 350°F. Lightly butter two 8x4-inch baking pans. Combine milk and lemon juice in small bowl and let stand 5 minutes. Cream butter with sugar in medium bowl. Add eggs and vanilla and beat until smooth. Add milk mixture. Combine dry ingredients in another medium bowl and blend into butter mixture. Fold in chopped apples. Spoon batter into prepared pans. Bake until tester inserted in centers comes out clean, about 45 minutes. Cool in pans 10 minutes. Transfer to rack. Serve bread warm.

WHOLE WHEAT BANANA NUT BREAD

Makes 2 loaves

- Butter
- ¾ cup (1½ sticks) butter, room temperature
- 1 cup sugar
- ¼ teaspoon salt
- 2 eggs, beaten to blend
- 1 cup whole wheat flour
- 1 cup all purpose flour
- 1½ teaspoons baking powder
- ¼ teaspoon cinnamon
- ¼ teaspoon ground cloves
- ½ cup chopped walnuts
- 1½ cups mashed ripe bananas

Preheat oven to 325°F. Lightly butter two 4x8-inch loaf pans. Cream ¾ cup butter with sugar and salt in medium bowl. Add eggs, flours, baking powder, cinnamon and cloves and mix well. Stir in nuts. Blend in bananas. Divide batter between prepared pans. Bake until tester inserted in centers comes out clean, about 1 hour. Cool 15 minutes in pans. Transfer to rack to cool. Serve bread warm or at room temperature.

LOW-SUGAR PEAR NUT BREAD

Makes 1 loaf

 2 large ripe bartlett pears, cored and finely chopped
 2 eggs, beaten
 1 cup bran flakes cereal, crushed
 1 1/2 cups all purpose flour
 1/4 cup firmly packed brown sugar
 1 teaspoon baking powder
 1/2 teaspoon baking soda
 1/2 teaspoon salt
 1/4 rounded teaspoon cinnamon
 1/4 cup (1/2 stick) margarine
 1/2 cup chopped walnuts
 1 1/2 tablespoons freshly grated orange peel

Preheat oven to 350°F. Lightly grease 8 1/2x4 1/2-inch loaf pan. Combine pears, eggs and bran flakes in medium bowl and stir to moisten. Set aside. Mix flour, brown sugar, baking powder, baking soda, salt and cinnamon in large bowl. Cut in margarine until mixture resembles small peas. Stir in pear mixture, nuts and orange peel. Turn into prepared pan. Bake until tester inserted in center comes out clean, about 60 to 75 minutes; cover with foil if top browns too quickly during last few minutes of baking. Cool slightly before inverting loaf onto wire rack to cool completely.

WELSH TEA LOAF

Makes two 9x5-inch loaves

 2 3/4 cups water
 1 15-ounce package raisins
 4 teaspoons baking soda

 1 1/2 cups (3 sticks) butter or margarine, room temperature
 1 1/2 cups sugar
 3 eggs
 2 tablespoons molasses
 1 tablespoon vanilla
 1/8 teaspoon salt
 4 cups all purpose flour

Preheat oven to 350°F. Grease two 9x5-inch loaf pans. Combine water and raisins in medium saucepan. Bring to boil over high heat. Reduce heat to low and simmer 2 minutes. Stir in baking soda. Let cool.

Meanwhile, cream butter with sugar in large bowl of electric mixer. Add eggs 1 at a time, beating well after each addition. Add molasses, vanilla and salt and continue beating until well blended, 2 to 3 minutes. Beat in flour. Add raisin mixture and beat on low speed until well blended, about 2 minutes. Spoon batter into prepared pans. Bake until tester inserted in centers comes out clean, 50 to 60 minutes. Cool in pans on rack.

APRICOT-COCONUT BREAD

Makes 1 loaf

 3/4 cup (1 1/2 sticks) butter, room temperature
 3/4 cup sugar
 2 eggs, beaten to blend
 3/4 cup finely chopped dried apricots
 1/2 cup shredded unsweetened coconut
 1/4 cup fresh orange juice
 1 teaspoon grated orange peel
 1 1/2 cups all purpose flour
 1 1/2 cups whole wheat flour
 1 teaspoon salt
 1 teaspoon baking soda
 1 cup buttermilk
 1/2 cup chopped walnuts

Preheat oven to 350°F. Grease 9x5-inch loaf pan. Cream butter with sugar in large bowl. Mix in eggs. Stir in apricots, coconut, orange juice and orange peel. Sift together flours, salt and baking soda. Add to apricot mixture alternately with buttermilk, beginning with dry ingredients. Mix in nuts. Pour batter into prepared pan. Bake until tester inserted in center comes out clean, about 1 hour. Let stand in pan 10 minutes. Invert onto rack and cool. (*Can be prepared 2 days ahead. Wrap tightly; refrigerate.*)

HEARTY FRUIT AND NUT BREAD

Makes one 9x5-inch loaf

 1 1/2 cups all purpose flour
 1 1/4 cups whole wheat flour
 1/4 cup wheat germ

 2 1/2 teaspoons baking powder
 1 1/2 teaspoons cinnamon
 1/2 teaspoon salt
 1/4 teaspoon baking soda
 1 1/3 cups milk
 1/2 cup honey
 1/4 cup vegetable oil
 1 egg, beaten to blend
 1 cup raisins
 1 cup chopped dates
 3/4 cup chopped pecans

Preheat oven to 325°F. Butter 9x5-inch loaf pan. Combine first 7 ingredients in large bowl. Beat milk, honey, oil and egg in medium bowl until light and frothy. Stir raisins, dates and pecans into milk mixture. Add to dry ingredients and stir just until flour is moistened. Turn into prepared pan. Bake until golden brown and tester inserted in center comes out clean, about 1 hour. Cool on wire rack.

WALNUT-RAISIN ZUCCHINI BREAD

Makes 2 loaves

 1 cup vegetable oil
 1 cup sugar
 1 cup firmly packed light brown sugar
 3 eggs, beaten to blend
 1/4 cup dry Sherry
 2 teaspoons vanilla
 2 medium zucchini, grated
 1 1/2 cups chopped walnuts
 1 cup raisins
 3 cups all purpose flour
 1 teaspoon salt
 1 teaspoon baking soda
 1 teaspoon cinnamon
 1/2 teaspoon freshly grated nutmeg
 1/4 teaspoon baking powder

 1/2 cup powdered sugar
 2 tablespoons milk
 1 teaspoon vanilla
 Chopped walnuts

Preheat oven to 350°F. Grease and lightly flour two 9x5-inch loaf pans. Using electric mixer, combine first 6 ingredients in large bowl and beat on medium speed 2 minutes. Stir in zucchini, 1 1/2 cups walnuts and raisins. Combine flour, salt, baking soda, cinnamon, nutmeg and baking powder in medium bowl. Mix into batter just until blended. Divide batter between prepared pans. Bake breads until tester inserted in centers comes out clean, 1 hour. Cool on racks.

Meanwhile, combine 1/2 cup powdered sugar, milk and 1 teaspoon vanilla in small bowl. Drizzle over warm bread. Sprinkle with chopped nuts. (*Can be prepared 3 days ahead. Wrap loaves tightly in plastic and refrigerate.*)

BISHOP'S BREAD

Spread slices of this delicious bread with cream cheese or sweet butter, and serve with fresh fruit or chicken salad.

Makes one 9x5-inch loaf

2 1/2 cups cake flour, sifted
1/2 cup sugar
4 1/2 teaspoons baking powder
1/2 teaspoon salt
1/2 cup chopped walnuts
1/2 cup chopped dates
1/2 cup chopped candied orange peel
2 eggs
1 cup milk
1/4 cup solid vegetable shortening
1 ounce unsweetened chocolate

Preheat oven to 350°F. Grease and flour 9x5-inch loaf pan. Combine cake flour, sugar, baking powder and salt in large bowl. Stir in walnuts, dates and orange peel. Beat eggs and milk in small bowl until frothy. Blend into flour mixture. Melt shortening with chocolate in small saucepan over low heat. Add to flour mixture and blend well. Spoon into prepared pan, spreading evenly. Bake until brown and toothpick inserted in center comes out clean, about 50 minutes. Serve warm.

BUTTERMILK APPLE MUFFINS

Rhubarb may be substituted for the apple in these muffins.

Makes 12

1 cup firmly packed brown sugar
1/3 cup vegetable oil
1 egg, beaten to blend
1 teaspoon vanilla
1 1/2 cups unbleached all purpose flour
1/2 teaspoon baking soda
1/4 teaspoon salt
1 cup peeled chopped apples
1/2 cup buttermilk
1/4 cup walnuts, chopped
1/2 teaspoon cinnamon

Preheat oven to 325°F. Place paper liners in muffin tins. Blend 3/4 cup brown sugar, oil, egg and vanilla in large bowl. Add flour, baking soda and salt. Add apple and buttermilk and mix thoroughly. Divide among lined muffin tins. Combine remaining 1/4 cup brown sugar, walnuts and cinnamon in small bowl. Sprinkle over batter. Bake until muffins are browned and toothpick inserted in centers comes out clean, 30 to 35 minutes.

BANANA CHOCOLATE MUFFINS

Makes 12

1 3/4 cups plus 2 tablespoons all purpose flour
1/3 cup sugar
2 tablespoons unsweetened cocoa powder
1 tablespoon baking powder
1 cup mashed bananas
2/3 cup milk
1/3 cup safflower oil
1 egg, beaten to blend
1 cup semisweet chocolate chips

Preheat oven to 425°F. Line 12-cup muffin tin with paper liners. Combine flour, sugar, cocoa powder and baking powder in large bowl. Blend in banana, milk, oil and egg until just moistened. Mix in chocolate chips. Spoon batter into prepared tin. Bake until tester inserted in center comes out clean, about 20 minutes. Invert muffins onto wire rack. Serve warm or at room temperature.

LEMON-BLUEBERRY MUFFINS

Makes 12

2 eggs, beaten to blend
1/2 cup sugar
3/4 cup vegetable oil
3 tablespoons fresh lemon juice
1 teaspoon grated lemon peel
1 1/4 cups all purpose flour
1 teaspoon baking soda
1/2 teaspoon freshly grated nutmeg
1/2 teaspoon ground ginger
1/8 teaspoon salt
3/4 cup fresh blueberries

Preheat oven to 350°F. Line 12-cup muffin tin with paper liners. Using electric mixer, beat eggs and sugar until pale and thick, about 2 minutes. Add oil in thin stream. Stir in lemon juice and peel. Sift together 1 cup flour, baking soda, nutmeg, ginger and salt. Mix into batter. Dredge blueberries in remaining 1/4 cup flour. Fold into batter. Pour into prepared tin. Bake until lightly browned, about 25 minutes. Transfer muffins to rack. Serve warm or at room temperature.

RAISIN BRAN MUFFINS

This batter will keep in the refrigerator for several weeks.

Makes 12 cups batter (about 48 muffins)

1 cup solid vegetable shortening, melted and cooled
1 cup sugar
1 cup firmly packed dark brown sugar
4 eggs, beaten to blend
4 cups buttermilk
5 cups all purpose flour
1 15-ounce box raisin bran cereal
1/2 cup raisins
5 teaspoons baking soda
2 teaspoons salt

Preheat oven to 400°F. Grease 12-cup muffin tin. Mix shortening with sugars in large bowl. Stir in eggs. Gradually add buttermilk. Add remaining ingredients and mix just until blended. Spoon some batter into prepared tin, filling each cup 3/4 full. Bake until tester inserted in centers comes out clean, about 20 minutes. Serve warm. Refrigerate remaining muffin batter in airtight container.

FRESH HERB MUFFINS

Makes 12

- 1 cup milk
- 1/4 cup (1/2 stick) butter, melted
- 2 eggs, beaten to blend
- 2 cups all purpose flour
- 2 teaspoons baking powder
- 2 teaspoons ground cumin
- 1/2 teaspoon salt
- 1/2 cup chopped fresh cilantro

Preheat oven to 400°F. Grease 12-cup muffin tin. Combine milk, butter and eggs in medium bowl. Combine flour, baking powder, cumin and salt in another bowl. Add to milk mixture and stir just until blended. Mix in cilantro. Spoon into prepared tin. Bake until tester inserted in centers comes out clean, about 15 minutes. (*Can be prepared 3 days ahead. Cool. Refrigerate in airtight container.*) Serve warm.

OATMEAL MUFFINS

Makes 12

- 1 cup old-fashioned oatmeal
- 1 cup buttermilk

- 1/2 cup firmly packed brown sugar
- 1/2 cup vegetable oil
- 1 egg, beaten to blend
- 1 cup all purpose flour
- 1 teaspoon baking powder
- 1/2 teaspoon baking soda
- 1/2 teaspoon salt

Combine oatmeal and buttermilk in large bowl. Let stand 30 minutes.

Preheat oven to 400°F. Generously butter 12-cup muffin tin. Blend sugar, oil and egg into oatmeal mixture. Add remaining ingredients and stir just until moistened. Spoon into prepared tin, filling cups 2/3 full. Bake until muffins are golden brown and tester inserted in centers comes out clean, about 20 minutes. Cool 5 minutes. Remove from tin. Serve muffins warm.

TRIPLE NUT MUFFINS

Makes 8

- 1 egg
- 1/2 cup milk
- 1/4 cup (1/2 stick) margarine, melted

- 1 1/2 cups all purpose flour
- 1/2 cup sugar
- 1/4 cup pine nuts, lightly toasted
- 3 tablespoons chopped pecans, lightly toasted
- 3 tablespoons sunflower seeds
- 2 tablespoons baking powder

Preheat oven to 400°F. Lightly grease muffin tins. Beat egg until foamy using electric mixer. Blend in milk and margarine. Stir in remaining ingredients. Spoon evenly into prepared tins. Bake muffins until golden brown and tester inserted in centers comes out clean, 20 to 25 minutes.

CARROT BRAN MUFFINS

Makes 10

- 1 cup bran flakes cereal, crushed
- 1 cup all purpose flour
- 1/4 cup firmly packed light brown sugar
- 2 teaspoons baking powder
- 1/2 teaspoon baking soda
- 1/2 teaspoon salt
- 1/2 teaspoon cinnamon
- 1/4 teaspoon freshly grated nutmeg
- 1 cup milk
- 1 egg
- 3 tablespoons vegetable oil
- 1 cup grated carrots
- 1/4 cup chopped walnuts
- 1/4 cup raisins

Preheat oven to 400°F. Generously grease muffin tins. Combine first 8 ingredients in large bowl. Blend milk, egg and oil. Stir into dry ingredients, mixing well. Stir in carrots, walnuts and raisins. Spoon batter into prepared tins. Bake muffins until golden and toothpick inserted in centers comes out clean, about 15 minutes. Remove from tins. Cool slightly on racks.

PEPPER WREATHS

Sprinkle these pretzel-like bread wreaths with coarse salt if desired.

Makes 32

- 2 envelopes dry yeast
- 1 cup warm water (105°F to 115°F)

- 1/3 cup olive oil
- 1 teaspoon salt
- 3/4 teaspoon freshly ground pepper
- 1/2 teaspoon fennel seeds
- 4 cups (about) all purpose flour

- 1 egg, beaten to blend
- 1 1/2 teaspoons water

Sprinkle yeast over warm water in large bowl; stir to dissolve. Let mixture stand 5 minutes.

Add oil, salt, pepper and fennel seeds to yeast mixture. Mix enough flour into yeast mixture 1 cup at a time to form dough. Gather dough into ball. Knead on lightly floured surface until smooth and elastic, adding more flour if dough is sticky.

Grease large bowl. Add dough, turning to coat entire surface. Cover with towel. Let dough rise in warm draft-free area until doubled in volume, about 2 hours.

Divide dough into 4 pieces; divide each quarter into 4 pieces. Divide each dough piece in half, forming 32 pieces. Roll 1 piece into 16-inch-long rope. Fold rope in half and pinch ends to seal. Twist dough, then bring ends together to form wreath. Place on baking sheet. Repeat with remaining dough pieces. Let rise in warm draft-free area 20 minutes.

Preheat oven to 400°F. Combine egg and water. Brush wreaths with egg wash. Bake until light brown, about 20 minutes. Cool on rack. (*Pepper Wreaths can be prepared 2 days ahead. Store in airtight container.*)

BUTTER-GLAZED SESAME SEED ROLLS

Poppy seeds can be used instead of sesame for a change of pace.

Makes 20

- **Butter**
- 1/4 cup (1/2 stick) butter, melted and cooled
- 1 egg, beaten to blend
- 1 1-pound loaf frozen bread dough, thawed

- 1 tablespoon sesame seeds

Butter 9-inch round cake pan. Combine 1/4 cup butter with 1 tablespoon beaten egg (reserve remainder for another use) in small bowl. Cut dough into 20 pieces. Shape into balls. Dip into butter mixture. Arrange in single layer in prepared pan. Cover and let rise in warm draft-free area until doubled, about 2 1/2 hours.

Preheat oven to 350°F. Sprinkle rolls with sesame seeds. Bake until golden brown, about 25 minutes. Let cool 10 minutes. Turn out onto rack. (*Rolls can be prepared 1 day ahead. Cool completely; cover and refrigerate. Rewarm before serving.*)

QUICK EGG BREAD

Makes 16 rolls

> 3 to 3 1/2 cups unbleached all purpose flour
> 2 tablespoons sugar
> 2 envelopes fast-rising dry yeast
> 1 1/2 teaspoons salt
> 2 eggs
> 1 cup hot water (120°F to 130°F)
> 2 tablespoons vegetable oil
>
> 2 teaspoons sesame seeds

Grease 9-inch round cake pan. Combine 3 cups flour, sugar, yeast and salt in large bowl and mix well. Separate 1 egg; set white aside. Add yolk and remaining egg, hot water and oil to dry ingredients. Mix vigorously with wooden spoon until smooth. Turn dough out onto lightly floured surface. Knead until smooth and elastic, kneading in additional flour if necessary. Cover dough with mixing bowl and let rest 5 minutes.

Divide dough into 16 pieces. Arrange pieces in prepared pan. Beat reserved egg white until foamy. Brush over rolls and sprinkle with sesame seeds. Set wire rack in 9x13-inch baking dish. Add enough boiling water to come just below rack. Set pan on rack. Cover with towel and let rise in warm draft-free area until doubled in volume, about 25 minutes.

Preheat oven to 350°F. Bake until rolls are deep golden and sound hollow when tapped on bottom, about 20 minutes. Serve rolls warm.

FINGER BISCUITS

12 servings

> 2 cups all purpose unbleached flour
> 2 cups cake flour (do not use self-rising)
> 1 teaspoon salt
> 2 tablespoons plus 2 teaspoons baking powder
> 8 tablespoons (1 stick) well chilled unsalted butter
> 1 1/4 to 1 1/2 cups chilled milk

Preheat oven to 425°F. Grease baking sheet. Combine dry ingredients in deep bowl. Using pastry blender, cut in butter until mixture resembles coarse meal. With fork, add milk and toss gently; *do not overmix* (use only enough milk to make dough moist but not wet). Turn onto floured board and gently knead only 2 or 3 times. Roll or pat into rectangle 1/2 inch thick. Cut into 1-inch squares. Transfer to prepared sheet, spacing about 1/8 inch apart. Bake until puffed and golden brown, 10 to 15 minutes.

BUTTERMILK BISCUITS

These large, soft biscuits are a natural with butter and honey. Serve straight from the oven with fried chicken, barbecued ribs, or on their own.

Makes 6

> 2 cups sifted unbleached all purpose flour
> 2 teaspoons baking powder
> 1/4 teaspoon baking soda
> 1/4 teaspoon salt
> 6 tablespoons solid vegetable shortening, room temperature
> 1 cup buttermilk

Position rack in center of oven and preheat to 450°F. Sift flour, baking powder, baking soda and salt into medium bowl. Cut in shortening until mixture resembles coarse meal. Make well in center. Add buttermilk to well. Stir just until mixture is moistened.

Generously flour hands. Divide dough into 6 pieces. Lightly toss each piece back and forth between hands to form ball. Arrange on ungreased baking sheet. Flatten to 1-inch rounds; sides should touch. Bake until light brown, 18 to 20 minutes. Cool biscuits for 5 minutes on rack before serving.

QUICK PROCESSOR BISCUITS

Makes 1 dozen

> 2 cups all purpose flour
> 1/4 cup (1/2 stick) butter, chilled and cut into thirds
> 2 teaspoons baking powder
> 1/4 teaspoon salt
> 2/3 cup milk

Preheat oven to 450°F. Combine flour, butter, baking powder and salt in processor and blend using on/off turns until mixture resembles coarse meal, about 15 seconds. With machine running, add milk through feed tube and mix just until dough forms ball, about 7 seconds; *do not overmix*. Turn dough out onto lightly floured surface and knead gently 10 times. Roll dough to thickness of 1/2 inch. Cut into rounds using 2-inch floured biscuit or cookie cutter. Transfer rounds to baking sheet with sides almost touching. Bake until biscuits are golden, about 10 to 12 minutes. Serve hot.

MINI CARAWAY BISCUITS

Makes 16

> 2/3 cup all purpose flour
> 1/3 cup whole wheat flour
> 1 1/4 teaspoons baking powder
> 1/2 teaspoon salt
> 3 tablespoons butter, room temperature
> 1 teaspoon caraway seeds, crushed
> 6 tablespoons lowfat milk
> Milk

Preheat oven to 450°F. Lightly butter baking sheet. Combine flours, baking powder and salt. Cut in butter until mixture resembles coarse meal. Mix in caraway seeds. Blend in 5 tablespoons lowfat milk. If dough is dry, add remaining 1 tablespoon lowfat milk and mix well. Turn out onto lightly floured surface. Pat gently into 1/2-inch-thick rectangle. Fold in thirds, as for letter. Roll out to thickness of 1/2 inch. Cut into 16 rounds using floured 11/2-inch biscuit cutter. Arrange on prepared baking sheet. Brush tops with milk. Bake until lightly browned, 15 to 20 minutes. Serve biscuits warm.

QUICK CORN SAVORIES

Makes about 3 dozen small biscuits

      6 tablespoons (3/4 stick) butter
  11/2 cups buttermilk baking mix
      1 81/2-ounce can cream-style corn

Preheat oven to 400°F. Melt butter in 11x17-inch jelly roll pan. Combine baking mix and corn in medium bowl. Drop biscuits onto pan by heaping teaspoons. Turn in butter to coat well. Bake until golden, 20 minutes.

MILE-HIGH POPOVERS

These popovers are also delicious served warm with maple syrup and butter for a quick hot breakfast.

6 servings

      2 eggs
      1 cup milk
      1 cup sifted all purpose flour
  1/2 teaspoon salt

Grease custard cups and arrange on baking sheet. Combine eggs and milk in medium bowl and mix well. Gradually whisk in flour and salt until flour is well incorporated; batter may be lumpy. Fill each cup 3/4 full. Place baking sheet in cold oven, then turn temperature to 425°F. Bake 30 minutes; *do not open oven door.* Turn off oven. Let popovers stand in oven 10 minutes. Loosen popovers from cups and turn out onto racks.

HERB-CHEESE POPOVERS

6 servings

      2 eggs, beaten to blend
      1 cup milk
      1 cup all purpose flour

  1/2 cup grated sharp cheddar cheese
  1/2 teaspoon salt
  1/2 teaspoon dried thyme, crumbled
  1/4 teaspoon dried sage, crumbled
  1/4 teaspoon dried basil, crumbled

Position rack in lower third of oven. Generously grease muffin pan or twelve 5-ounce custard cups. Combine all ingredients in medium bowl and mix until blended; batter may appear lumpy. Pour into prepared pan or cups, filling 2/3 full. Place in cold oven and set temperature at 450°F. Bake 30 minutes without opening oven door. Remove popovers from oven and turn off heat. Puncture 4 sides of each popover down into pan at angle. Return to oven, close door and dry 10 minutes. Unmold and pull apart to open slightly. Serve immediately. (*Can be prepared up to 2 days ahead; wrap airtight and refrigerate. Reheat in 350°F oven about 5 minutes.*)

YOGURT SCONES

Makes 12

  22/3 cups unbleached all purpose flour
      3 tablespoons sugar
      1 teaspoon baking powder
      6 tablespoons (3/4 stick) well-chilled butter, cut into small pieces
      1 egg
      1 egg, separated
      1 cup plain yogurt
      1 tablespoon water

Preheat oven to 400°F. Grease baking sheet. Combine first 3 ingredients in large bowl. Using pastry blender or two knives, cut in butter until mixture resembles coarse meal. Mix whole egg and yolk. Stir into batter. Blend in yogurt. Turn mixture out onto lightly floured surface. Knead briefly until dough comes together. Roll out to thickness of 1 inch. Cut with 2-inch biscuit cutter. Gather scraps; reroll and cut additional scones. Place on prepared sheet. Mix egg white with water. Brush tops with glaze. Bake until golden brown, about 20 minutes.

GINGER CREAM SCONES

Makes 20

      2 cups sifted unbleached all purpose flour
      6 tablespoons sugar
      1 tablespoon baking powder
  1/4 teaspoon salt
  1/4 cup minced crystallized ginger
  11/3 cups chilled whipping cream
        Melted butter
        Sifted dark brown sugar

Position rack in center of oven and preheat to 425°F. Sift flour, 6 tablespoons sugar, baking powder and salt into medium bowl. Mix in ginger. Beat cream in large bowl until soft peaks form. Gently fold in dry ingredients in 2 additions. Turn dough out onto lightly floured surface and knead gently just until dough holds together, about 10 times. Cut into 5 pieces. Gently pat each piece into 1/2-inch-thick round. Cut each round into fourths, pushing straight down with floured knife. Arrange on ungreased baking sheets, spacing 3/4 inch apart. Brush tops with butter and sprinkle lightly with brown sugar. Bake until just beginning to color, 12 to 14 minutes. Let Ginger Cream Scones cool for 5 minutes on rack before serving.

CURRANT-MARSALA SCONES

Marsala adds a twist to this traditional scone. Perfect at tea time.

Makes 12

  3/4 cup dried currants
  1/3 cup sweet Marsala

  11/2 cups sifted unbleached all purpose flour
  1/2 cup whole wheat flour
      1 tablespoon baking powder
  1/4 teaspoon salt
  1/3 cup dark brown sugar
      1 teaspoon grated lemon peel
      6 tablespoons (3/4 stick) unsalted butter, chopped, room temperature
      1 egg, beaten to blend

3/4 cup (about) half and half
Melted butter
Sugar

Combine currants and Marsala in heavy small saucepan and bring to boil, stirring constantly. Cover and let stand overnight, stirring occasionally.

Position rack in center of oven and preheat to 450°F. Sift flours, baking powder and salt into medium bowl. Add any large pieces of wheat caught in sifter. Mix in brown sugar and peel. Cut in butter until mixture resembles coarse meal. Drain currants; stir into mixture. Make well in center. Place egg in measuring cup. Blend in enough half and half to equal 3/4 cup. Add to well. Stir just until dough comes together. Turn out onto well-floured surface and knead gently just until dough holds together, about 12 times. Cut dough into 3 pieces. Gently pat each piece into 3/4-inch-thick round. Cut each round into quarters, pushing straight down with floured sharp knife. Arrange on ungreased baking sheet, spacing 1/2 inch apart. Brush tops with melted butter and sprinkle with sugar. Bake until light brown, about 14 minutes. Cool for 5 minutes on rack before serving.

LEMON PANCAKES

Makes about 16 pancakes

  2 cups all purpose flour
2 1/2 tablespoons sugar
1 1/2 tablespoons baking powder
  1/2 teaspoon salt
2 1/2 cups milk
  2 egg yolks, lightly beaten
  2 tablespoons (1/4 stick) butter, melted
  2 tablespoons fresh lemon juice
  1 teaspoon freshly grated lemon peel
  2 egg whites, stiffly beaten
  1 teaspoon oil
  Powdered sugar

Sift flour, sugar, baking powder and salt into large bowl. Combine milk, egg yolks, butter, lemon juice and lemon peel in another bowl and mix thoroughly. Stir milk mixture into dry ingredients until just moistened; *do not overmix*. Gently fold in egg whites. Preheat griddle or electric skillet to 400°F. Brush with oil. Using about 1/4 cup batter for each, cook pancakes until done, turning once, about 3 to 4 minutes. Transfer to heated platter. Sprinkle with powdered sugar.

PANCAKE PUFF

4 servings

  1/2 cup (1 stick) butter
  1 cup all purpose flour
  1 cup milk
  4 eggs
  1/4 teaspoon salt

  2 10-ounce packages frozen mixed fruit, thawed and drained
  2 tablespoons firmly packed brown sugar
  Pinch of freshly grated nutmeg

Preheat oven to 425°F. Melt 1/4 cup butter in heavy 10-inch skillet in oven, 3 to 5 minutes. Mix flour, milk, eggs and salt in blender until smooth. Pour batter into hot skillet. Bake until pancake is puffed and golden brown, approximately 20 minutes.

Meanwhile, combine remaining 1/4 cup butter, fruit, brown sugar and nutmeg in medium saucepan. Stir over low heat until butter is melted and sauce is warm, about 5 minutes. Place pancake on serving plate. Cut into 4 wedges. Top with fruit, using slotted spoon, and serve, passing fruit sauce separately.

SOUFFLE PANCAKES

Serve these with butter and assorted syrups, or fresh fruit and a light sprinkling of powdered sugar.

6 servings

  6 eggs, separated
  1/3 cup pancake mix
  1/3 cup sour cream
  1/4 teaspoon salt
  1/8 teaspoon cream of tartar

Preheat griddle or skillet. Beat yolks in large bowl of electric mixer until thick and lemon colored. Stir in pancake mix, sour cream and salt. Beat whites with cream of tartar in another large bowl until stiff. Fold into yolk mixture. Grease griddle generously. Drop batter onto griddle by tablespoons and cook until golden, turning once, about 1 to 1 1/2 minutes per side. Serve hot.

APPLESAUCE PANCAKES WITH APPLE SYRUP

8 servings

  2 cups buttermilk baking mix
  1 cup milk
  2 eggs, beaten to blend
  1 cup applesauce
  1 tablespoon (or more) butter
  Apple Syrup (see recipe)

Combine first 4 ingredients in large bowl and mix well. Melt 1 tablespoon butter in large skillet or griddle over high heat. Add batter to skillet 1/4 cup at a time. Cook pancakes until browned, turning once, about 1 minute per side. Repeat with remaining batter, adding more butter if necessary. Serve, passing syrup separately.

Apple Syrup

Makes about 1 cup

  1/2 10-ounce jar apple jelly
  1/2 cup applesauce
  1/4 teaspoon cinnamon
  Pinch of ground cloves

Melt jelly in saucepan over low heat. Add remaining ingredients. Stir Apple Syrup until heated through.

EASY CINNAMON PUFF

6 to 8 servings

  Butter
  2 tablespoons (1/4 stick) butter, room temperature
  1 cup sugar
  1 teaspoon vanilla
2 1/2 cups all purpose flour
  2 teaspoons baking powder
  1/8 teaspoon salt
  1 cup milk
  1/4 cup (1/2 stick) butter, melted
  1/2 cup firmly packed brown sugar
  1 teaspoon cinnamon

Preheat oven to 350°F. Butter and lightly flour 8-inch square ovenproof glass baking dish. Using electric mixer, cream 2 tablespoons butter in large bowl until smooth, 2 to 3 minutes. Add sugar and vanilla. Continue beating until light, 4 to 5 minutes. Sift together flour, baking powder and salt. Add to butter mixture in 2 batches alternately with milk, blending well after each addition. Spoon batter into prepared pan. Brush top with melted butter. Sprinkle with brown sugar and cinnamon. Bake until golden brown and puffy and tester inserted in center comes out clean, 25 to 30 minutes.

ALMOND FRENCH TOAST

6 servings

> 3 eggs
> 1/2 cup half and half
> 1 teaspoon dark brown sugar
> 1/2 teaspoon almond extract
> 1/2 teaspoon freshly grated nutmeg
> 6 1-inch-thick slices French bread
> 2 tablespoons (1/4 stick) butter (or more)
> 1/4 cup sliced toasted almonds
>   Powdered sugar
>   Maple syrup

Beat eggs and half and half in small bowl. Mix in brown sugar, almond extract and nutmeg. Pour into large shallow dish. Soak bread in egg mixture 5 minutes, turning at least once. Melt 2 tablespoons butter in very large skillet over medium-low heat. Add bread and cook until golden, adding more butter if necessary, 3 to 4 minutes on each side. Sprinkle with nuts and sugar. Serve with syrup.

PINEAPPLE FRENCH TOAST WITH COCONUT

4 to 6 servings

> 4 eggs
> 1 8-ounce can crushed pineapple, drained
> 1/4 cup milk
> 1 tablespoon sour cream
> 1 tablespoon maple syrup
> 1 tablespoon sugar
> 1 teaspoon vanilla
> 6 tablespoons (3/4 stick) butter or margarine
> 8 slices day-old egg bread
>   Powdered sugar
>   Toasted shredded coconut

Combine first 7 ingredients in blender and whip until smooth. Transfer to shallow dish. Melt 4 tablespoons butter in large heavy skillet over medium heat. Cut bread diagonally; dip quickly into egg mixture, covering completely. Arrange bread in skillet (do not crowd) and cook until browned, about 3 to 4 minutes per side. Transfer to heated platter. Repeat with remaining bread, adding more butter to skillet as necessary. Sprinkle with powdered sugar and coconut.

BACON-CHEESE WAFFLES

Makes 5

> 1 1/2 cups all purpose flour
> 1 1/2 cups milk
> 1/4 cup (1/2 stick) butter or margarine, melted
> 2 eggs, beaten to blend
> 1 tablespoon baking powder
> 1/4 teaspoon salt
> 8 bacon slices, crisply cooked, crumbled
> 2/3 cup grated cheddar cheese
>   Butter
>   Maple syrup

Preheat waffle iron. Whisk flour, milk, melted butter, eggs, baking powder and salt in medium bowl. Stir in bacon and cheese. Bake batter in waffle iron according to manufacturer's instructions. Serve waffles immediately with butter and maple syrup.

8 ❖ Sauces and Condiments

Often it is the little extra touches that set a meal apart from the ordinary: the spicy condiment, the tangy relish, the perfect sauce. And while these little touches add so much to the meal, they are eminently quick and easy to make, and can be prepared days, weeks and even months in advance.

Condiments and pickles are do-ahead by their very nature—they benefit from the extra time to allow their flavors to develop fully. Their flexibility makes them suitable accents for almost any meal. Greek olives with the added zip of fresh orange juice, wine vinegar, garlic, hot red peppers and cloves, are excellent with cocktails, or as a tidbit to accompany a Greek menu. Spinach Pesto is a delicious flavor accent in chicken salad; it can also be tossed with freshly cooked pasta or used as a pizza topping. To add fire to a Mexican fiesta, serve Chili and Cilantro Salsa or Hot Tomato Salsa with tortilla chips for dipping.

What hamburger or barbecue dish would be complete without sweet relishes and crunchy pickles? Bread and Butter Pickles are made in the microwave in about fifteen minutes, then cooled and refrigerated until ready to serve. Colorful Green and Red Bell Pepper Relish and Eggplant-Tomato Relish would add spark to any grilled meats— serve them from large glass jars to show off the vibrant colors of summer.

Quick sauces are versatile accents to have on hand for dressing up a main dish, or even a dessert. Both savory and sweet sauces are included here, and range from Microwave Mornay Sauce, perfect for tossing with pasta or with freshly steamed vegetables, to Spiked Pineapple Dessert Sauce, a sweet complement to ice cream, pound cake or gingerbread.

PIQUANT OLIVES

These will keep for a month in the refrigerator. Excellent with cocktails.

12 to 16 buffet servings

    1 11-ounce jar Greek olives,
         undrained
    1 cup light olive oil
         Juice and peel of one large
         orange
    3 tablespoons wine vinegar
    6 garlic cloves, lightly crushed
    2 dried hot red peppers, broken
         or 1 tablespoon hot red pepper
         flakes
    6 whole cloves

Combine all ingredients. Cover and refrigerate at least 4 days, stirring daily. Drain, discarding peel, garlic, peppers and cloves. Serve in shallow bowl.

WINE-MARINATED SUN-DRIED TOMATOES WITH HERBS

For a delicious appetizer, slice a baguette, spread the slices with Montrachet cheese and top each with one of these tomatoes. They can also be tossed with salads, freshly cooked pasta or vegetables.

Makes about 1 1/2 cups

    1 3-ounce package sun-dried
         tomatoes
  1/2 cup olive oil
  1/2 cup dry red wine
    4 shallots, minced
    1 teaspoon salt
    1 bay leaf
  1/2 teaspoon dried thyme,
         crumbled
  1/4 teaspoon dried marjoram,
         crumbled
  1/8 teaspoon cayenne pepper

Combine all ingredients in medium nonaluminum bowl. Cover and let stand overnight, stirring occasionally. Transfer to jar and seal tightly. Refrigerate until ready to use. (*Can be prepared up to 2 weeks ahead.*)

CHILI AND CILANTRO SALSA

Makes 3 cups

    3 medium tomatoes, finely
         chopped
    1 cup tomato sauce
  1/2 cup finely chopped onion
    2 jalapeño chilies, minced
    1 tablespoon vegetable oil
    1 tablespoon red wine vinegar
    1 tablespoon minced fresh
         cilantro
  1/4 teaspoon garlic salt
         Salt and freshly ground pepper

Combine all ingredients in serving bowl. Let stand 15 minutes. Serve at room temperature. (*Can be prepared 1 day ahead, covered and refrigerated.*)

HOT TOMATO SALSA

Makes 5 cups

    2 14 1/2-ounce cans stewed
         tomatoes, chopped (liquid
         reserved)
    2 cups chopped onions
 1 1/4 cups chopped green bell peppers
  2/3 cup chopped green onions
    6 dried tepin chilies,* crushed, or
  1/2 teaspoon cayenne pepper
  1/2 teaspoon salt
  1/4 teaspoon dried oregano,
         crumbled
         Freshly ground pepper

Mix all ingredients in bowl. Serve chilled or at room temperature. (*Can be prepared 1 day ahead and chilled.*)

*Available at Latin American markets.

PARSI PICKLE

Makes about 2 cups

    3 large cucumbers, peeled and
         thinly sliced (about 6 cups)
    1 cup water
  1/2 cup white vinegar
    2 canned pickled jalapeño
         peppers, finely chopped
 1 1/2 tablespoons salt
    2 garlic cloves, minced
    1 teaspoon minced fresh ginger

Combine all ingredients in medium saucepan and bring to boil. Cook 1 minute. Cool; transfer to large jar with tight-fitting lid. Cover and refrigerate at least 1 hour, or overnight. Serve with slotted spoon. (*Can be prepared up to 1 week ahead and refrigerated. Jalapeño pepper flavor will become stronger with storage.*)

BREAD AND BUTTER PICKLES

MICROWAVE

Makes about 2 quarts

    2 cups water
    1 cup sugar
    1 cup white vinegar
    2 teaspoons pickling spice
    1 teaspoon salt
    1 teaspoon turmeric
    1 teaspoon dry mustard
    4 large cucumbers, peeled and
         sliced
    1 large onion, sliced

Combine first 7 ingredients in 2-quart glass measuring cup or bowl. Cook on High until mixture boils, about 6 to 7 minutes. Stir in cucumber and onion. Continue cooking on High until mixture comes to rolling boil, about 6 to 8 minutes. Transfer mixture to jars. Let cool. Cover and refrigerate until ready to serve.

TOMATO PICKLE

Makes about 4 cups

    3 large ripe tomatoes, seeded,
         juiced and cut into 1/2-inch dice
         (about 3 cups)
  1/3 cup finely chopped green bell
         pepper
    3 tablespoons minced onion
    3 tablespoons fresh lemon juice
    1 tablespoon white vinegar
    1 teaspoon salt

Combine all ingredients in bowl and mix thoroughly. Cover and refrigerate at least 1 hour. Drain tomatoes thoroughly before serving. (*Can be prepared 3 days ahead and refrigerated.*)

GREEN AND RED BELL PEPPER RELISH

Makes about 4 cups

- 3 green bell peppers, seeded and finely chopped
- 3 red bell peppers, seeded and finely chopped
- 2 medium onions, finely chopped
- 3 quarts boiling water
- 3/4 cup red wine vinegar
- 1/2 cup sugar
- 1 tablespoon salt

Combine bell peppers and onions in large saucepan. Pour 1 1/2 quarts boiling water over. Let stand 5 minutes. Drain. Pour remaining 1 1/2 quarts boiling water over and let stand 10 minutes. Drain. Return to saucepan. Stir in vinegar, sugar and salt. Bring to boil over high heat. Reduce heat and simmer until relish thickens slightly, about 15 minutes. Cool completely. Cover and refrigerate. Serve chilled.

EGGPLANT-TOMATO RELISH

Serve with grilled meats or bread.

MICROWAVE

Makes about 3 cups

- 1 large eggplant (about 1 1/4 pounds)
- 2 teaspoons vegetable oil
- 1 medium onion, chopped
- 1 jalapeño chili, seeded and finely chopped
- 1/2 teaspoon mustard seeds
- 1/2 teaspoon cumin seeds
- 1 medium tomato, chopped
- 1 teaspoon sugar
  Salt and freshly ground pepper
- 1 tablespoon chopped fresh cilantro

Brush eggplant with 1 teaspoon oil. Cook on High 9 minutes. Cool. Scoop flesh from skin into medium bowl. Mash pulp. Heat remaining 1 teaspoon oil in heavy medium skillet over medium-high heat. Add onion, chili, mustard and cumin seeds and cook until onion softens, stirring frequently, 3 to 4 minutes. Stir in eggplant, tomato and sugar. Season with salt and

pepper. Cook until thickened, stirring frequently, about 5 minutes. (*Can be prepared 3 days ahead and refrigerated.*) Garnish with cilantro.

SPINACH PESTO

Use this pesto as a flavor accent in chicken noodle soup and chicken salad. It would also be delicious tossed with freshly cooked pasta or on pizza.

Makes about 2 cups

- 4 medium garlic cloves
- 1 10-ounce package frozen spinach, thawed and squeezed dry
- 1 cup chopped fresh parsley
- 1/2 cup pine nuts
- 3 ounces freshly grated Parmesan cheese
- 2 tablespoons dried basil, crumbled
- 1 teaspoon salt
- 1 cup (or more) olive oil

Mince garlic finely in processor. Add spinach, parsley, pine nuts, cheese, basil and salt and process until well blended. With machine running, pour 1 cup oil through feed tube in thin stream. Process just until well mixed, adding more oil if thinner consistency is desired. Cover and refrigerate up to 1 week or freeze up to 3 months. To serve, bring pesto to room temperature and stir well.

CONEY ISLAND SAUCE

Kids (and adults) will love this with hot dogs and hamburgers.

Makes about 2 1/2 cups

- 1 1/2 cups water
- 1 6-ounce can tomato paste
- 1/4 pound ground beef
- 1/4 cup sweet pickle relish
- 1 tablespoon minced onion
- 1 tablespoon Worcestershire sauce
- 1 tablespoon mustard
- 1 tablespoon chili powder
- 1/2 teaspoon sugar

Combine all ingredients in heavy large saucepan over medium heat. Cook until beef is no longer pink, stirring occasionally. Reduce heat and simmer

until sauce is brown and thickened, about 30 minutes. (*Can be prepared 3 days ahead. Cover and chill. Rewarm sauce before serving.*)

WESTERN-STYLE BARBECUE SAUCE

Delicious with both ribs and chicken.

Makes about 2 1/3 cups

- 1 cup catsup
- 1/2 cup dark molasses
- 1/2 cup finely chopped onions
- 1/4 cup firmly packed brown sugar
- 2 tablespoons cider vinegar
- 1 tablespoon steak sauce
- 1 teaspoon chili powder
- 3/4 teaspoon cayenne pepper
- 1/8 teaspoon hot pepper sauce
  Salt and freshly ground pepper
- 1/2 cup raisins

Combine first 9 ingredients in blender or processor. Season with salt and pepper and blend. Add raisins and mix using 4 on/off turns. (*Can be prepared 3 days ahead and refrigerated.*)

CHUNKY TOMATO SAUCE

This tasty vegetable sauce is perfect over spinach fettuccine.

Makes 5 cups

- 1/4 cup (1/2 stick) butter
- 1 large onion, finely chopped
- 2 carrots, peeled and shredded
- 1 celery stalk, finely chopped
- 5 garlic cloves, finely chopped
- 1 28-ounce can tomatoes, seeded and chopped (juice reserved)
- 2 cups chicken broth
- 1 cup dry white wine
- 1/4 cup fresh lemon juice
- 1/4 cup fresh orange juice
- 1/4 cup chopped fresh parsley
- 1 teaspoon dried marjoram, crumbled
- 3/4 teaspoon salt
- 1/2 teaspoon dried basil, crumbled
- 1/2 teaspoon dried thyme, crumbled
- 1/2 teaspoon dried oregano, crumbled
  Freshly ground pepper

Melt butter in Dutch oven over medium-low heat. Add onion, carrots, celery and garlic and sauté 10 minutes. Add remaining ingredients and bring to boil. Cook 10 minutes, stirring occasionally. Reduce heat and simmer until thickened, about 30 minutes. Serve tomato sauce hot. (*Can be prepared 1 week ahead and refrigerated.*)

MICROWAVE MORNAY SAUCE

An excellent sauce with egg and pasta dishes and over freshly steamed vegetables.

MICROWAVE

Makes about 2 1/2 cups

   2 cups milk

   1/4 cup (1/2 stick) unsalted butter
   1/4 cup all purpose flour
   1 cup shredded Swiss cheese
   2 tablespoons fresh lemon juice
   Freshly grated nutmeg
   Salt and freshly ground pepper

Cook milk in 1-quart glass bowl on High until hot, about 2 minutes. Set aside and keep warm.

   Combine butter and flour in another 1-quart glass bowl. Cook on High 1 minute; stir. Cook on High 1 more minute; stir. Whisk in hot milk. Cook on High 3 minutes; stir. Continue cooking on High until thickened, about 1 minute. Whisk in remaining ingredients. Taste and adjust seasoning. Use immediately.

PEANUT BUTTER SAUCE

Excellent with lamb, chicken or pork.

Makes about 3 cups

   1 cup creamy peanut butter
   1 cup cream of coconut
   1/3 cup fresh lemon juice
   1/4 cup soy sauce
   1 tablespoon Worcestershire sauce

   Dash of hot pepper sauce
   3/4 to 1 cup water

Combine first 6 ingredients in medium saucepan. Stir in 3/4 cup water. Add more water 1 tablespoon at a time until sauce is desired consistency. Warm over medium-low heat until smooth, 3 to 5 minutes. Serve hot.

FAST APPLESAUCE

Makes about 1 cup

   1/2 cup water
   4 large apples, peeled, cored, halved and chopped
   2 tablespoons brown sugar
   1 teaspoon fresh lemon juice
   1 teaspoon vanilla
   Cinnamon

Bring water to boil in 2-quart saucepan over medium-high heat. Add apples and cook until soft, about 15 to 18 minutes. Transfer to processor or blender. Add sugar, lemon juice and vanilla and puree until smooth. Turn into serving bowl. Dust top with cinnamon. Serve warm.

DIXIE CHOCOLATE SAUCE

Makes 3/4 cup

   1/2 cup water
   1/3 cup sugar
   1 1-ounce square unsweetened chocolate
   1 tablespoon light corn syrup
   Dash of salt
   1/4 cup smooth or chunky peanut butter
   1/4 teaspoon vanilla
   Vanilla ice cream

Combine water, sugar, chocolate, corn syrup and salt in medium saucepan. Bring to boil over medium heat, stirring constantly until sugar dissolves and chocolate melts. Reduce heat to low and simmer 3 minutes. Remove from heat and whisk in peanut butter and vanilla. Serve hot over ice cream.

SPICY APPLE SYRUP

Makes about 1 1/2 cups

   1 cup cold water
   1 6-ounce can frozen unsweetened apple juice concentrate, thawed
   1/4 cup sugar
   1 1/2 tablespoons cornstarch
   1/2 teaspoon cinnamon
   1/2 teaspoon vanilla
   Ice cream, pancakes or crepes

Combine first 6 ingredients in 1 1/2-quart saucepan and stir over medium heat until mixture simmers and clears, about 10 to 12 minutes. Serve warm over ice cream, pancakes or crepes. Refrigerate extra in jar.

SPIKED PINEAPPLE DESSERT SAUCE

A perfect accent to ice cream, pound cake or gingerbread.

Makes about 3 cups

   1 cup pineapple juice
   1/2 cup water
   1/2 cup lightly packed brown sugar
   1 tablespoon cornstarch
   Pinch of salt
   1/2 cup Drambuie
   1/2 cup chopped dates
   1/2 cup chopped canned pineapple, drained
   1/2 cup chopped pecans
   2 tablespoons (1/4 stick) butter
   1/4 teaspoon freshly grated nutmeg
   1/8 teaspoon grated lemon peel

Combine juice, water, sugar, cornstarch and salt in medium saucepan over medium heat. Stir until smooth and thickened, about 7 minutes. Gradually add Drambuie. Bring to boil and continue boiling 1 minute. Add remaining ingredients and cook 1 more minute. Serve warm.

9 ◆ Desserts

You'll recognize some of your favorite desserts here, but you'll be surprised at just how quick and easy they are. Ranging from classics to new creations, with some delightful surprises in between, these desserts provide the busy cook with a perfect fast finish for any occasion.

Many are updated renditions that cut down on preparation time but not on old-time flavor. Next time your menu calls for an all-American dessert, try Banana Custard Pie, Yankee Devil's Food Cake or Blueberry Buckle. Other down-home treats include the comforting creaminess of old-fashioned Quick Custard Bread Pudding and sumptuous Strawberry-Sour Cream Ice Cream.

Some occasions call for a more sophisticated finale, and you'll find a veritable dessert cart of selections here. For an impressive flourish, serve Chocolate Mousse Pie with Raspberry Sauce, which uses the food processor to make it even easier, or our fast version of a heavenly classic, Quick Coupe Melba. Equally festive is Mocha Amaretto Soufflé—a speedy yet elegant ending to a special dinner.

Of course, a dessert chapter wouldn't be complete without everybody's favorites, cookies and candy. In addition to being deliciously satisfying as after-meal treats, the cookies and candies included here are quick, easy and perfectly suited to preparing ahead. Many of the cookie doughs can be refrigerated, so you can keep them on hand, ready to be baked whenever you need a speedy dessert or snack. Most cookies and candies can be stored for several weeks in an airtight container or frozen for several months. And both make delightful hostess or holiday gifts. You may want to make a double batch in some cases—they're irresistible and have a tendency to disappear before you have a chance to wrap them up!

This tempting assortment of desserts for any occasion—from family casual to elegant dinner party—will inspire even the busiest of cooks to a grand finale.

Pies, Tarts and Pastries

PISTACHIO LIME PIE

8 servings

>   1 cup sugar
>   1 envelope unflavored gelatin
> 1/4 teaspoon salt
>   4 eggs, separated, room temperature
> 1/2 cup fresh lime juice
> 1/4 cup water
>   Green food coloring (optional)
>
>   1 cup whipping cream, whipped
>   1 baked 9-inch pie crust
> 1/3 cup coarsely ground pistachio nuts

Mix 1/2 cup sugar, gelatin and salt in medium saucepan. Blend yolks, lime juice and water and stir into gelatin mixture. Place over medium heat and stir just until mixture thickens and coats back of spoon, 3 to 4 minutes; *do not boil.* Transfer to bowl; stir in food coloring if desired. Refrigerate, stirring occasionally, until mixture mounds slightly on spoon, approximately 1 1/2 hours.

Beat egg whites in large bowl of electric mixer until soft peaks form. Gradually add remaining 1/2 cup sugar and beat until stiff and glossy. Fold gelatin mixture into egg whites. Gently fold in whipped cream. Transfer to pie crust. Sprinkle with nuts. Refrigerate until firm.

LIME MERINGUE PIE

Makes one 9-inch pie

>   2 cups sugar
> 1/3 cup sifted cornstarch
> 1 1/2 cups hot water
>   3 egg yolks, beaten to blend
> 1/4 cup fresh lime juice
> 1 1/2 tablespoons grated lime peel
>   1 baked 9-inch pie crust
>
>   3 egg whites
>   Pinch of salt

Preheat oven to 350°F. Combine 1 1/2 cups sugar and cornstarch in medium saucepan. Add hot water and mix well. Stir over medium heat until thickened, 6 to 7 minutes. Boil 1 minute, stirring constantly. Remove from heat. Whisk about 1/3 of hot mixture into yolks, then whisk yolks back into saucepan. Bring to boil over medium heat. Boil 1 minute, stirring constantly. Remove from heat. Stir in lime juice and peel. Pour into crust.

Beat whites with salt until soft peaks form. Gradually add remaining 1/2 cup sugar and beat until stiff but not dry. Spread over hot pie filling, sealing carefully to edges of crust. Bake until meringue is just golden, 12 to 15 minutes. Cool slightly.

SHERRY-PUMPKIN CHIFFON PIE

8 servings

>   3 eggs, separated
> 1/2 cup sugar
>   1 cup canned pumpkin
> 1/2 cup half and half
>   1 teaspoon cinnamon
> 1/2 teaspoon freshly grated nutmeg
> 1/2 teaspoon salt
> 1/8 teaspoon ground ginger
>   1 tablespoon unflavored gelatin
> 1/2 cup sweet Sherry
>   2 tablespoons (1/4 stick) butter, room temperature
>   1 teaspoon vanilla
>
>   1 baked 9-inch pie crust
>   Whipped cream

Beat yolks with sugar in medium bowl of electric mixer. Add pumpkin, half and half, cinnamon, nutmeg, salt and ginger and mix well. Transfer to medium saucepan and stir over low heat until mixture thickens, 4 to 5 minutes. Soften gelatin in Sherry. Stir into pumpkin mixture. Blend in butter and vanilla. Transfer filling to bowl. Cover and refrigerate filling mixture until thickened but not set, stirring occasionally, about 40 minutes.

Beat egg whites until stiff but not dry. Fold into filling. Spoon into pie crust. Refrigerate until firm. Decorate pie with whipped cream and serve.

BANANA CUSTARD PIE

6 to 8 servings

>   3 cups milk
>   4 egg yolks, beaten to blend
> 2/3 cup sugar
> 1/4 cup cornstarch
>   1 8-ounce package cream cheese, cut into chunks
>   1 tablespoon vanilla
>
>   1 cup all purpose flour
> 1/2 cup finely chopped walnuts
> 1/2 cup (1 stick) butter, room temperature
>   2 tablespoons sugar
>
>   2 large bananas, peeled and sliced
>   1 cup shredded coconut, toasted

Combine first 4 ingredients in heavy medium saucepan over medium heat. Bring to boil, stirring constantly. Add cream cheese and stir until melted. Mix in vanilla. Remove from heat. (*Custard can be prepared 1 day ahead. Cover and refrigerate.*)

Preheat oven to 350°F. Combine flour, walnuts, butter and sugar in bowl of electric mixer and beat at medium speed until dough forms. Press into 9-inch round tart pan with removable sides. Bake until golden, about 25 minutes. (*Can be prepared 1 day ahead. Cover and refrigerate.*)

Place bananas in crust. Top with custard. Sprinkle with coconut. Refrigerate until well chilled, at least 1 hour. (*Can be prepared 8 hours ahead.*)

Rosemary Rösti, page 121

Onion Cheese Custard Bread, page 139

Vegetable Fettuccine Carbonara, page 98

Linguine with Bell Pepper Julienne
and Tomato and Basil Sauce, page 97

Quick Egg Bread, page 143

Quick Tomato, Cheese and
Mushroom Pizza, page 103

PETER·A·HOGG

BLUEBERRY-GLAZED PEACH BOTTOM PIE

8 servings

- 12 ounces cream cheese, room temperature
- 1/2 cup sugar
- 1 cup well-chilled whipping cream
- 3/4 pound frozen peach slices, thawed
- 1 9-inch baked pie crust
- 1 12-ounce bag frozen blueberries, thawed
- 1/3 cup sugar
- 1 tablespoon cornstarch

Blend cream cheese with 1/2 cup sugar in medium bowl. Whip cream to stiff peaks. Fold into cheese mixture until well blended. Pat peach slices dry and arrange over bottom and up sides of crust. Spoon filling over peaches. Refrigerate until firm, about 30 minutes.

Meanwhile, combine blueberries, 1/3 cup sugar and cornstarch in heavy medium saucepan. Stir over low heat until thickened, being careful to keep berries whole, about 7 minutes. Cool to room temperature. Pour over pie. Chill at least 1 hour or overnight.

RHUBARB-CUSTARD PIE

Makes one 9-inch pie

- 3 cups rhubarb, cut into 1-inch pieces
- 2 frozen 9-inch deep-dish pie shells, thawed
- 1 cup sugar
- 3 tablespoons all purpose flour
- 1 tablespoon butter, room temperature
- 1 teaspoon grated orange peel
- 2 eggs, beaten to blend

Preheat oven to 450°F. Arrange rhubarb in 1 pie shell. Blend sugar, flour, butter and orange peel in medium bowl. Add eggs and blend well. Pour over rhubarb. Remove remaining pie shell from pan and place on lightly floured board. Gently roll dough flat. Cut into 1/2-inch-wide strips. Arrange strips over top of pie in lattice design. Trim off excess. Pinch edges to seal. Bake 10 minutes. Reduce temperature

to 350°F and continue baking until bubbly and golden, about 30 minutes. Serve at room temperature.

LEMON SPONGE AND CUSTARD PIE

8 servings

- 1 unbaked 9-inch deep-dish pie shell
- 1 cup sugar
- 1/4 cup (1/2 stick) butter, melted
- 3 tablespoons all purpose flour
- 1 1/2 cups milk
- 3 egg yolks, beaten to blend
- 1/4 cup fresh lemon juice
- 2 1/2 teaspoons freshly grated lemon peel
- 3 egg whites, room temperature

Position rack in lower third of oven and preheat to 350°F. Line shell with parchment or foil. Fill with dried beans or pie weights. Bake until pastry is set, about 10 minutes. Remove beans and paper. Continue baking 3 minutes. Set aside crust to cool.

Increase temperature to 450°F. Blend sugar, butter and flour in large bowl. Add milk, yolks, juice and peel and mix well. Beat egg whites until stiff but not dry. Gently fold 1/2 cup lemon batter into whites. Fold in remaining batter, being careful not to overmix. Pour into crust. Bake 8 minutes. Reduce temperature to 325°F. Cover edges of crust with foil if browning too quickly. Continue baking until knife inserted in center comes out clean, 25 to 30 minutes. Cool on rack. Serve at room temperature.

PEACHES AND CREAM PIE

6 to 8 servings

- 1 unbaked 9-inch pie shell
- 3/4 cup sugar
- 1/4 cup all purpose flour
- 1/4 teaspoon salt
- 1/4 teaspoon freshly grated nutmeg
- 1/4 teaspoon cinnamon
- 3 cups peeled sliced peaches (about 5 medium)
- 1 cup whipping cream
  Whipped cream (garnish)

Preheat oven to 350°F. Prick pie shell with fork. Bake 10 minutes. Cool. (Increase oven temperature to 400°F.)

Combine sugar, flour, salt, nutmeg and cinnamon in large bowl. Add peaches and toss gently. Spoon mixture into pie shell. Pour whipping cream over top. Bake until set, about 40 to 45 minutes. Let cool to room temperature. Serve with whipped cream.

GINGER-PUMPKIN PIE

MICROWAVE

8 to 12 servings

Crust
- 1/3 cup butter or margarine
- 1 1/4 cups gingersnap cookie crumbs (about 20 cookies)

Filling
- 1 8-ounce package cream cheese
- 1 cup canned pumpkin
- 3/4 cup firmly packed brown sugar
- 3 eggs, beaten to blend
- 1 1/2 tablespoons all purpose flour
- 1 teaspoon ground ginger
- 1 teaspoon cinnamon
- 1/4 teaspoon ground allspice or ground cloves
  Candied ginger and chopped nuts (garnish)

For crust: Melt butter on High in 9-inch microwave-safe pie plate, about 1 minute. Stir in crumbs; press firmly into bottom and sides of plate. Cook on High 1 to 1 1/2 minutes. Set crust aside to cool completely.

For filling: Place cream cheese in medium-size glass bowl and soften on Medium (50 percent power), about 1 1/2 to 2 minutes. Beat until smooth. Add pumpkin, sugar, eggs, flour, ginger, cinnamon and allspice or cloves and continue beating until smooth. Cook filling on Medium (50 percent power) until thickened, about 7 to 9 minutes, stirring frequently. Pour filling into crust. Cook on Medium (50 percent power) until firm, about 10 minutes. Let cool (pie will continue to set as it cools). Refrigerate until ready to serve. Garnish with candied ginger and chopped nuts.

LEMON CHEESE PIE

6 to 8 servings

- **3 eggs**
- **1/2 cup sugar**
- **1 8-ounce package cream cheese, room temperature**
- **1/2 cup cottage cheese**
- **1 9-inch graham cracker pie crust**

- **1 14-ounce can sweetened condensed milk**
- **1/3 cup fresh lemon juice**
  Grated lemon peel

Preheat oven to 350°F. Using electric mixer, beat eggs until thick, 2 to 3 minutes. Gradually beat in sugar. Add cheeses and blend until smooth. Pour into cracker crust. Bake 35 minutes. Cool pie 15 minutes.

Combine condensed milk and lemon juice. Spread over top of pie. Cover and refrigerate overnight. Garnish with grated peel.

COLONIAL INNKEEPER'S PIE

8 to 10 servings

- **1 1/2 ounces unsweetened chocolate**
- **1/2 cup water**
- **2/3 cup sugar**
- **8 tablespoons (1 stick) butter, room temperature**
- **2 teaspoons vanilla**

- **1 cup all purpose flour**
- **3/4 cup sugar**
- **1 teaspoon baking powder**
- **1/2 teaspoon salt**
- **1/2 cup milk**
- **1 egg**
- **1 unbaked 9-inch pie shell**
- **1/2 cup chopped walnuts**
- **1 cup whipping cream, whipped**

Preheat oven to 350°F. Melt chocolate with water in small saucepan over hot water, stirring frequently. Add 2/3 cup sugar. Remove from over water, increase heat to medium-high and bring to boil, stirring constantly. Remove from heat. Add 4 tablespoons butter and stir until melted. Add 1 1/2 teaspoons vanilla. Set aside.

Combine flour, 3/4 cup sugar, baking powder and salt in medium bowl

of electric mixer. Add milk and remaining butter and vanilla and beat 2 minutes. Add egg and beat 2 more minutes. Pour batter into pie shell. Stir chocolate sauce and carefully pour over batter. Sprinkle with nuts. Bake until tester inserted in center comes out clean, about 55 minutes. Serve warm with whipped cream.

BLUE RIBBON PECAN PIE

6 to 8 servings

- **1 cup light corn syrup**
- **1 cup firmly packed dark brown sugar**
- **3 eggs**
- **1/3 cup butter, melted**
  Dash of vanilla
  Pinch of salt
- **1 1/2 cups coarsely chopped pecans**
- **1 unbaked 9-inch pie shell**
- **16 pecan halves (garnish)**
  Whipped cream or ice cream

Preheat oven to 375°F. Combine first 6 ingredients in medium bowl and mix well. Stir in chopped pecans. Pour batter into pie shell. Arrange pecan halves decoratively around top of pie, spacing evenly. Bake until center is set and crust is golden brown, 1 hour. Serve with whipped cream or ice cream.

CHOCOLATE MOUSSE PIE WITH RASPBERRY SAUCE

6 to 8 servings

- **4 ounces semisweet chocolate**
- **2 tablespoons milk**

- **1 8-ounce package cream cheese, room temperature**
- **3 tablespoons sugar**
- **1/3 cup Grand Marnier**
- **1 3/4 cups whipping cream, whipped**
- **1 9-inch graham cracker crust**

- **2 10-ounce packages frozen raspberries, thawed and drained**
- **1/4 cup Grand Marnier**

- **1 cup whipping cream, whipped**
- **2 ounces semisweet chocolate, grated**

Combine 4 ounces chocolate and milk in small saucepan over very low heat. Stir until chocolate melts, 1 to 2 minutes. Set aside to cool.

Beat cream cheese and sugar until smooth and well mixed, 2 to 3 minutes. Add 1/3 cup Grand Marnier and cooled chocolate mixture and blend well. Gently fold in whipped cream. Spoon into crust. Cover and refrigerate at least 2 hours or overnight.

Combine raspberries and Grand Marnier in food processor and puree. Strain into small bowl to eliminate seeds. Refrigerate raspberry puree at least 2 hours or overnight.

Just before serving, pipe rosettes of whipped cream around outside edge of pie. Sprinkle with grated chocolate. Pass sauce separately.

FUDGE PIE

6 to 8 servings

- **Butter**
- **1/2 cup (1 stick) unsalted butter**
- **2 ounces bittersweet (not unsweetened) or semisweet chocolate, chopped**
- **2 eggs**
- **1 cup sugar**
- **1/4 cup sifted all purpose flour**
  Vanilla ice cream

Preheat oven to 350°F. Butter 9-inch pie pan. Melt butter with chocolate in top of double boiler over barely simmering water. Stir until smooth. Whisk eggs in large bowl. Mix in sugar and flour. Add chocolate mixture. Pour batter into prepared pan. Bake until tester inserted in center comes out clean, about 40 minutes. Cool. (*Can be prepared 1 day ahead. Cover and refrigerate.*) Serve pie at room temperature with ice cream.

CHOCOLATE CHIP-PEANUT BUTTER PIE

8 servings

- **3 eggs, beaten to blend**
- **1 cup dark corn syrup**
- **1/2 cup sugar**
- **1/2 cup creamy peanut butter**
- **1 teaspoon vanilla**

**2/3 cup salted peanuts
1 unbaked 9-inch pie shell, chilled
1 cup semisweet chocolate chips**

Preheat oven to 400°F. Using electric mixer, beat first 5 ingredients until smooth, 1 to 2 minutes. Stir in peanuts. Sprinkle pie shell with chocolate chips. Pour filling over. Bake 15 minutes. Reduce oven temperature to 350°F and continue baking until tester inserted in center of pie comes out clean, 30 to 35 minutes. Cool. Cover with plastic and refrigerate overnight. Serve at room temperature.

EASY APPLE TART

6 to 8 servings

**1 sheet frozen puff pastry, thawed
3 Rome Beauty apples, peeled, cored and thinly sliced
2 tablespoons (1/4 stick) butter, melted
2 tablespoons sugar**

**1/4 cup apricot preserves
1 teaspoon honey**

Preheat oven to 400°F. Place pastry in 91/2-inch tart pan. Trim edges. Pierce pastry with fork. Arrange apple slices on pastry in overlapping concentric circles. Brush butter evenly over apples. Sprinkle with sugar. Bake until pastry is golden brown and apples are soft, approximately 35 minutes.

Stir preserves and honey in small saucepan over medium-low heat until warmed through, 1 to 2 minutes. Strain. Brush over hot tart.

APRICOT TART

6 to 8 servings

Filling
**1 pound dried apricots
1 cup (or more) water
1 cup sugar**

Crust
**1 cup (2 sticks) unsalted butter, room temperature
1 cup sugar
2 egg yolks
1 cup ground almonds**

**1 teaspoon vanilla
Dash of cinnamon
2 cups sifted all purpose flour**

1 egg white, lightly beaten

For filling: Combine apricots, 1 cup water and sugar in medium saucepan over medium-high heat and cook until tender, stirring occasionally and adding more water if necessary. Transfer to processor or blender and puree. Return to pan and set aside.

For crust: Position rack in center of oven and preheat to 350°F. Cream butter with sugar in medium bowl until smooth. Add egg yolks, almonds, vanilla and cinnamon, mixing well after each addition. Gradually blend in flour and knead until dough is smooth.

Divide dough in half. Press half onto bottom and sides of 9-inch springform pan. Pour apricot mixture into pan, spreading evenly. Pat remaining pastry out into rectangle. Cut into 1-inch-wide strips. Arrange in lattice pattern over filling. Brush strips with egg white. Bake until top is golden, about 45 minutes. Transfer to rack and let cool completely. Just before serving, remove springform and transfer tart to platter. Slice into wedges.

MINIATURE CHERRY TARTS

Makes 12

**21/4 cups sifted all purpose flour
1 teaspoon salt
3/4 cup solid vegetable shortening
6 tablespoons ice water**

**1 16-ounce can tart cherries in water, drained (liquid reserved)
3/4 cup sugar
2 tablespoons cornstarch
1/4 teaspoon salt
2 tablespoons (1/4 stick) butter
Whipped cream (optional)**

Preheat oven to 400°F. Lightly butter *outside* of 12 muffin tin cups. Combine flour and salt in medium bowl. Cut in shortening using pastry blender or 2 knives until mixture resembles coarse meal. Set 2/3 of dough aside. Add ice water to remaining 1/3 and blend well.

Return reserved dough to bowl and mix well. Gather pastry into ball. Roll out on lightly floured surface to thickness of 1/8 inch. Cut out 12 circles, using 31/2-inch round cutter. Mold circles around outsides of prepared muffin cups. Prick pastry shells with fork. Bake until lightly browned, about 25 minutes. Cool crusts briefly on cups, then transfer to rack to cool.

Heat reserved liquid from cherries in medium saucepan over medium heat. Add sugar, cornstarch and salt. Cook just until thickened, clear and smooth, 4 to 5 minutes. Remove from heat. Add cherries and butter and mix well. Cool to room temperature. Spoon cherry filling into crusts. Top each with whipped cream.

RUM AND PINE NUT TARTLETS

Chopped walnuts or pecans can be substituted for the pine nuts.

Makes 12

**6 16x17-inch phyllo pastry sheets
3/4 cup (11/2 sticks) butter, melted**

**1/2 cup light corn syrup
1/2 cup sugar
5 tablespoons butter, melted
1 egg, beaten to blend
3 tablespoons dark rum
1/4 teaspoon salt
1 cup pine nuts**

Preheat oven to 450°F. Grease 12-cup muffin tin. Brush 1 sheet of phyllo with butter. Top with second sheet and brush with butter. Fold in half crosswise. Brush with butter. Fold in half again. Brush with butter and cut into fourths. Place 1 portion in each prepared cup, forming shell. Repeat process with remaining phyllo. Bake until light golden, 5 minutes. Reduce oven temperature to 350°F.

Meanwhile, combine corn syrup, sugar, 5 tablespoons butter, egg, rum and salt in medium bowl. Stir in nuts. Spoon into phyllo shells. Bake until tester inserted in center comes out clean, 10 to 15 minutes.

STRAWBERRY PIZZA

A unique and very pretty dessert that is a snap to prepare.

10 servings

- 1/2 cup (1 stick) butter, room temperature
- 1 cup sugar
- 1 egg, beaten to blend
- 1/4 cup milk
- 1/4 teaspoon vanilla
- 2 cups all purpose flour
- 1 teaspoon baking powder

- 11 ounces cream cheese, room temperature
- 1/2 cup sugar
- 1 teaspoon vanilla
- 6 cups strawberries, sliced

Using electric mixer, cream butter with 1 cup sugar. Add egg, milk and 1/4 teaspoon vanilla. Sift flour with baking powder. Blend into butter mixture. Cover dough and refrigerate 25 minutes or overnight.

Preheat oven to 375°F. Generously butter 14-inch round pizza pan. Press dough evenly into pan. Bake until lightly browned, 15 to 20 minutes. Cool to room temperature in pan.

Combine cream cheese, 1/2 cup sugar and vanilla. Spread over crust. Cover with strawberry slices, overlapping slightly. Cut into wedges.

GOLDEN CHOCOLATE PASTRY PUFFS

Makes 6

- 1 17 1/4-ounce package frozen puff pastry (2 sheets)
- 6 tablespoons semisweet chocolate chips
- 1 egg beaten with 1 teaspoon water (glaze)

Preheat oven to 350°F. Thaw pastry 20 minutes. Cut each sheet into 3 pieces along folds. Thaw until flexible, about 10 more minutes. Place 1 tablespoon chocolate chips in center of 1 piece. Fold pastry in half crosswise to enclose chocolate, pinching edges to seal. Repeat with remaining pastry. (*Can be prepared 1 day ahead, covered and refrigerated.*) Arrange on un-

greased baking sheet. Brush tops with glaze. Bake until golden brown, about 20 minutes. Serve hot.

DESSERT TORTILLA

1 serving

- Butter
- 1 8-inch flour tortilla
- 1 tablespoon honey
- 1/4 teaspoon cinnamon
- Vanilla ice cream

Butter both sides of tortilla. Transfer to skillet or griddle and cook over medium heat until golden, about 3 minutes. Turn tortilla over; transfer to plate. Drizzle with honey and cinnamon. Spoon ice cream down center of tortilla. Roll up and serve.

ROLLED BAKLAVA

An easy rendition of the classic Greek nut and honey dessert.

Makes 35

- 2 cups finely chopped walnuts
- 1 cup sugar
- 1 tablespoon (generous) cinnamon
- 1/8 teaspoon freshly grated nutmeg
- 1 pound phyllo pastry sheets
- 2 cups (4 sticks) butter, melted

- 1 cup honey
- 1 cup sugar
- 1 cup water
- 1 tablespoon fresh lemon juice

Combine first 4 ingredients in medium bowl. Place 1 pastry sheet on towel. Brush with butter. Top with another pastry sheet and brush with butter. Repeat with two more pastry sheets. Place about 1/4 cup nut mixture along one short end of pastry. Fold long edges in and over filling. Roll up jelly roll fashion, starting at end with filling and using towel as aid. Place seam side down in ungreased baking dish. Brush top with butter. Repeat with remaining pastry sheets and nut mixture, forming 6 more rolls. Refrigerate 30 minutes. (*Can be prepared 1 month ahead. Place pastries close together in*

parchment-lined pan. Cover and freeze.)

Preheat oven to 350°F. Cut each roll diagonally into 5 pieces without cutting through to base. Bake until golden, about 35 minutes. Cool.

Meanwhile, cook remaining ingredients in heavy medium saucepan over low heat, swirling pan occasionally, until sugar dissolves. Simmer 5 minutes. Separate baklava pieces, cutting through base of cooled pastries. Using slotted spoon, dip each pastry into syrup and place on serving platter. (*Can be made 1 day ahead. Store in airtight container at room temperature.*)

CREAM PUFFS CHAMBORD

Makes about 30

- 1/4 cup (1/2 stick) butter
- 1/2 cup water
- 1/2 cup all purpose flour
- 1/2 teaspoon sugar
- 1/8 teaspoon salt
- 2 eggs

- 1 cup whipping cream
- 2 tablespoons plus 1 1/2 teaspoons powdered sugar
- 2 tablespoons plus 1 1/2 teaspoons Chambord liqueur

- Powdered sugar

Preheat oven to 400°F. Line baking sheets with parchment paper. Melt butter with water in medium saucepan. Bring to boil. Remove from heat. Add flour, sugar and salt. Stir vigorously until mixture leaves sides of pan. Transfer to food processor. Add 1 egg and process until well blended. Repeat with remaining egg. Spoon mixture into pastry bag fitted with large star tip. Pipe onto prepared sheets forming 1 1/2-inch balls. Bake until golden, about 15 minutes. Transfer to racks. Slice in half horizontally. Cool. (*Puffs can be prepared 1 week ahead. Wrap tightly and freeze. Thaw, then recrisp in 300°F oven for 5 minutes. Cool completely.*)

Whip cream until soft peaks form. Blend in 2 tablespoons plus 1 1/2 teaspoons sugar and liqueur. (*Cream should be soft.*) Spoon cream into pastry bag fitted with large star tip. Pipe about 1 tablespoon cream onto bottom half of 1 puff. Set top half over. Repeat with remaining cream and puffs. Dust with additional powdered sugar. Serve immediately.

ROLLED RASPBERRY CREPES

Makes 24

1 1/2 cups milk
3 eggs, beaten to blend
3/4 cup all purpose flour
1 teaspoon vanilla
1/4 teaspoon salt
4 to 6 tablespoons butter, melted
1 cup raspberry or apricot jam
1 cup walnuts, toasted and coarsely chopped
Powdered sugar

Preheat oven to 200°F. Lightly grease 9x13-inch ovenproof glass baking dish. Combine milk and eggs in large bowl or blender. Gradually add flour, vanilla and salt, mixing until smooth. Heat 8-inch skillet over medium-high heat. Lightly brush bottom of skillet with melted butter. Add enough batter to cover bottom of skillet, tilting to spread evenly. Cook crepe until bottom is golden brown. Turn or flip and cook second side until golden brown. Turn out onto plate. Spread 2 teaspoons jam over crepe and roll up, enclosing jam. Transfer to prepared baking dish. Repeat with remaining batter, brushing skillet with butter as needed. Sprinkle crepes with walnuts. Warm in oven until heated through, 10 to 15 minutes. Sprinkle with powdered sugar. Serve immediately.

Cakes

  ◆

APPLE CAKE WITH HOT CARAMEL SAUCE

The sauce also is delicious when poured over vanilla ice cream.

16 servings

1/4 cup (1/2 stick) butter, room temperature
1 cup sugar
1 egg
1 cup all purpose flour
1/2 cup coarsely chopped walnuts
1 teaspoon cinnamon
1 teaspoon freshly grated nutmeg
1 teaspoon baking soda
1/4 teaspoon salt
3 medium cooking apples, peeled and grated
Hot Caramel Sauce (see recipe)

Preheat oven to 350°F. Lightly grease 8-inch square baking dish. Cream butter with sugar in large bowl. Beat in egg. Add flour, walnuts, cinnamon, nutmeg, baking soda and salt and mix well. Stir in grated apple. Spoon mixture into prepared dish. Bake until golden brown and toothpick inserted in center comes out clean, 35 to 40 minutes. Cool completely in dish. Cut into squares. Pour some of Hot Caramel Sauce over each and serve.

Hot Caramel Sauce

Makes 1 1/3 cups

1/4 cup (1/2 stick) butter
1/2 cup firmly packed brown sugar
1/2 cup sugar
1/2 cup whipping cream
1 teaspoon vanilla
Pinch of salt

Melt butter in heavy medium saucepan over low heat. Add remaining ingredients. Bring to boil slowly, stirring constantly. Continue stirring until sauce thickens, 5 to 6 minutes.

APPLESAUCE SPICE CAKE

12 to 16 servings

2 1/2 cups all purpose flour
2 cups sugar
2 cups applesauce
1/2 cup solid vegetable shortening, room temperature
1/2 cup water
2 eggs, beaten to blend
1 1/2 teaspoons baking powder
1 1/2 teaspoons baking soda
1 teaspoon vanilla
1 teaspoon salt
1 teaspoon cinnamon
1/2 teaspoon ground cloves
1/2 teaspoon ground allspice
1/2 teaspoon freshly grated nutmeg
1 cup chopped walnuts
1 cup raisins
Vanilla Frosting (see recipe)
Walnut halves

Preheat oven to 350°F. Grease and flour two 9-inch-diameter cake pans with 2-inch-high sides. Combine all ingredients except walnuts, raisins and frosting in large bowl of electric mixer and beat well. Stir in chopped walnuts and raisins. Turn into pans, spreading evenly. Bake until golden brown and toothpick inserted in centers comes out clean, 30 to 35 minutes. Cool completely. Spread frosting between layers and over top and sides. Arrange nuts around bottom of cake.

Vanilla Frosting

Makes about 3 1/4 cups

3/4 cup (1 1/2 sticks) butter, room temperature
5 cups sifted powdered sugar
1/4 cup milk
2 teaspoons vanilla

Using electric mixer, beat butter in small bowl until light and fluffy, 3 to 4 minutes. Add remaining ingredients and beat frosting mixture until smooth, about 3 minutes.

UPSIDE-DOWN HUNGARIAN DATE CAKE

10 to 12 servings

1 1/2 cups chopped dates
1 1/4 cups boiling water

3/4 cup (1 1/2 sticks) butter, room temperature
1 1/2 cups sugar
2 eggs, beaten to blend
1 teaspoon vanilla
1 1/2 cups all purpose flour
1 teaspoon cinnamon
1 teaspoon salt
1 teaspoon baking soda
3/4 cup semisweet chocolate chips
1/2 cup chopped walnuts
Whipped cream

Place dates in bowl. Pour water over and let stand until dates are plump, about 30 minutes.

Preheat oven to 350°F. Grease and lightly flour 8-inch bundt pan. Cream butter with 1 cup sugar in medium bowl until light and fluffy. Mix in eggs and vanilla. Sift flour, cinnamon, salt and soda together in another bowl. Add dates and water to flour mixture. Stir into butter mixture. Pour into prepared pan. Combine chocolate chips, walnuts and remaining 1/2 cup sugar in small bowl. Sprinkle over batter. Bake until tester inserted in center comes out clean, 35 to 40 minutes. Cool completely. (*Can be prepared 1 week ahead and frozen.*) Invert cake onto plate; invert again onto platter. Serve slices of cake with whipped cream.

TRIPLE LEMON CAKE

10 to 12 servings

1 18 1/2-ounce package yellow cake mix
1 3-ounce package lemon-flavored gelatin
3/4 cup vegetable oil

4 eggs, beaten to blend
1/2 cup water
1/4 cup fresh lemon juice

1 cup sifted powdered sugar
3 tablespoons fresh lemon juice
1 tablespoon grated lemon peel

Preheat oven to 350°F. Grease and flour 10-cup bundt pan. Using electric mixer, beat first 6 ingredients in large bowl until smooth, about 4 minutes. Pour batter into prepared pan. Bake until tester inserted in center comes out clean, about 45 minutes. Cool cake in pan 25 minutes. Invert cake onto wire rack and cool completely.

Stir together sugar, 3 tablespoons lemon juice and peel in medium bowl until sugar dissolves. Pierce cake with fork. Spoon glaze over, allowing some to drip down sides.

RAISIN-ORANGE CAKE

8 to 10 servings

1 medium orange
1 cup raisins
2 cups all purpose flour
1 1/2 cups sugar
3/4 cup sour milk*
2 eggs
1/2 cup (1 stick) butter or margarine, room temperature
2 teaspoons fresh lemon juice
1 teaspoon baking soda
1/4 teaspoon salt

Preheat oven to 350°F. Grease 9x13-inch glass baking dish. Squeeze juice from orange and reserve. Chop peel and rind into 1-inch dice. Transfer to processor or blender. Add raisins and chop finely. Transfer to large mixing bowl. Stir in flour, 1 cup sugar, sour milk, eggs, butter, lemon juice, baking soda and salt and mix thoroughly. Pour batter into prepared dish. Bake until tester inserted in center comes out clean, about 40 to 45 minutes. Immediately pour reserved orange juice over top of cake. Sprinkle with remaining sugar. Let cake cool in dish on rack. Cut into squares.

*For sour milk, combine 1 tablespoon lemon juice or distilled white vinegar in measuring cup with enough milk to equal 3/4 cup liquid.

CREAM CHEESE-TOPPED PINEAPPLE CAKE

8 to 10 servings

2 eggs
2 cups sugar
2 cups all purpose flour
1 20-ounce can crushed pineapple packed in its own juice, undrained
1/2 cup chopped pecans
2 teaspoons baking soda
1 teaspoon vanilla

Cream Cheese Frosting

2 cups powdered sugar
1 8-ounce package cream cheese, room temperature
1/4 cup (1/2 stick) butter, room temperature
1 teaspoon vanilla

Additional chopped nuts (garnish)

Preheat oven to 350°F. Lightly grease 9x13-inch baking pan. Beat eggs in large bowl until light and fluffy. Add sugar and continue beating until thick. Stir in flour, pineapple, pecans, baking soda and vanilla and mix thoroughly. Pour batter into prepared pan. Bake until tester inserted in center comes out clean, about 40 to 45 minutes. Let cake cool in pan on rack.

For frosting: Combine powdered sugar, cream cheese, butter and vanilla in large bowl and mix until fluffy. Spread evenly over cooled cake.

Sprinkle nuts over cake. Cut into squares. Serve at room temperature.

RASPBERRY COFFEE CAKE

12 servings

Butter
1 cup (2 sticks) butter, room temperature
4 eggs
1 1/2 cups sifted all purpose flour
1/2 cup sugar
1/2 cup firmly packed light brown sugar

2 teaspoons baking powder
Pinch of salt
1 10-ounce package frozen raspberries in syrup, thawed and drained

1 cup all purpose flour
1/2 cup (1 stick) butter, melted
1/3 cup firmly packed light brown sugar
1 teaspoon cinnamon

Preheat oven to 350°F. Butter 9x13-inch baking pan. Cream 1 cup butter in large bowl of electric mixer on low speed. Add eggs 1 at a time, beating well after each addition. Mix 1½ cups flour, sugar, 1/2 cup brown sugar, baking powder and salt in medium bowl. Add to butter mixture and beat on medium-low speed until well blended, about 6 minutes. Spoon into prepared pan. Cover with raspberries.

Blend remaining flour, melted butter, brown sugar and cinnamon in another bowl. Spoon over raspberries. Bake until light golden and tester inserted in center comes out clean, 35 to 40 minutes. Cool slightly; serve.

STRAWBERRY-TOPPED NUT CAKE

8 servings

4 eggs, beaten to blend
1 cup sugar
1 1/3 cups walnuts, ground
6 tablespoons all purpose flour
1 teaspoon baking powder
1 teaspoon vanilla
1/2 cup strawberry jam

1/2 cup sifted powdered sugar
1 tablespoon fresh orange juice

Preheat oven to 350°F. Grease 9-inch springform pan. Beat eggs and 1 cup sugar in large bowl of electric mixer until pale yellow and slowly dissolving ribbon forms when beaters are lifted, about 4 minutes. Blend in ground nuts, flour, baking powder and vanilla on low speed until well combined. Pour batter into prepared pan. Bake until tester inserted in center comes out clean, about 30 minutes. Cool 10 minutes. Spread jam over. Cool.

Remove pan edges. Mix powdered sugar and orange juice until sugar dis-

solves and glaze is smooth. Drizzle over cake and down sides, allowing some jam to show through. Let stand at least 1 hour or overnight. Serve at room temperature.

BUTTERMILK-GLAZED CARROT CAKE

To save time, shred the carrots and chop the walnuts in the food processor.

10 to 12 servings

2 cups all purpose flour
1 1/2 cups sugar
2 teaspoons cinnamon
1 teaspoon baking soda
1/2 teaspoon salt
3/4 cup buttermilk
3 eggs, beaten to blend
1/2 cup vegetable oil
2 teaspoons vanilla
2 cups finely shredded peeled carrots
1 8-ounce can crushed pineapple, drained
1 cup chopped walnuts
Buttermilk Glaze (see recipe)

Preheat oven to 350°F. Combine first 5 ingredients in medium bowl. Stir together buttermilk, eggs, oil and vanilla in large bowl. Add dry ingredients and stir until well blended. Mix in carrots, pineapple and walnuts. Pour batter into 9x13-inch ovenproof glass baking dish. Bake until tester inserted in center comes out clean, about 45 minutes. Cool cake completely. Drizzle with hot Buttermilk Glaze. Let glaze cool slightly before serving cake.

Buttermilk Glaze

Makes about 1 1/4 cups

2/3 cup sugar
1/3 cup butter, melted
1/3 cup buttermilk
2 tablespoons light corn syrup
1/4 teaspoon baking soda
1/2 teaspoon vanilla

Combine first 5 ingredients in heavy medium saucepan. Bring to boil over medium heat, stirring frequently. Boil

until slightly thickened, about 5 minutes. Remove from heat. Stir in vanilla. Use glaze immediately.

ZUCCHINI CHOCOLATE CAKE

12 servings

1 1/3 cups sugar
1/2 cup (1 stick) butter, room temperature
1/2 cup vegetable oil
1/2 cup milk
1 teaspoon fresh lemon juice
2 eggs
1 teaspoon vanilla
2 1/2 cups all purpose flour
6 tablespoons unsweetened cocoa powder
1 teaspoon baking soda
1/2 teaspoon cinnamon
1/2 teaspoon baking powder
Pinch of salt
2 cups grated zucchini
Powdered sugar

Preheat oven to 325°F. Grease and flour 9x13-inch baking pan. Mix sugar, butter and oil in large bowl. Combine milk and lemon juice in small bowl and add to sugar mixture. Add eggs and vanilla and blend well. Sift together flour and cocoa. Add baking soda, cinnamon, baking powder and salt to dry ingredients and blend well. Stir into sugar mixture. Mix in zucchini. Pour into prepared pan. Bake until tester inserted in center comes out clean, about 40 minutes. Cool to room temperature. Sprinkle top with powdered sugar before serving.

LITTLE DUTCH CAKE

For a light dessert, try serving this tasty cake with fresh fruit.

4 to 6 servings

1/2 cup (1 stick) butter, room temperature
1/2 cup sugar
2 teaspoons finely grated lemon peel
Pinch of salt
3/4 cup all purpose flour
1 egg, beaten to blend

Preheat oven to 400°F. Lightly butter 8-inch round cake pan. Cream first 4 ingredients. Blend in flour and egg. Spread batter evenly in pan. Bake until lightly browned, about 20 minutes. Cool in pan on rack.

ALMOND CHEESECAKE

12 servings

Crust

1¹/₂ cups graham cracker crumbs
¹/₄ cup (¹/₂ stick) butter, melted
2 tablespoons sugar
1 teaspoon all purpose flour

Filling

4 8-ounce packages cream cheese, room temperature
1 cup sugar
2 eggs, lightly beaten
1 teaspoon vanilla
1 teaspoon almond extract

2 cups sour cream
³/₄ cup sugar
³/₄ teaspoon almond extract
¹/₂ teaspoon fresh lemon juice

For crust: Preheat oven to 350°F. Combine crumbs, melted butter, sugar and flour in medium bowl and mix thoroughly. Pat mixture onto bottom and sides of 10-inch springform pan. Bake 5 minutes. Let crust cool completely. Turn off oven to cool.

For filling: Beat cream cheese, 1 cup sugar, eggs, vanilla and almond extract at low speed in large bowl of electric mixer until smooth. Pour into crust. Place in oven; turn temperature back to 350°F. Bake until firm and set, about 30 minutes. (Maintain oven temperature at 350°F.)

Combine remaining ingredients in medium bowl and blend well. Using rubber spatula, spread mixture over cheesecake to within ¹/₂ inch of edge. Bake 8 minutes. Cool completely, about 2 hours. Refrigerate overnight. Just before serving, remove springform; set cake on platter. (*Cheesecake can be prepared up to 1 week ahead. Cover and refrigerate.*)

BUTTERMILK-BROWN SUGAR CHEESECAKE

8 servings

1 8-ounce package cream cheese, room temperature
2 eggs, beaten to blend
³/₄ cup firmly packed light brown sugar
¹/₄ cup buttermilk
2 tablespoons amaretto liqueur
1 teaspoon vanilla
1 unbaked 9-inch graham cracker pie shell
¹/₃ cup lightly toasted slivered almonds
¹/₄ teaspoon cinnamon

Preheat oven to 350°F. Combine first 6 ingredients in blender and mix until creamy, about 1 minute. Pour into pie shell. Top with almonds and cinnamon. Bake until lightly browned, about 30 minutes. Cool. Cover and refrigerate until set. Serve chilled.

ITALIAN POUND CAKE

Irresistible when served with strawberries and sweetened sour cream or almond-flavored chocolate sauce.

10 to 12 servings

1 2³/₄-ounce package sliced almonds
1¹/₂ cups (3 sticks) butter or margarine, room temperature
2¹/₄ cups sugar
6 eggs
³/₄ cup milk
2 teaspoons almond extract
3 cups sifted all purpose flour
1 tablespoon baking powder

Preheat oven to 350°F. Grease and flour bundt pan. Sprinkle ¹/₂ cup almonds over bottom of pan. Using electric mixer, cream butter with sugar in large bowl until fluffy. Add eggs 1 at a time, beating well after each addition. Beat in milk, then extract. Sift flour and baking powder over; mix well. Pour batter into prepared pan. Bake until tester inserted near center comes out clean, about 1 hour. Invert onto rack to cool. Serve at room temperature.

GOOEY BUTTER CAKE

10 to 12 servings

1 18-ounce box yellow cake mix
¹/₂ cup (1 stick) unsalted butter, melted
¹/₂ cup chopped almonds
1 egg, beaten to blend
1 16-ounce box powdered sugar
1 8-ounce package cream cheese, room temperature
2 eggs, beaten to blend

Preheat oven to 350°F. Grease 9x13-inch ovenproof glass baking dish. Using electric mixer, blend cake mix, butter, almonds and 1 egg 1 minute. Pat mixture into bottom of prepared dish. Using electric mixer, beat sugar, cream cheese and 2 eggs 1 minute. Pour over cake. Bake until lightly browned, about 50 minutes.

PI PHI CAKE

12 servings

3 6-ounce packages semisweet chocolate chips
¹/₄ cup sugar
3 tablespoons water
5 eggs, separated
1³/₄ cups whipping cream, whipped

1 prepared 8-inch angel food cake

¹/₂ cup whipping cream, whipped
Grated chocolate

Combine chocolate chips, sugar and water in top of double boiler set over hot (but not boiling) water. Cook until chocolate is melted. Beat yolks in small bowl until thick and lemon colored, about 1¹/₂ minutes. Add to chocolate mixture and stir 3 minutes. Transfer to large bowl. Beat whites until stiff but not dry. Fold into chocolate. Fold in whipped cream.

Slice cake into thin wedges. Arrange enough slices in bottom of 10-inch springform pan to cover completely. Spread with some of chocolate filling. Repeat layering, ending with filling. Refrigerate overnight.

Just before serving, remove sides of springform pan. Top cake with remaining whipped cream. Sprinkle with grated chocolate.

PEANUT BUTTER CAKE

12 servings

- 2¼ cups all purpose flour
- 2 cups lightly packed dark brown sugar
- 1 cup smooth peanut butter
- ½ cup (1 stick) butter or margarine, room temperature
- 1 cup milk
- 3 eggs, beaten to blend
- 1 teaspoon vanilla
- 1 teaspoon baking powder
- ½ teaspoon baking soda
- 1 cup semisweet chocolate chips

Preheat oven to 325°F. Grease bottom only of 8x12-inch glass baking dish. Combine first 4 ingredients in large mixing bowl and blend until crumbly. Set aside 1 cup flour mixture. Add next 5 ingredients to remaining flour mixture and blend well. Spoon batter into pan and sprinkle with reserved flour mixture. Top with chocolate chips. Bake until tester inserted in center of cake comes out clean, 45 to 50 minutes. Let cool slightly. Cut cake into squares and serve.

YANKEE DEVIL'S FOOD CAKE

Makes one 9x13-inch cake

Cake
- ½ cup (1 stick) butter, room temperature
- 2 cups sugar
- 3 eggs, separated
- ½ cup sour cream
- ¾ teaspoon baking soda
- ¼ cup unsweetened cocoa powder
- ¾ cup boiling water
- 2 cups sifted cake flour
- 1 tablespoon vanilla
- ⅛ teaspoon salt

Icing
- 2½ cups powdered sugar
- 6 tablespoons unsweetened cocoa powder
- 5 tablespoons butter, room temperature

- 1 teaspoon vanilla
- ⅛ teaspoon salt
- 2 tablespoons hot milk

For cake: Preheat oven to 350°F. Grease and flour 9x13-inch metal baking pan. Cream butter with sugar in large bowl of electric mixer. Add yolks and beat on medium speed 2 minutes. Combine sour cream and baking soda in small bowl and stir until baking soda is dissolved. Beat into butter mixture. Dissolve cocoa in boiling water in another small bowl. Add to butter mixture. Beat in flour, vanilla and salt. Beat whites until stiff but not dry. Fold into batter. Pour into prepared pan. Bake until tester inserted in center comes out clean, about 30 minutes. Cool in pan on rack.

For icing: Combine powdered sugar, cocoa, butter, vanilla and salt in medium bowl and mix thoroughly. Add hot milk and stir until smooth. Frost top of cake in pan and serve.

BLACK RUSSIAN CAKE

8 to 10 servings

- 1 18½-ounce package devil's food cake mix
- 1 4-ounce package instant chocolate pudding mix
- 4 eggs, beaten to blend
- ¾ cup brewed strong coffee, room temperature
- ¾ cup coffee liqueur
- ¾ cup crème de cacao
- ½ cup vegetable oil

- 1 cup sifted powdered sugar
- 2 tablespoons brewed strong coffee, room temperature
- 2 tablespoons coffee liqueur
- 2 tablespoons crème de cacao
- Additional powdered sugar

Preheat oven to 350°F. Grease and lightly flour 10-inch bundt pan. Using electric mixer, blend first 7 ingredients at medium speed until batter forms. Pour into prepared pan. Bake until tester inserted in center comes out clean, about 45 minutes. Let cake cool in pan 10 minutes.

Meanwhile, combine all remaining ingredients except additional powdered sugar in small bowl. Invert cake onto rack. Pierce top surface of cake with fork. Spoon glaze over. Cool completely. (*Can be prepared 3 days ahead. Store in airtight container.*) Dust cake with powdered sugar before serving.

MOCHA BROWNIE CAKE

12 to 15 servings

- Butter
- 1 cup (2 sticks) unsalted butter
- 4 1-ounce squares unsweetened chocolate
- 4 eggs
- 2 cups sugar
- 1 cup sifted all purpose flour
- ½ cup chopped walnuts
- Pinch of salt

- 1½ cups whipping cream
- ⅓ cup firmly packed brown sugar
- 1 tablespoon instant coffee powder
- 2 1-ounce squares semisweet chocolate, shaved

Preheat oven to 350°F. Generously butter two 9-inch round baking pans. Melt 1 cup butter and unsweetened chocolate in double boiler over simmering water. Cool. Using electric mixer, beat eggs until frothy, about 3 minutes. Gradually add sugar and beat well, 2 to 3 minutes. Carefully stir in cooled chocolate mixture. Fold in flour, nuts and salt; do not overmix. Pour into prepared pans. Bake until tester inserted in centers comes out clean, 20 to 25 minutes. Do not overbake; if edges crisp they will crumble. Cool in pans 5 minutes. Turn out onto racks and cool completely.

Using electric mixer, whip cream until beginning to thicken, 2 to 3 minutes. Gradually add brown sugar and instant coffee. Continue beating until stiff peaks form. Spread cream between layers and over top and sides of torte. Sprinkle shaved chocolate over top. Refrigerate at least 1 hour or overnight. Serve chilled.

FESTIVE CHOCOLATE COOKIE ROLL

8 servings

Creamy Chocolate Frosting
  1 cup semisweet chocolate chips
  2/3 cup firmly packed brown sugar
  3 ounces cream cheese, room temperature
  1/2 teaspoon vanilla
  1/2 teaspoon cinnamon
     Pinch of salt
  1 egg yolk
  1 cup whipping cream, whipped

Cake
  1/3 cup all purpose flour
  1/2 teaspoon baking powder
  14 chocolate sandwich cookies, crushed
  5 eggs, separated, room temperature
  1/2 cup sugar
  1 teaspoon vanilla

  2 tablespoons powdered sugar

Cream Filling
  1 cup whipping cream, whipped
  1/2 cup slivered almonds, toasted
  1/4 teaspoon almond extract

  Meringue mushrooms

For frosting: Melt chocolate chips in small saucepan over low heat. Combine brown sugar, cream cheese, vanilla, cinnamon and salt in large bowl. Add yolk and beat until fluffy. Stir in chocolate; fold in whipped cream. Chill 1 to 1 1/2 hours or overnight.

For cake: Preheat oven to 350°F. Grease 10 1/2x15 1/2-inch jelly roll pan. Line pan with foil; lightly grease foil. Sift flour and baking powder into medium bowl. Stir in cookie crumbs and set aside. Beat yolks with sugar at medium speed in large bowl of electric mixer until just blended. Stir in vanilla and set aside. Beat whites in another bowl until stiff. Stir 1/3 of crumbs into yolk mixture. Gently fold in 1/3 of

whites. Repeat twice. Spread batter evenly into prepared pan. Bake until tester inserted in center comes out clean, approximately 15 minutes.

Sprinkle powdered sugar over towel. Remove cake from oven and cover pan with towel, sugar side down, then top with cutting board, if desired. Invert cake onto towel and board or other flat surface. Remove pan and gently peel off foil. Carefully roll up cake starting from short end, using towel as aid. Cool on rack 30 minutes.

For filling: Combine whipped cream, almonds and almond extract in small bowl. Set aside.

To assemble: Unroll cake and remove towel. Spread filling evenly, almost to edges of cake. Gently reroll cake. Transfer to serving platter. Spread frosting over top and ends. Make log-like marks using fork tines. Garnish with meringue mushrooms and refrigerate until ready to serve.

Fruit Desserts

JAMAICAN APPLES

6 servings

  6 medium Granny Smith apples, peeled and cored
  1 cup firmly packed light brown sugar
  3/4 cup apricot jam

  3 tablespoons dark rum
  1/4 cup slivered almonds
     Whipped cream

Preheat oven to 375°F. Stand apples in 9x13-inch glass baking dish. Combine sugar and jam in small bowl. Place 1 to 2 tablespoons sugar mixture in center of each apple, filling halfway (you will have sugar mixture left over). Add 1/4 inch of water to baking dish. Bake apples 20 minutes, basting with cooking liquid occasionally.

Add rum to remaining sugar mixture. Brush apples with sugar-rum mixture. Continue baking until soft, about 25 minutes. Top with almonds. Continue baking until almonds are toasted, about 2 minutes. Transfer apples to plates. Pour cooking liquid into heavy small saucepan and boil to thicken, if necessary. Pour sauce over apples. (*Can be prepared 1 day ahead. Cover and refrigerate.*) Serve apples warm with whipped cream.

FRUIT-STUFFED BAKED APPLES

8 servings

  6 pitted dates, sliced
  1/4 cup raisins
  1/4 cup chopped walnuts

  2 tablespoons light brown sugar
  1 teaspoon cinnamon
  8 large Golden Delicious apples, cored, top 1/2 inch peeled
  1/4 cup water
  1/4 cup brandy
  1/4 cup (1/2 stick) butter, melted
     Vanilla ice cream

Preheat oven to 400°F. Combine first 5 ingredients in small bowl. Place apples in 9x13-inch glass baking dish. Fill apples with date mixture. Combine water, brandy and butter in small bowl. Pour over apples. Cover and bake until apples are tender, basting occasionally with cooking liquid, about 1 1/4 hours. Transfer apples to plates. Pour cooking liquid over. Serve baked apples with ice cream.

ROCKY MOUNTAIN HIGH APPLE CRISP

6 to 8 servings

- 5 cups peeled, sliced tart apples
- 1 teaspoon cinnamon
- 1 teaspoon grated lemon peel
- 1 teaspoon grated orange peel
- 2 tablespoons Grand Marnier
- 2 tablespoons almond liqueur
- 3/4 cup sugar
- 3/4 cup all purpose flour
- 1/2 cup (1 stick) butter or margarine
- 1/4 cup firmly packed brown sugar
- 1/4 teaspoon salt
  Cream, whipped cream or ice cream (garnish)

Preheat oven to 350°F. Grease 2-quart round baking dish. Arrange apple slices in bottom of dish. Sprinkle evenly with cinnamon, lemon peel, orange peel, Grand Marnier and almond liqueur. Combine sugar, flour, butter or margarine, brown sugar and salt in medium bowl and mix until crumbly. Sprinkle over apples. Bake until golden, about 1 hour. Spoon into bowls. Garnish each serving with cream, whipped cream or ice cream.

RHUBARB-APPLE CRUNCH

4 to 6 servings

- 2 cups sliced fresh or frozen rhubarb
- 1 cup sliced apples (about 1/4 pound)
- 1 cup sugar
- 3 tablespoons all purpose flour
- 1/2 teaspoon cinnamon

- 1 1/2 cups quick-cooking oats
- 1 cup firmly packed light brown sugar
- 1 cup all purpose flour
- 1/2 cup (1 stick) butter, cut into 1-inch pieces
  Vanilla ice cream

Preheat oven to 375°F. Grease 10x10-inch baking dish. Combine first 5 ingredients in large bowl and mix thoroughly. Spoon evenly into dish.

Combine oats, brown sugar, flour and butter in another large bowl (or processor) and mix until crumbly. Sprinkle over rhubarb-apple mixture. Bake until top is lightly browned, about 40 minutes. Serve dessert warm with vanilla ice cream.

MOCK DEEP-DISH APPLE PIE

6 to 8 servings

- 6 medium Granny Smith apples, peeled, cored and sliced
- 1 cup golden raisins
- 1/2 cup firmly packed light brown sugar
- 2 tablespoons all purpose flour
- 2 tablespoons water
- 2 tablespoons applejack
- 1 teaspoon cinnamon
- 1/2 cup chopped pecans

Brown Sugar Topping
- 1 1/2 cups firmly packed light brown sugar
- 1 cup all purpose flour
- 1/2 cup (1 stick) butter

Preheat oven to 350°F. Butter 9 1/2-inch deep-dish pie pan. Toss apples, raisins, brown sugar, flour, water, applejack and cinnamon in large bowl. Spoon

FRESH FRUIT FINISHERS

Nothing could be simpler and more appealing for dessert than an attractively arranged serving of fruit. Take advantage of the season's bounty and try some of the combinations suggested below:

Apples cored and baked in a 350°F oven for 35 minutes in a bath of red wine sweetened with sugar.

Bananas baked in their skins for 20 minutes in a 350°F oven, peeled and served with a squeeze of lemon.

Cantaloupe diced and marinated in Port wine with a sprig of fresh mint.

Cherries pitted and macerated in a mixture of 2 parts cassis syrup and 1 part framboise eau-de-vie, then served with crème fraîche or ice cream.

Figs mixed with yogurt and sprinkled with raw or brown sugar, or doused with kirsch-flavored heavy cream.

Grapefruit sections drizzled with grenadine, or halves sprinkled with brown sugar and cinnamon and then broiled until top is caramelized.

Melon balls sprinkled with anisette and orange juice, or with sugar served in a goblet with champagne and mint.

Orange slices splashed with Grand Marnier or Cognac, or with a combination of crème de cassis and fresh lemon juice.

Papaya drenched in plum wine, or sliced and served simply with a squeeze of lime and/or zest.

Peaches peeled and marinated to cover in red or white wine sweetened with sugar to taste.

Pears peeled, halved, cored and baked in a 375° oven until tender, about 50 minutes, with brown sugar, Poire Williams eau-de-vie and nuts.

Pineapple sliced thinly and drizzled with honey and fresh lime juice.

Strawberries splashed with balsamic vinegar and sweetened with sugar to taste.

Tangerines peeled and segmented, then sprinkled with sifted powdered sugar and kirsch.

Watermelon sprinkled with sugar and dry Sherry.

into prepared pan. Sprinkle apple mixture with chopped pecans.

For topping: Blend brown sugar, flour and butter until crumbly. Sprinkle evenly over apples. Bake until brown and bubbly, 50 minutes.

BLUEBERRY BUCKLE

6 servings

    Butter
1/2 **cup (1 stick) butter, room temperature**
1/2 **cup sugar**
  1 **egg, beaten to blend**
  1 **cup all purpose flour**
1 1/2 **teaspoons baking powder**
1/4 **teaspoon salt**
1/2 **cup milk**
  2 **cups fresh or frozen, thawed blueberries**

1/4 **cup (1/2 stick) butter, room temperature**
  1 **cup sugar**
1/2 **cup all purpose flour**
1/2 **teaspoon cinnamon**
    Whipped cream

Preheat oven to 375°F. Butter 9-inch square baking pan. Using electric mixer, cream 1/2 cup butter with 1/2 cup sugar 3 minutes. Add egg and continue beating 1 minute. Combine 1 cup flour, baking powder and salt. Add to butter mixture in 4 batches, alternating with milk. Turn into prepared pan, spreading evenly. Top with berries.

Using electric mixer, cream 1/4 cup butter with 1 cup sugar. Add 1/2 cup flour and cinnamon and blend until crumbly. Sprinkle over blueberries. Bake until golden brown and bubbly, about 45 minutes. Serve immediately with whipped cream.

FLAMING BANANAS OVER ICE CREAM

4 servings

1/3 **cup sweetened shredded coconut**
1/3 **cup chopped pecans**
1/4 **cup firmly packed light brown sugar**
  1 **teaspoon grated orange peel**
1/4 **cup (1/2 stick) butter**

  4 **firm but ripe bananas, peeled and sliced**
  4 **tablespoons dark rum**
  1 **pint vanilla ice cream**

Combine first 4 ingredients in medium bowl. Melt butter in heavy large skillet over low heat. Add bananas. Sprinkle coconut mixture over. Add 2 tablespoons rum. Cook until bananas are tender, stirring occasionally, about 3 minutes. Tilt skillet. Add remaining rum. Heat slightly and ignite with match. Scoop ice cream into bowls. When flames subside, spoon bananas and sauce over ice cream.

RUM-ORANGE BANANAS

This is a lovely salt-free dessert when served by itself and deliciously indulgent when it is spooned over vanilla ice cream.

4 servings

  2 **tablespoons (1/4 stick) unsalted margarine**
  5 **tablespoons light rum**
1/4 **cup fresh orange juice**
  3 **tablespoons firmly packed brown sugar**
1/4 **teaspoon allspice, ground mace or freshly grated nutmeg**
  4 **firm ripe bananas, peeled and halved lengthwise**

Melt margarine in 12-inch skillet over low heat. Add 3 tablespoons rum, orange juice, brown sugar and allspice. Simmer until slightly thickened, 1 to 2 minutes. Add bananas and turn to coat. Add remaining 2 tablespoons rum. Heat and ignite, shaking skillet gently until flames subside. Serve hot.

LIQUEUR-MARINATED PEACHES

The Grand Marnier-grenadine syrup gives the fruit a pretty pink blush.

6 servings

1 1/4 **cups water**
1/2 **cup sugar**
  2 **tablespoons thinly sliced lemon peel**

  6 **large peaches, peeled, halved and pitted**
  3 **tablespoons Grand Marnier**
  1 **tablespoon grenadine syrup**
1/4 **cup toasted almond slivers**

Heat water, sugar and lemon peel in 2 1/2-quart saucepan over low heat, swirling pan occasionally, until sugar dissolves. Add peaches, cover and cook until just soft, about 10 minutes. Transfer peaches to serving bowl, using slotted spoon. Cook syrup over medium heat until reduced to 3/4 cup, 7 to 10 minutes. Strain syrup. Stir in Grand Marnier and grenadine. Pour over peaches. Refrigerate until chilled. Sprinkle with almond slivers and serve.

QUICK COUPE MELBA

4 servings

2/3 **cup seedless raspberry jam**
  2 **tablespoons Grand Marnier**
  1 **16-ounce can sliced peaches in juice, drained or 4 ripe fresh peaches, peeled, pitted and sliced**
  1 **quart French vanilla ice cream, slightly softened**

Combine jam and liqueur in medium bowl. Add peaches and mix thoroughly. Scoop ice cream into dessert dishes. Spoon raspberry mixture over top, dividing evenly among servings.

UNCOOKED NECTARINE COMPOTE

8 servings

1/3 **cup firmly packed light brown sugar**
1/4 **cup dark rum**
  2 **tablespoons fresh lemon juice**
  6 **cups sliced nectarines (about 8 large)**

    Vanilla ice cream
  1 **cup fresh blueberries**

Blend first 3 ingredients in large bowl. Mix in sliced nectarines. Cover tightly and refrigerate 1 hour.

Soften ice cream slightly in refrigerator. Spoon nectarines into shallow bowls. Top with scoops of ice cream. Sprinkle with blueberries.

RASPBERRY-RHUBARB COMPOTE

Serve as a topping for vanilla ice cream or thin slices of pound cake.

6 servings

- 10 ounces frozen unsweetened rhubarb, thawed, juice reserved
- 1/2 cup sugar
- 1 10-ounce package frozen raspberries, thawed, juice reserved
- 1/4 cup Grand Marnier

Cook rhubarb in juice with sugar in heavy medium saucepan over medium heat until rhubarb is softened, 4 to 5 minutes. Stir in raspberries with their juice and liqueur. Cook until warm. Serve immediately.

STRAWBERRY AND ICE CREAM CLOUD

10 to 12 servings

- 2 quarts strawberries, hulled
- 1 tablespoon sugar
- 1 cup well-chilled whipping cream
- 1 pint vanilla ice cream, softened
- 1/2 cup Triple Sec

Arrange strawberries on platter. Sprinkle with sugar. Refrigerate until chilled.

Whip cream to soft peaks. Fold into ice cream. Stir in Triple Sec. Spoon over berries and serve.

CHOCOLATE-DIPPED STRAWBERRIES

Makes 24

- 1/2 pound white chocolate
- 24 strawberries with stems
- 3/4 pound walnuts, pecans or almonds, finely chopped

Line baking sheet with waxed paper. Melt chocolate in double boiler over hot water. Dip bottom half of each strawberry in chocolate. Roll in chopped nuts. Arrange on prepared sheet. Cool until set.

SPIRITED FRUIT SUNDAES

Makes 2 cups

- 1/2 cup sugar
- 1 cup fresh orange juice
- 1 8¼-ounce can crushed pineapple, drained
- 1 small banana, chopped
- 1/4 cup Grand Marnier
  Vanilla ice cream

Heat sugar in heavy medium saucepan over low heat. Cook, swirling pan gently, until sugar dissolves and just turns rich caramel color, about 8 minutes; do not burn. Add orange juice (sugar will harden). Stir gently with wooden spoon until sugar dissolves again, 10 to 15 minutes. Increase heat to medium-low and simmer 6 minutes. Stir in pineapple, banana and Grand Marnier. Cool mixture to room temperature or refrigerate overnight. Serve fruit over vanilla ice cream.

TROPICAL SUNDAE

MICROWAVE

4 servings

Topping
- 3 medium-size slightly green bananas, chopped
- 1/4 cup apricot preserves
- 1/4 cup Cointreau or other orange liqueur
- 1/4 teaspoon grated orange peel
- 4 scoops vanilla or coffee ice cream
  Whipped cream

For topping: Combine all ingredients in glass dish and stir. Cover with waxed paper. Cook on Medium 1½ minutes.

Place ice cream scoops in individual dishes. Pour warm topping over. Garnish each with whipped cream.

AUTUMN FRUITS WITH SHERRY SABAYON SAUCE

6 servings

- 3 egg yolks
- 2 tablespoons sugar
- 2/3 cup cream Sherry (preferably imported)
- 2/3 cup chilled whipping cream
- 1 teaspoon grated orange peel
- 1 large cantaloupe, seeded, cut into thin slices and peeled
- 8 figs, each cut into 4 wedges or 2 baskets of strawberries, halved
- 2 cups seedless green grapes
  Toasted sliced almonds

Whisk yolks and sugar to blend in top of large stainless steel double boiler. Gradually whisk in 1/3 cup Sherry. Set over simmering water and whisk until mixture holds shape for 3 seconds when drizzled from whisk, about 5 minutes. Remove from over water and refrigerate until cool, whisking occasionally. Beat cream until soft peaks form. Fold into sabayon with remaining 1/3 cup Sherry and orange peel. (*Can be prepared 6 hours ahead; chill.*)

Just before serving, arrange cantaloupe slices around center of plates. Combine figs and grapes and mound in center. Spoon sauce over and sprinkle with toasted almonds.

CHERRY SOUP

A refreshing, slightly sweet soup that is perfect for a light summer dessert.

6 servings

- 1 1-pound bag frozen pitted cherries, thawed
- 1/2 cup black cherry juice
- 1/2 cup whipping cream
- 1/2 cup plain lowfat yogurt
- 1 teaspoon grated orange peel
  Pinch of cinnamon
- 1 orange, peeled and thinly sliced

Combine first 6 ingredients in blender and mix until smooth, about 1 minute. Pour into serving bowl. Refrigerate overnight. Float orange slices on top.

ICED PLUM SOUP

6 to 8 servings

- 1 30-ounce can purple plums, drained (reserve syrup), pitted and finely chopped
- 1 cup water
- 1/2 cup sugar
- 1 cinnamon stick
- 1/4 teaspoon freshly ground white pepper
  Pinch of salt
- 1/2 cup whipping cream
- 1/2 cup dry red wine
- 1 tablespoon cornstarch
- 2 tablespoons fresh lemon juice
- 1 teaspoon freshly grated lemon peel
- 1 cup sour cream
- 1/3 cup black raspberry liqueur

  Sour cream (garnish)
  Cinnamon (garnish)

Combine plums, reserved syrup, water, sugar, cinnamon stick, pepper and salt in 3 1/2-quart saucepan and bring to boil over medium heat. Reduce heat to low and simmer 5 minutes. Combine cream, wine and cornstarch in small bowl. Stir into soup. Continue cooking until thickened, about 2 to 3 minutes. Add lemon juice and peel. Remove from heat. Whisk 1/3 cup soup into 1 cup sour cream in small bowl. Whisk in liqueur until smooth. Add sour cream mixture to soup and blend thoroughly. Discard cinnamon stick. Cover and refrigerate several hours until chilled or overnight.

Ladle soup into individual bowls. Garnish each serving with sour cream and cinnamon and serve.

SPICED FRUIT ON SKEWERS

Also delicious served over ice cream.

4 to 6 servings

Marinade
- 1/2 cup firmly packed light brown sugar
- 1/4 cup pineapple juice
- 1/4 cup fresh orange juice
- 1 tablespoon vegetable oil
- 1/8 teaspoon ground cloves
  Pinch of ground cardamom

- 1/4 medium pineapple, cut into 1-inch chunks
- 2 medium nectarines, peeled and cut into 1-inch chunks
- 2 medium peaches, peeled and cut into 1-inch chunks
- 2 large plums, cut into 1-inch chunks

For marinade: Whisk all ingredients in large shallow glass dish.

Add fruit to marinade and stir to coat. Cover and chill overnight, stirring once or twice.

Preheat broiler. Thread alternating chunks of fruit on four 10-inch skewers. Broil until edges of fruit begin to brown, basting frequently with marinade and turning skewers occasionally, about 10 minutes. Serve hot.

QUICK RUM SAUCE FOR FRUIT

Makes about 3 cups

- 1 13-ounce can evaporated milk
- 1 cup milk
- 1 tablespoon dark rum
- 1 teaspoon vanilla
- 1 3 3/4-ounce package vanilla instant pudding mix
- 1 tablespoon sugar
  Sliced strawberries, peaches or blueberries

Combine first 4 ingredients in blender and mix on medium speed until blended. Gradually add pudding mix and sugar and blend well. Transfer to bowl. Cover and refrigerate until set, about 1 hour. Serve over fruit.

FRUIT SALAD TOPPING

Delicious on any fresh fruit.

Makes 1 quart

- 2 egg yolks
- 1/4 cup sugar
- 3 tablespoons fresh lemon juice
- 1 cup unsweetened pineapple juice
- 1 tablespoon cornstarch
- 2 teaspoons butter

- 1 cup whipping cream, whipped

Mix yolks, sugar and lemon juice in top of double boiler set over hot (but not boiling) water. Stir in pineapple juice, cornstarch and butter. Cook, stirring occasionally, until mixture thickens, about 20 minutes. Transfer to medium bowl and cool.

Just before serving, fold whipped cream into topping.

Custards, Mousses and Soufflés

BLENDER LEMON BAVARIAN CREAM

Serve this quick-to-make dessert with fresh berries or an easy fruit sauce.

8 servings

> 2 envelopes unflavored gelatin
> 1/4 cup cold water
> 2 tablespoons thinly sliced lemon peel (yellow part only)
> 1/2 cup boiling water
> 1/4 cup fresh lemon juice
> 1 cup sugar
> 1 cup whipping cream
> 3 eggs
> 1/4 teaspoon salt
> 1 1/4 cups crushed ice

Sprinkle gelatin over cold water in blender. Let stand until gelatin softens, about 5 minutes. Add lemon peel. Pour in boiling water and lemon juice. Blend until gelatin is dissolved. Add sugar, cream, eggs and salt. Blend at high speed 2 minutes. Add ice and blend until melted. Immediately pour into 4-cup ring mold. Refrigerate until set, at least 1 hour or overnight. Serve bavarian cream chilled.

ITALIAN CREAM WITH RASPBERRY SAUCE

4 to 6 servings

> 1 8-ounce package cream cheese, room temperature
> 1 cup (2 sticks) butter, room temperature
> 1 cup powdered sugar
> 1/2 cup golden raisins
> 1/2 cup raisins
> 2 tablespoons fresh lemon juice
> 1 1/2 teaspoons vanilla
> 1 8-ounce package frozen raspberries, thawed (undrained)

Using electric mixer, beat cream cheese and butter until well combined. Beat in sugar, raisins, lemon juice and va-nilla. Refrigerate until well chilled. Scoop onto plates. Surround with raspberries and berry juice.

AMARETTO CUSTARD WITH HOT FUDGE

MICROWAVE

4 servings

> 3 eggs, beaten to blend
> 1/3 cup sugar
> 1 teaspoon vanilla
> 1/4 teaspoon almond extract
> 1/8 teaspoon salt
> 1 1/4 cups milk
> 1/4 cup amaretto liqueur
>
> 1 12-ounce jar hot fudge topping, heated
> Sliced almonds

Lightly butter four 6-ounce custard cups. Blend first 5 ingredients. Set aside. Combine milk and liqueur in 2-cup glass container. Cook on High until tiny bubbles form around edge, about 4 minutes. Gradually stir into egg mixture, blending well. Pour into prepared cups. Place cups in circle in microwave. Cook on Low 6 minutes. Rotate cups. Continue cooking on Low until tester inserted halfway between center and edge of custards comes out clean, about 6 minutes. Refrigerate overnight.

Unmold custards onto plates. Pour heated fudge topping over each. Sprinkle with sliced almonds.

MICROWAVE POTS DE CREME

MICROWAVE

4 servings

> 1 6-ounce package semisweet chocolate chips
> 1 egg
> 2 tablespoons sugar

> 1 teaspoon vanilla
> Pinch of salt
> 3/4 cup milk
>
> Whipped cream
> Chocolate shavings

Mix first 5 ingredients in processor. Heat milk in ovenproof glass bowl on High until just boiling, about 2 minutes. With processor running, pour milk through feed tube and mix until smooth, stopping occasionally to scrape down sides of work bowl. Pour into 1/2-cup ramekins. Cover and refrigerate overnight.

Top each with whipped cream and chocolate shavings and serve.

LEMON MOUSSE WITH RASPBERRY SAUCE

You can present this lovely, rich mousse in a large bowl instead of individual glasses, although it will take an additional three hours to set.

8 to 10 servings

> 6 large eggs
> 6 large egg yolks
> 1 1/2 cups sugar
> 1 cup fresh lemon juice, strained
> 2 tablespoons minced lemon peel
> 14 tablespoons (1 3/4 sticks) well-chilled unsalted butter, cut into small pieces
>
> 3/4 cup chilled whipping cream
>
> 1 1/2 cups fresh raspberries or frozen unsweetened, thawed
> 2 tablespoons (or more) sugar
>
> Fresh mint sprigs

Whisk eggs and yolks in heavy non-aluminum saucepan until foamy. Whisk in 1 1/2 cups sugar, then lemon juice. Mix in peel. Stir over low heat until mixture thickens to consistency of heavy custard, about 10 minutes; do not boil. Remove from heat and whisk in butter. Transfer mixture to bowl and cool until very thick, stirring occasionally, about 50 minutes.

Whip cream in medium bowl to soft peaks. Fold cream into lemon mixture just until combined. Spoon mousse into individual serving glasses. Cover and chill until set, about 2 hours. (*Can be prepared 1 day ahead.*)

Coarsely mash berries in small bowl using fork. Mix in 2 tablespoons sugar. Taste, adding more sugar if desired. Cover and refrigerate 1 hour to release juices. (*Can be prepared 1 day ahead.*)

Spoon sauce over center of mousse. Garnish with mint sprigs.

CHOCOLATE WALNUT PUDDING

MICROWAVE

4 servings

  2/3 **cup sugar**
  5 **tablespoons unsweetened cocoa powder**
  3 **tablespoons cornstarch**
     Pinch of salt
2 1/4 **cups milk**
  2 **tablespoons (1/4 stick) butter, room temperature**
  1 **tablespoon dark rum**
  1/2 **cup chopped walnuts or shredded coconut or combination**

Combine sugar, cocoa, cornstarch and salt in glass bowl. Gradually stir in milk and blend well. Cook on High 7 minutes, stirring 3 times during cooking. Mix in butter and dark rum. Stir in nuts and/or coconut. Divide among 4 ramekins, spreading evenly. Serve hot or chilled.

QUICK CHOCOLATE MOUSSE

This easy, elegant dessert looks pretty when garnished with shaved chocolate, fresh berries or whipped cream rosettes.

Makes about 7 cups

  1 **12-ounce package semisweet chocolate chips**
  1/2 **cup half and half, scalded**

  1/3 **cup hot brewed strong coffee**
  4 **eggs, room temperature, beaten to blend**
  1/4 **cup coffee liqueur**
  2 **cups whipping cream, whipped**

Chop chocolate chips in blender until powdery, about 1 minute. Add hot half and half and hot coffee and blend until smooth, about 1 minute. Add eggs and liqueur and blend until smooth, 1 to 2 minutes. Transfer chocolate mixture to medium bowl. Cool to room temperature. Gently fold in whipped cream. Spoon into individual ramekins or 1 1/2- to 2-quart serving dish. Refrigerate at least 1 hour. (*Can be prepared 1 day ahead.*) Serve chilled.

TORTA MASCARPONE

Mascarpone, a fresh triple cream cheese, lends texture and richness to this simple Italian layered dessert.

6 servings

  1 **cup mascarpone cheese***
  1/2 **cup powdered sugar, sifted**
  1/3 **cup dry Marsala**
  1 **teaspoon vanilla**
  3 **ounces bittersweet (not unsweetened) or semisweet chocolate, grated**
  1 **cup well-chilled whipping cream**
  2 **egg whites, room temperature**
 20 **amaretti (Italian macaroons), crushed**
     Fresh strawberries or raspberries (optional)

Beat mascarpone in large bowl until smooth. Stir in sugar, Marsala and vanilla. Fold in chocolate.

Beat cream in medium bowl until soft peaks form. Using clean dry beaters, beat whites in another bowl until stiff but not dry. Gently fold cream into mascarpone mixture, then fold in whites. Divide 1/3 of mascarpone mixture evenly among 6 goblets. Sprinkle with 1/3 of crushed amaretti. Top with 1/3 of mascarpone mixture. Sprinkle with 1/3 of amaretti. Top with remaining mascarpone mixture. Sprinkle with remaining amaretti. Cover

and chill 3 to 24 hours. Top with berries. Serve immediately.

*Italian cream cheese available at Italian markets. If unavailable, blend 3/4 pound cream cheese with 6 tablespoons whipping cream and 1/4 cup sour cream. Measure 1 cup of mixture for recipe. Reserve remainder for another use.

BOURBON, PEACH AND SHORTBREAD FOOLS

"Foolishly simple" is the only way to describe this old-fashioned layered combination of fresh peaches, buttery shortbread cookies and whipped cream. Prepare individual servings using tall wine glasses.

6 servings

  4 **pounds fresh ripe peaches**
  2/3 **cup sugar**
  1/3 **cup bourbon**

  1 **package shortbread cookies (about 5.5 ounces), crumbled**

  3/4 **cup chilled whipping cream, whipped to soft peaks**
     Additional shortbread cookies (optional)

Blanch peaches in batches in large pot of boiling water 30 seconds. Drain; transfer to bowl of cold water. Slip skins off peaches using fingertips. Halve peaches; cut into wedges. Stir peaches, sugar and bourbon in heavy large saucepan over low heat until sugar dissolves and mixture comes to simmer. Cover and cook until peaches are very tender, about 15 minutes. Cool to room temperature. Cover and refrigerate until well chilled.

Drain peaches; reserve syrup. Coarsely mash in large bowl using potato masher or fork. Pour syrup into glasses. Spoon half of mashed peaches over. Cover with shortbread crumbs. Top with remaining mashed peaches. Refrigerate 1 hour to mellow flavors.

Top each serving with dollop of whipped cream and cookie. Serve, passing additional cookies separately.

Strawberry-Sour Cream Ice Cream, page 188

Applesauce Spice Cake, page 165

Chocolate Chip Almond
Cookies, page 192

RICHARD CLARK

Clockwise from bottom:
Uncooked Nectarine Compote with
Vanilla Ice Cream, page 172;
Bourbon, Peach and Shortbread Fools, page 176;
Lemon Mousse with Raspberry Sauce, page 175

IRWIN HOROWITZ

Almond-Walnut Butter Toffee, page 196

Blue Ribbon Pecan Pie, page 162

DICK SHARPE

Cream Puffs Chambord, page 164

Fast Holiday Trifles, page 185

PETER A. HOGG

FAST HOLIDAY TRIFLES

6 servings

> 1 16-ounce frozen pound cake, thawed, crust trimmed
> 12 tablespoons brandy
> 12 tablespoons raspberry jam
> 2 12-ounce packages frozen raspberries, thawed, or 3 cups fresh
> 1 5¼-ounce package instant vanilla pudding prepared according to package instructions
> 1½ cups whipping cream, whipped
> Toasted slivered almonds
> Mint leaves

Cut pound cake crosswise into ½-inch-thick slices. Cut each slice crosswise into ½-inch-wide pieces. Line bottom of 12-ounce goblet with cake. Drizzle 1 tablespoon brandy over cake. Spread 1 tablespoon jam over. Top with 1 heaping tablespoon raspberries. Spoon ¼ cup pudding over. Repeat procedure once. Pipe whipped cream over in spiral fashion. Repeat with remaining ingredients to make 5 more trifles. Refrigerate 1 hour. Garnish with remaining berries, toasted almonds and mint leaves.

APRICOT FANTASY

6 servings

> 1 10½-ounce can apricot halves, drained
> 2 tablespoons unflavored gelatin
> 1 12-ounce can apricot nectar
> ½ cup water
> 1 3⅝-ounce package vanilla pudding mix
> 1½ to 2 teaspoons fresh lemon juice
> 1 cup whipping cream, whipped
> 1 cup fresh strawberries or ½ cup chopped toasted pecans (garnish)

Mash apricot halves in small bowl and set aside. Combine gelatin and ¼ cup nectar in large bowl, stirring until gelatin is dissolved. Blend remaining nectar with ½ cup water in small bowl. Prepare pudding mix according to package instructions, substituting nectar-water mixture for milk. Add hot

pudding to gelatin mixture in thin stream, stirring constantly. Add apricots and lemon juice and mix thoroughly. Let cool slightly. Gently fold in whipped cream. Turn apricot mixture into 1-quart soufflé dish or spoon into 6 wine goblets. Cover and refrigerate until set, at least 30 minutes. Garnish with berries or pecans.

QUICK CUSTARD BREAD PUDDING

MICROWAVE

6 servings

> 5 slices white bread, crusts removed, torn into pieces
> 2 cups milk
> ½ cup sugar
> ⅛ teaspoon salt
> 3 eggs, beaten until frothy
> 1 teaspoon vanilla
> Cinnamon

Butter 2-quart round glass baking dish. Blend bread and milk in medium bowl of electric mixer at low speed. Stir in sugar and salt until dissolved. Blend in eggs and vanilla. Pour into prepared baking dish. Sprinkle with cinnamon. Cook on High until set, 17 to 18 minutes. Serve bread pudding hot or chilled.

COSTA RICAN BREAD PUDDING

12 servings

> 1 medium loaf white bread, torn into small pieces
> 4 cups milk
> 1 cup whipping cream
> 5 eggs, well beaten
> 1½ cups sugar
> ½ cup (1 stick) butter or margarine, melted
> 1 tablespoon grated orange peel
> 1 teaspoon vanilla
> ½ teaspoon cinnamon
> ¼ teaspoon freshly grated nutmeg

Topping
> ½ cup sugar
> ¼ cup water
> 1 teaspoon cinnamon
> ¼ cup (½ stick) butter
> Whipped cream

Preheat oven to 400°F. Generously butter 9x13-inch ovenproof glass baking dish. Combine bread, milk and cream in large bowl. Chop finely with 2 knives or pastry blender. Let stand 10 minutes. Stir in eggs, sugar, melted butter, orange peel, vanilla, cinnamon and nutmeg. Pour into prepared dish.

For topping: Combine sugar, water and cinnamon in small bowl. Spoon over bread mixture. Dot with butter. Bake until tester inserted 2 inches from side of dish comes out clean, 35 to 40 minutes. (If top browns too quickly, cover loosely with foil.) Cool in pan on rack. Cut into squares. Top each serving with whipped cream.

BLUEBERRY PUDDING

6 servings

> 1 cup sugar
> ½ cup water
> 4 cups fresh or frozen blueberries
> 6 slices white bread, crusts trimmed
> 2 tablespoons (¼ stick) butter
> 1 tablespoon cinnamon
>
> Whipped cream or crème fraîche

Bring sugar and water to boil in medium saucepan over high heat. Reduce heat to medium. Stir in blueberries and cook 10 minutes. Spread bread slices with butter and sprinkle with cinnamon. Arrange 2 slices in bottom of 9x5-inch loaf pan. Cover with ⅓ berry mixture. Repeat with remaining bread and berry mixture, making 6 layers. Cover and chill overnight.

To serve, spoon pudding from pan. Top with whipped cream.

CUSTARD KUCHEN

8 servings

> 2 cups soft breadcrumbs
> ½ cup shredded coconut
> 3 eggs, beaten to blend
> 2 cups milk
> 1 cup sour cream
> ½ cup honey
> 1 teaspoon vanilla
> ½ teaspoon salt
> ½ teaspoon ground ginger

Preheat oven to 350°F. Butter shallow 9-inch round ovenproof glass baking dish. Mix breadcrumbs and coconut in prepared dish. Combine remaining ingredients in large bowl and beat until well blended. Pour over crumb mixture. Place dish in roasting pan. Transfer to oven. Pour enough boiling water into pan to come 2/3 way up sides of dish. Bake until custard is set and tester inserted in center comes out clean, 55 to 60 minutes. Cool slightly in water bath. Serve kuchen warm or at room temperature.

RICOTTA-FRUIT TORTE

6 to 8 servings

- 1¹/2 cups ricotta cheese
- 6 tablespoons powdered sugar
- 2 teaspoons vanilla
- 1 10³/4-ounce frozen pound cake, partially thawed
- 1 large banana, peeled and thinly sliced
  Juice of ¹/2 lemon
- 1¹/2 cups fresh blueberries, raspberries or sliced strawberries

Beat ricotta cheese, powdered sugar and vanilla in small bowl until smooth. Slice cake horizontally into 3 layers using serrated knife. Dip banana slices in lemon juice. Reserve several banana slices and berries for garnish. Arrange remaining banana slices over bottom cake layer. Spread ¹/3 of cheese mixture over banana. Top with half of berries. Set second cake layer over. Spread with half of remaining cheese mixture. Arrange berries over cheese. Add final cake layer and frost top with remaining cheese mixture. Garnish with reserved banana and berries and serve.

ALMOND MOCHA PUDDING

8 servings

- ³/4 cup coarsely chopped toasted almonds
- ¹/2 cup plus 1 tablespoon sugar
- 1¹/2 cups whipping cream
- 1¹/2 cups milk
- 2 eggs

- 2 tablespoons brandy
- 2¹/2 teaspoons instant coffee powder dissolved in 1 tablespoon water
- 1¹/2 teaspoons vanilla
- ¹/4 teaspoon almond extract
- ¹/4 teaspoon freshly grated nutmeg

- 2 cups diced pound cake
- 1 6-ounce package semisweet chocolate chips

  Whipped cream
  Instant espresso or cappuccino powder

Preheat oven to 325°F. Grind almonds with sugar in processor. Add cream, milk, eggs, brandy, coffee, vanilla, almond extract and freshly grated nutmeg and blend thoroughly.

Arrange pound cake in bottom of 7x11-inch baking dish. Sprinkle with chocolate chips. Pour almond mixture over. Place dish in large baking pan. Transfer to oven. Add boiling water to pan to come halfway up sides of dish. Bake until set, 50 to 55 minutes. Remove from water bath and cool to room temperature. Cover mocha pudding and refrigerate overnight.

Cut pudding into squares. Top each serving with dollop of whipped cream and sprinkle with espresso powder.

CREAM CHEESE AND NOODLE KUGEL

10 to 12 servings

- ¹/2 pound fine egg noodles, cooked
- 3 eggs, beaten to blend
- ¹/2 cup sugar
- 1 teaspoon vanilla
- 2 cups milk
- 4 ounces cream cheese, room temperature
- ¹/2 cup cottage cheese
- 1 cup golden raisins
- ¹/2 cup (1 stick) butter, melted
- ¹/4 teaspoon cinnamon

  Sour cream

Preheat oven to 350°F. Butter 9x13-inch glass baking dish. Combine noodles, eggs, sugar and vanilla in large bowl. Blend milk, cream cheese and cottage cheese in blender or processor until creamy, 3 to 4 minutes. Add to noodle

mixture. Stir in raisins, butter and cinnamon. Transfer to prepared dish. (*Can be prepared 1 day ahead. Cover and refrigerate.*) Bake until tester inserted in center comes out clean, approximately 45 minutes.

Cut kugel into squares. Serve warm with sour cream.

COCONUT RICE PUDDING

6 servings

- 2¹/2 cups water
- 1 cup long-grain white rice
- 2 cups milk, room temperature
- ¹/2 cup shredded coconut
- ²/3 cup sugar
- 1 teaspoon rose water
- ¹/2 teaspoon vanilla
  Cinnamon
  Chopped unsalted pistachio nuts

Bring water to boil in medium saucepan. Stir in rice. Reduce heat to low, cover and cook 10 minutes. Add milk and coconut. Increase heat to medium and cook, stirring constantly, 20 minutes. Blend in sugar. Remove from heat. Mix in rose water and vanilla. Divide pudding evenly among dessert cups or bowls. Sprinkle with cinnamon and pistachio nuts. Refrigerate until ready to serve.

CHOCOLATE AND ORANGE MARMALADE SOUFFLE

4 servings

- ¹/2 cup whipping cream
- 6 ounces bittersweet (not unsweetened) or semisweet chocolate, coarsely chopped
- 3 tablespoons orange marmalade
- 3 egg yolks
- 2 teaspoons Triple Sec or Grand Marnier

  Sugar
- 5 egg whites, room temperature
- ¹/4 teaspoon cream of tartar
- 1 tablespoon sugar
  Powdered sugar
  Whipped cream

Combine cream, chocolate and marmalade in heavy medium saucepan over low heat. Stir until chocolate and marmalade melt and mixture is smooth. Remove from heat and beat in yolks 1 at a time. Mix in Triple Sec. Cool to tepid. (*Can be prepared 4 hours ahead. Press piece of plastic onto surface and let stand at room temperature. Stir mixture over low heat until tepid before continuing.*)

Preheat oven to 425°F. Butter 2-quart soufflé dish. Sprinkle generously with sugar. Beat whites and cream of tartar in large bowl until stiff but not dry. Beat in 1 tablespoon sugar. Fold 1/4 of whites into chocolate. Gently fold into remaining whites. Transfer to prepared dish. Bake until soufflé rises but center is not firm when touched, about 20 minutes. Dust top with powdered sugar. Serve, passing whipped cream separately.

GRAND MARNIER SOUFFLE

6 servings

Butter
1/4 cup (1/2 stick) butter
1/3 cup all purpose flour
1/8 teaspoon salt
1 1/2 cups milk
4 egg yolks, beaten to blend
1/3 cup Grand Marnier
3 tablespoons sugar
1 tablespoon grated orange peel
1/2 teaspoon vanilla
6 egg whites
1/4 teaspoon cream of tartar
Powdered sugar

Preheat oven to 375°F. Butter 2-quart soufflé dish. Melt 1/4 cup butter in medium saucepan over low heat. Whisk in flour and salt. Increase heat to medium. Add milk and stir until smooth, thick and bubbly. Remove from heat. Add yolks, Grand Marnier, sugar, peel and vanilla. Using electric mixer, beat batter until thoroughly combined. Using clean dry beaters, beat whites with cream of tartar in large bowl to moderately stiff peaks. Gently fold whites into batter. Pour into prepared dish. Bake until golden and tester inserted in center comes out clean, 30 to 35 minutes. Sprinkle with powdered sugar. Serve immediately.

MOCHA AMARETTO SOUFFLE

4 servings

1/2 cup lowfat milk
1/4 cup evaporated lowfat milk
1 tablespoon cornstarch
1 tablespoon sugar
1/4 cup semisweet chocolate chips
1 tablespoon unsweetened cocoa powder
2 teaspoons amaretto liqueur
1 teaspoon instant coffee powder
1 teaspoon vanilla

3 egg whites, room temperature
1/4 teaspoon cream of tartar

Preheat oven to 325°F. Butter 1-quart soufflé dish. Whisk first 4 ingredients in small saucepan over medium heat until cornstarch dissolves. Bring to boil. Reduce heat to low and stir until thickened, about 1 minute. Remove from heat. Add chocolate chips, cocoa, amaretto, coffee powder and vanilla and stir until chocolate melts and mixture is smooth, about 2 minutes.

Beat whites until foamy. Add cream of tartar and continue beating until stiff but not dry. Fold 1/4 of whites into chocolate mixture, then fold in remaining whites. Gently turn into prepared dish, using rubber spatula. Bake until puffed and set, about 40 minutes.

Frozen Desserts

❖ ❖ ❖

PINEAPPLE-ORANGE ICE

If you do not have an ice cream maker, freeze the mixture in ice cube trays. When hard, mix it in the processor or blender until smooth, then freeze until firm. Serve with fortune cookies.

8 servings

2 cups water
3/4 cup sugar
1 20-ounce can crushed pineapple packed in juice
3 cups fresh orange juice
2 tablespoons fresh lime juice

Toasted coconut

Cook water and sugar in heavy medium saucepan over low heat until sugar dissolves, swirling pan occasionally. Bring to boil. Reduce heat and simmer 5 minutes. Cool completely.

Puree undrained pineapple in processor or blender. Pour into bowl. Blend in sugar syrup, orange and lime juices. Transfer to ice cream maker and freeze according to manufacturer's instructions. Spoon into airtight container. Freeze at least 3 hours.

To serve, scoop ice into bowls. Sprinkle with toasted coconut.

ROSE SORBET

4 servings

- 1/2 cup cold water
- 1 envelope unflavored gelatin
- 2 cups rosé wine
- 3/4 cup sugar
- 1 10-ounce package frozen raspberries in syrup, thawed and drained
- 1/4 cup fresh lime juice

Combine water and gelatin in small bowl. Let stand 10 minutes. Heat wine in medium saucepan over medium heat until hot, about 5 minutes. Add sugar and stir until dissolved. Add gelatin mixture and stir until dissolved. Mix in raspberries and lime juice. Transfer to medium bowl and freeze until just frozen, about 1 hour.

Beat frozen mixture with electric mixer until berries are evenly blended and mixture is just frothy. Freeze overnight. Serve sorbet in long-stemmed glasses or compote dishes.

MANGO ICE CREAM

Makes about 1 1/2 quarts

- 2 medium mangoes, peeled and pitted
- 1 14-ounce can sweetened condensed milk
- 1 cup whipping cream

Puree mangoes in blender or processor. Combine milk and cream in large bowl. Stir in mango puree. Strain through fine sieve. Transfer mixture to ice cream maker and process according to manufacturer's instructions. Freeze in covered container several hours to mellow. If ice cream is frozen solid, soften in refrigerator before serving. (*Ice cream can be prepared 1 week ahead.*)

STRAWBERRY-SOUR CREAM ICE CREAM

Makes about 1 quart

- 1 cup whipping cream
- 1/2 cup milk
- 1/2 cup sour cream
- 1/2 cup sugar

- 1 egg, beaten to blend
- 1/8 teaspoon vanilla
- 6 large strawberries, hulled and finely diced, juice reserved
  Sliced strawberries

Combine first 6 ingredients in large bowl, stirring until sugar dissolves. Mix in diced berries and juice. Transfer mixture to ice cream maker and process according to manufacturer's instructions. Freeze in covered container until ready to use. If ice cream is frozen solid, soften in refrigerator before serving. Garnish with berries.

BAILEYS ORIGINAL IRISH CREAM ICE CREAM

Makes about 1 1/2 quarts

- 2 cups whipping cream
- 2 cups half and half
- 1 cup sugar
- 1/2 cup Baileys Original Irish Cream liqueur
  Additional Baileys Original Irish Cream liqueur (optional)

Combine first 4 ingredients in large bowl, stirring until sugar dissolves. Transfer mixture to ice cream maker and process according to manufacturer's instructions. Freeze in covered container until ready to use. (*Can be prepared 1 week ahead.*) If ice cream is frozen solid, soften in refrigerator slightly before serving. Scoop into serving bowls. Drizzle additional liqueur over tops if desired.

FROZEN COFFEE CREAM

7 six-ounce servings

- 8 egg yolks, room temperature
- 1/4 cup sugar
- 1/4 cup water
- 1/2 cup coffee liqueur
- 1 cup whipping cream
- 1/2 cup chopped pecans

Beat egg yolks in large bowl of electric mixer until lemon colored and tripled in volume, about 10 minutes. Mean-while, combine sugar and water in small saucepan and cook over low heat, stirring just until sugar is dissolved. Increase heat to medium, bring to boil and let boil 5 minutes without stirring. With mixer running, pour syrup into egg yolks in thin steady stream and continue beating until cold. Stir in coffee liqueur. Whip cream in chilled bowl until soft peaks form. Gently fold cream and pecans into yolk mixture. Spoon into 6-ounce custard cups and freeze overnight.

FROZEN ORANGE MERINGUES

4 servings

- 4 large oranges
- 2 cups vanilla ice cream, slightly softened
- 3 ounces Triple Sec
- 1 egg white
- 2 tablespoons sugar
  Mint sprigs

Slice tops off oranges. Scoop out pulp. Set shells aside. Coarsely chop pulp in processor using 1 or 2 on/off turns; drain well. Transfer 1/4 cup pulp to medium bowl; discard remainder. Add ice cream and Triple Sec and mix well. Divide ice cream mixture among orange shells. Freeze overnight.

Preheat oven to 400°F. Beat egg white with sugar until stiff peaks form. Arrange oranges on baking sheet. Top each with some of meringue, sealing to edges. Bake until meringue browns slightly, 4 to 5 minutes. Garnish with mint sprigs. Serve oranges immediately.

QUICK TORTONI

12 servings

- 1 quart vanilla ice cream, slightly softened
- 1/2 cup dry macaroon crumbs
- 1/4 cup chopped candied cherries
- 1/4 cup mini semisweet chocolate chips
- 1 tablespoon brandy
- 1/2 cup whipping cream, whipped

BUTTER PECAN COOKIES

Makes about 30

Butter
1/2 cup (1 stick) butter, room temperature
3 tablespoons powdered sugar
1 cup chopped pecans
3/4 cup all purpose flour
1 teaspoon vanilla
1/4 cup powdered sugar

Preheat oven to 300°F. Lightly butter baking sheets. Using electric mixer, cream 1/2 cup butter with 3 tablespoons powdered sugar. Mix in pecans, flour and vanilla. Form dough into 1-inch balls and place on prepared sheets. Bake until lightly browned, 20 to 25 minutes. Transfer to rack to cool. Roll in 1/4 cup sugar to coat. Store cookies in airtight container.

THUMBPRINT POPPY SEED COOKIES

Makes about 3 1/2 dozen

1 cup (2 sticks) butter, room temperature
1/2 cup sugar
2 egg yolks
1 teaspoon vanilla
2 cups all purpose flour
3 tablespoons poppy seeds
1/8 teaspoon salt

Strawberry jelly

Using electric mixer, cream butter with sugar in large bowl. Add yolks and vanilla and beat until light and fluffy, about 3 minutes. Add flour, poppy seeds and salt and blend well. Cover and chill overnight.

Preheat oven to 375°F. Form dough into 1-inch balls. Arrange on ungreased baking sheets, spacing about 2 inches apart. Let soften several minutes at room temperature. Make indentation in center of each using thumb. Bake cookies until lightly browned, 12 to 15 minutes. Transfer to racks. While still warm, press centers again with thumb. Just before serving, fill centers with jelly.

BUTTER "SCOTCH" BALLS

Makes about 48

1/2 cup chilled butterscotch chips

1 cup (2 sticks) butter, room temperature
6 tablespoons powdered sugar
1 tablespoon Scotch whisky
2 cups all purpose flour
1/2 cup finely chopped walnuts
1/2 cup finely chopped pecans

1/2 cup powdered sugar

Finely chop butterscotch chips in blender or processor.

Preheat oven to 350°F. Cream butter with 6 tablespoons sugar in large bowl. Mix in whisky. Stir in flour, walnuts, pecans and butterscotch chips. Roll dough into 1-inch balls. Place on ungreased baking sheets. Bake until light brown, 12 to 15 minutes. Transfer cookies to rack to cool.

Roll balls in 1/2 cup sugar. (*Can be prepared 3 days ahead.*)

MAPLE CRUNCH COOKIES

Makes about 30

1 cup (2 sticks) butter, room temperature
3/4 cup sugar
1 1/2 teaspoons maple extract
2 cups all purpose flour
1/4 teaspoon salt
2/3 cup pecan halves

Preheat oven to 350°F. Grease baking sheet. Using electric mixer, cream butter with sugar and maple extract. Combine flour and salt; slowly blend into butter mixture on low speed. Roll 1 tablespoon dough into ball. Place on prepared sheet. Gently press pecan half into top. Repeat with remaining dough and pecans. Bake until cookies are golden brown, about 17 minutes. Transfer to rack and cool completely. (*Can be prepared 1 week ahead. Store in airtight container at room temperature.*)

FROZEN DATE NUT COOKIES

Makes about 55

1/2 cup (1 stick) butter, room temperature
1 cup firmly packed light brown sugar
1 egg, beaten to blend
1 1/2 teaspoons whipping cream
1 1/2 teaspoons milk
1/2 teaspoon vanilla
1/4 teaspoon black walnut flavoring
2 cups all purpose flour
1/2 teaspoon baking soda
1/2 teaspoon cream of tartar
1/2 teaspoon salt
1/2 cup chopped dates
1/2 cup chopped walnuts

Sugar

Cream butter with brown sugar in large bowl. Add egg, cream, milk, vanilla and walnut flavoring and beat until smooth. Combine dry ingredients in medium bowl and mix into butter mixture. Mix in dates and walnuts. Shape dough into 2 logs 2 inches in diameter and 6 to 7 inches long. Wrap logs in waxed paper and freeze until firm. (*Can be prepared 1 month ahead.*)

Preheat oven to 350°F. Lightly grease baking sheets. Do not defrost logs. Cut into 1/4-inch-thick slices. Place on prepared baking sheets. Sprinkle with sugar. Bake until cookies are light golden, 16 to 18 minutes. Cool on sheets 2 to 3 minutes. Transfer to cooling racks.

LEMON-GLAZED BUTTER COOKIES

Makes 3 dozen

1 cup (2 sticks) unsalted butter, room temperature
1/3 cup powdered sugar
1 cup all purpose flour
2/3 cup cornstarch

2 1/2 cups powdered sugar, sifted
1/2 cup (1 stick) butter, melted
2 tablespoons fresh lemon juice

Preheat oven to 350°F. Using electric mixer, beat butter and 1/3 cup sugar on medium speed 1 minute. Sift together flour and cornstarch. Add to butter. Blend until dough is soft, about 1 minute. Drop by teaspoonfuls onto ungreased baking sheet. Bake until very lightly browned, about 15 minutes. Transfer cookies to racks to cool.

Meanwhile, combine 2½ cups sugar, melted butter and lemon juice. While cookies are still warm, mound ½ teaspoon icing on each; icing will melt. Cool cookies completely.

NO-BAKE COCOA OATMEAL DROPS

Makes 4 dozen cookies

  2 cups sugar
  ½ cup milk
  ½ cup (1 stick) butter
  ½ cup unsweetened cocoa powder
  3 cups quick-cooking oats
  2 teaspoons vanilla

Generously butter baking sheets. Combine first 4 ingredients in medium saucepan and bring to boil. Reduce heat and simmer until smooth and thick, about 3 minutes. Remove from heat; add oats and vanilla and mix well. Drop by teaspoon onto prepared sheets. Cover and refrigerate at least 1 hour or overnight. Serve chilled.

CHINESE RAISIN-OATMEAL COOKIES

Makes 4 dozen

  ⅔ cup solid vegetable shortening, room temperature
  1 cup firmly packed brown sugar
  ⅔ cup sugar
  2 eggs, beaten to blend
  1 teaspoon vanilla
  2 cups all purpose flour
  1 cup rolled oats
  1 teaspoon baking soda
  1 teaspoon five-spice powder
  ½ teaspoon ground cloves
  ½ teaspoon cinnamon
  1 cup raisins
  1 cup chopped walnuts

Preheat oven to 350°F. Grease baking sheets. Cream shortening and both sugars in large bowl until light and fluffy. Mix in eggs and vanilla. Add

flour, oatmeal, baking soda and spices and blend well. Stir in raisins and nuts. Drop batter onto baking sheets by heaping teaspoons. Bake until lightly browned, 10 to 12 minutes; do not overbake. Cool on racks.

JUMBO OATMEAL-PEANUT BUTTER COOKIES

Makes about 40 cookies

  1 cup sugar
  1 cup firmly packed light brown sugar
  ¾ cup (1½ sticks) margarine, room temperature
  ½ cup chunky peanut butter
  2 eggs
  ¼ cup milk
  1 teaspoon vanilla
  2 cups all purpose flour
  1 teaspoon baking soda
  1 teaspoon cinnamon
  1 teaspoon salt
  1½ cups quick-cooking oats
  1 cup raisins

Preheat oven to 350°F. Grease baking sheets. Cream sugars with margarine and peanut butter in large bowl of electric mixer on medium speed. Add eggs 1 at a time, beating well after each addition. Beat in milk and vanilla. Mix in flour, baking soda, cinnamon and salt. Stir in oats and raisins. Drop dough onto prepared sheets by heaping tablespoons, spacing 2 inches apart. Bake until golden brown, about 15 minutes. Transfer to waxed paper and cool. Store in airtight container.

FANTASY FUDGE COOKIES

Makes about 5 dozen

  1 cup (2 sticks) butter, room temperature
  1½ cups sugar
  2 eggs, room temperature
  1 teaspoon vanilla
  2 cups all purpose flour
  ⅔ cup unsweetened cocoa powder

  ¾ teaspoon baking soda
  ½ teaspoon salt
  1 8-ounce package Reese's Pieces candy
  ¼ cup semisweet chocolate chips

Preheat oven to 350°F. Lightly grease baking sheets. Cream butter with sugar in large bowl. Blend in eggs 1 at a time. Stir in vanilla. Combine flour, cocoa powder, baking soda and salt. Slowly beat into creamed mixture. Stir in candy and chocolate chips. Drop dough by teaspoonfuls onto prepared sheets, spacing 2 inches apart. Bake until set, but still very soft, 10 to 12 minutes. (Cookies will firm as they cool.) Transfer to racks to cool.

MOCHA CHIP COOKIES

Makes about 20

  1 12-ounce package semisweet chocolate chips
  1¼ cups all purpose flour
  ½ cup (1 stick) butter, cut into 8 pieces, room temperature
  ½ cup sugar
  ½ cup firmly packed light brown sugar
  1 egg, beaten to blend
  2 teaspoons instant coffee crystals

Preheat oven to 350°F. Melt ½ cup chocolate chips in top of double boiler over barely simmering water. Transfer to processor. Add all remaining ingredients except unmelted chips and blend well, about 20 seconds. Stir in remaining chips. Drop by heaping tablespoon onto ungreased baking sheets. Bake until set, about 15 minutes. Cool on sheet 2 to 3 minutes. Transfer to rack. Serve at room temperature.

CHOCOLATE CHIP ALMOND COOKIES

Makes about 12

  Butter
  ½ cup (1 stick) butter, room temperature
  ½ cup firmly packed brown sugar
  ⅓ cup sugar
  1 egg, beaten to blend
  1 teaspoon vanilla

1 cup plus 2 tablespoons
all purpose flour
1/2 teaspoon salt
1/4 teaspoon baking soda
1 cup sliced almonds
1 6-ounce bag milk
chocolate chips

Preheat oven to 375°F. Lightly butter baking sheets. Cream 1/2 cup butter with sugars in processor. Blend in egg and vanilla. Sift together flour, salt and baking soda; add to processor and mix until just combined. Add almonds and chocolate chips and mix in using 20 on/off turns.

Form dough into 2-inch balls and place on prepared baking sheets. Bake until golden, about 10 minutes. Cool on rack. Store in airtight container. (*Can be prepared 1 week ahead.*)

PUMPKIN-CHOCOLATE CHIP COOKIES

Makes about 6 dozen

Butter
1/2 cup (1 stick) butter, room
temperature
1 1/2 cups sugar
1 cup canned solid pack pumpkin
1 egg, beaten to blend
1 teaspoon vanilla
2 1/2 cups all purpose flour
1 teaspoon baking soda
1 teaspoon baking powder
1 teaspoon cinnamon
1 teaspoon freshly grated nutmeg
1/2 teaspoon salt
1 6-ounce package semisweet
chocolate chips

Preheat oven to 350°F. Lightly butter baking sheets. Cream 1/2 cup butter with sugar in large bowl until fluffy. Blend in pumpkin, egg and vanilla. Sift flour, baking soda, baking powder, cinnamon, nutmeg and salt into medium bowl. Add to butter mixture, blending well. Stir in chocolate chips. Drop batter by heaping teaspoons onto prepared sheets. Bake until lightly browned, about 15 minutes. Cool cookies on wire rack.

DOUBLE CHIP COOKIES

Makes 6 dozen

Butter
1 cup (2 sticks) butter, room
temperature
1 cup chunky peanut butter
1 cup sugar
1 cup firmly packed brown sugar
2 eggs, beaten to blend
2 cups all purpose flour
1 teaspoon baking soda
1 6-ounce package semisweet
chocolate chips
1 6-ounce package peanut butter
chips

Preheat oven to 325°F. Butter baking sheets. Using electric mixer, cream 1 cup butter with peanut butter. Gradually beat in sugars and eggs until smooth. Beat in flour and baking soda until well blended. Stir in chocolate and peanut butter chips. Drop by rounded teaspoonfuls onto prepared sheets, spacing 2 inches apart. Flatten cookies slightly with fork. Bake until golden, 12 to 15 minutes. Cool cookies completely on racks.

ANISEBRODT

Makes about 6 dozen cookies

1 cup sugar
3/4 cup plus 2 tablespoons
vegetable oil
4 eggs
2 tablespoons water
2 tablespoons poppy seeds
4 teaspoons baking powder
1 teaspoon vanilla
1 teaspoon anise extract
4 1/2 cups all purpose flour

Preheat oven to 325°F. Grease baking sheets. Combine first 8 ingredients in large bowl and beat well. Stir in flour and knead until dough is no longer sticky, about 10 minutes. Shape dough into 5 strips about 2 inches wide, 14 inches long and 1/3 inch high. Arrange on baking sheets. Bake until golden, about 20 minutes. Cut strips diagonally into 1-inch-wide bars. Return to oven and bake 5 minutes. Turn

cookies on side and bake another 5 minutes. Let cool on rack. Store in airtight container.

APRICOT-OATMEAL BARS

Makes 24

3 cups dried apricots
3 cups water
1/2 cup sugar

2 cups all purpose flour
1 3/4 cups rolled oats
1 cup firmly packed brown sugar
3/4 cup (1 1/2 sticks) butter, melted
1/4 cup wheat germ
1 teaspoon baking soda
1 teaspoon vanilla

Combine first 3 ingredients in medium saucepan over medium-high heat. Stir until sugar dissolves, about 5 minutes. Reduce heat and simmer until almost all water is absorbed, about 15 minutes. Remove saucepan from heat. Mash apricots. Set aside.

Preheat oven to 350°F. Combine remaining ingredients in large bowl and mix well. Press half of crumb mixture into bottom of 9x13-inch baking pan. Spread evenly with apricot filling. Top with remaining crumb mixture, pressing down lightly to flatten. Bake until lightly browned, 30 to 35 minutes. Cool in pan. Cut into bars.

COCONUT-WALNUT CHEWS

Makes twenty-four 2-inch squares

3/4 cup (1 1/2 sticks) butter, room
temperature
3 tablespoons powdered sugar
1 2/3 cups all purpose flour

1 16-ounce box light brown sugar
3 eggs, separated
1 cup chopped walnuts
1/2 cup shredded coconut
Additional powdered sugar

Preheat oven to 350°F. Cream butter with 3 tablespoons powdered sugar in medium bowl. Mix in flour. Press dough into 9x13-inch glass baking dish. Bake until lightly browned, 15 to

20 minutes. Remove crust from oven. Retain oven temperature.

Combine brown sugar and yolks in large bowl. Mix in nuts and coconut. Beat whites until stiff. Fold into brown sugar mixture. Spread filling over crust. Bake until firm and browned on top, about 20 minutes. Cool completely. Cut into squares. Dust with powdered sugar. (*Can be prepared 1 week ahead. Refrigerate in airtight container.*)

LEMON SQUARES

Makes about 2 dozen

> 2 cups all purpose flour
> 1/2 cup sugar
> 1 cup (2 sticks) butter, well chilled
>
> 4 eggs
> 2 cups sugar
> 1/4 cup all purpose flour
> 1 teaspoon baking powder
> 6 tablespoons fresh lemon juice

Preheat oven to 350°F. Combine 2 cups flour and 1/2 cup sugar in medium bowl. Cut in butter using pastry blender or 2 knives until consistency of coarse meal. Press into bottom of 9x13-inch baking dish. Bake crust until golden, 20 minutes.

Meanwhile, beat eggs in large bowl of electric mixer on medium speed. Gradually add 2 cups sugar, beating constantly. Mix in 1/4 cup flour and baking powder. Add lemon juice and blend well. Pour into crust, spreading evenly. Bake until set, about 25 minutes. Cool in pan on rack. Cut into squares. Store in airtight container.

PINEAPPLE SCOTCHIES

Makes 12 to 16 bars

> 1 1/2 cups all purpose flour
> 1 1/2 cups quick-cooking oats
> 1 cup firmly packed light brown sugar
> 3/4 cup (1 1/2 sticks) butter or margarine
> 1/2 teaspoon baking soda
> 1 16-ounce can crushed pineapple, drained

> 1/4 cup sugar
> 3 tablespoons apricot or grape jam

Grease 9-inch square ovenproof glass baking dish. Combine flour, oats, brown sugar, butter and baking soda in processor and mix until crumbly using on/off turns (or mix using pastry blender or fork). Combine pineapple, sugar and jam in medium saucepan. Bring to boil over medium heat, stirring. Remove from heat. Let cool.

Preheat oven to 375°F. Sprinkle half of flour mixture in prepared dish. Top with pineapple filling. Spread remaining flour mixture over pineapple. Pat down gently. Bake until golden brown, 35 to 40 minutes. Cool to room temperature. Cover with plastic wrap and let stand at room temperature overnight. Cut into bars to serve.

PECAN PIE TOFFEE BARS

Makes about 25

> 1 1/2 cups all purpose flour
> 1/3 cup powdered sugar
> 3/4 cup (1 1/2 sticks) well-chilled butter, cut into pieces
>
> 1 14-ounce can sweetened condensed milk
> 1 egg, beaten to blend
> 1 teaspoon vanilla
> 1 cup chopped pecans
> 5 1 1/8-ounce English toffee candy bars, cut into 1/4-inch dice

Preheat oven to 350°F. Combine flour and sugar in medium bowl. Cut in butter until mixture resembles coarse meal. Press firmly into bottom of 9x13-inch baking pan. Bake until lightly golden and edges begin to darken, 15 to 20 minutes.

Meanwhile, combine milk, egg and vanilla in medium bowl. Stir in nuts and English toffee. Pour into prepared crust. Bake until golden brown, 20 to 23 minutes. Cool. Refrigerate until well chilled. Cut into bars.

CHOCOLATE AND BUTTERSCOTCH BARS

Makes about 36

> 1/2 cup (1 stick) unsalted butter
> 1 1/2 cups graham cracker crumbs
> 1 cup semisweet chocolate chips
> 1 cup butterscotch chips
> 1 1/3 cups shredded coconut
> 1 cup toasted hazelnuts, chopped
> 1 14-ounce can sweetened condensed milk

Preheat oven to 350°F. Place butter in 9x13-inch baking pan and melt in oven. Swirl pan to coat bottom and sides with butter. Spread crumbs evenly over bottom of pan. Layer chocolate chips, butterscotch chips, coconut and nuts over crumbs. Pour condensed milk over nuts. Bake until edges are golden brown, about 25 minutes. Cool. Cut into bars.

OATMEAL FUDGE BARS

Makes about 5 dozen

> 1 cup (2 sticks) margarine, room temperature
> 2 cups firmly packed light brown sugar
> 2 eggs
> 3 cups rolled oats
> 2 1/2 cups all purpose flour
> 2 teaspoons vanilla
> 1 teaspoon baking soda
> 1 teaspoon salt
> 1 cup chopped walnuts
>
> 1 14-ounce can sweetened condensed milk
> 1 12-ounce package semisweet chocolate chips
> 1 1/2 cups chopped walnuts
> 2 tablespoons (1/4 stick) margarine
> 2 teaspoons vanilla
> 1/2 teaspoon salt

Lightly grease 10x15x2-inch baking pan. Cream 1 cup margarine with sugar in large bowl. Add eggs one at a time, beating well after each addition. Mix in oats, flour, vanilla, baking soda and salt. Stir in 1 cup walnuts.

Combine milk and chocolate in top of double boiler set over hot water and stir until chocolate melts. Add remaining ingredients and blend well.

Preheat oven to 350°F. Spoon 2/3 of oat mixture into prepared pan, compacting with fork. Spread chocolate mixture over top. Crumble remaining oat mixture over chocolate and spread with fork. Bake until golden brown, 25 to 30 minutes. Cool completely. Cut into 1½-inch bars.

GOLD RUSH BROWNIES

Graham crackers lend a different nuance to these treats.

Makes about 24

   2 cups coarsely ground graham
      cracker crumbs (about
      20 crackers)
   1²/3 cups sweetened condensed milk
   1 6-ounce package semisweet
      chocolate chips
   ½ cup coarsely chopped pecans

Preheat oven to 350°F. Lightly butter 8-inch square ovenproof glass baking dish. Line with parchment paper; butter paper. Combine all ingredients in medium bowl. Pour batter into prepared dish. Bake until lightly browned, 30 minutes. Cool in pan 10 minutes. Cut into squares. Store in airtight container.

GLORIFIED BROWNIES

Makes about 36

      Butter
   ½ cup (1 stick) butter, room
      temperature
   1¼ cups sugar
   1½ cups all purpose flour
   4 eggs, beaten to blend
   ½ cup milk, room temperature
   4 ounces unsweetened chocolate,
      melted and cooled
   2 teaspoons vanilla
   ½ teaspoon salt
   2 cups chopped walnuts

   16 large marshmallows, halved
      Chocolate Glaze (see recipe)

Preheat oven to 350°F. Lightly butter 9x13-inch ovenproof glass baking dish. Cream ½ cup butter with sugar in large bowl. Blend in flour, eggs, milk, chocolate, vanilla and salt. Stir in walnuts. Pour into prepared dish. Bake until tester inserted in center comes out clean, about 15 minutes. Cool slightly in pan. Invert onto rack; cool.

Rinse marshmallows under cool water and drain. Arrange atop brownies. Set rack over sheet of waxed paper. Pour glaze over brownies. Cut into bars. Store in airtight container.

Chocolate Glaze

Makes about 1½ cups

   4 ounces unsweetened chocolate,
      coarsely chopped
   ½ cup (1 stick) butter
   1 cup sugar
   ½ cup milk
   2 teaspoons vanilla

Melt chocolate with butter in heavy medium saucepan over low heat, stirring constantly. Mix in sugar, milk and vanilla. Increase heat and boil 1 minute, stirring constantly. Remove from heat. Whisk until glaze forms heavy ribbon, 10 minutes.

FAST PEANUT BUTTER CANDY

MICROWAVE

Makes about 36 pieces

   1 cup creamy peanut butter
   ½ cup (1 stick) margarine
   2³/4 cups powdered sugar
   1 6-ounce package semisweet
      chocolate chips
   1 tablespoon margarine

Combine peanut butter and ½ cup margarine in large glass bowl. Cook on High 1½ minutes. Stir in powdered sugar. Spread on 9-inch plate. Combine chocolate chips and remaining margarine in medium glass bowl. Cook on Medium until softened, about 4 minutes. Spread chocolate over peanut butter mixture. Refrigerate at least 1 hour or overnight. Cut into 1-inch pieces.

QUICK AND EASY PEANUT BRITTLE

MICROWAVE

Makes about ³/4 pound

   1 cup sugar
   ½ cup light corn syrup
   1 cup roasted unsalted peanuts
   2 tablespoons (¼ stick) butter
   1 teaspoon vanilla
   1 teaspoon baking soda

Line 10x15-inch jelly roll pan with foil. Generously butter foil. Combine sugar and corn syrup in deep 2-quart glass bowl. Cook on High 5 minutes. Stir in peanuts, butter and vanilla with wooden spoon. Cook on High 5 minutes. Stir in baking soda. Spoon onto prepared pan, spreading evenly. Refrigerate 10 minutes, then cool at room temperature. Turn out of pan and peel off foil. Break into large pieces. Store in airtight container.

CHOCOLATE PEANUT BUTTER BALLS

Makes about 3½ dozen

   1 cup chopped dates
   1 cup chopped walnuts
   1 cup powdered sugar, sifted
   1 cup chunky peanut butter
   2 tablespoons (¼ stick) butter,
      melted
   12 squares semisweet chocolate

Line baking sheets with waxed paper. Combine dates and walnuts in large bowl. Add powdered sugar. Blend in peanut butter and melted butter and mix thoroughly. Shape into 1- to 1½-inch balls. Melt chocolate in top of double boiler set over hot (not boiling) water, stirring occasionally to prevent lumping. Dip balls into chocolate with fork, turning to coat evenly. Transfer to baking sheets. Refrigerate until chocolate is set, about 1 hour. If desired, trim bottoms of candies with knife and place in miniature muffin cup liners. Refrigerate candies until ready to serve.

KENTUCKY COLONELS

Makes about 3 dozen

- 1 16-ounce box powdered sugar
- 1 cup finely chopped pecans
- 1/2 cup (1 stick) butter, room temperature
- 1/4 cup green crème de menthe
- 1 6-ounce package semisweet chocolate chips, melted

Mix first 4 ingredients in medium bowl until well blended. Cover and refrigerate pecan mixture until firm, about 30 minutes.

Line large baking sheet with foil. Shape pecan mixture into 1 1/4-inch rounds and place on sheet. Refrigerate until firm, about 15 minutes. Dip half of each round into melted chocolate. Return to sheet. Refrigerate until set, about 1 hour. (*Can be prepared ahead. Place in airtight container and refrigerate 5 days or freeze up to 1 month.*)

ALMOND-WALNUT BUTTER TOFFEE

Makes about 2 pounds

- 2 1/4 cups sugar
- 1 1/4 cups (2 1/2 sticks) butter
- 1/2 cup water
- 1 teaspoon salt
- 1 1/2 cups chopped blanched almonds (about 1/2 pound)
- 1 cup chopped walnuts (about 6 ounces)
- 6 ounces semisweet or milk chocolate, melted

Generously butter 9x13-inch baking dish and set aside. Combine sugar, butter, water and salt in 3-quart saucepan and bring to boil over medium-high heat. Continue cooking, stirring constantly with wooden spoon, until mixture registers 325°F on candy thermometer. Stir in almonds and 1/2 cup walnuts. Pour into prepared pan, spreading evenly. Let cool. Spread with melted chocolate and sprinkle with remaining walnuts. Break toffee into pieces before serving.

MACADAMIA BRITTLE

Makes about 1 pound

- 1 cup unsalted macadamia nuts, coarsely chopped
- 1/2 cup (1 stick) butter, room temperature
- 1/2 cup sugar
- 1 tablespoon light corn syrup
- 3/4 cup semisweet chocolate chips

Line bottom and sides of 9-inch round cake pan with aluminum foil. Butter foil generously. Cook nuts, butter, sugar and corn syrup in heavy large skillet over low heat, stirring until butter melts and sugar dissolves. Increase heat and boil until mixture turns golden brown and begins to mass together, stirring constantly, about 5 minutes. Pour into prepared pan, spreading evenly. Sprinkle with chocolate chips; let melt. Spread evenly over top. Cool 15 minutes. Remove candy from pan. Peel off foil. Cool completely. Break into pieces.

MARSHMALLOW CREME FUDGE

Makes about 8 dozen

- 2 cups coarsely chopped pecans
- 6 tablespoons (3/4 stick) unsalted butter, melted

- 3 cups sugar
- 3/4 cup (1 1/2 sticks) unsalted butter
- 1 5-ounce can evaporated milk
- 1 12-ounce package semisweet chocolate chips
- 1 10-ounce jar marshmallow creme
- 1 teaspoon vanilla

Preheat oven to 375°F. Place pecans in 9x13-inch glass baking dish. Pour melted butter over. Bake until pecans are golden and butter is browned, stirring occasionally, about 10 minutes. Transfer mixture to medium bowl. Cool dish, then place in freezer.

Stir sugar, 3/4 cup butter and evaporated milk in heavy large saucepan over low heat until sugar dissolves. Increase heat to medium and bring to boil. Let boil 5 minutes. Remove from heat. Stir

in chocolate chips, marshmallow creme and vanilla. Mix in pecans. Spread in chilled baking dish. Refrigerate until firm, about 3 hours. Cut into 1-inch squares. Store in airtight container.

PEANUT BUTTER FUDGE

Makes about 6 dozen squares

- 1 16-ounce box powdered sugar
- 2 cups graham cracker crumbs
- 1 18-ounce jar chunky peanut butter
- 1 cup (2 sticks) butter, melted
- 1 12-ounce package semisweet chocolate chips
- 1/2 cup (1 stick) butter

Mix first 4 ingredients in medium bowl. Firmly press into 9x13-inch glass baking dish. Chill 1 hour.

Meanwhile, melt chocolate with 1/2 cup butter in small saucepan over low heat, stirring until smooth. Pour over peanut butter mixture, smoothing with spatula. Refrigerate 20 minutes. Cut into 1-inch squares. Refrigerate until firm, about 20 minutes. (*Fudge can be prepared up to 3 days ahead. Store in airtight container.*)

COCONUT TRUFFLES

Makes 3 dozen

- 1/2 cup (1 stick) butter
- 3 cups sweetened shredded coconut
- 2 cups powdered sugar
- 6 ounces semisweet chocolate, melted

Line baking sheet with waxed paper. Melt butter in large saucepan. Remove from heat. Stir in coconut and powdered sugar. Shape heaping teaspoonfuls of mixture into balls. Dip bottom of each ball into melted chocolate. Arrange chocolate side down on sheet. Refrigerate until firm, about 30 minutes. Serve truffles chilled.

Menus

On the following pages, we've put together menus for entertaining at any time of year and on any occasion. For those times that call for a special meal, look to these pages for ideas and inspiration. You'll find everything from a Country Weekend Lunch for Six to a Holiday Dessert Party for Twelve.

Whether you choose one of the menus here or create your own, a few tips will help make entertaining even easier. Keep the pantry well stocked with a variety of vinegars and oils, beef and chicken stock, dried mushrooms, pasta, rice, and herbs and spices. Plan ahead whenever possible, and take advantage of the do-ahead steps that are included in many of the recipes.

With the following selection of easy menus and a little organization, all that's left to do is gather family and friends and enjoy the party.

SPECIAL SUNDAY BREAKFAST FOR 6

Hot Mulled Cranberry Orange Juice (pg 14)
Almond French Toast (pg 146)
Sausage Patties
Sautéed Cinnamon Apples

◆

SUPER BOWL BRUNCH FOR 10

Sliced Melon
Chili Puffed Eggs (pg 88)
Hash Browns
Raspberry Coffee Cake (pg 166)

◆

LUNCHEON ON THE TERRACE FOR 6

Chilled Ginger Carrot Soup (pg 16)
Warm Chicken and Walnut Salad (pg 43)
Fresh Herb Muffins (pg 142)
Miniature Cherry Tarts (pg 163)

◆

COUNTRY WEEKEND LUNCH FOR 6

Creamy Greens Soup (pg 19)
Bacon, Pimiento and Cheddar Cheese
Sandwiches (pg 104)
Chocolate Chip Almond Cookies (pg 192)

◆

ALL-AMERICAN PICNIC FOR 6

Chili Deviled Eggs (pg 7)
Down-home Fried Chicken (pg 60)
Blue Cheese Apple Slaw (pg 38)
Potato Salad
Fresh Fruit
Apricot-Oatmeal Bars (pg 193)

◆

CASUAL SUNDAY SUPPER FOR 8

Pork Loin with Creamy Mustard Sauce (pg 57)
Steamed Spinach
Baked Sweet Potatoes
Yankee Devil's Food Cake (pg 169)

◆

PATIO PARTY FOR 6

Springtime Spaghettini (pg 98)
Grilled Salmon with Tarragon Mayonnaise (pg 80)
Positively West Coast Salad (pg 33)
Fresh Fruit Tarts

EVENING UNDER THE STARS FOR 4

Hummus Dip (pg 2)
Yogurt Cucumber Soup (pg 16)
California Pasta Salad with Pecan-Cilantro Pesto (pg 43)
Gold Rush Brownies (pg 195)

◆

EAST-WEST DINNER FOR 8

Lemon, Corn and Shrimp Broth (pg 22)
Pecan-crusted Pork Cutlets with Ginger Mayonnaise (pg 57)
Stir-fried Romaine, Sugar Snaps and Green Onions (pg 121)
Steamed Rice
Pineapple-Orange Ice (pg 187)
Fortune Cookies

◆

ITALIAN ROMANCE FOR 2

Prosciutto and Fresh Figs
Arugula Salad
Breadsticks
Veal Chops with Tomatoes and Artichoke Hearts (pg 54)
Buttered Peas with Chives
Cannoli

◆

ELEGANT ALFRESCO SUPPER FOR 6

Yellow Pepper Soup (pg 17)
Fresh Tuna with Piquant Sauce (pg 82)
Crusty Italian Bread
Torta Mascarpone (pg 176)

◆

SUMMER BARBECUE FOR 4

Ranch Crackers (pg 10)
Steamed Artichokes with Herb Mayonnaise
Lemon-Pepper Seafood Kebabs (pg 84)
Rice Pilaf with Pine Nuts
Tropical Sundaes (pg 173)

◆

HEARTY RANCH SUPPER FOR 6

Spicy Meat Loaf (pg 52)
Corn Soufflé-filled Bell Peppers (pg 120)
Spinach and Butter Lettuce Salad
Biscuits
Buttermilk Brown Sugar Cheesecake (pg 168)

◆

ORIENTAL ONE-DISH DINNER FOR 2

Hot and Spicy Shrimp with Noodles (pg 84)
Pound Cake with Fresh Fruit Compote

AFTER THEATER SUPPER FOR 4

Mussels Vinaigrette (pg 9)
Pasta with Walnut Sauce (pg 96)
Chocolate-covered Strawberries

SPECIAL ANNIVERSARY DINNER FOR 4

Radicchio, Endive and Fennel Salad (pg 24)
Roast Tenderloin with Pancetta,
Marjoram and Red Wine (pg 48)
Tomato Bruschetta (pg 138)
Herbed Turnips Dauphinois (pg 124)
Chocolate and Orange Marmalade Soufflé (pg 186)

AUTUMN FIRESIDE DINNER FOR 6

Brie and Herb Cheeses in Pastry (pg 5)
Lamb and Green Bean Stew with Rice (pg 55)
Butter-glazed Sesame Seed Rolls (pg 142)
Mixed Greens with Herb Vinaigrette
Chocolate Mousse Pie with Raspberry Sauce (pg 162)

SPRING CELEBRATION DINNER FOR 4

Watercress, Pear and Blue Cheese Salad (pg 34)
Cucumber Sole (pg 81)
Sautéed Cherry Tomatoes (pg 123)
Steamed New Potatoes
Strawberry-Sour Cream Ice Cream (pg 188)
Butter Pecan Cookies (pg 191)

EXOTIC INDIAN DINNER FOR 6

Pakoras Fritters with Tomato Pickle (pg 6)
Keema Beef Curry Matar (pg 51)
White Rice
Parsi Pickle (pg 148)
Ginger Ice Cream

◆

COLUMBUS DAY CELEBRATION FOR 6

Florentine Appetizer Puffs (pg 6)
Penne with Spicy Red Sauce (pg 97)
Roman-style Veal (pg 53)
Sautéed Zucchini
Rum and Pine Nut Tartlets (pg 163)

TASTES OF THE MIDDLE EAST FOR 6

Caponata
Baked Chicken with Saffron
and Yogurt Marinade (pg 61)
Butternut Squash and Shallots with
Cumin and Turmeric (pg 122)
Spiced Couscous (pg 127)
Autumn Fruits with Sherry Sabayon Sauce (pg 173)

SOUTH OF THE BORDER SUPPER FOR 4

Guacamole Picante (pg 2)
Rio Grande Beef Burritos with Creamed Peppers (pg 48)
Refried Beans
Vanilla Ice Cream Topped with Kahlúa

HOLIDAY COCKTAIL PARTY FOR 16

Easy Artichoke Dip (pg 2)
Stuffed Snow Peas (pg 4)
Caviar and Chopped Egg Appetizer (pg 4)
Zucchini Appetizer Squares (pg 7)
Tangy Sweet and Sour Meatballs (pg 8)
Oriental Chicken Wings (pg 7)
Assorted Pâtés and Cheeses

HOLIDAY DESSERT PARTY FOR 12

Rum and Pine Nut Tartlets (pg 163)
Chocolate-dipped Strawberries (pg 173)
Lemon Cheese Pie (pg 162)
Black Russian Cake (pg 169)
Buttermilk-glazed Carrot Cake (pg 167)
Pecan Pie Toffee Bars (pg 194)
Chocolate Peanut Butter Balls (pg 195)

❖ Index

Credits & Acknowledgments

❖   ❖   ❖   ❖

The following people contributed the recipes included in this book:

Betty Ackermann
Jan Adams
Linda Anderson
Sandi Anderson
Paula Ayers
Melissa Baker
Leslie Balick
Elga Balodis
Nancy Verde Barr
Marilyn Bartley
Christine Baumhefner
Susan Beegel
Yvonne Bendler
Freddi Bercovitch
Vincent Bianco
Louise Blackwell
Johanne Blais
Adrienne Blocker
Mary Lou Boone
Carol Bowen
Naila Britain-Callahan
Jeffree Brooks
Sheila Browitt
Ann Brown
Ron Brown
Susie Kritini Brown
Mary Bryant
Susan Bullard
Sue Cam
Jim Cameron
Larry and Vicki Cansler
Lois Carita
Beth Carlson
John Carter
Sharlyn Carter
Diane Castelli
Marina Castle
Terrie Cave
Diana Cavey
Rebecca Chase
Nona Chern
Linda Chrisey
Cheryl Clairardin
Dana Clayton
Norma Clipperton
Elaine Colgan
Jo Colter
Dale Cowan
Christa Craig
Eric Crespel
Kerry Ann Crovello
Evelyn Cunha
Sandre Cunha
John Cusimano
Maggi Dahlgren
Mary Dame
Katie Nunes-Danca

Karen Danielson
Detra Denay Davis
Connie De Brenes
Suzanne Delaney
Rita Denitti
Stephanie Dent
Marion Dewar
Veronica Di Rosa
Dorothy Diliddo
Barbara Dobson
Kay Domurot
Kathy Donahue
Janet Dorfman
Leslie Dougan
Alice Selby Douglas
Meryl Dun
Claudia Ebeling
Gail Ellerbrake
Sue Ellison
Mary Ernst
Selma Estrem
Jeanne Fadely
Barbara Feldstein
Adrienne Flor
Kevin Forsberg
Chester Fortun
Cindy Freeman
Nancy Friedlander
Gail Frizzell
Beth and Bruce Ganem
Dorothy Garrison
Kay Garrity
Linda George
Judith Gerstein
Marilyn Gibfried
Terry Gilbertson
Sid Goldstein
Aida Gonzalez
Corinne Gomo
Joan Good
Barbara Goodman
Julie Gordon
Phyllis Gorenstein
David Grant
Freddi Greenberg
Sara Moore Greene
David Griffin
Tori Griffin
Rhonda Gritzmacher
Hugh Grogan
Karen Grosso
Sharon Guizzetti
Rick Guldan
Penny Gunkler
Carol Haggett
Laura Halloran
Dorothy Hamilton

Malcolm Hamilton
Barbara Hansen
Susan Hare
Gloria Harris
Ingrid Harrison
John Hartman
Jerry Hashimoto
Marie Hasman
Mark Hawthorne
Victoria Hayne
Rae McIntee Hermens
Mary Hildebrand
Laxmi Hiremath
Sandy Hoffman
Jim Holmes
Linda Hummel
Karen Hurwitz
Ed Hussian
Maria Jacketti
Nehama Jacobs
Ellie Johnson
Katherine Fortino Johnston
Carolann Jones
Ronda Jones
Virgil Carrington Jones
Kathy Kahan
Cyndee Kannenberg
Karen Kaplan
Lynne Rossetto Kasper
Marlene Kellner
Nancy Kern
Kristine Kidd
Marie Zralek King
Bharti Kirchner
Barbara Kleinman
Kay Koch
Maureen Kolis
Emily Koltnow
Skippy Krohn
Alan Kunz
Dona Kuryanowicz
Michele La Haise-Bates
Heidi Landers
Arlie Lane
Annemarie Latimer
Lesley Lawson
Aiko Lee
Linda Lee
Mary Lefever
Clara Less
Vivian Levine
Louanne Lind
Portia Little
Robert Magretta
Saleh Makar
Dani Manilla
Pamela Manning

Sandra Mansfield
Debbie Marsh
Rosalie Marsh
Sunny Marx
Norma Matlin
Robert McClellan
Richard McCullough
Marty McDaniel
Michael McLaughlin
Barbara McRae
Anne Meeker
Carmela Meely
Catherine Merlo
Shirley Metropoulis
Perla Meyers
Sara Meza
Melinda Miller
Toni Milto
Nancy Mock
Jefferson and Jinx Morgan
Janice Mulligan
Bren Murphy
Dick Murphy
Dee Nimmo
Ruta Nonacs
Dorry Norris
Jeri Otteson
Daniel Pannebaker
Lamar Parker
Mary-Ann Parshall
Irene Patchett
Suzanne Paulson
Kathryn Pease
Robin Peek
Sharon Perlman
Martha Peters
Marcia Pilgeram
Alison Poccia
Janet Potter
Lisa Pundeff
Maria Laudisi Purwin
Emily Rapp
Carolyn Reagan
John Reaves
Ruedell Reaves
Joyce Resnick
Lucy Rice
Bryan Richey
Phyllis Rizzi
David Robare
Michele Roberts
Carol Robertson
Joan Robinson
Concepcio Roca
Roberta Roche
Susan Rosenfeld
Dahlia Ross

Linda Rosso
Marlene Ruderman
Susan Runkle
Liisa Salosaari-Jasinski
Bess Samaras
Louise Sargent
Richard Sax
Carolyn Schneider
Gary Selden
Marilyn Shaffer
Edena Sheldon
Elizabeth Sheley
Morgan Sheridan
Judy Sherman
Nancy Sherman
Karen Sherwood
Wendy Silverman
Marie Simmons

Ann Siner
Carol Slocum
Jan Smith
Rose Smith-Brydon
Susan Snyder
Maggi Sokolik
Peter Spechler
Elena Speedling
Dorothy Stanaitis
Frank Steele
Anne Stewart
Margee Striler
Sonya-Ariel Sugarman
Jo Ellen Susman
Norman Swanson
Pat Tanner
Stella Theokas
Ezell Thomas-Bell

Carol Tokay
Alzina Toups
Louise Brooks Town
Jane Trittipo
Jo Tunnell
Brenda Tunstill
Susan Turok
Mary Umenhoffer
Nicole Urdang
Peter Valenti
Nancy Ellard Vass
Carol Lee Veitch
Jane Vogel
Janet Voyna
Dorothy Vusich
Jere Wade
Grace Ann Walden
Julie Summers Walker

Nellie Wallace
Marty Waring
Marilyn Waugh
Darlene Weaver
Marty Westerman
Barry Wine
Zita Wilensky
Debbie Winbigler
Lynn Wolkerstorfer
Isabel Wood
Karen Woodin
Roy Yamaguchi
Lin and Rex Young
Andrew Younghusband
Lynda Younghusband
Gilda Zimmar

Merchandise pictured on cover:
Cuisinarts "Commercial" paella pan available at *Montana Mercantile,* 1500 Montana Avenue, Santa Monica, CA 90403. *Jean Couzon "Cardinal"* serving fork available at *Gumps,* 9560 Wilshire Boulevard, Beverly Hills, CA 90212. All other accessories are privately owned.

Editorial Staff:
William J. Garry
Barbara Fairchild
Nancy D. Roberts
MaryJane Bescoby

Graphic Design:
Bernard Rotondo
Robert S. Tinnon

Rights and Permissions:
Karen Legier

Indexer:
Rose Grant

Special thanks to
Lane S. Crowther

Composition by Andresen's Tucson Typographic Service, Inc., Tucson, Arizona